PADDLING ꞋꞋꞋꞋ ꞋꞋꞋꞋ ꞋꞋꞋꞋ ꞋꞋꞋꞋ

The Times and Texts of
E. Pauline Johnson
(Tekahionwake)

Frequently dismissed as a 'nature poet' and an 'Indian Princess,'
E. Pauline Johnson (1861–1913) was not only an accomplished thinker
and writer but a contentious and passionate personality who 'talked
back' to Euro-Canadian culture. *Paddling Her Own Canoe* is the only
major scholarly study that examines Johnson's diverse roles as a First
Nations champion, New Woman, serious writer and performer, and
Canadian nationalist.

A Native advocate of part-Mohawk ancestry, Johnson was also an independent, self-supporting, unmarried woman during the period of first-
wave feminism. Her versatile writings range from highly erotic poetry to
polemical statements about the rights of First Nations. Based on thorough research into archival and published sources, this volume probes
the meaning of Johnson's energetic career and addresses the complexities of her social, racial, and cultural position. While situating Johnson
in the context of turn-of-the-century Canada, the authors also use current feminist and post-colonial perspectives to reframe her contribution. Included is the first full chronology ever compiled of Johnson's
writing.

Pauline Johnson was an extraordinary woman who crossed the racial
and gendered lines of her time, and thereby confounded Canadian society. This study reclaims both her writings and her larger significance.

(Studies in Gender and History)

VERONICA STRONG-BOAG is a professor of Women's Studies and Educa-
tional Studies, University of British Columbia.
CAROLE GERSON is a professor, Department of English, Simon Fraser
University.

STUDIES IN GENDER AND HISTORY

General editors: Franca Iacovetta and Karen Dubinsky

Paddling Her Own Canoe

The Times and Texts of
E. Pauline Johnson
(Tekahionwake)

Veronica Strong-Boag and Carole Gerson

UNIVERSITY OF TORONTO PRESS
Toronto Buffalo London

© University of Toronto Press Incorporated 2000
Toronto Buffalo London
Printed in Canada

ISBN 0-8020-4162-0 (cloth)
ISBN 0-8020-8024-3 (paper)

Printed on acid-free paper

Canadian Cataloguing in Publication Data

Strong-Boag, Veronica Jane, 1947–
Paddling her own canoe : the times and texts of
E. Pauline Johnson (Tekahionwake)

(Studies in gender and history series)
Includes bibliographical references and index.
ISBN 0-8020-4162-0 (bound)   ISBN 0-8020-8024-3 (pbk.)

1. Johnson, E. Pauline (Emily Pauline), 1861–1913 – Criticism and
interpretation.   I. Gerson, Carole.   II. Title.   III. Series.

PS8469.O283Z85 2000   C811'.4   C99-933046-2
PR9199.2.J64Z85 2000

University of Toronto Press acknowledges the financial assistance to its publishing program of the Canada Council for the Arts and the Ontario Arts Council.

This book has been published with the help of a grant from the Humanities and
Social Sciences Federation of Canada, using funds provided by the Social
Sciences and Humanities Research Council of Canada.

University of Toronto Press acknowledges the financial support for its
publishing activities of the Government of Canada through the Book Publishing
Industry Development Program (BPIDP).

As we study the past in the hope of bettering the future, we dedicate this book to our students and especially to our children: Daniel and Rebekah Gerson; Christopher, Dominic, and Gabriel Ross.

Contents

Acknowledgments

Almost everyone we know has assisted in some way with this book, as have many people we have met only on paper or through e-mail. We are indebted to all the friends, colleagues, students, archivists, and librarians, across Canada and beyond, who constituted an informal 'Pauline Patrol,' alerting us to many sightings and citings of references to Johnson that we would not otherwise have found. In some instances we do not know the names of the staff (often student assistants) who helped out; other omissions may be attributed to inadvertent misfiling or our aging memories.

We are grateful to Jean Barman, Gillian Creese, Julie Cruikshank, Margery Fee, Nitya Iyer, Jane M. Jacobs, Arlene McLaren, Kathy Mezei, Dorothy Seaton, Donald B. Smith, Wendy Wickwire, and Donald Wilson for reading and commenting on early versions of portions of the manuscript. Students who directly assisted with the research or provided insights into Johnson's works include Kim Doucette, Sandra Even, Marie Howton, Phyllis Mancini, Sarah Parry, Larissa Petrillo, Wendy Plain, Christopher Ross, Ruth Darkson Siemans, Wendy Smith, Lorraine Snowden, Jenn Suratos, and Sandra Walker. We also thank Erika Aigner-Varoz, Sheila Johnston, Betty Keller, and Christine Marshall for sharing their research on Johnson.

At the University of Toronto Press, we are indebted to Gerry Hallowell for shepherding us through the various phases of manuscript preparation, and to Jill McConkey, Frances Mundy, and Barbara Tessman for seeing the book through later stages of production. Special thanks to Sandra Even, who prepared the index. Our intrepid copy editor, Diane Mew, incited us to cut, clarify, and justify; the book is better for her efforts.

This project would have been impossible without the assistance of myriad archivists, librarians, and other staff in museums and libraries: Wayne Crockett at the Archives of Ontario; Elizabeth Hunter and Sonia Mirva at the Brant County Museum; Paula Whitlow at Chiefswood; Lynne Prunskis at Brock; Richard Virr at McGill; Gayle Ball and Martin Miller at Miami University; Anne Goddard, Alain Lamarche, Roanne Mokhtar, and Sarah Montgomery at the National Archives of Canada; Brian A. Young and others at the Provincial Archives of British Columbia; George Henderson at Queen's University; staff at St Mary's Museum; Todd Mundle and Christine Stojakovic of Inter-Library Loans at Simon Fraser University; Jodi Aoki and Joe Kennedy at Trent University; Patricia Belier at the University of New Brunswick; Sandra Alston at the University of Toronto; Bruce Whiteman at UCLA; staff at the Vancouver Museum and Archives; Susan Bellingham at Waterloo University; and Tom Hill, director of the Woodland Cultural Centre Museum. We owe special thanks to Renu Barret and Carl Spadoni for ongoing assistance with the Johnson Collection at McMaster University, and to Susan Manakul, who painstakingly researched Johnson's contributions to serials in the Library of Congress, Washington, D.C.

Many other friends, acquaintances, colleagues and strangers answered queries, alerted us to Johnson materials, or otherwise contributed to this project. We appreciate the collegial support provided by the Simon Fraser University English Department, and the University of British Columbia's Women's Studies Program, Faculty of Education, and First Nations House of Learning. For sharing conversation and information we thank Marie Baker, Scott Calbeck, Gail Campbell, Blanca Chester, Ann Cowan, Joan Crate, Gwendolyn Davies, Betty Donaldson, James Doyle, Klay Dyer, Doug Francis, Janet Friskney, Mary Ann Gillies, Polly Howells, Wayne Hunter, Margo Kane, Marjory Lang, Margaret Linley, George Littlechild, Loryl MacDonald, Mary Lu MacDonald, Jim Miller, Nicholas Mount, Trudy Nicks, Richard Plant, Scott Plear, Julie Rak, Marilyn Rose, Don Stewart, David Stouck, Loretta Todd, Tom Vincent, John Wadland, John B. Wilkes, and Margaret Williams. Thanks, as always, to Martin and to Daphne for their unflagging support.

Early versions of several portions of this book were published in two essays: Veronica Strong-Boag, '"A Red Girl's Reasoning": E. Pauline Johnson Constructs the New Nation,' in *Painting the Maple: Essays on Race, Gender, and the Construction of Canada*, ed. Srong-Boag et al. (Vancouver: UBC Press, 1998), 130–54, and Carole Gerson, '"The Most

Canadian of All Canadian Poets": Pauline Johnson and the Construction of a National Literature,' *Canadian Literature*, no. 158 (Autumn 1998): 90–108. Research for this book was supported by grants from the Social Sciences and Humanities Research Council, the Hampton Place Fund at the University of British Columbia, and the Publication Fund at Simon Fraser University.

PADDLING HER OWN CANOE

The Times and Texts of
E. Pauline Johnson
(Tekahionwake)

Introduction

Emily Pauline Johnson, the writer and performer Tekahionwake, has captured the imagination of Canadians since the 1880s and 1890s. Her life continues to inspire popular biographers and aspiring Native writers and, at the turn of the millennium, she is being rediscovered by a generation of feminist and post-colonial critics. Few of her Canadian contemporaries have enjoyed such a hold on the public mind and heart. What accounts for this appeal? *Paddling Her Own Canoe: The Times and Texts of E. Pauline Johnson (Tekahionwake)* begins to answer that question. In the high age of Anglo-Saxon imperialism and patriarchy she was, we argue, a figure of resistance, simultaneously challenging both the racial divide between Native and European, and the conventions that constrained her sex. Her vision of Canada, of First Nations, and of women, articulated in print and on stage, was very different from that set forth by the Fathers of Confederation in 1867.

This book tells that alternate story. It is a story that properly begins in the Six Nations territory in Ontario, although its roots lie deeper still in the original meeting of First Nations and Europeans many centuries before Johnson's birth. By Canadian law, she was Mohawk. But crossing boundaries as intrepidly as she ran rapids, she also merged with a community of Euro-Canadian women who challenged misogynous conventions in their transatlantic, turn-of-the-century world. As well, she was one of a small Canadian elite who employed poetry, prose, and theatre to shape the new Dominion. Pauline Johnson was a complicated, contentious, and passionate personality whose life blurs the borders of what it means to be Native, a woman, and Canadian.

This volume demonstrates how Johnson 'talked back' to the dominant culture. Like the Knights of Labor or the suffragists of her day, who

too 'dreamed of what might be,' she chronicled and questioned prejudice and oppression. While not always consistent or unambiguous, her
writing and performances disturbed and remade the conventions that
saw First Nations peoples and women as properly subject to an imperial,
and imperious, masculinity. Her resistance to demeaning narratives is
sometimes blunt, sometimes ironical, and sometimes so subtle as to be
barely perceptible, but rarely entirely absent. Like Emma LaRocque and
other later Native thinkers similarly 'caught within the confines of ideo-
logically rooted, Western-based canons, standards, and notions of objec-
tivity and research,' Johnson walked in the 'shadow [of colonial history]
on a daily basis.'[1] Furthermore as a woman forced to make a living in a
man's world, she could not afford to be entirely straightforward or
uncompromising. Her public championship of a more inclusive and tolerant nationality incorporating dignity and respect for the First Nations
and for women, her claim of both the 'shadows and the dreaming,'[2]
was a fragile but recurring accomplishment that threatened powerful
conventions. In her own way, Pauline Johnson presaged such end-of-
the-twentieth-century First Nations writers as Lee Maracle and Jeannette Armstrong, who too are 'storytelling for their lives.'[3]

Throughout her public life Pauline Johnson played with the fundamental question of identity posed by her dual heritage from an English
mother and a mostly Mohawk father. On stage she appeared one
moment as the Mohawk woman warrior or storyteller, and at another as
the supposed opposite, the refined Euro-Canadian lady. She could highlight her Native credentials in her writing, or omit them altogether. To
both contemporaries and later observers who ascribed great importance to racial identity, her ability to blur the boundaries between the
races enhanced her appeal. The very ambiguity of her person summed
up the quandary of living in an imperial world that, willingly or not, was
increasingly multicultural and multiracial. Perhaps observers were puzzled not so much that she appeared to cross the racial line at will, moving from Native 'Other' to imperial 'I' with the change of a dress, but
that she made the return voyage. If she could pass as one of the dominant, what then drew her back to the margin?

In the face of European arrogance about First Nations, Johnson regularly encountered problems of credibility. While she insisted, 'Never let
anyone call me a white woman,'[4] her authenticity was questioned. As
with subsequent Mixed-race generations, she frequently received the
treacherous compliment, 'You don't look a bit like that!'[5] Critics have
rarely known how to make sense of the two aspects of her background

that she variously chose to emphasize. There has been a recurring temptation to suggest masquerade, a fraudulent presentation of either the 'lady' or the 'savage.' By claiming and expressing the sensibilities of both Aboriginal margin and European centre, Johnson ultimately confounds the simple dichotomies that underpin Western consciousness.

Debates about authenticity continue at the end of the twentieth century. Serious questions of entitlement and appropriation feed fierce battles both inside and outside First Nations communities. Who is the 'real' Native? Who speaks as a 'real' Indian? Who gets to claim tribal membership when this may, at long last, mean material benefits in oil-rich lands, or housing, or affirmative action or even sales of books and paintings? Who is allowed to share in traditions of Native spirituality when the West's religious heritage seems in some eyes all too bankrupt? And equally important, who makes these decisions? Questions about partial or total inclusion in what is defined as 'race,' a concept that has little biological significance but tremendous social meaning, trouble scholars, activists, artists, and citizens in general. There was no unanimity in Johnson's time, nor is there now or likely to be in the foreseeable future.

As Euro-Canadian feminist academics – a literary critic and an historian – we ask what it means for us to take up the story of a Mohawk-English Canadian woman. We respect the concerns of those like Ethel Gardner and Lenore Keeshig-Tobias who rightly worry about the motives and results of non-Natives taking up Native subjects.[6] Like Kathleen Donovan, we distinguish the analytical mode of 'speaking about' from the appropriative mode of 'speaking for.'[7] The problem of mainstream feminist scholars focusing on First Nations topics, that of 'appropriation of voice,' has been particularly well articulated by Christine St. Peter:

> One cannot appropriate others' stories. But to back guiltily away from them is to allow the hegemonic relations to continue unchecked ... As feminist scholars we wish not just to name the social whole but to change its configuration. This requires creative thinking about enabling rather than blocking ... we need to find ways of legitimating that struggle in professional terms. But finally, we need always to think about our shared terrain as 'the colonial bench.' Keeping the consequences of such divisions firmly in mind will keep us honest.[8]

Unlike First Nations people who, as Celia Haig-Brown has noted, 'are border workers by the nature of their aboriginal claims and their persisting marginalization by Canadian society' and 'some non-Native people who choose to remain in the border area,' we presume to be no more than occasional visitors.[9] As visitors, we see our position as 'speaking nearby,' to borrow a phrase from Trinh T. Minh-ha.[10] This book recuperates an under-acknowledged Canadian historical figure; it also offers restitution, a giving back, to the First Nations of Canada. The next time that Canada's leading national magazine, *Maclean's*, publishes a list of the hundred most important Canadians in history, Pauline Johnson should take her rightful place alongside the selected Native figures of Tecumseh, Pontiac, Tom Longboat, Bill Reid, and Tomson Highway, activists Louis Riel and Nellie McClung, author Catharine Parr Traill, and celebrity Grey Owl. In *Maclean's* compilation, Aboriginals and women are sparse enough, but First Nations women are utterly absent.[11]

In our research, we have worked almost exclusively with textual records, both published and archival, and have sought out publications from First Nations sources, especially the Iroquois. We have discussed this project with Native scholars and audiences but have not conducted the interviews that would have brought us into the domain of oral history.[12] Our contacts with individuals at the Chiefswood Museum, the Woodland Cultural Centre, the University of Toronto's Native Studies Program, and the University of British Columbia's First Nations House of Learning have been helpful and supportive. We decided that whatever stories about Pauline Johnson lie in Native oral history must be told by others with skills and knowledge different from our own. What follows is a discussion of Pauline Johnson's extended conversation with European Canada. Somewhat like end-of-the-twentieth-century Métisse author Maria Campbell, who in *Halfbreed* (1973) writes 'for all of you,'[13] Johnson addressed all who wished to listen.

Sources for this study therefore must begin with Pauline Johnson's writings. This is more difficult than it sounds. Various volumes, published during her lifetime and later, contain selections of her work but none, including the best-selling so-called complete poems, *Flint and Feather* of 1912, encompasses all examples in any genre. As our appendix indicates, we have sought, not always successfully, the original dates of Johnson's published verse and prose. Unpublished, ephemeral, and sometimes partial pieces from her pen surfaced from our explorations in archives and collections across Canada. Skits and dramatic presentations composed for performance experienced a particularly high mortality rate, surviving only in accounts by newspaper reviewers. The likelihood that much more may be found is rather slim. We have identified and perused more of Johnson's writings than have previous critics and biographers. We anticipate that a further volume which assembles Johnson's collected poetry and selected prose will appear in the near future with the University of Toronto Press.

In preparing *Paddling Her Own Canoe*, we each drew on our own two and a half decades of experience in Canadian women's and literary history and our wide reading in history, literature, anthropology, Native studies, and women's studies. We are acutely conscious, particularly as new publications daily appear in these and other fields, that we will have missed important work. However, we know from past experience that no scholarly endeavour is ever truly finished. We believe that we have discovered new ways to think about Pauline Johnson that merit dissemination at this moment of enhanced attention to First Nations history and culture, and we fully expect others to improve on what we have produced.

We have learned a great deal from recent Canadian writing on the First Nations by scholars such as Jean Barman, Jennifer Brown, Sarah Carter, Julie Cruikshank, Olive Dickason, Cole Harris, Jim Miller, Donald Smith, Georges E. Sioui, Sylvia Van Kirk, Winona Stevenson, and others. We hope that Barman's and Carter's particular sensitivity to the significance of sexuality in shaping race relations informs the entire volume. We have benefited extensively from our generation's recovery of literature and history, in Canada and elsewhere, which now properly includes women in every aspect of their lives. Our notes and bibliography record the mass of material written in the last decades that has transformed our understanding of Canada and the larger imperial world, and that permits us to situate Pauline Johnson in ways that have not previously been possible.

We have also been much influenced by feminist and post-colonial theoretical writing in many fields, including that by Janice Acoose, Jeannette Armstrong, Margery Fee, Franz Fanon, Barbara Godard, Celia Haig-Brown, Lee Maracle, Trinh T. Minh-ha, and Robert Young. These and others have helped us better understand the meaning of existence on the margins of empire, both for the 'Other' and the 'I.' We are intensely aware of feminist and post-colonial reminders about the constructed and situated nature of all knowledge. We know ourselves as authors to be deeply imbued with the ideas and values of the end-of-the-twentieth-century western world. We have endeavoured to be conscious of our own 'making' and what this may mean for our investigation of a Mixed-race woman who died in 1913.

Nevertheless, if we cannot recognize all evidence that may shed light on Johnson's life or understand fully all the meanings of what we have found, we remain committed to the view that it is possible to assemble more complete and accurate portraits of the past. We believe that scholars have an essential contribution to make to popular understanding of our world and we have endeavoured to produce an engaging and readable story. Thus theory informs our analysis but is rarely addressed in and of itself. Readers in search of our theoretical foundations should consult the notes.

A few words need to be said about terminology or the problem which one Native writer has labelled 'An Indian By Any Other Name.'[14] Distinctions among and proper capitalization of Aboriginal, First Nations, Indigenous, Indian, Mixed-race, Métis/Métisse, Native, and White, not to mention the terms 'red,' 'redskin,' 'savage,' and 'paleface' which Johnson and her contemporaries used and which we quote but do not ourselves employ, repeatedly troubled us. Guidance is not readily found. Usage varies among individual authors, scholars, and disciplines, and from one nation to another. What is acceptable in one time or place may well turn out to be deeply prejudicial in another. We prefer the Canadian use of 'First Nations' with its recognition of 'first presence' and nationality. When writing in our own voice, we have sought language that connotes inclusion and respect. We use Aboriginal, Indigenous, Indian, and Native, all capitalized, as nouns and adjectives to refer to peoples and communities of First Nations origin. Where we wish to specify that ancestry is both First Nations and European, we have employed Mixed-race, and more particularly Métis/Métisse when referring to those of French–First Nations origin. We have also chosen to treat Whites similarly, as we have Blacks in more occasional references. But to avoid perpetuating oppositional categorization, we prefer, if possible, to use terms that are less racially charged, such as 'European settler' and 'Euro-Canadian.' We reserve 'English' to identify the British imperial presence or to specify speakers of the English language. While these decisions are necessarily imperfect, all are intended to denote equality among groups of variously distinguished people. Nowhere do we wish to reify supposed racial categories which, like gender, are constructed largely in the human mind.

While Pauline Johnson has intrigued observers since her first public appearances in writing and in person in the 1880s, few have known the scope of her productivity. Famous for her verse, especially the poems featuring nature, notably 'The Song My Paddle Sings' (1892), and the First Nations, such as 'Ojistoh' (1895), she was far more than a poet. By the 1890s, as she set about to make a living, she was composing travel sketches, humorous accounts, outdoor pieces, short stories, and realistic portraits of Native peoples, especially the Six Nations. In the new century, she produced stories for children's and women's magazines and turned to the interpretation of Native legends, most obviously in *Legends of Vancouver* (1911), most of which were first published in the *Vancouver Province Magazine*. She also wrote and performed pieces such as 'His Sister's Son' of which we have no more record than the title and a few reviewers' comments.

We have tried to engage seriously and systematically with the entire body of Johnson's work. Her writings and performances were necessarily tailored to available markets and opportunities, but this is so with most public utterances, whether they come from politicians or poets. We have looked for recurring themes and values that appear over the thirty years of Johnson's surviving output. At the same time, we realize that inconsistency is a necessary feature of her diversified career and identity. As she herself said, 'one of the secrets of good writing of any kind is the power of being someone else ... How can one be consistent until the world ceases to change with the changing days? It always amuses me when some very clever critic undertakes to tell you exactly what kind of person you are "under the skin."'[15]

Johnson also said, 'there are two of me,' both the Native and the European.[16] Even that was an underestimation. Like everyone, she was many people. We do not forget, nor did she, the significance and the value of a superior class position. This has sometimes encouraged later critics, unaware of Johnson's departures from conventionality and misunderstanding the term 'poetess,' to dismiss her as a 'lady poet.' Social class, like race and gender, is experienced and employed in diverse ways that defy summary in a simple phrase. In light of the destruction of Johnson's intimate records, we do not presume to know who Pauline Johnson was 'under the skin.' But we do believe that our examination of the particular social contexts in which she wrote, and of the issues that repeatedly preoccupied her writing and performance, brings greater understanding of her ideas and her actions.

While especially attentive to her poetry and prose, we have also searched widely for Johnson's private correspondence. Letters survive in the collections of her contemporaries, ranging from Wilfrid Laurier to Frank Yeigh and Kate Simpson-Hayes. We also looked for commentary about Johnson's person, writing, and performances in private observations and public sources. These exchanges and reflections tell us much about how she survived and how she was perceived. Johnson, however, left no diaries and few personal papers. The largest archive, at McMaster University, consists mostly of press clippings about her activities, and copies of her periodical publications. Her sister Evelyn, like the protective and suspicious relatives who destroyed the diaries of Nellie McClung after her death, culled Pauline's effects. Years later, Evelyn instructed her executor to burn her own journals. The Johnson family kept many secrets to the end. Rather than report rumours or engage in idle speculation, we chose to respect their privacy.

Since Pauline Johnson was very much a product of a particular Mixed-race family, we have attempted to think more critically about her parents, Emily Howells and George Henry Martin Johnson, and their three other children. We have been especially struck by the significance of her sister, Evelyn Johnson, and her extensive efforts to express the meaning of the Native/non-Native binarism she too experienced in her youth at Chiefswood. Beyond the importance of the Johnsons as individuals, there is the wider issue of what a First Nations identity meant for settler society and imperial observers in the years after Canada's Confederation in 1867. To begin to understand that picture, we read as much as possible of the local press in Brantford and Vancouver, the annual reports from the Department of Indian Affairs, and a great deal about the Iroquois and the First Nations in general from the mid-nineteenth century to the First World War.

We have also attempted to understand Johnson as a woman living in the midst of urgent debates about the meaning of femininity and masculinity in the modern world. As a working woman and an ambitious writer, she joined many of her generation in questioning traditions and practices that designated one sex subordinate. To understand this experience better, we looked for evidence of interest in First Nations on the part of first-wave Canadian feminists. However, we found little sign of this. Occasional friendships never seemed to translate into Euro-Canadian feminist critiques of the racial politics of the British Empire. Although Johnson pursued her career alongside and to some extent assisted by a pioneer generation of women professionals and reformers, who supported expanded rights for their sex, her interests and theirs, while sometimes coinciding, ultimately separated in critical ways.

Although loyalty to the British Crown could conflict with Native advocacy, Pauline Johnson herself was often a fervent imperialist. Her loyalty invoked the spirit of the traditional Iroquois alliance with the British Empire, but more than this it reflected her hope for a multinational state united by a common allegiance to a set of ethical principles embodied in the monarchy and its institutions. Canada, especially the west, lay at the core of this vision of a fair deal. Johnson's contribution to Canadian imperialism was to imagine a nationality which could embrace the difference of the First Nations.

We have been interested in how Johnson and her work, especially her poetry, were incorporated into the literary history of Canada. The evolving reception, from celebration as 'Canada's poetess'[17] to subsequent trivialization as an artificial Indian princess, has underscored the general failure to recognize Johnson's contribution to the national imaginary. We have been struck by how little either her literary detractors or her champions identified or addressed the broader implications of her work. We have also observed a tendency by American scholars in particular to ignore Johnson's relationship to Canada and the British Empire. Both ironically and straightforwardly, she told a particular story about Natives, women, and Canadians. *Paddling Her Own Canoe* recovers the particularities that made Johnson a unique figure in the North American landscape.

Johnson was, moreover, much more than a writer. Like Jeannette Armstrong at the end of the twentieth century, who is 'a First Nations poet, sculptor and educator of the Okanagan people' and reciter,[18] Johnson explored different forms of communication, drawing from both Native and Euro-Canadian traditions. For many in her own time, she was first of all a mesmerizing performer who roused audiences across North America and Britain. The power of her direct appeal in the days before radio and television can never be recovered. Pauline Johnson's storytelling of a different world wove a connection with many in her audiences that helped keep her memory alive, for decades after her death. How much her charismatic presentation of the First Nations perspective furthered greater understanding in Canada is, unfortunately, unmeasurable.

We have also been interested in the shifts in Johnson's work over time. Having compiled as complete a chronology of her textual production as is possible at present, we have been struck by the patterns of emphasis and omission that emerge. The creative life that extended from at least 1884, the date the first of her works seems to have met public scrutiny, until her death in 1913, encompassed many different forms and issues. A close reading of poetry and prose reveals the evolution of an author and performer who had much more to say about the First Nations, women, and nationality than previous scholars have suspected.

We have been continually fascinated by how Pauline Johnson chose to present herself and by the possible meanings attached to her performance of race, gender, and social class. Multiple and simultaneous identities informed Johnson's comprehension of herself and others' views of her. Scholars of First Nations oral traditions and European popular culture remind us that meaning is continuously negotiated and that understandings shift and develop along with performance. We have endeavoured to read sources with sensitivity to what Johnson's public acts of telling meant and how these may have evolved over time. We attempted to take the same care with the visual record, recognizing that publicity photos and sketches carry their own negotiated meanings of race, gender, and class.

The conversation between Johnson and her audiences did not end with her death. Authors from Earle Birney to Ethel Wilson, Margaret Atwood, and Beth Brant continued to address her contribution. Their varying attention reflects their knowledge, mostly fragmentary, of her work and history, their own investment in particular literary perspectives, and their feminist and First Nations sympathies (or lack thereof). Johnson's name has also been attached to a machine-gun, public schools, a luxury yacht, and a Vancouver chocolate company, evidence of the more popular story that threads through these pages.

Throughout the course of our research, we have looked for responses from First Nations individuals and communities, both during Johnson's lifetime and subsequently. In particular, we have been moved and informed by her significance in inspiring subsequent Native artists such as Frances Nickawa shortly after World War One, Bernice Loft Winslow (Dawendine) in the 1920s and 1930s, and Beth Brant in the 1980s and 1990s. More than one generation of First Nations women has looked to Johnson for evidence that they too can survive and thrive as creative artists. That story is still in progress and is only suggested here.

We are acutely conscious of the disparagement that Johnson has received over the years. Much less common has been a systematic effort to explain why she generated so many positive responses. What, in the 1885 poem, 'A Cry from an Indian Wife,' prompted the anonymous 'B' to write back,

> Let white men scoff and scorn, with taunts and jeers,
> For them, as for your Noble Brave, is stored
> Some racial conflict in a coming age
> Such as the past doth show on every page,
> The vengeful justice hist'ry shall record;[19]

Again, after a sold-out performance in the 1890s, who was the admirer
who addressed the following verse to Brantford's woman poet?

> Speak out, brave girl; speak, speak for the nation,
> Of wrongs it has suffered, the woes it hath braved.
> Tell simply the story of sad desolation;
> Of forest crowned heroes who can't be enslaved.
>
> Speak, speak, for the nation which smiles in its hardships,
> Usurped of its plenty, crushed, dogged and debased.
> For the spirit of freedom swells high with emotion,
> And wild torrents murmur, 'we will not be slaves.'
>
> Pale faces may sneer, and our brave spirits rankle;
> The self 'christened' Christians may dig our last grave;
> And the hero whose soul was the pride of our fathers
> Be crushed under might, but can ne'er be a slave.[20]

Such passionate lines, with their reminder of the refrain from 'Rule, Bri-
tannia!' – 'Britons never will be slaves' – testify to Johnson's ability to
mobilize resistance to European domination.

When, years later, a well-travelled Pauline Johnson, 'the only woman
in town,' sat in the bar of a small western community exchanging stories
with miners and prospectors, she forged still another type of connection.[21] An imperial male frontier committed to the brutal submission of
all in its way stopped for a moment to consider other alternatives. What
might these have seemed to be, we wondered? We also wanted to understand what so 'fascinated' Mary Edgar, a young woman from Canada's
European elite, that she wished she were related to the Mohawk poet.
This admirer went on to establish a girls' camp that echoed Johnson's
advocacy of outdoor pursuits for young women.[22] Ethel Wilson, British
Columbia author and a prominent member of Vancouver society, similarly never forgot a youthful meeting with Johnson, years afterwards
saluting the courageous independence of a sister artist who 'pursued a
path of her own making, and did this with integrity until the last day of
[her] life.'[23] Later still, a young Cree writer, Loretta Jobin, on the Red
Pheasant Reserve, 'was first inspired, at the age of eight, by the poetry of
Pauline Johnson.'[24] What drew such diverse audiences together in their
appreciation of a woman who died at the age of fifty-one, far from sure
of her achievements? Johnson's search for answers to hard questions

about human value and community resonates with some part of the experience and hopes of many people living in Canada during her own time and subsequently. That resonance too helps explain her continuing popularity.

Above all *Paddling Her Own Canoe* reflects our desire to place Johnson in a number of critical contexts that together illuminate her experience and her significance. We started off trying to think about what it meant to be a member of the First Nations, more particularly Iroquois and Mohawk, in post-Confederation Canada. This thinking is most evident in chapter 1, which sets out European Canada's ideas about race, the place of the Iroquois, and the role of the Johnson family, but it also pervades every chapter. Pauline Johnson believed that being 'Canadian Born' was significant for Natives as well as newcomers. We agree, although we do not think that our differences from the United States have always benefited the First Nations.

We are also especially sensitive to Pauline Johnson as a woman of her time, someone struggling to find a voice and make a living in an English-speaking imperial world governed by the conventions of patriarchy. This preoccupation particularly inspired our discussion of her as a New Woman in chapter 2. As a prominent example of an independent, self-sufficient single woman, Johnson was a significant advocate for her sex. Again, however, we intend the entire volume to reflect our sustained interest in women and gender as categories of analysis.

We also take Pauline Johnson seriously as an intellectual and a published and performing artist who made a contribution significantly beyond what she has been credited with as a supposedly minor figure among the Confederation poets. Chapters 3 and 4 take up critical questions about the meaning of literature and performance, highlight the shifting interests and forms of cultural expression that Johnson embraces, and suggest the different ways in which she has sometimes been understood in Canada and the United States. Chapter 5 turns to her views of Canada itself and identifies her as a provocative and serious champion of a new nationality, inclusive of Native and European, women and men, and expressive of something resembling the red toryism which some commentators have believed to distinguish Canada. While Pauline Johnson has been popular with investigators keen to add Aboriginal voices to the American literary landscape, her life and works are finally best comprehended as part of Indigenous Canada's encounter with imperialism.

This is a study of an extraordinary woman. While hoping to be inclusive and fair-minded, we are also unashamedly partisan. We both came to this shared project with long-standing commitments to recovering women in Canadian literature and history. If, as we argue, Johnson had a long love affair with Canada, we have in turn developed an enduring commitment to her. While the historical and literary canon of our day has largely slighted Johnson, she has persisted in slipping in and out of our consciousness, never entirely to be forgotten, in ways that many other Canadians would understand. For us, her return to centre stage seemed at first largely serendipitous. But was it, we wonder? Like her, we too are trying to envision a world in which the First Nations and newcomers, women and men, can live together in equality and community.

At the Centre for Research in Women's Studies and Gender Relations at the University of British Columbia, one of us, Veronica Strong-Boag, began to think seriously about post-colonial theory as part of an interdisciplinary team examining 'race, gender and the construction of Canada' in 1992–5. Inspired to consider how race and gender interact to shape representations and experiences of the nation she found an old fascination rekindled. Unknown to her, on the other side of Vancouver at Simon Fraser University, Carole Gerson was stirring the same embers in her research on Canada's early women authors. This partnership has proven an invigorating interdisciplinary exercise. We have inspired and challenged each other, disagreed, and come back to reconsider. We each wrote individual chapters which were then revised, often substantially, by the other. The result, combining our individual knowledges of history and literature, is a substantially better volume than either of us could have achieved alone.

We know that our organizing structure does not make for an easy reading of Pauline Johnson's life. For this reason, we have provided two aides-memoire: a time line listing key dates in Johnson's life, and an appendix giving an unprecedented listing of her publications and as many of the untraced titles, by date and place, as could be identified.

Time Line

1853   Marriage of George Henry Martin Johnson (1816–84) and
         Emily Susanna Howells (1824–98)
1854   Birth of Henry Beverly Johnson

1856   Birth of Eliza Helen (Evelyn) Johnson
1858   Birth of Allen Wawanosh Johnson
1861   Birth of Emily Pauline Johnson
c.1876–7 Johnson attends school in Brantford
1884   Death of George Henry Martin Johnson
1885   Move of Emily Howells Johnson and daughters from Chiefs-
          wood to Brantford
1886   Death of Pauline Johnson's grandfather, Chief Smoke
          Johnson or Sakayengwaraton (b. 1792)
          Interview in Toronto *Globe* (October 14) by 'Garth Grafton'
          (Sara Jeannette Duncan), the day after Johnson's memorial
          ode was read at the unveiling of the monument to Joseph
          Brant in Brantford
1886–7   Appeared as a member of the Brant Amateurs in several plays
          in Brantford
1889   Publication of W.D. Lighthall, ed., *Songs of the Great Dominion*,
          with two poems by Johnson
1892   Pauline Johnson's performance at Frank Yeigh's 'Canadian
          Literature Evening' in Toronto (18 January)
          Beginning of Pauline Johnson's tours as a performer
1894   Pauline Johnson's first visit to London, its publishing houses,
          and its salons (April–July)
1894–7   Johnson tours with Owen Smily
1894   First tours of the Canadian west and British Columbia; she
          meets the suffragist Nellie L. McClung on an early tour of
          Manitoba
          Death of Johnson's oldest brother, Henry Beverly Johnson
1895   Publication of *The White Wampum* by the Bodley Head Press,
          London
1897   Johnson begins to use Winnipeg as the base of her perform-
          ing career and about this time meets Charles Drayton
1898   Death of Emily Susanna Howells
          Loss of home in Brantford
          Engagement with Charles Drayton announced; it was dis-
          solved in late 1899 or early 1900
1900   Beginning and end of mysterious relationship with her man-
          ager, Charles H. Wuerz
1901   Beginning of performing partnership with Walter McRaye
          which continued until 1909
1903   Publication of *Canadian Born*, Toronto

1906	Second visit to Britain, this time with Walter McRaye (April–November)

1906   Second visit to Britain, this time with Walter McRaye (April–
       November)
       Meeting with Chief Su-á-pu-luck (Joe Capilano) and B.C.
       chiefs during their visit to London to petition King Edward
       VII on behalf of B.C. First Nations
       Begins publishing in *Boys' World*
1907   Johnson's last visit to London (April-June)
       Begins publishing in the *Mother's Magazine*
1908   Publication of *When George Was King* by Brockville *Times*
1909   Moves her base to Vancouver and gives up regular perform-
       ing to concentrate on writing; shortly thereafter she is diag-
       nosed with breast cancer
1910   Death of Su-á-pu-luck
       Johnson's articles on Native legends begin to appear in Van-
       couver *Province*
1911   Publication of *Legends of Vancouver*
1912   Publication of *Flint and Feather*
1913   Death of Johnson in Vancouver on March 8 and her civic
       funeral in the same city on March 10
       Posthumous publication of *The Shagganappi* and *The Moccasin
       Maker*
1922   Erection of monument in Stanley Park, Vancouver, to
       Johnson
1923   Death of her brother, Allen Wawanosh
1929   Publication of *Town Hall Tonight* by her partner Walter
       McRaye
1931   Publication of the first book-length study, *The Mohawk Princess:
       Being Some Account of the Life of TEKAHION-WAKE
       (E. Pauline Johnson)* by Mrs W. Garland Foster
1937   Death of Eliza Helen (Evelyn) Johnson
1947   Publication of *Pauline Johnson and Her Friends* by Walter
       McRaye
1961   Appearance of a Canadian stamp to commemorate the
       centennial of Johnson's birth
1965   Publication of *Pauline Johnson: Her Life and Work* by Marcus
       Van Steen
1981   Publication of *Pauline: A Biography of Pauline Johnson* by Betty
       Keller
1987   Republication of *The Moccasin Maker,* with introduction, anno-
       tation, and bibliography by A. LaVonne Brown Ruoff

1989   Publication of *Pale as Real Ladies: Poems for Pauline Johnson* by
        Joan Crate
1997   Publication of *Buckskin and Broadcloth: A Celebration of E.
        Pauline Johnson – Tekahionwake 1861–1913* by Sheila Johnston

CHAPTER ONE

'One of Them':
The Politics of Race, the Six Nations,
and the Johnson Family

The Politics of Race

In the nineteenth century, English-speaking Canadians set about establishing who they were and, by extension, who they might become. In their quest for community, for future superiority over Great Britain and the United States, women and men turned to ideologies of race for answers. Race, many believed, ultimately determined the authentic Canadian. Yet Britain's 'great imperial race' faced rivals. There were, of course, the French Canadians and the Americans, but before them came the Dominion's First Nations, the peoples indigenous to the land. This priority had to be addressed, and dismantled, before Canada could become a European 'home and native land.'[1] The efforts of Canada's colonists to claim pre-eminence in the North American landscape were, from the first, resisted by the First Nations. As Pauline Johnson reminded her audiences, Aboriginal residents had their own views of what it meant to share Canada.

During much of the nineteenth and twentieth centuries, the Iroquois, more particularly the Six Nations of Grand River, stood near the centre of the recurring Aboriginal challenge to European dominion. While the community had many voices, the family of Pauline Johnson embodied a long-standing conversation with English Canada on the role of Aboriginal peoples in the new nation. Their efforts to preserve a collective Indian identity took place within a deepening gulf between Native and non-Native worlds. That gulf kept many in Pauline Johnson's audiences, then and today, ignorant of the Indigenous politics which informed her life and work. This chapter's discussion of English-Canadian debates about Indians and the mingling of the races, the re-

sponse of the Six Nations to repression, and the significance of the
Johnson family in these controversies highlights issues that shaped the
most famous daughter of the Grand River territory, someone who, as
the novelist Sir Gilbert Parker declared, remained a 'rare creature who
had the courage to be glad of her origin.'[2]

From the confederation of four British colonies in 1867 until the First
World War, different demands from diverse populations of retreating
Natives and surging newcomers, the difficulty of charting a distinctive
course between the two powerful empires of Britain and the United
States, and the uncertainties and inequities of economic development
kept the fledgling Canadian state an uncertain enterprise. In their assertion of superior claims to land and power, Euro-Canada's settler society
readily took up and embellished discourses on race that conveyed inestimable advantages on British peoples.[3] Rivals, whether European or
Aboriginal, were readily categorized as inferior 'races.' While French
and English were uneasily joined within a single state, the Native nations, like most immigrant communities, were targeted for absorption
and disappearance.

By the time of Pauline Johnson's birth in 1861 and increasingly thereafter, academic and popular commentators explored and explained the
evolving relationship between Natives and Europeans in terms of a
racial dialectic that validated the Europeans' claims to Canada's imaginative and physical space. Two different opinions of First Nations
emerged. The dominant view pictured Indian societies as the inverse of
middle-class Victorian propriety, censuring them for debauchery, sloth,
and violence. Such a trilogy of vices consigned them to inferiority alongside the Irish peasantry and the impoverished urban working class. The
century's notions of racial hierarchy used Celtic origin to explain the
failings of such British groups, but Indians often rated lower still.
Although contact with Europeans, notably their introduction of alcohol,
was acknowledged as one potent source of decline, Aboriginal shortcomings were also reckoned as innate. While valour, eloquence, and
generosity were regularly acknowledged, particularly of Natives prior to
or during the early period of contact, Euro-Canadians ultimately characterized the tribes as lacking the physical, moral, and intellectual
resources to compete with a more virile civilization.[4] In the contest for
North America, Native nations were regarded as outmoded. After Confederation, the Dominion government largely embraced this conclusion; provincial administrations were seldom better and sometimes a
good deal worse in their dealings with Native peoples.[5]

First Nations women were key figures in this negative portrayal, and efforts to control female sexuality, especially that of Aboriginals, stood near the heart of imperial dominion in Canada.[6] The cultural and physical reproduction of Native societies was systematically undermined by persistent portrayals of women as inadequate and degenerate wives and mothers. There was also the steady hemorrhage caused by the 1869 provision of the Canadian Indian Act, which denied status to Native women marrying White men, in much the same way in which their British counterparts lost their nationality on wedding a foreigner. In the United States, in contrast, Indian women, regardless of husbands, retained tribal membership. In time, some of their American Mixed-race daughters and granddaughters proved effective champions of Native people. In Canada, however, women whose Indian inheritance came from mothers were largely lost to tribal communities until the 1985 reform of the Indian Act. In contrast, women of European origin were cast as moral superiors, essential harbingers of imperial civilization. A clear distinction between the two types of women, the wild and the civilized, was critical in justifying the defeat of Natives and the triumph of Europeans. By confounding this boundary Pauline Johnson called into question the logic of the imperial project.

A different perspective was adopted by a few Euro-Canadian observers who were captivated by the promise of Native culture for a modern world struggling, it was believed, with effeminacy and materialism. Like early investigators of pre-industrial Maritime and Quebec folklore, they sought inspiration for western civilization in the supposed 'primitivism' of others.[7] Their search for Native myth, a 'golden age' prior to European contact, and Indian heroes, 'noble savages' such as the imperial loyalists Joseph Brant and Tecumseh, acknowledged desirable qualities that deserved imitation and in the process appropriated new imaginative space for British newcomers. A glorious Iroquoian past fit the bill perfectly for the romantically inclined, like William D. Lighthall, author of *The Master of Life: A Romance of the Five Nations and of Prehistoric Montreal* (1908), editor of *Songs of the Great Dominion* (1889), and friend of Pauline Johnson.[8] Fantasies about primitivism, current in Western civilization since at least the Enlightenment, kept such Canadians enthralled as the problems of urban industrial life loomed larger in the Dominion.

Occasional expressions of concern for actual Native peoples came from the missionary efforts of Christian churches. As the frontier of contact retreated and most Euro-Canadians appeared to forget the land's original residents, 'home-based' missionaries emerged as the uncertain mainstay of the atrophied Euro-Canadian conscience. Clergy-men such as Adam Elliott and Abram Nelles at Six Nations, friends of the Johnson family, helped train Native leaders in the skills they would use to defy Ottawa and the provinces. Typical of clergy-led initiatives was the Canadian Indian Research and Aid Society (CIRAS), founded in 1890 by a missionary from northwestern Ontario. Attracting the gover-nor general as patron, the society was dominated by sympathetic churchmen and anthropologists and received support from a few Natives, notably from the Ontario Iroquois. While that effort failed, later groups such as the Society of the Friends of the Indians of British Columbia (1910) similarly appealed to church people committed to ameliorating some of the effects of contact.[9] Traditions of Christian paternalism and occasional evidence of respect and friendship helped keep some Natives loyal to churches. Pauline Johnson's elite Mohawk family found comfort and encouragement at the Church of England's Mohawk chapel at Six Nations.

However, with Pauline Johnson, religion, like virtually every abstrac-tion, is never simple. Some of her early poems, such as 'Easter Lilies' (1886), 'A Request' (1886), 'Christmastide' (1889) and 'Brier' (1893) suggest heartfelt Christian belief. Later on, Christian hypocrisy and betrayal become targets in poems such as 'The Cattle Thief' (1894) and '"Give Us Barabbas"' (1899), as well as in stories such as 'The Derelict' (1896) and 'As it was in the Beginning' (1899). The latter, with its title invoking the familiar words of the Anglican creed, recounts betrayal by a Protestant minister who, garbed in the 'blackcoat' normally associated with Catholic priests, embodies all Christian missionaries. Many readers would be able to add the following words, 'and ever shall be,' a powerful accentuation of the author's indictment of religious racism. Johnson's telling alteration in 1895 of the last lines of 'A Cry from an Indian Wife' to challenge the 'white man's god,' and her ostensible declaration of personal paganism in 'A Pagan in St Paul's' (1906), both discussed in more detail later, similarly chart the public alienation of the formerly 'earnest member of the Church of England.'[10] Whether such shifts rep-resented Johnson's private beliefs, rhetorical experiments, or political acts, we do not know. Her death was apparently eased by the presence of the Church of England's C.C. Owen, whose family was well known at Six Nations,[11] and of her doctor, Thomas Nelles, a relative of the Anglican clergyman she had known in childhood. Johnson's differing approaches confirm that Christianity supplied an uncertain ally for many Native champions. Their struggle, as a political reading of Johnson's late poem, 'And He Said, Fight On' might suggest, was ultimately a lonely crusade.

While few Canadians foresaw the long-term survival of distinct Indian communities, some imagined the survival of superior Aboriginal individuals and traits in a population amalgamated under Anglo-Canadian suzerainty. The extensive racial mixing that began when Europeans first touched North America always raised at least the question of a new 'hybrid' people claiming the virtues of both founding races, a possibility tested in fictional accounts such as the anonymously authored 'Azakia: A Canadian Story' (1791), Catharine Parr Traill's *Canadian Crusoes: A Tale of the Rice Lake Plains* (1852), and Gilbert Parker's *The Translation of a Savage* (1893). In Canada, as elsewhere in the imperial world described by Robert Young in *Colonial Desire*, 'hybridity was a key issue for cultural debate.' Fear of an inability to control the northern half of the continent made Euro-Canadians increasingly anxious, as Young has noted more generally of these years, 'about racial difference and the racial amalgamation that was apparent as an effect of colonialism and enforced migration.'[12] Just what could be the contribution of other races to empires fashioned by and for Europeans? What was the result of long-standing racial mixing? The Mohawks of Six Nations, for example, were said to have no 'pure-bloods' left.[13]

In the thirty years after Confederation, uncertainty about the viability of British North America, together with the presence of the Iroquois among the nation's increasingly mythologized United Empire Loyalist (UEL) founders, the persistence of powerful tribes, and an outspoken Métis presence in the west, combined to raise the possibility of other recruits to the national community.[14] According to Pauline Johnson's admirer, Charles Mair, a founding member of the Canada First movement of the 1870s and and the author of a laudatory poetic drama about the War of 1812 Indian hero Tecumseh, 'in our history, the Indians hold an honoured place, and the average reader need not be told that, at one time, their services were essential to Canada.'[15] No comparable imaginative space for a loyalist Native warrior existed in the United States, which in the latter part of the nineteenth century continued genocidal Indian wars and dispossessions.

Anthropologists were particularly keen early observers of the Canadian racial experiment. In his influential assertion of humanity's common origin, *Prehistoric Man: Researches into the Origin of Civilisation in the Old and the New World* (1876), Daniel Wilson, Fellow of the Royal Society of England and Professor of History and Literature at the University of

Toronto, commented, 'I have recognized the semi-Indian features in the gay assemblies at a Canadian Governor-General's receptions, in the halls of the Legislature, among the undergraduates of Canadian universities, and mingling in selected social circles.' Although he discerned significant flaws in hybrid races, Wilson concluded that 'Canadian half-breeds' supplied numerous 'men at the bar and in the Legislature; in the church; in the medical profession; holding rank in the army; and engaged in active trade and commerce' and he noted the emergence of a new 'Native stock' in Red River.[16] That flourishing settlement supplied not only its own Mixed-race elite, but also a test of the ethical and physical results of intermarriage.[17] Pauline Johnson's Manitoba Métis hero in her short story 'The Shagganappi' (1913) captures the promise of this moment in Canada's development.

A small number of nineteenth-century intellectuals such as Wilson, John Reade, the assistant editor of the *Montreal Gazette*, and the author Catharine Parr Traill, herself the grandmother of Native-European children, appear to have contemplated intermarriage with relative equanimity.[18] Canada could integrate Europeans from beyond the British Isles and draw on the best of the Native peoples. Here seemed both a more humane remedy for the 'Indian problem' and a solution to Canada's continuing crisis of viability. Reade emphasized that racial mixture, with its confirmation of the essential unity of the human race,[19] was a long-standing fact of life as 'the inhabitants of the earth are, slowly in some places, with surprising rapidity in others, undergoing transformation by interfusion of blood.'[20] Canadians, like the British themselves, were a composite people, a fact that Pauline Johnson also emphasized in discussions of her family. This view also presumed the ultimate fate of the Indian. Duncan Campbell Scott, the deputy superintendent general of Indian affairs, waxed as positive as he ever was about his charges in the magisterial *Canada and Its Provinces* (1914), decreeing that 'the great forces of intermarriage and education will finally overcome the lingering traces of Native culture and tradition.'[21] In the union of Indian and White, the former, like a married woman in the legal fiction of the day, would at best effectively disappear in the person of the superior partner.

What proponents of intermarriage rarely acknowledged was continuing prejudice. As Pauline Johnson's last partner, Walter McRaye, recalled of journeys around the Dominion, hybrid races contributed some of 'the leading families of the west,' yet suffered 'the odium of being indexed as belonging to neither the white nor the red race.'[22]

In her stories 'A Red Girl's Reasoning' (1893), 'As It Was in the Beginning' (1899), and 'My Mother' (1909), Johnson dramatized this hostility. Racial mixing remained intensely problematic in an era coloured by increasing acceptance of racial hierarchy. The 'country-born,' the prairie offspring of Native-British marriages, like Ontario's Pauline Johnson and others at Six Nations, had incentives to downplay or deny their non-European heritage. In contrast, the Métis, stigmatized as Native, Catholic, and French in provinces that were increasingly Anglo-centric and Protestant, had every reason to declare themselves a new nation.[23] More difficult to achieve, as Louis Riel and others learned in two rebellions, was recognition and respect. The particular meanings of couplings that flourished along the borders of contact were always mediated by the realities of power. Once the sex ratios of the advancing settler population stabilized, Native mates received scant courtesy.

European men were sometimes faulted for the occurrence of interracial unions but, as in cases of rape, they rarely bore the brunt of society's disapproval. The scapegoats were, as Jean Barman has cogently set forth for British Columbia, almost invariably Native women who were portrayed as deviant, debauched, and dangerous.[24] Doubly degraded, Native women were assumed ultimately to be victims not so much of predatory European males, although they might well have been, but of the misogynist traditions of their own people. They were assumed to have a clear interest in pursuing European partners, whether it be to reap better rewards for debauchery, to escape the attentions of their own menfolk, or to raise themselves and their offspring above Native barbarism.

If the attachment of Native women and White men was understood as a common, if largely unfortunate, occurrence, that between a White woman and a Native man was considered extraordinary. On the one hand, there was the possibility, as Daniel Wilson argued, that this was 'the true test of equality of races ' In making such a match, Native men supposedly demonstrated their capacity for civilization. The innate superiority of the European spouse promised, optimists believed, improved offspring. Others concluded, far less positively, that only an inferior specimen could be attracted to Native men.[25] However construed, unions like that of George Johnson and Emily Howells, Pauline's parents, were closely scrutinized.

As the products of Native-White intercourse, Mixed-race children were expected to forget their supposedly inferior ancestry. As one correspondent to the *Toronto News* in 1885 insisted, Mixed-race individuals

honor and nobility when absolute starvation gnaws out his body and he
sees the food he rightfully owns being swallowed by another, who like the
man in Holy Writ possessed flocks of his own but took his poor neighbor's
one ewe lamb and served it for his guest.

Exploring Squamish legends almost two decades later, she again
reflected on the denigration of Native culture. Even a sympathetic
listener found 'it becomes harder and harder to induce the old people
to talk, while the young folk are silent because so often they are
ignorant.'[34]

Yet even if demoralization was widespread, Indian and Mixed-race
peoples actively rejected extinction and inferiority and explored other
scenarios for interaction. In 1860 the Ojibway Nahnebahwequay (1823–
65), known as Catherine Soneegoh Sutton, took the case for Native
rights to Queen Victoria, receiving an audience never granted to
Johnson. Returning to Ontario, she continued to denounce colonial
greed and intolerance, reminding settlers that Indians were 'human
beings, possessing living souls.'[35] An early death ended her calls for justice. Shortly thereafter the 1869 Indian Act denied women like her,
Native wives of Whites, their nationality and their right to similar protest. Bitter experience prompted Ontario chiefs to boycott an 1891 conference planned by the Canadian Indian Research and Aid Society, as 'a
mere ruse on the part of the Government to draw out from them what
they have to say, and that nothing will come of it.'[36] Such Native advocates used improving English and better formal education to mount
sophisticated campaigns for redress. Like their feminist contemporaries, they became experts on their legal status and held their own with
politicians and bureaucrats who attempted to employ laws to further
their own hegemonic racial interests.[37] Pauline Johnson's example may
have encouraged Native champions to master the imperial language.
At the end of the twentieth century, Cree writer and activist Emma
LaRocque summed up the result: 'Colonization works itself out in
unpredictable ways. The fact is that English is the new Native language,
literally and politically. English is the common language of Aboriginal
peoples. It is English that is serving to raise the political consciousness
in our community; it is English that is serving to de-colonize and to
unite Aboriginal peoples. Personally, I see much poetic justice in this
progress.'[38] Johnson's performances and texts lie near the beginning of
the emergence of English as a common language of resistance for
North America's First Nations.

In their struggle to be heard and to make larger sense of their struggle, Indigenous peoples also maintained links across the British Empire and the English-speaking world. Britain's anti-slavery community provided an important reference point for those like the Anglo-Ojibwa Kahkewaquonaby, known also as Reverend Peter Jones (1802–56), who traced the struggle of colonized peoples in Asia, Africa, Australia, New Zealand, and California. Natives criss-crossed borders, comparing notes on situations and strategies. The Iroquois in Ontario and New York State kept old ties alive in recurring campaigns for financial compensation.[39]

No province entirely escaped Native agitation in the years after Confederation but as a contributor to the *Canadian Magazine* sourly observed in 1921, 'the Indians of British Columbia and the Six Nations tribes, more particularly, have for some time been showing symptoms of unrest in respect of supposed grievances.'[40] By the end of the nineteenth century, multi-tribe alliances were typical of both Ontario and British Columbia. As the struggle against racism intensified, pan-Indian sentiments spread. Even before the First World War, when enlistment and overseas service linked a diverse community of Native activists, wider travel was forging new collective identities. As Pauline Johnson noted in her 1907 story 'The Haunting Thaw,' for example, some Iroquois had moved to the prairies where they had 'grown into manhood, learned in the wisdom of the great Six Nations Indians of the east, and in the acquired craft and cult of the native-born plainsman of the west.'

By 1906 Johnson readily drew on a sense of shared identity in her London meeting with Squamish Chief Su-á-pu-luck, who was there to muster support from King Edward VII. Two years later, Su-á-pu-luck, known in settler society as Joe Capilano, the most prominent B.C. Indian champion of his day and the bête noire of the Vancouver press, confirmed the friendship with Johnson and the public relations benefits of contact with Anglo-Canada's most popular Indian.[41] As mainstream culture welcomed Johnson to Vancouver when she decided to make it her home in 1909, the province's First Nations claimed equality as hosts. Honouring her as 'none of the eastern tribes' had done, Su-á-pu-luck led four local chiefs in telling her 'that she came into the west and into their hearts at the same time.'[42] This highly symbolic gesture linked two of Canada's most active Native groups, the Iroquois and the Squamish. Between Johnson's arrival and the Squamish chief's death at the age of fifty-six in 1910, the two met often. From Su-á-pu-luck and his wife Líxwelut (baptized Mary Agnes), Johnson learned tribal stories, the counterparts of those she regretted not learning from her own grandfather. Versions of these legends were first published in the *Vancouver Province Magazine*, where the narrative role of the Squamish champion is diminished. In the book, titled against Johnson's express wish *The Legends of Vancouver* (1911) rather than *The Legends of the Capilano*, he and to a lesser extent Líxwelut resurface as dignified representatives of their people. In 1910 Johnson took a prominent place in Su-á-pu-luck's funeral and later introduced his son Mathias Capilano to Prime Minister Sir Wilfrid Laurier.

Monarchs, governors general, lieutenant-governors, premiers, and prime ministers regularly received Native petitions and delegations employing the conservative language of deference and reciprocal obligation. In the east, the Iroquois were expert at respectfully but firmly asserting their claims as long-term allies. During the 1885 revolts, many prairie tribes insisted that, 'loyal till death,' they merited fair and generous treatment. Pauline Johnson's continuing avowal of Iroquois fidelity and her personal pleas for elite patronage sprang from the same tory tradition, according to which the powerful are expected to succour loyal subordinates. Such strategies, much like those of female petitioners in the days before their own enfranchisement,[43] reflected a pragmatic recognition of the imbalance of military and economic power and at least some hope of manipulating a reciprocal relationship.

While willing to exploit relations with the mighty, Natives dismissed many aspects of settler society. Proud of their own traditions, some shared with conservative White critics a profound distrust of the modern world. Materialism, excessive individualism, and violence towards women and children joined the long litany of European failings identified by Aboriginal peoples. Johnson's retelling of the legend of 'The Sea-Serpent' (1910) captured just such condemnation. The thrust of Native criticism was that 'Indian country' had been conquered because of European numbers and duplicity, rather than through any intrinsic shortcomings of the original inhabitants.[44]

Mixed-race individuals in Canada, as in the United States, were often near the centre of resistance to settler society's dismissal of Native virtue. Like Kahkewaquonaby, better known as Peter Jones, son of an Ojibwa mother and a Welsh father and friend of the Johnson family, they symbolized the fusion of two cultures and frequently saw themselves as especially equipped to take the lead in encounters between Natives and Whites. While male champions such as Jones and Louis Riel have attracted more attention, women were also involved in resistance. Their activity was often local and barely documented,[45] but Johnson was not alone in developing a national voice. Amelia McLean Paget, daughter of a part Aboriginal mother and a Hudson's Bay Company employee, presented a sympathetic portrait of the prairie Cree, Saulteaux, and Assiniboine in *The People of the Plains* (1909). Her subjects retain a 'natural sensitiveness and inherent dignity'[46] and successfully evade the efforts of Duncan Campbell Scott, who wrote the introduction and edited the volume, to impose a negative interpretation of Plains people.[47] Women emerge as hard workers not victims in a far more attractive portrait than that provided by most European commentators. Unfortunately, Paget seems to have had no further public occasion to tell this alternate story.

By the time of Johnson's birth in 1861, something of a Mixed-race aristocracy had emerged in North America. This multi-heritage people were a diverse group about whom Natives, as well as Euro-North Americans, harboured ambivalence. Recently, one Indigenous American scholar has bluntly generalized that 'mixed-bloods had more money and material goods than fullbloods, and they maneuvered themselves into tribal leadership positions.'[48] The prominence of Mixed-race persons was interpreted somewhat differently by Maria Houghton, the daughter of an elite Okanagan tribe woman and an early Anglo-Canadian member of Parliament: 'They seem to possess a certain mental aloofness, a freedom and independence and judgment which makes them different from the whites, pure bloods; and these qualities make for leadership among men ... if he takes part in community life at all, he is apt to forge to the front. These men are in a sense "well-born."'[49] Certainly some favourable combination of character and circumstances helped produce politicians such as Manitoba premier John Norquay, and American vice-president Charles Curtis, as well as a host of writers, performers, and professionals. In the United States the sisters Susette and Susan LaFlesche (Omaha, 1854–1903 and 1865–1915), and Laura Cornelius Kellogg (Oneida, 1880–1949) formed a generation of 'Native women journalists [who] attempted both to legitimate a Native identity and to argue for inclusion as equals in the dominant culture.'[50] In Canada many such women, whose fathers and grandfathers were often Euro-Americans, would not have been status Indians. With her personal history of a Dutch great-great-grandmother and a middle-class English mother married to Mohawk men, Pauline Johnson was a highly unusual Mixed-race advocate of her day.

At what point persons of Mixed-race ancestry can claim to be Native or White, or whether indeed they constitute a separate nationality as the Métis in Canada have argued, remains unsettled. Parents and communities have tried to situate offspring advantageously with respect to their own perception of the meaning of racial categorization. Sylvia Van Kirk has suggested that Mixed-race sons had more difficulty than daughters in passing into the dominant European society.[51] But for her own and her family's insistence on a Native identity, Pauline Johnson might well have slipped relatively unnoticed into the settler community. The elusiveness of her identity was summed up in one contemporary's memory of her first stage appearance: 'She then struck me as a very beautiful English lady, of whom you might have had no thought of her Indian blood unless told.'[52]

The Six Nations

Johnson was especially fortunate in growing up on the Six Nations territory near Brantford, Ontario, a community widely acknowledged as 'populous, multinational, and wealthy,' a showpiece of both Native talent and the supposed success of Canadian Indian policies.[53] This pre-eminence was so marked that the Department of Indian Affairs arranged for the principal loyal chiefs during the rebellions of 1885 to tour Six Nations and take part in unveiling a monument to Joseph Brant in Brantford. The visit, including a side trip to meet Pauline Johnson, her widowed mother and sister, was carefully orchestrated to highlight civilization under European suzerainty.[54]

Notwithstanding nods of imperial approval, the Six Nations operated as a centre of Native resistance. Since at least the seventeenth century the Iroquois Confederacy had been acknowledged as an extraordinary community, not to say a worthy and dangerous foe. Early English colonists, eager to secure allies against the French, readily hailed the Iroquois as 'naturally akin to us'[55] and 'imperial republics.'[56] Later American anthropologists like Lewis Henry Morgan (1818–81) and Henry Rowe Schoolcraft (1793–1864) expressed similar admiration, naming the Iroquois the Romans or sometimes the Greeks of the New World.[57] Such praise helped inspire Longfellow's famous poem *Hiawatha*, with its Onondaga hero. Canada's leading early scholar of the Six Nations and a close friend of Johnson's parents, Horatio Hale (1817–96), was equally complimentary in drawing a somewhat different comparison: 'We see in them many of the traits which Tacitus discerned in our ancestors of the German forests, along with some qualities of a higher caste than any he has delineated.'[58] Still later, the National Museum's Diamond Jenness in his canonical *The Indians of Canada*

(1932) confirmed long-standing praise. He declared that the Iroquois stood out as a 'democratic,' 'virile' community, with 'political genius' and the 'spirit of empire builders.'[59] Even writers in the *Canadian Magazine*, rarely friendly to Indians, were likely to concur. In attempting to understand why they caused so much 'trouble' to Ottawa, a March 1921 reviewer reminded readers that the Iroquois were after all 'the intellectuals of North America, as the Greeks were of the Ancient World.' Objectionable, from his point of view, was that 'as a people they had a good conceit of themselves, thinking they were 'by nature superior to the rest of mankind, and call themselves Onguehonwe; that is, "men surpassing all others."'[60] As one speaker in Pauline Johnson's 'The Haunting Thaw' (1907) observes, 'you can't boss an Iroquois.'

An especially intriguing aspect of Iroquois superiority was its matrilineal, or even matriarchal, traditions. The prospect of matrons with important political and economic roles raised troubling questions. Few commentators imagined that virile, responsible men could live alongside powerful women or that male success could exist without female dependence. One result, as Martha Harroun Foster has concluded, was that 'Indian progress' was interpreted by anthropologists 'as male progress' and women were 'consciously programmed' out of the picture.[61] Like other dissenting Mohawks, Pauline Johnson entered a debate about the future of Native peoples whose very terms made strong women a threat to community improvement.

The Iroquois Confederacy of first five tribes (Cayuga, Mohawk, Oneida, Onondaga, Seneca) and then six, with the addition of the Tuscarora around 1722, had been founded in the seventeenth century by the near-mythological Hiawatha. The Six Nations Council House at Ohsweken, Ontario, where Pauline Johnson's father, grandfather, and male kin debated and legislated, suggested a model for multi-cultural alliances. Within the Confederacy, tribes often assumed different roles. The Onondaga were commonly regarded as the guardians of tradition. The powerful Mohawks were considered risk-takers and innovators, characteristics which perhaps also explain their reputation for intermarriage with the European community. Euro-Canadian observers have regularly singled out the Mohawks for special regard. The author of *Prehistoric Man*, Daniel Wilson 'distinguished' them 'for the readiness with which, from the earliest date of their intercourse with whites, they have allied themselves with them, and adopted them into their tribes.' He qualified this admiration in adding that Mohawks were particularly 'wealthy, opinionated and litigious, and vexing the soul of [their] friendly superintendent by choosing to have a will and an opinion' of their own in terms of their long history of assimilation and intermarriage.[62] Mohawk prominence and outspokenness also owed much to the fact that they made up a majority of the Iroquois United Empire Loyalists who came north following the American Revolution. They included the war chief Joseph Brant, celebrated by Canadian ethnologist, John MacLean, in 1889, as 'a sagacious leader ... the Indian Loyalist of Canada, hated by his foes, and admired and loved by his friends.'[63]

As refugees and allies, the Six Nations sought out privileges within the British Empire. During the War of 1812, when their warriors could still make a difference, they considered neutrality and then intervened effectively against the Americans. Settling in as heroic founders, the Iroquois established two significant communities, one at Deseronto on the Bay of Quinte and another which would coalesce after 1847 on the Grand River near Brantford, around the Confederacy's major settlement of Ohsweken. From the beginning and to the present day, they have insisted on their special status among Native peoples. Once the Iroquois had ceased to be useful in guaranteeing Canada against the United States, however, governments downsized claims to status as well as to land. Governor General Lord Dufferin conveyed this changing politics in 1874. While acknowledging the Iroquois as a 'distinct nationality,' he hailed them as 'happily incorporated with the British Empire,' no different from the 'French, English, Irish, and Scot' who had also chosen to come to Canada.[64]

For all such assertions of equality, the Six Nations had good cause for disenchantment. While Ontario lands given in recompense for the losses of the American Revolution had once been vast, by 1847 little over 22,000 hectares remained. At the end of the century these had dwindled to 17,960. Property and funds were eaten up by land speculators and settlers. Pauline Johnson's grandfather, John Smoke Johnson, a hero of the War of 1812, was far from unusual in surrendering his holding in the 1870s.[65] White bootlegging and illegal sales of timber invoked further tension, as did Ottawa's recurring efforts to enfranchise Natives and impose elected councils, and its passage of the 1869 Indian Act. The latter's attack on matrilineal inheritance, like federal legislation's general assumption of Indian submission, fuelled resistance as the Six Nations saw self-government steadily eroded.

Relations with Brantford, the nearest settler community, reflected the difficulties of sovereignty. While the city originated to serve the nearby Native market, it soon looked enviously at Six Nations territory, first trying to incorporate parcels of Native land in the 1850s. Conflicting claims kept relations uneasy and sometimes angry. The visit of Buffalo Bill's Wild West show in August 1885 occasioned a revealing comment on race relations. Noting that a local boy had died at the Battle of the Little Big Horn, the *Brantford Expositor* surmised that the audience 'heartily enjoyed' the moment when Wild Bill enacted the defeat of Sitting Bull, Custer's nemesis. The city's best-known author, Sara Jeannette Duncan, signalled the dominant point of view in *A Social Departure* (1890). Dismissing a Native as 'not noble, aquiline, or red, but basely squat,' the novel's American narrator informs readers that James Fenimore Cooper's idealized fictional Indians were not encountered in real life.[66]

To be sure, friendship and mutual interest sometimes linked ambitious city folk and local Natives. In 1886 Brantford citizens joined the Iroquois in commemorating Joseph Brant with a larger-than-life statue and a poem composed by Pauline Johnson. Eight years later they presented Johnson, now their leading poet, with gold sovereigns to assist her trip to England. Some children from the Grand River territory attended the local collegiate and Natives of all ages played lacrosse and baseball with other Canadian enthusiasts. By the beginning of the twentieth century, however, a long history lay behind the local Indian superintendent's lament that 'a spirit of fault finding, of antagonism, and I will also say, of jealousy, has been growing in this city and county against the Six Nations.'[67] Brantford's 1917 request for the donation of Johnson's old home, Chiefswood, to the town, to be maintained as a park in her honour, was rejected out of hand as just one more attempt at a land grab.[68]

Iroquois efforts to negotiate with European Canada were spearheaded by a powerful and articulate elite, often dominated by, but not restricted to, Christian Mohawks. Well before Johnson's birth and throughout her lifetime, the Confederacy Council was largely managed by a group which included her father and grandfather. On the side, but never removed from power, were her grandmother and aunts. Bolstered by fluency in Mohawk, the official language of council meetings, which contributed to their reputation as outstanding orators, the Johnsons and their kin attempted to direct the Confederacy.

This Christian elite appeared confident pragmatists, working with missionaries and imperial authorities while championing sovereignty. While the Johnsons were notable members of this group, Oronhyatekha (1841–1908), known as Dr Peter Martin, and John Ojijatekha Brant-

Sero (1867–1914) were also highly visible. Although neither was a chief, these multi-talented men were well-travelled Mohawk advocates. During the period when Pauline Johnson was establishing herself as a writer and performer, they too developed reputations as effective spokesmen, informing the imperial world of Iroquois virtues.[69] In common with B.C. Native leaders in the first decades of the next century, they believed it possible to 'choose between tradition and assimilation, [and] they chose tradition, but they sought to widen it, to adapt it, and to integrate it within the white political system.'[70]

In the decades after Confederation, such successors of Joseph Brant, often dubbed progressive by settlers, would find negotiation of what post-colonial critics call subaltern space increasingly difficult. The Iroquois and the Mohawks in particular reveal that '"peculiar intimacy" of colonizer and colonized,' which explains the complicated play of resistance and attraction which characterizes relationships between the imperial power and the colonial 'other.'[71] Like many colonized people around the globe, the Iroquois anticipated selecting the useful from European civilization while maintaining their own culture's claims to legitimacy and autonomy. The history of the Johnson family, and the Mohawks in general, with its appropriation of signs, notably of the cultivated intellectual, reveals what Homi Bhabha has called 'a mixed economy of not only power and domination but also desire and pleasure.'[72] The position of such elites is notoriously unstable, relying as it does on consent, from those who are led as well as from the imperial power and its delegates.

By the second half of the nineteenth century, the Mohawks were encountering significant Six Nations resistance to their leadership and to the high levels of acculturation evidenced by their command of English, their intermarriage, their education, their Christianity, and their material prosperity.[73] Before, during, and after Pauline Johnson's lifetime the reserve was deeply divided between those who, like her father, were for the most part Christian and responsive, albeit critically, to the opportunities of European contact and others, notably the Onondaga, commonly styled traditionalists who held firmly to Longhouse values, including language, customary law, and religion. In the face of European advance, traditionalists were anxious and suspicious. Often followers of Handsome Lake (1735–1815), the post-American Revolutionary War Iroquois religious reformer who had spoken out against intermarriage and in favour of restricted contact with settlers, they particularly questioned Mixed-race ambitions. For example, one self-styled

'Six Nations' writer summed up reservations in his attack on Oron-hyatekha: 'This latter doctor is of the Martin family of our Tuscarora reserve and has perhaps not more than one-eight part of Indian blood in his veins.'[74] Given the long-standing multiculturalism of Grand River, with its traditions of adoption and intermarriage, such views were highly divisive and constituted a direct attack on Mohawk leadership.

Economic differences reinforced these divisions. Disputes over permission for private timber sales after Confederation appear rooted in the determination of the progressives to have the hereditary council (where they were powerful) control sales; the traditionalists, on the other hand, with plenty of timber left to sell, more often favoured unrestricted marketing. Seneca, Onondaga, and Cayuga speakers summed up the bitter grievance: 'A few of the chiefs who are tools of the superintendent, J.T. Gilkison (not the majority of chiefs) have taken upon themselves to appoint twelve men to seize our timber and wood. We, the Lower Indians, do not approve of this course of the Upper Indians who, having disposed of their timber and wood, now wish to prevent us from doing as we like with what we consider our own property. The Interpreter, G.H.M. Johnson, a person not at all popular with us, also busied himself with our matters.'[75] Opponents challenged each other in the Confederacy Council in what has been described by one subsequent Native commentator as 'crippling political conflict.'[76] Brutal attacks on Pauline's father, George Johnson, the appointed forest warden, in 1865, 1873, and 1878, suggest the complex nature of this struggle. As the daughter of a highly partisan family active in fierce debates, Pauline Johnson roused mixed feelings among the people she publicly celebrated as her own. In time, her visits home grew fewer and she elected to die and leave her ashes in British Columbia.

While the Longhouse community maintained a relatively low profile beyond Grand River, the Christian elite included a prosperous community of farmers, professionals, and officials. Families displayed success in large brick and stone homes furnished similarly to those of their affluent Euro-Canadian neighbours. The Johnson home, Chiefswood, regularly described as a mansion, with its 'lovely Native park ... 800 walnut, 300 butternut, and about 200 hickory trees of various kinds,' hosted politicians, academics, churchmen, and members of the British aristocracy. Its comforts, apparently funded in part from family legacies to Emily Howells, Pauline's mother, were comparable to those of 'Echo Villa,' a neo-classic residence with Doric columns built for the Methodist minister and Mississauga chief Kahkewaquonaby, or Peter Jones, on the same

northeast corner of the reserve and, for that matter, the Victorian gin-
gerbread homestead of Alexander Graham Bell a few miles away. All
three middle-class families were friends, and friendly with those similarly situated in Brantford.

While precise numbers are difficult to ascertain, Euro-Canadian
women were included among the Mixed-race elite who moved on and
off the reserve during these years.[77] In addition to Eliza Field (1804–
90), the wife of Kahkewaquonaby, and Emily Howells, the mother of
Pauline Johnson, there were Frances Baynee Kirby, the widow of an
English clergyman, who married John Ojijatekha Brant-Sero, and Affa
Northcote Gease, a British-Canadian woman who wed Frederick Ogilvie
Loft (1861–1934), another Iroquois activist, in 1898.[78] The tendency of
such women, once widowed, to desert Grand River, taking their children with them, complicated the inheritance of lands, where the usual
practice favoured matrilineal succession. White relatives might convey
status in some quarters but they also compromised membership in the
Native community.

The children of elite Christian families sometimes attended local
schools, including the Mohawk Institute run by the Anglican New
England Company, but they were more likely to be sent elsewhere. Run-
aways and arson at the institute were signs of problems that anxious parents sought to avoid by enrolling their offspring in local fee-paying
collegiates or even in private schools such as the Brantford Young
Ladies' College or London's Hellmuth College which welcomed Pauline's siblings, Evelyn and Beverly. Some women, such as Johnson's
sister-in-law Floretta Maracle, like their Euro-Canadian contemporaries,
turned to teaching or clerical work. Mixed-race students who attended
institutions such as the Ontario Agriculture College, Queen's University,
Ohio State University, McGill University, and the University of Toronto
contributed to a generation of journalists, teachers, government officials, and doctors who had begun to appear on and off the Iroquois territory by the last quarter of the nineteenth century.[79] There was,
however, no equivalent to Oklahoma's Cherokee Female Seminary
which from 1851 dedicated itself to a Mixed-race elite of young women,
many descendants of Euro-American men, who were groomed to lead
their nation in its interactions with American society.[80] But Six Nations,
like the more numerous Cherokee, was deeply divided about those who
adopted too many settler ways. One Iroquois critic summed up misgivings: 'As time went on there arose an intellectual elite who had won for
themselves a place in the whiteman's world, but they did not impress
Ohsweken.'[81] Notably, Pauline Johnson does not seem to have per-

formed in her 'home' town on the reserve, although nearby Brantford welcomed her on stage.

Connected to the outside world by interests and often by family ties, the Six Nations Christian elite cultivated powerful friends and protectors in a tradition that went back at least to the days of Sir William Johnson, Britain's Indian superintendent in New York before the American Revolution. With visiting dignitaries such as governors general, British aristocrats, and military and religious officials, Canadian politicians, and even such members of the British royal family as the Prince of Wales and the Duke of Connaught, the Confederacy Council employed time-honoured customs of ceremonial adoption. Ties with missionaries and Indian superintendents, as well as long-standing military traditions that drew many Iroquois men into local militia regiments, presented similar opportunities for patronage. Such connections, with their exploitation of conservative notions of deference and obligation as well as fictive kinship, were decried by at least one non-Native commentator who cited the 'capture ... of the inestimable occupant of Rideau Hall, Lord Aberdeen' to demonstrate the calculated nature of the ploy and the naiveté of the prey.[82] Whatever the reality of such relationships, Pauline Johnson regularly drew on them to further her career and overcome economic and social embarrassment.

Recognizing their strength relative to other tribes, the Six Nations chiefs often looked beyond their own territories to speak for indigenous peoples as a whole. This role frequently led the Six Nations to voice the concerns of all Native Americans in international conventions. As early as 1840, at an historic assembly of Ontario tribes, John Smoke Johnson unsuccessfully urged other Indians to cooperate in demands for land title. On the same occasion, he enjoined the Ojibwa to cease referring to the British governor as 'Father' and to employ the term 'Brother,' with its connotation of equality.[83] Grand River hosted other such assemblies and maintained Native networks well into the United States. The repetition of such contacts over the years encouraged the pan-Indian sentiments and protests that would, after World War One, increasingly characterize First Nations politics in Canada. Hardly surprisingly, the founder of the first nation-wide Native federation, the League of Indians of Canada (1919), was Frederick Ogilvie Loft of Six Nations.

The Iroquois shored up claims to equality with Europeans and superiority among Native peoples in a variety of ways, notably in their recourse to history.[84] They argued that their civilization predated European contact and was comparably endowed both in culture and governance, and

also pointed to their alliances with the British, against first the French
and then the Americans. On both counts, the Six Nations merited preference.

The emerging discipline of anthropology was central to these claims.
The Six Nations consciously cultivated, and were in turn cultivated by, a
long line of pioneer practitioners, some of them Iroquois. In this way,
they asserted a distinguished genealogy and a unique relationship with
the British Empire. Lewis Henry Morgan, the author of *League of the Ho-
dé-no-sau-nee, or Iroquois* (1851), made a series of visits in his construction
of a powerful story of Aboriginal genius. Still more closely bound to the
community was the Ontario-based Horatio Hale, a familiar guest at
Chiefswood. His 'long love affair with the Iroquois'[85] was unmatched by
any of the other early anthropologists, such as Harriet Maxwell Converse (1836–1903), Erminnie A.P. Smith (1836–86), David Boyle (1842–
1911), Diamond Jenness (1886–1969), and William Fenton (1908–).
Also remarkable was a group of Mixed-race scholars, notably the American Seneca, Arthur Parker (1881–1955) and the American Tuscarora,
J.B. Hewitt (1859–1937), who explored Grand River's artifacts and histo-
ries on behalf of the New York State and Smithsonian museums.[86]

Pauline Johnson hints at the emotional links that bound some 'Indi-
anologists' to the tribes in her story 'A Red Girl's Reasoning.' Her character, Charlie McDonald, had 'as a boy ... the Indian relic-hunting craze,
as a youth he had studied Indian archaeology and folklore, as a man he
consummated his predilections for Indianology by loving, winning and
marrying the little daughter of the English trader, who himself had married a Native woman.' The fact that the story recounts his betrayal of his
wife certainly suggests how professional interest can miscarry when it
crosses into personal involvement. There is a similar tone of bitterness
in her comment in her non-fiction account, 'A Brother Chief' (1892),
that 'the researches made in archaeology and ethnology benefit not the
subjects studied.'

The Six Nations were active participants in anthropology's recovery
of their past. They told stories, corrected accounts, and gave and sold
wampum belts, ceremonial masks, and other artifacts. Some, like the
Onondaga-Mohawk, Seth Newhouse, and the Seneca chief, John A. Gibson, asserted their own accounts of tribal government.[87] A prime example was the Mohawk Oronhyatekha, who assisted anthropologists and
became a collector himself, not only of First Nations but also of European and African artifacts. Iroquois recognition of the significance of
recovering the past on their own terms was underlined by a later anthro-

pologist who pointed out that it was 'not at all uncommon to be asked whether one wishes the answer in terms of Parker's, Hale's, Hewitt's, or Fenton's description.'[88]

Although Native participants often attempted to control early social scientists, some desperately needed cash, misunderstood the significance of what they sold, or chose to make a living as 'pickers.' Whatever the process of transfer, Iroquois goods and stories fed a market which cared little about ongoing Aboriginal culture. As an anthropologist of his day, the Royal Ontario Museum's David Boyle was not unusual in his faith in a racial hierarchy topped by Anglo-Saxons, nor in the criticism he received from the Six Nations.[89] Evelyn Johnson, Pauline's sister, bitterly recalled the abuse of hospitality enacted by another researcher, Erminnie Smith, who paid a mere ten dollars to ninety-year-old John Smoke Johnson for a copy of the original *Iroquois Book of Rites*: 'As she was leaving our home, Chiefswood, for her home in New York, we learned of the transaction of our American guest, and, although we made every effort to recover the book from her, we were unsuccessful. I was told ... that she, who loved the Indians so much, made some hundreds of dollars by the sale. ... to the Smithsonian Institution in Washington.'[90] Yet hard times, as when Pauline Johnson herself had trouble paying bills, meant that artifacts passed out of tribal hands, in her case to Boyle and Converse, among others. Her story 'Hoolool of the Totem Poles' (1911) dramatizes the quandary posed by the choice between poverty and sales to eager collectors. The decision of the heroine to carve and sell miniature replicas of the great family totems is an unusually happy solution in which she simultaneously expresses her personal artistry, protects and communicates tribal heritage, and earns a living.

By the end of the nineteenth century, a small group of Iroquois were committed to producing more inclusive accounts of Ontario and Canadian history. These enthusiasts seized opportunities to emphasize their community's contribution to the Dominion's survival. In 1874, some years before the formation of the Brant Historical Society, they initiated efforts to raise a memorial to Joseph Brant. His statue in the heart of Brantford, dedicated in the presence of settler and Native dignitaries in 1886 and the occasion of a memorial ode by Pauline Johnson, supplied a powerful visual symbol of the nation's Indian heritage. Pauline's interpretation of the stories of the Squamish people near the end of her life offered a further reminder that First Nations history and the First Nations themselves constituted an essential moral and mythical resource.

Recurring contributions to the Ontario Historical Society (OHS)

Over the nineteenth century, female authority and status in Iroquois society appear to have declined in response both to European opposition and to the influence of the religious and cultural code of the conservative reformer Handsome Lake. His attacks on so-called witches and emphasis on female obedience aimed to shore up masculinity at the expense of women.[101] Iroquois women nevertheless continued to wield power as clan matrons and retained prominence in tribal cosmology. Their importance underlay the strong opposition in 1869 to Ottawa's 'denaturalization' of Iroquois women marrying Whites. As chairman of the Grand Indian Council of Ontario and Quebec in 1872, Oronhyatekha petitioned to strike this section from the Indian Act. Later, as president of the Independent Order of Foresters, he campaigned more successfully to have women admitted as members in 1898.

Not surprisingly, the prestige and power of Iroquois women were also admired by North American feminists.[102] The freedom of Native women from the social and material restraints of middle-class convention appealed to literary writers across the whole spectrum of female advocacy. In 1769 Frances Brooke (1724–89) celebrated the right of Indian women to travel alone; in the words of her lively character, Arabella Fermor: 'they talk of French husbands, but commend me to an Indian one, who lets his wife ramble five hundred miles, without asking where she is going.' A century later Rosanna Leprohon (1829–79) invoked an Aboriginal example to argue for a purer domestic life in her poem 'The White Maiden and the Indian Girl.' A forest maiden, whose wampum belts suggest the Iroquois, debates the merits of her freer life with a pampered White woman and emerges triumphant in the last verse:

No, sister, it cannot my heart engage,
I would worry to death of this gilded cage
And the high close walls of each darkened room,
Heavy with stifling, close perfume;
Back to the free, fresh woods let me hie,
Amid them to live, – amid them to die.[103]

While Leprohon follows conventions in her infantilization of the Indian, who hails the other as 'sister' but is referred to in turn as 'child,' she also admires another way of life. White female authors' recurring interest in such Mohawk United Empire Loyalist 'founders' as Molly and Catharine Brant echoes early enthusiasm.[104]

Drawing on indigenous traditions as well as sharing in evolving Euro-

Canadian middle-class practice, Native women played active community roles in the post-Confederation decades. Where property and status for themselves and their children, legitimate and illegitimate, was concerned, Iroquois women demanded a hearing from the Confederacy council.[105] They also maintained the Ohsweken Women's Institute and organized and raised funds for causes ranging from public health to sports and education. In many ways such women seemed, as Pauline Johnson insisted in 'Iroquois Women of Canada' (1895), like 'daughters of one of Ontario's prosperous farmers.' The outspoken defence of Iroquois land claims by the American Oneida, Minnie Kellogg, like the contribution of Six Nations resident Sophie Martin to the creation of the Indian Defense League of America in the 1920s,[106] reflected a self-confidence rooted in custom and affirmed in twentieth-century practice. Growing up on the Grand River, Pauline Johnson had a first-hand view of women's ability to employ long-standing traditions as a source of power. When she moved to British Columbia in 1909, she encountered another region with its own history of female authority.[107] In *Legends of Vancouver* she frequently credits coastal women with considerable influence. Like the Iroquois matrons she also celebrates, these women draw significant power from their role as mothers.

Iroquois cultural energy and resources were further demonstrated in the appearance of what the American scholar L. C. Moses has termed 'show Indians.' While there is a long tradition of 'wannabees' masquerading as Natives, notably Long Lance and Grey Owl,[108] the years from Confederation to the First World War proved the heyday of Indian performers in wild west shows, international expositions, and congresses, theatres, and sporting events. Subject to the ambitions of managers and agents and the preferences of audiences, Natives were exploited and stereotyped. For some there was also money, excitement, fame, and the opportunity to develop talent. As entertainers, they might find moments when it was possible, as the later Mohawk singer-songwriter Murray Porter explained, to 'play a part and put down in words and music the feelings of what it's like to grow up on a reserve, what it's like to go to a residential school, what it's like to be looked down upon as a second-class [Canadian] citizen.'[109] Given common prejudices and limited opportunities, the career of a 'show Indian' held obvious attractions.

Invigorated both by the determined engagement of some Iroquois with European Canada and by the refusal of both Christians and Longhouse factions to surrender prized traditions, the Six Nations constituted a powerful, if sometimes conflicted, community. By the 1890s the

Ohsweken Farmer's Institute, the Agricultural Society, and the Agricultural Fair demonstrated that local farmers could match farmers elsewhere in Canada. The emergence of temperance and other moral reform groups testified to the activist orientation shared with the non-Native community. By the end of the nineteenth century, Council government had also initiated public works, education, and social assistance programs. Such a thriving community was not likely to disappear, despite the 1876 recommendation of anthropologist Daniel Wilson: 'Better far would it be for them to accept the destiny of the civilized half-breed, and mingle on equal terms with settlers many of whom have yielded up a nationality not less proud than theirs ... each survivor of the Old Indian Confederacy would be the gainer by the abandonment of what is worse than an empty name. While the Euromerican race would take once more into its veins the red blood of the ancient aristocracy of the forest.'[110]

The Johnson Family

The story of the Johnson family, George, Emily Howells, and their daughters and sons, captures the energy and the difficult choices facing the Six Nations. Onwanonsyshon, or George Henry Martin Johnson (1816–84) was the son of Helen or Nellie Martin (1798–1866) and Sakayengwaraton, or 'Smoke' Johnson (1792–1886). The forceful Nellie Martin was the eldest daughter of a noble Mohawk family. Her mother, Wan-o-wen-re-teh or Catherine Rollston Martin, was a Dutch-American captive adopted into the tribe. Sensitive to suspicions evoked by such ancestry, her great-granddaughter, Evelyn Johnson, insisted that Rollston was 'an Indian in all but blood.'[111] Certainly her Mixed-race daughter, Nellie, never spoke English and took considerable pride in her status as a senior matron of the Wolf Clan with the right to select chiefs.

Named by the Six Nations Council as a Pine Tree, or elected, chief at the request of the British government for his support during the War of 1812, Smoke Johnson did not come from a high-ranking family. He was, nevertheless, as Evelyn Johnson emphasized, of pure Mohawk blood.[112] There were, however, always rumours that his family was descended, through an unformalized marriage with a Mohawk woman, from the New York Indian superintendent, Sir William Johnson.[113] Speaker of the Confederacy Council, and a noted orator in both Mohawk and English, Smoke Johnson proved a determined leader of the so-called progressive forces. George, the eldest son of his union with Nellie Martin, was educated by Anglican missionaries, a testament to his father's continuing commitment to negotiating a place within the British Empire.

After training at the Mohawk Institute, where he revealed the linguistic talent that would make him fluent in all the Iroquois languages and English, George Martin Johnson considered becoming an Anglican clergyman but he elected instead to assist the Church of England missionaries, Abram Nelles and Adam Elliott. Young Johnson's continuing fervour was demonstrated by his public destruction of a religious idol of the Delawares, a minor tribe at Six Nations.[114] A favourite of the missionaries, he became an interpreter for the Anglican Church. In the Elliott parsonage, Johnson found the atmosphere, as his daughter Evelyn noted, of 'an English Gentleman's home. Father was brought up in it at Uncle's [Elliott] quite as much as mother.'[115] Affinities with the settler community were further reinforced by marriage to Emily Howells, the sister of Elliott's wife Eliza, in 1853. To brave his new wife's friends and relatives, some of whom were overtly hostile, Johnson garbed himself in the height of British 1850s fashion, replete with black silk hat and satin waistcoat, a presentation which marked his claim to superiority before a sceptical Euro-Canadian audience.[116] The union was also strongly opposed by his mother. An English daughter-in-law meant grandchildren who could not, according to traditional law, inherit Mohawk rank. At a time when issues of tribal loyalty were fiercely debated at Grand River, the presence of Emily Howells reminded critics that the Johnson family had a full measure of European blood.

After his marriage, the younger Johnson continued to improve his position. In 1859 he emerged as interpreter for the superintendent of Indian affairs. As his close friend Horatio Hale took pride in observing, 'Mr Johnson is an educated gentleman ... the chief executive officer of the Canadian government on the reserve.' In a memorial testament, Hale reflected further that 'few have done more than he accomplished in his humble sphere, in breaking down the absurd and wicked prejudices of race, and proving the essential unity and brotherhood of the human family.'[117] What he failed to note was that Johnson, for all his talent, was ultimately only the assistant to the Indian superintendent who lived off the reserve and who remained the final official authority. Whatever his ambitions, Pauline's father worked very effectively with imperial authorities, enthusiastically opposing the Rebellions of 1836–7 and, some thirty years later, joining the hunt for the Irish Fenians when they attacked from the United States.

A Scottish Rite Mason, an ardent Anglican, and a proud member of the provincial Horticultural Society, this 'Iroquois Chief' and 'Anglo-Canadian gentleman,'[118] self-styled 'Esquire of Onondaga,' embodied his family's close ties to Euro-Canadian society. Yet his captaining of Native men in a mock battle to entertain the governor general, Lord Dufferin, in 1874 also suggested that he never escaped his ambiguous status as a 'savage' gentleman.[119] While it is impossible to know, it is tempting to wonder if George Johnson's regularly expressed admiration for Na-poleon, Britain's once-powerful enemy (he named Pauline after the emperor's favourite sister and nicknamed his elder son 'Boney'), gave a hint of ambivalence concerning his affiliations with imperial, as well as Iroquois, authority.

Despite his controversial marriage, George H.M. Johnson was selected by his mother to succeed his uncle, Jacob Martin, as a hereditary Mohawk chief. Although his daughter Evelyn claimed that his simultaneous tenure of the roles of translator and chief was at issue, as was the presence of both a son and a father in the Confederacy Council, at least as disquieting for Iroquois traditionalists was the growing power of this Mohawk family with its strong identification with imperial interests. Led by the Longhouse conservatives, the Wolf clan meeting prepared to depose him as chief. In a highly unusual action, the Mohawk matron Nellie Martin asserted her right to name chiefs and insisted that no one would replace her son. If he were not confirmed, her nation would forego a representative on the Council. The result was compromise. Johnson became a chief but while he remained a government official, his vote would not count.[120]

That resolution foreshadowed his more famous daughter's ambiguous place in the Confederacy. Since her father was Native, Pauline Johnson was Mohawk according to federal law but, since her mother was English, never in tribal law. Emily Howells' status was likewise problematic, as the refusal of the Indian superintendent and the Confederacy Council to grant her a widow's pension confirmed. Not even her relative impoverishment, nor the fact that her husband's 1884 death occurred in large part through injuries inflicted by timber smugglers, released purse strings.

Like Eliza Field who wed the Ojibwa-Welsh Methodist minister Kahke-waquonaby in 1833, Emily Howells (1824–98) came from an economically comfortable English family sympathetic to evangelical and anti-slavery campaigns. Such progressive antecedents were important in encouraging favourable responses to Native suitors. Both women were in their late twenties at the time of marriage, old enough to know their own minds but also mature enough to sense dimming marital prospects. Her father's early Quakerism and move to the United States as an active abolitionist may underlie Emily Howells's willingness to consider an unconventional match. At the same time, his authoritarian, even brutal, parenting apparently also encouraged her to seek refuge with older sisters until her marriage, which was described by her daughters as being deeply affectionate. She and her children were later welcomed into the homes of her close kin. However, the most famous Howells relation, American writer W.D. Howells, kept his distance.

Years on the Anglican mission, a possible stint as a teacher at Six Nations, and regular visits to family in Ontario and the northern states, not to mention contact with the Jones family, introduced Emily Howells to racism's hard realities.[121] The idea that rumours were circulating about her initially secret courtship caused much anxiety. Faced with briefly leaving Six Nations, she jested: 'now be careful my old boy how you act for how do you know that should you wait too *long* ... I may be tempted to ... trot off with a "*pale white face.*" What a shock that would be to your nerves my poor old fellow.' She then quickly asserted: 'dear no face is so dear to me as yours ... how happy I should be to think that I shall again so soon see my *dearest friend*. But God's will must be done dear George ... trust to God alone for *our future happiness*. God bless thee my dear George ... May God guide my wandering feet through this world and grant that we may live happily together til death shall separate us ... then ... meet in heaven.' Two years after their marriage, Emily was still offering reassurance: 'All my friends are delighted to see me, they say I look as well as ever, and "just like old times" ... I do not see that I am *treated* with the least *disrespect* because I am the *wife of an Indian Chief.*'[122]

According to their daughters, this love, as well as a shared commitment to Native peoples, music, literature, and the Anglican religion, sustained the happy couple. Devotion was facilitated by the maintenance of a middle-class lifestyle, complete with piano, silver tea service, books, and Black, White, and Indian servants. Money from the Howells relatives helped keep up appearances, subsidizing, for example, Emily Johnson's music lessons. The architecture of the substantial family home, Chiefswood, with doors facing both the Grand River and the county concession road, opposite entrances symbolically welcoming both Native and White, confirmed the couple's determination to combine worlds.[123]

mal schooling offered the boys other avenues, but that course was not
without problems. Like many a Mixed-race and Indian child, Allen ran
away from the Mohawk Institute. White institutions were not necessarily
better: Beverly threatened truancy from Hellmuth College.[132] Eventually, however, both secured formal educations which equipped them for
Canada's commercial middle class.

The attractive Beverly, or 'Hell' Johnson as he was nicknamed,
became a talented musician and well-known lacrosse player before moving on to a series of positions with life insurance companies, first in Canada and then in the United States. Allen, after boarding with his
Hamilton uncle, Dr T.B. Howells, while he attended the local collegiate,
became a cashier in the warehouse of Senator James Turner, a family
friend. As a young businessman, he lived in rented rooms that he deco-
rated with valuable Indian artifacts, and took up membership in Hamilton's rowing and lacrosse clubs, and the Garrick Dramatic Club. In 1891
one observer hailed the brothers, 'whose handsome and distinguished
appearance would attract attention anywhere. They hold good positions
in insurance companies and move in the best society.'[133]

Ultimately, however, both men found it difficult to unite their dual
heritage. Allen's efforts to host gatherings where he dressed in Iroquois
garments were not palatable to polite society. When his so-called wig-
wam parties came 'to the ears of his employers through some of their
daughters being guests, he lost his position and the parties were discon-
tinued.'[134] Apparently disappointed in love for a Euro-Canadian
woman, he returned to Brantford. There Allen remained, unemployed
and supported by his mother and sisters until Emily's death in 1898.
Beverly relinquished his family's traditional support for the Conservative party when John A. Macdonald's government brutally suppressed
the starving prairie tribes during the Northwest Rebellions of 1885.[135]
Whatever his brother's disillusionment, however, Allen went on to
become vice-president of the United Empire Loyalist Association.

Beverly and Allen Johnson never settled permanently among their
Native relatives. Both brothers, like their sisters, lived much of their
later lives, as Pauline put it, as 'waifs and strays ... in hotels and rooming
houses.'[136] The elder ultimately died a bachelor in his forties, dropping
dead of a heart attack, alone and anonymous in an American city. Late
in life Allen married Floretta Maracle, a longtime friend of his sisters,
and lived in Ottawa and Toronto. He died in his sixties without issue.

Like her brothers, Evelyn Charlotte Johnson, the second of the four
children, has almost been forgotten. Pauline's biographers claim that

she and her sister did not agree, their conflicts largely blamed on the elder's supposedly domineering nature. Evelyn, in turn, chided Pauline's spendthrift habits. There have also been suggestions that while 'Evelyn had some very fine characteristics ... [she] was chiefly English – while Pauline was nearly all Indian.'[137] Such comments reveal more about the observers' attachment to the charismatic poet than about her sister. Despite her modest, or bitter, comment that she was unknown 'because I never did anything,'[138] Evelyn, too, was a significant product of Chiefswood's bicultural experiment. Worth recalling are the views of one rare public admirer, a Brantford citizen transplanted to Vancouver, that

> this sister was as remarkable and out-of-the-ordinary in her own sphere as Pauline was famous in the fields of literature and the histrionic arts ... She was a great student of Indian folk-lore and biography, and had an unrivaled knowledge of her father's people. Pauline on the other hand, skimmed over the surface of these subjects more lightly, but had a keen insight for any dramatic situations that might be welded into poetic form ... a critical historian like Evelyn will probe to the very bottom of a subject before he leaves it. She was long a valued member of the Brant Historical Society.[139]

Unfortunately, the sources for Evelyn's life are scanty. Her surviving publications and personal notes provide glimpses of a woman with a strong sense of middle-class morality, whose attempts to defend the First Nations, especially the Iroquois, are worth recovering. They remind us that Pauline Johnson moved within a kin group that shared many concerns.

Evelyn Johnson was educated at Hellmuth College, the Anglican boarding school in London, Ontario, where she spent some of her happiest days. She was subsequently engaged briefly to an Indian doctor who remains unidentified. That relationship ended for obscure reasons that may have stemmed from her temperance sympathies. Like her sister, she never married. Years later, she remembered an epigram, coined by the teenage Pauline, which revealed their shared attractiveness and hinted at sibling rivalry: 'Eva is like the sun, she dazzles the men, but I am like the moon, I send them crazy.'[140]

Like many a spinster daughter, Evelyn remained a mainstay of her widowed mother. And unlike her sister who, upon the move to a rented home in Brantford in 1885, settled down to writing, visiting kin, canoeing with friends, and developing a local reputation for amateur dramatics while waiting for a suitable husband, Evelyn performed clerical duties in the office of the Waterous Engine Works, where she remained until her mother's death.

Like many ambitious women before her, she then elected to leave small town Ontario. In 1901–2 she completed a course in domestic science at Toronto's Technical School. By 1903 she had moved to New York State in search of employment as a matron, housekeeper, or lady's companion – occupations that often signalled genteel poverty. Always short of money, she travelled about for work but never lost her ties with Six Nations, well meriting her reserve name, Ka-nah-kah-lay-hah, 'one whose home is here, but goes away for a time to different places then home again.'[141] While matron of a YWCA residence in Troy, New York, she was so shocked by what she regarded as improper behaviour by young Iroquois women that she helped found Ohsweken's Indian Moral Association. This initiative, typical of turn-of-the-century middle-class activism, won the support of Dr Helen MacMurchy, one of Canada's leading moral reformers. Evelyn's papers also suggest American contacts with both Whites and Indians active in the cause of Native rights, including the prominent feminist and Iroquoian scholar, Harriet Maxwell Converse, who hosted Pauline on her visits to New York City.[142]

While coping with chronic financial insecurity, Evelyn Johnson maintained her commitment to setting straight the historical record on her people and defending their interests. Rarely able to attend meetings, she was nonetheless an involved member of the Brant County and Ontario Historical Societies and an outspoken United Empire Loyalist. In articles, addresses, and letters to the editors she championed Grand River and the Martin and Johnson families. She took considerable pride in her accuracy. In an annotation to her sister's memoir 'My Mother,' she observed, somewhat self-righteously, 'Paul could write poetry and fiction – but not history. She imagines so much that is not fact.'[143] More explicitly historical than her sister's writings, Evelyn's articles regularly linked the past to the present. A 1911 account of her Mohawk grandmother's family urged the Brant Historical Society to rescue the historic Martin homestead from destruction. Her arguments revealed awareness of what was happening south of the border and interest in women's role in nation-building:

In the United States the women everywhere are saving for posterity every possible relic of the wars of the Revolution and 1812, and a future generation for whom these loyal women are indeed conservateurs will assuredly appreciate and value these efforts to preserve to them the historic sites and relics of their forebears.

This, then, is applicable to the U.E. Loyalists, and the Six Nations, the allies of Great Britain, the price of whose suffering and losses, both of homes and country, cannot, in these blessed times of peace, be too justly estimated, nor too greatly honored.[144]

While this plea proved fruitless, Evelyn's approach would have received approval from the Women's Historical Society of Ontario and other middle-class women of her day who were mobilizing in the cause of Canadian heritage.

This daughter of Six Nations did more than resurrect the past. She also challenged conventions that denigrated Native peoples. 'Indians,' she was known to insist, 'produce many of the most beautiful women and the handsomest men in the world. Undoubtedly the assertion of so many visitors to the United States that it has the most beautiful women of all countries is owing to the mixture of blood of practically every nation around the Globe.' After Pauline's death Evelyn renewed her commitment. To a friendly American supporter, she explained, 'my people in whose welfare I am bound up are so dear to me that my life from now on I have consecrated to them. At least, neither of us has been called upon to bear what our poor people have been compelled to endure in loss of homes, land, hunting grounds, and their several nations themselves almost exterminated ... The losses they have sustained with *scarcely a murmur.*'[145]

Although her papers suggest support of the Native American rights campaigns, this Johnson daughter retained her commitment to her home. She applauded the Confederacy Council's 1914 efforts to cultivate the Duke of Connaught: 'the Chiefs have added another link to the chain which binds him closer to us, a brother Chief of Six Nations and that is well, particularly in these days of uncertainty regarding the question of our land holdings when we need all the friendship we can retain of those who are in sympathy with Indians in their fight for justice.'[146] Efforts at intervention went beyond Grand River. During the First World War, she lectured Prime Minister Robert Borden on the politics of conscription. The Six Nations had once again resisted Canadian claims to sovereignty and were deeply divided over participation, torn between martial traditions, not to mention much needed wages, and the failure to have their previous sacrifices in the name of empire properly

rewarded. If Borden urged King George V to request their support as
long-time allies, the matter would, Evelyn assured him, be resolved.
What she did not emphasize was that such a resolution would also
favour long-standing demands for national recognition.[147]

In 1919, Evelyn Johnson again attempted to educate the Confederacy.
At a time when Six Nations was in turmoil over elected versus hereditary
government, she defended women who could, under the pressure of
the Indian Act's support for patrilineal inheritance, be forgotten. She
instructed Iroquois leaders, including some of her own kin,

> to remember the land was given to the Six Nations Indians – that is to the
> people and not to the males only; therefore I believe that no land can be
> rightly surrendered by the vote of the Council alone, nor of the males
> alone, but only by a vote of the people both male and female ... women's
> suffrage has been practically recognized by the Six Nations for all of these
> centuries ... the great civilized countries of the world are only at this later
> date now giving their women the right to vote. The Six Nations should feel
> a great and just pride in thus being in advance of all other nations of the
> world in women's suffrage.

Unimpressed by the Council's defence of its sovereignty and firm in her
own convictions, Evelyn Johnson dismissed those who would not fight:
'We are now one of the small nations but we can fight for our freedom
and refuse to surrender the land that is left to us.'[148]

Age slowed Evelyn Johnson down but, like many a mature Iroquois
woman, she exercised her right to voice opinion. In 1921 she let the
Hamilton Spectator's readers know of her sympathies for Chief Frederick
O. Loft, founder of Canada's first pan-Indian organization and later a
pallbearer at her brother Allen's funeral. In the same year she
attempted to set the Imperial Order Daughters of the Empire (IODE)
straight about Iroquois opposition to any policy which entailed private
land tenure and the loss of communal territory. 'The allies of Great Britain,' the Six Nations were protecting the last of their territory. 'It is
because of the rapacity of white people round about the Reserve who
want to wrench the land from the nation; and it is for our very existence
that the Six Nations are fighting perhaps their greatest fight since the
Confederacy came into being ...' She capped her arguments by appealing to other Loyalists: 'We are different from any other Indians in Canada ... Every man, woman and child of the Six Nations is a United
Empire Loyalist and I call upon that patriotic association of U.E. Loyal-

ists ... to come to our aid, to encourage and co-operate with their fraternity in our fight for British justice.'[149] Two years later, in her late sixties,
she was still campaigning, this time targeting the instruction offered by
the Mohawk Institute.[150]

Poor and blind, Evelyn retired to Brantford in the 1920s, to become
something of a landmark, passing lonely days in a local park. Here she
dreamed of writing her memoirs but, like her sister, she finally left her
story to others.[151] Her will recalled many themes that also marked
Pauline's life. The trustees included Six Nations friends as well as the
regent of the Brantford chapter of the IODE. She requested three
White and three Native pallbearers and desired to preserve Chiefswood
as a refuge for elderly Indian women and, potentially, a bird sanctuary.
Kindnesses were returned with gifts to the Chinese manager and his
wife and the three Chinese boy waiters of the Patricia Café where she
took her meals. Finally, in a last effort to protect the privacy of a family
whose history had made them the object of so much interest, she
instructed a friend to burn 'all my diaries, unread.'[152]

Like her sister and brothers, Pauline Johnson was the product of a
country, Canada, which was, for the most part, committed to a politics
of racism; of a nation, the Six Nations, which desperately sought accommodation for its own traditions; and of a family which was hard put to
maintain itself within a Mixed-race elite. A literary-minded youngest
child, Johnson had to make sense of a complicated heritage, full of con-
tradictions and ambiguities. Chiefswood's bicultural experiment force-
fully shaped her imagination and her understanding of both the British
Empire and Canada itself. In time she would regret not learning more,
for allowing her 'grandfather [to] die, with his wealth of knowledge,
without trying to find out something of what he knew.'[153]

Like the legendary Pocahontas, whose dramatic rescue of Captain
John Smith she youthfully re-enacted with a cousin at Chiefswood,
Pauline Johnson embraced the possibility of a Native-European alliance.
In 1884 and 1886, memorial odes to the heroes Red Jacket and Joseph
Brant initiated her public commitment to the Iroquois. Intensely sensi-
tive to the racial politics of her age, Johnson also took up the cause of
other Indian nations. Rage at imperial Canada's response to the North-
west tribes and Métis during the 1885 rebellions inspired her extraordi-
nary poem 'A Cry from an Indian Wife' (1885), which still shocked
audiences at the 1892 Ontario performances that marked her as a major
Canadian personality of her day. Soon caught up in making a living,
Johnson did not forget the desperate situation on the prairies, docu-

menting the starvation of those who had once depended on the buffalo in the poem 'The Cattle Thief' (1894). By the end of her life, when Johnson turned to British Columbia tribes for intimacy and inspiration, anger at injustice still echoed through her words even while sadness dominated her narratives. As *Legends of Vancouver* made very clear, First Nations peoples were perishing at the hands of greedy and brutal invaders. Too often she feared she was observing their final moments. The prospect of that bleak future haunted Pauline Johnson even as she established herself as a career woman questioning the conventions that hobbled her sex in the Euro-Canadian world to which she also belonged.

CHAPTER TWO

'I am a woman':
Finding Her Way as a New Woman

The Canadian New Woman

Pauline Johnson flourished amid a post-Confederation generation of middle-class women who puzzled and disturbed their contemporaries. Unlike her mother, who chose to avoid 'public life' and 'the glare of the fierce light that beat upon prominent lives, the unrest of fame, the disquiet of public careers,'[1] the daughter elected to make her way as a New Woman in North America and Britain. An amateur performer and enthusiastic writer since her teens, Johnson resisted maternal opposition to a stage career and self-consciously seized opportunities to occupy the spotlight. Her sister Evelyn remembered a quick retort to a query about accepting Frank Yeigh's invitation to join other literary personalities in a prestigious Canadian Literature Evening in Toronto in 1892: 'You bet. Oh Ev, it will be such a help to get before the profession.'[2] By the time of her encore on that occasion, Johnson was well on the way to taking her place in a community of New Women who advanced the frontiers of respectable activity. Although connected to the Native community, she was also a career-minded woman with bohemian aspirations and close ties to the Anglo-imperial world.

Often identified with feminism, although not always a suffragist, the New Woman appeared in the Western world in the 1880s and survived into the 1920s. The leitmotif of this international phenomenon was independence. In real life, as well as in writing and on stage, the New Woman signalled modernity in her espousal of many causes, including better education, paid work, egalitarian marriage, and health and dress reform, to improve her own lot and that of her sex in general. In the 1880s the Canadian version appeared in the persons of teachers, businesswomen, doctors, and artists. For the first time, significant numbers of middle-class women set about to earn their own living, able to assert both respectability and some independence from their families. By the time the term 'New Woman' had stabilized, its implications were being explored through the depiction of fictional heroines, including such Canadian characters as Sara Jeannette Duncan's Advena Murchison in *The Imperialist* (1904) and Amelia Fytche's Dorothy Pembroke in *Kerchiefs to Hunt Souls* (1895). While the vast majority of women continued to link their fates to husbands and children, many expressed more than a hint of independence, and even rebellion.

Debates about women's role appeared regularly in Canada's leading magazines, including *The Week*, *Saturday Night*, and the *Canadian Magazine*, all of which published Johnson's work. Kingston writer Agnes Maule Machar, well-known to Pauline Johnson, was an early champion of employment, education, and enfranchisement. She had many successors across the country, including such popular journalists as Flora MacDonald Denison, Francis Beynon, Cora Hind, and Isabel MacLean.[3] While the women's movement which helped sustain these activists largely accepted the prevailing power structure which marginalized non-White women, the Eurasian-Canadian Edith Eaton (1865–1914) (or, to employ her Chinese pseudonym, Sui Sin Far) also invoked the image of the emancipated female as she struggled to win a living as a writer in Canada and, later, south of the border.[4] In the United States, writers of Indian-European background, such as Susette and Susan La Flesche, S. Alice Callahan, and Zitkala-Sa among others, also challenged conventions limiting their sex, again seemingly largely unnoticed by White feminists.

In Canada, as elsewhere, New Women were 'violently abused by many, ridiculed by the less hysterical, and championed by a select few.'[5] In tones reminiscent of the horror reserved for so-called barbarian races, independent, rebellious middle-class females who dared to transgress conventional gender norms were occasionally referred to as 'wild women.' Like their sisters among the Aboriginal peoples of the Empire, they were castigated as a throwback to a matriarchal stage of human development. In confirmation of the inter-relation of prejudices, the 'unwomanly' of their sex 'were commonly compared by their denigrators in academic circles to Jews, blacks, and native American Indians.'[6] All such malcontents were unwanted challengers to the White male body politic.

The illegitimacy of any challenge was detailed by one 1893 writer in the *Canadian Magazine*. In typical fashion, he decried the 'displacement of young men,' arguing that women's 'unnatural' desires for independence were generated by 'considerations of cupidity, selfishness and pride' and the search for 'luxurious living.'[7] Leading Canadian intellectuals such as editor and author Goldwin Smith, doctor and McGill professor Andrew Macphail, and humorist and McGill economist Stephen Leacock, composed similar anti-feminist jeremiads while claiming to defend western civilization. Like Native rebels, insubordinate women had to find their way in a country where powerful forces opposed their assault on entrenched privilege.

However, hostility was never universal. Some Canadians were intrigued by the promise of female emancipation, albeit for the most part in small doses. A youthful Hector Charlesworth, later a leading theatre critic and cultural administrator, outlined an attractive and unthreatening case for his adventuresome compatriot, 'the Canadian Girl'. Appealing to the patriotism of readers, who like him shrank from the supposed excesses of 'the American girl' of their era, he reassured his audience that the local version was quite unlike her British contemporary as well. Superior Canadians did not cling to 'the Anglo-Saxon belief that woman is the weaker vessel.' As a result, Charlesworth cheerfully concluded, the 'woman's rights movements make small progress ... [and] because the Canadian woman gets what she wants without let or hindrance: because she has so many privileges, the right to vote on a subject in which she takes little or no interest seems not worth striving for.' Still better, for those who feared the sex wars which were believed to harry less fortunate nations, the 'average girl' of the Dominion, while possessing 'a decided aptitude for commanding,' had also 'an impulsive force or magnetism that makes its conquests without strife.' The ultimate expression of this well-mannered 'child of nature' was 'a lively girl in boating flannels.' Charlesworth, whom we consider again in chapter three, completed his celebration and coincident domestication of one of his era's most threatening spectres, the New Woman, by hailing E. Pauline Johnson as among the 'most Canadian of Canadian girls.'[8]

This critic subsequently set out the terms of Johnson's acceptance as an artist. Denying any 'haughty male prejudice,' Charlesworth declared that women must find their chief reward in the approval of men: 'Mankind is for womankind, the ultimate court of appeal, and one is giving Miss Johnson the very best of praise, and setting her on a pedestal high above most other feminine wielders of the pen in saying that her songs will meet with the deepest appreciation from all song-loving men ... a natural, generous, healthful woman has, already, won over a large and appreciative audience of men who find something lasting and moving in her music.'[9] Readers were bluntly reminded that despite the increasing visibility of women writers, men remained the critical power-brokers in the literary world.

Ambitious Brantford cultivated its own New Women. In 1873 the city that had produced the Dominion's first female school principal, Emily Howard Stowe, heard from 'Evy' who chastised critics of so-called old maids. Many spinsters, this correspondent to the *Expositor* pointed out, had 'experienced "storms of passion."' They had no desire 'to be a slave to ... some lord of creation who fetters their every thought and action;' for 'all females do not require a male appendage to drag them through the years.'[10] In later years, the Brantford standard for the New Woman was upheld by Sara Jeannette Duncan, as she plied her writing career in Canada, the United States, Britain, and India. Nor was small-town Ontario immune to humorous manifestations of the modern 'regiment of women' so feared by John Knox in an earlier era. What are we to make of the 'Lady Dufferin Guards?' Christened after an energetic governor general's lady of the 1870s, some thirty-five of Brantford's most respectable young women, headed by Captain Gussie Gilkison, daughter of Indian Superintendent Jasper Gilkison and Johnson's friend, and armed with 'brooms and bright red dustpans,' were known on occasion 'to storm' Hamilton, their community's mercantile and industrial rival.[11] While such shenanigans were all in fun, they reminded citizens that their own daughters might question convention.

Building Networks as a New Woman

Even before she left Chiefswood for Brantford's Napoleon Street in 1885, Pauline Johnson had begun to forge a life that associated her closely with the Euro-Canadian world and the New Woman. Her own mother, raised as an English Quaker, had rebelled on several fronts by marrying a Native member of the Church of England. For all her reservations about her daughter's choice of career, Emily Howells Johnson nourished Pauline's love of literature and took pride in her talents. The extended Howells family, despite Pauline's unhappiness with its best-known representative, the American novelist, W.D. Howells, continued influential. Before she took to the road as a performer, Johnson resembled many marriageable young women, enjoying a regular pattern of family visiting which could extend to weeks or even months. Useful and effervescent, she visited brothers, cousins, aunts, and uncles in Hamilton, Montreal, and Kingston, not to mention an occasional American mid-west city.

She was a regular guest at the home of her cousin Kate Howells, first in Paris, Ontario, and later, after Kate married Stephen Frederick Washington, in Hamilton. Her affection for this good friend and her new husband permeates an 1890s canoeing sketch for the American magazine *The Rudder.* Here Pauline and a thinly disguised Owen Smily, her first stage partner, enjoy a camping holiday with the newlyweds, Kathie and Freddy.[12] In Ottawa, another Howells cousin, Annie, sister of the notorious W.D. and wife of Achille Fréchette, translator to the House of Commons and brother of the more noted poet Louis, provided occasional accommodation and financial help.[13] Such highly respectable relatives knit Johnson more closely to the middle-class community of her day than would be suggested by her emerging public persona as half-White but wholly Indian.

Friendships with other White women grew naturally from Pauline's social and cultural interests, creating a continuing network of affection. She appears to have acted on her mother's advice to 'make friends – she said she never made many friends and as they grew old and died she had none left.'[14] In Brantford, family friends boarded Johnson as a student at the local collegiate. Later, her own intimates, including actors such as Mr and Mrs Charles Bell of the Vokes theatrical company, who were in Toronto in October 1890, regularly welcomed her arrival. Despite memories of shyness, Johnson had a particular capacity for friendship.

In her student days Johnson turned to verse to memorialize early affections. Written for 'My Little Jean,' or Jean Morton, her 'bonny girl' and best friend at Brantford Collegiate, one poem includes the lines

Your friendship has sufficed, and held its own
Unsullied still,
What manly voice upon my heart has grown,
What stronger hand can soothe like yours alone
My headstrong will?

Life offers me no love but love for you,
My woman's thought
Was never given to test a faith untrue.[15]

Such lines capture the intense feelings that characterized many female friendships of the day. By sharply distinguishing the emotional and moral potential of the two sexes, Victorian middle-class sexual ideologies heightened the appeal of homosocial bonds. Margaret Conrad's studies of Atlantic Canada during the same period illustrate how women commonly turned to one another for affection and support; the advent of husbands and children need not break those close ties.[16]

The daughter of the Brantford family with whom Pauline had first boarded, Mary Elizabeth (May) Curtis, later wife of Judge A.D. Hardy, never forgot that earlier intimacy. When close to death, Johnson thanked her for mobilizing a gift of $500 from her old circle: 'You have remembered me, fought for me, worked for me, even while I have drifted far from the old life, the old "towns-folk," and today I am a grateful woman because of that ... womanhood, and fellowship which you have shown to me.'[17] Warm memories also underlie the Brantford Local Council of Women's contribution of a further $125 to the Pauline Johnson Trust Fund to assist their old companion in her last days.

For whatever reason, no Native friend or relative other than her father and grandparents emerges in Johnson's published narratives before the appearance of Squamish chiefs Su-á-pu-luck (Joe Capilano) and Mathias Capilano, and a woman informant, probably Líxwelut (Mary Agnes Capilano), in the British Columbia legends published in the *Mother's Magazine* and the *Vancouver Province Magazine* in 1909 and 1910. Until then, whenever Johnson is present as narrator, her only significant companions are Euro-Canadian women or men, such as her stage partners Owen Smily and Walter McRaye, or her much admired literary mentor, the poet Charles G.D. Roberts. While tantalizing traces of Native friends surface occasionally in the limited surviving private correspondence, that story awaits pursuit.

When she went on to become the Dominion's most famous travelling performer, Johnson turned regularly to Euro-Canadians for intimacy and support. Encountering her during a tour of Manitoba in the 1890s, the suffragist Nellie McClung recalled her first impressions: 'she was the first great personage we had met, and we knew it was time for white gloves and polished shoes.'[18] Such formality soon dissolved before the force of Pauline's engaging personality. No stranger to hostile reviews and near-empty houses, Johnson fostered and appreciated friends across the country. In a letter typical of those exchanged among the often besieged writing sisterhood, she thanked Kate Simpson-Hayes of Saskatchewan warmly for support: 'And now my loyal friend to your "bully" write-up of me in the Free Press. It was splendid of you, and will

help me so much. You dear girl, with your strong true heart, always pulsing I believe to help your fellow kind, I owe you much, much more than
I can ever thank you for ... And I know you fought bravely for me with
the bearded lions – it was just like you – you great-hearted warrior
woman.' Pauline reciprocated with advice on writing and publishing her
correspondent's play.[19] Toronto's better-known feminist journalist,
Faith Fenton (Alice Fenton Freeman), saluted by Pauline as a 'fellow
craftsman or rather woman,' and columnist Kit Coleman, another
friend, were highly visible members of the same self-conscious community that would coalesce in the Canadian Women's Press Club
(CWPC).[20] Johnson manifested such loyalties early on when she pressed
hard for the inclusion of women poets in J.E. Wetherell's anthology,
Later Canadian Poems (1893).

Not surprisingly, when she settled permanently in Vancouver, Pauline
Johnson quickly became a popular member of the local branch of the
CWPC. Like many early professional women's organizations, it offered
opportunities for companionship, networking, and affirmation. Such
support was demonstrated by the genial introduction of the poet-performer when she was hosted by the Pacific coast club in 1910: 'It is very
true that the hand that rocks the cradle rules the world, but is it not also
true that the hand which wields the pen directs the world, and our
guests of today have all earned honors for themselves through their pen
points.'[21]

Her loyalty and generosity, including cash gifts from her own meagre
resources, continually broadened Johnson's circle. From the theatrical
community, particularly the Webling sisters, recitalists from London,
England, and Eileen Maguire, a contralto from Vancouver, arose intimates who understood the trials of the itinerant life. With friends like
Henry O'Brien, a Toronto lawyer, she shared enthusiasms for canoeing
and literature. Other non-Native admirers remembered repeated kindness. To a lonesome youngster from the prairies, coping with her first
teaching job in New Westminister, the poet was an utterly 'lovable
woman.'[22] Recalling moments together, an older Jean Stevinson
mourned a woman who 'taught me in many ways, steering me clear of
some things that could have been pitfalls to a girl alone in a big city –
she would have been a glorious mother.' The poet reciprocated with
friendly teasing, and when the prairie transplant found life hardgoing
she was instructed to 'bring an old gown as I go out rain or shine and
get my skirts wet every day; and you'll come with me. It is the only way to
chase the glooms away – go out, no matter what the weather.'[23]

As her health faltered after 1909, Johnson was aided by a 'host' of admirers. Regular visits, assistance with publishing, and timely cash kept the worst of loneliness and poverty from her door. The initial publication of *Legends of Vancouver* in the *Province* was ensured by the magazine editor, Lionel Makovski, who took dictation when she was too ill to continue. Society and professional women and men, including Vancouver-based journalists and entertainers, and the local chapter of the Imperial Order Daughters of the Empire (IODE), rallied to cheer her up and establish a nest egg. *Flint and Feather* (1912), which went on to become one of the country's best-selling volumes of poetry, was published and distributed through their efforts. Across the country women and men mobilized to a degree that was unprecedented on behalf of any public figure in the cultural sphere. Alerted to Pauline's precarious health, Nellie McClung expressed the sentiments of many,

> What a public you have, and how many real sincere admirers who are in such sympathy with you that no sorrow can come to you, without touching them: – this is your comfort, I know, and helps you to be brave and patient. It is easy to be brave, in the rush and roar of battle but it is not to be compared with that needed to face long nights of weariness and pain – I believe this is the courage which is yours. You are in my mind many times in the day, dear Pauline and it is my prayer that ministering angels may be with you in your lonely hours and that strength may come to you to bear all that comes to you of pain and loneliness. There are many prayers for your recovery. You have more friends than you can ever know. My love to you ever.[24]

The prairie suffragist followed up her kind words with concrete help. Determined to get *Flint and Feather* into as many homes as possible, she energetically set about contacting the Winnipeg newspapers. In response, Johnson cited McClung's loyal friendship in her final will.

Devotion continued after death. Pauline Johnson's public funeral in March 1913, with its closure of city offices and flags at half-mast and its celebration in Vancouver's most prestigious church, the Anglican cathedral, was supervised by the Women's Canadian Club (WCC). The president-elect gave the funeral oration. In Brantford, more modest memorial services, also supervised by Euro-Canadian admirers, similarly celebrated Johnson's life. The placing of her ashes in Stanley Park, a federal preserve, came about through the special intervention of the governor general, the Duke of Connaught, who had also visited during her final illness, and Sam Hughes, the minister of militia. Her will was prepared by the prestigious firm of Sir Charles Hibbert Tupper, son of the former prime minister. Later, despite Johnson's preference for an unmarked grave, the WCC sought a monument to confirm their regard. During World War One, part of the royalties from *Legends of Vancouver* went to purchase a machine gun inscribed 'Tekahionwake' for the 29th Battalion of the Canadian Expeditionary Force. In such practical and highly symbolic ways, Pauline Johnson was simultaneously succoured and recognized, firmly integrated into a Euro-Canadian world view that conveniently interpreted the noble Indian as a figment of the national past. From such a perspective, the Squamish people who lined the streets and followed her funeral cortège on 10 March 1913 supplied no more than a romantic backdrop for the best-known Canadian Native woman of her era. To the end, Johnson's life was mediated and appropriated by White admirers and friends.

Previous biographers emphasize Johnson's attraction to and for men. She tantalized and moved many, from those in public life such as Hector Charlesworth, Charles G.D. Roberts, Ernest Thompson Seton, and Charles Mair, who proved invaluable mentors as we shall see in the next chapters, to more anonymous canoe partners and members of her audiences. She worked closely with male performers, such as Smily and McRaye. Whatever the latter's personal and literary shortcomings, as perceived by Johnson's family and biographers, he shared more than a decade with her on the road and, albeit in his own self-interest, did much in later lectures and two books to keep his friend before the public eye. A late poem affirmed her fondness for 'the best friend I ever had':

... the friend I love, who up life's trail
Rode side by side with me through gallant days
... the friend who loves me, who would fain
Halt me from mounting for my lonely ride,
Who would give vast possessions to detain
Me on the range this side the Great Divide
... I shall not fail you at The Great Round Up
O! friend of mine, who never failed me yet.[25]

Pauline Johnson attracted many would-be lovers. Her sister remembered more than half a dozen marriage proposals from Euro-Canadians. While the inspiration for the passionate poetry of the 1880s and early 1890s, discussed in detail in chapter 4, remains a mystery, two later romances have been identified. As far as is known, Johnson returned the affection of Charles R.L. Drayton in the 1890s and Charles Wuerz in 1900, but both men proved unreliable.[26] The girl who had early teased boys on the Grand River and later composed intensely erotic poetry expected to marry. Unlike many other Mixed-race women, however, she became far too famous to set aside readily the racial heritage that the age frequently considered problematic, and to reappear as a respectable settler matron.

Ultimately, for all her romantic attachments, Johnson was nurtured throughout her life by a strong network of female friends who made their lives outside the Native community. Their importance is best attested in her own words: 'women are fonder of me than men are. I have had none fail me, and I hope I have failed none. It is a keen pleasure for me to meet a congenial woman, one that I feel will understand me, and will in turn let me peep into her own life – having confidence in me that is one of the dearest things between friends, strangers, acquaintances, or kindred.'[27] While she remained distinguished by her passionate commitment to the Native cause, she was very much part of another world as well, the world of Canada's pioneering New Women and their efforts to enlarge opportunities for their sex.

In some ways, Johnson's dual loyalties appear consistent. The overwhelmingly White and middle-class woman's movement of her time shared some issues with the Aboriginals' efforts to right their wrongs. Feminist and Aboriginal protests regularly disturbed the decades after Confederation, as each group attempted to make the new Dominion responsive to its wishes for education, economic opportunity, and political equality. They received similar denigration from anthropologists, churchmen, doctors, and politicians. Advocates of women and Natives, however, seldom connected directly. The everyday racism of the woman's movement kept it largely deaf to Native cries for justice.[28] Despite some suffragists' admiration for the matriarchal traditions of the Iroquois, most had too much invested in race privileges to accept Aboriginal peoples as their equals or to offer more than confused and ignorant commentary on the complex Native societies among which they lived.

By embodying and frequently defending the nation's Native inheritance, Pauline Johnson stood out as an anomalous member of the community of New Women with which she otherwise identified. However intense their feelings for her as an individual, Euro-Canadian women had personal and collective agendas which rarely, if ever, included acknowledgment of Native claims or much acquaintance with Aboriginal peoples. As she sought her foothold among their ranks, Johnson had to construct herself as an attractive blending of the familiar and the exotic. Double-garbed and double-voiced, she moved across Canada and beyond its boundaries embracing the memory of old British-Iroquois alliances and the evolving stereotype of the Indian princess, as well as the promise or threat of the independent career woman. Her ongoing dilemma remained: how to be true to herself as a woman of Aboriginal heritage with close personal and professional links to Anglo-Canadian feminists.

Despite a tendency in some quarters to downplay the political significance of women's writing, someone who attracted audiences as diverse as the American Canoe Association, the Canadian Manufacturing Association, the National Council of Women, the Canadian Women's Press Club, the Salem, Massachusetts, Women's Association (later the National Indian Association), a host of English and Canadian salons, and, far from least, listeners in town halls, churches, and theatres across North America, embodied a complicated message of resistance and accommodation which many wished to hear and some understood. Pauline Johnson's life and work suggest an implicit effort to reconcile and integrate the insights of Natives and New Women in a critique of the dominant race and gender politics of her day.

Not surprisingly, the dilemmas posed by multiple and sometimes conflicting identities surface as a major theme in some of Johnson's work. Like the disguised heroine of her short story 'The De Lisle Affair' (1897), Johnson put listeners on guard that things might not be quite as they seemed. In their role as mediators among groups of men, women need to practise a certain ambiguity, even the apparent betrayal of original loyalties. This shifting identification, as in 'The Ballad of Yaada' (1913), where a female character explains 'not to friend – but unto foeman I belong ... though you hate, / I still must love him,' generates the possibility of new understandings and communities. It can also prove fatal, as when Johnson's Mixed-race heroine Esther, in 'As It Was in the Beginning,' kills her unfaithful White lover. With the words 'I am a Redskin, but I am something else, too – I am a woman,' Esther demands recognition of multiple subjectivities. The world of real men and women was more complicated than the artificial divisions of race or nation laid down by authorities such as the racist Protestant minister in this story, revealingly nicknamed 'St Paul' after the biblical misogynist.

Like many of her characters, Johnson defied easy definition. On stage
and in print, she was simultaneously Native, female, and middle-class, a
claimant to the multinational heritage of empire presided over by
another woman, Queen Victoria, whom she celebrated in her poem
'For Queen and Country' (1890). A commentary in the widely circulated *Saturday Night* in December 1892 suggested that the contrast
between her two identities empowered Johnson's performance: 'Miss
Johnson on the platform is very different from the accomplished lady so
well known in social circles; when reciting one of her own fiery compositions on the wrongs suffered or heroism displayed by her Indian race,
she becomes the high-spirited daughter of her warrior sires and thrills
the reader through and through.' A later contributor to the same
weekly hailed her personality as 'essentially that of an Indian princess,
masterful and impulsive.'[29] A more knowledgeable admirer, the popular
nature writer Ernest Thompson Seton, saw a careful and courageous
mastery of very different environments. His friend was a 'world-woman,
at home equally in the salons of the rich and learned or in the stern of
the birch canoe, where, with paddle poised she was in absolute and fearless control.'[30]

In her efforts to work out a life and a profession in the midst of a
world which was only too likely to judge women and Natives harshly,
Johnson had to draw on all her resources, without appearing either cal-
culating or threatening. Her considerable talent for disguise was
summed up by the writer Arthur Stringer. After a conversation in a modest hotel room while she attended to her ironing, he concluded: 'She
was not quite as primitive as she pretended. Or, to put it more charita-
bly, she was not as elemental as her audiences liked to think her. She
was, in one way, quite patrician in mind and spirit.'[31] As this last observation implied, class was an essential part of the performer's repertoire. By
clinging to its privileges, she could hope to counteract other disadvantages.

Much like her friend Nellie McClung, Pauline Johnson learned to cir-
cumvent conventional prejudice against the New Woman, and, similarly,
against the Native, by creating attractive characters with whom it was difficult to take offence. This strategy was displayed in her 1896 sketch of a
canoe trip down the Saskatchewan River. Presenting herself as a fun-
loving but respectable young woman fully conscious of the proprieties
of travelling alone, she carefully notes the qualities of her chaperone.
The latter, a widowed 'lady of perhaps thirty-five' (in fact Pauline's own
age that year), is reassuringly 'garbed in the plain black frock, the spot-

less linen collar and cuffs that bespeak the professional nurse. She had one of the most attractive faces I ever saw, a sweet, laughing face, yet withal brave, strong, heroic as a man's.' This promising introduction to another of Canada's New Women is confirmed by a personal history which illustrates remarkable strength of character, tempered by sufficient self-sacrifice to win the hearts of all readers:

> So *this* was the woman who had Santa Filomena like braved two smallpox scourges in Montreal, living and serving in the fetid airs, the rotting alleys, the pestilential tenements of the French quarters, where overcrowding and filth vied grimly in horror with that grimest of all horrors – death from a loathsome disease. This was the woman who in her early twenties had nursed eleven cases of black diphtheria when the stricken district in western Ontario was paralyzed with fear, and isolated from all communication with surrounding towns, and she had come unscathed through it all, enveloped in the power of her beautiful self-forgetful humanity as though wrapped in the garments of Christ ... What a girl she was yet! ... Why, for a moment the thought hastened across my mind that people might shake their heads at the idea of this merry-voiced, laughing little widow being our chaperon. But the thought died at its birth. I knew that from end to end of Canada that woman's name could have lent respectability to a band of outlaws, a gang of jail birds.[32]

Whether featuring herself or others as heroines, Johnson was careful to guard against aspersions which might diminish audiences, and thus her livelihood. The obvious merits of her sympathetic subjects, even when these were disregarded by other characters, licensed exploration of new territory for women and Natives. Thus, in the opening instalment of 'Outdoor Pastimes for Women' (February 1892), she cleverly negotiates the dangerous 'rights' talk of her time when she uses humour to mitigate her challenge to the manly monopoly on 'the luxury of sports.' 'The day has departed,' she argues,

> when it was considered ungentle and masculine for women to participate in outdoor sports. Within the latter half of this practical century America, at least, has decreed that feminine beauty and feminine health are synonymous, and to attain these womankind clamored long and loudly at the iron portals so jealously closed by that most exacting of monsters, Good Form, betwixt her and her brethren, who themselves regarded the luxury of sports afield as their exclusive right ... And to-day there is little indeed from

which we are barred out – riding, sailing, swimming, rowing, paddling, cricketing, fishing, even shooting, and the latest thing approved – cycling; but in enumerating these all on a wild midwinter night one feels the pulse of a hot national blood athrob in one's veins, that demands with every heart beat a special mention of Canadian national winter sports in which both lads and lassies participate. And one instinctively yields to the impulse, saying, 'And now abideth these three – skating, tobogganing and snowshoeing,' but the greatest of these is snowshoeing ...

Johnson further displayed her sensitivity to her own reception as a New Woman, not to mention awareness of the market for magazine fiction, when she offered readers the romantic contrast of a seemingly less problematic age. While the author's references to the phrase 'New Woman' reveal her consciousness of her era as a time of social change, wives and mothers in her stories never question their consignment to the domestic sphere. Whether Aboriginal or White, these iconic figures stand at the heart of a stable social order, where maternity retains power. Her celebration of traditional Iroquois women, in 'Mothers of a Great Red Race' (1908) identifies powerful individuals who, secure in a forest home untouched by European intruders, have 'not yet joined the ranks of "new women."' Only when Johnson describes their losing battle to protect the manhood of Native sons from destruction due to White influence is the necessity of new strategies raised, and then only by implication in phrases such as 'not yet.' Read today, Johnson's discussion of the dilemmas of Native mothers offers a chilling prediction of alienation and despair. By the close of the twentieth century, another generation of Aboriginal women authors would document this dispossession, with its 'lost, stolen, abandoned, or dead children,' with 'protest, grievance and grief.'[33]

Johnson's effort to recast the masculine national narrative in 'Her Dominion – A Story of 1867, and Canada's Confederation' (1907) similarly portrays a heroine, in this instance White, who fears that sons may fall prey to modern corruptions. 'New women' not yet having come into existence, Mrs Fairleigh, the mother of Malcolm, a 'Father of Confederation,' is, the narrator ironically observes, neither advanced nor up to date. Throughout this story, Johnson extends a domestic metaphor in order to ground the young nation in women's reality. Still the mistress of her family and of her son, Mrs Fairleigh provides critical inspiration: 'It would be great Malcolm – a great thing for you to mother such an idea, to mother the scheme of confederation of those scattered provinces into one vast family.' Without an egalitarian tradition to guide him, the Euro-Canadian son must appropriate his mother's genius. His shift in language provides a further ironic commentary: 'To "father" such an idea, don't you mean, mother? ... Yes, it would be great to "father" the confederation of those provinces. Mother, you invented the right word – "Confederation." I'll make that word of yours go down in history.' While he later publicly acknowledges her role as a 'mother of Confederation,' the suspicious reader might wonder why so critical a character is not to direct, through the exercise of the franchise, the young nation which she has helped call into being. While Johnson repeatedly emphasizes women's domestic orientation and its value for the community, she clearly courts awareness of 'alternate representational possibilities.'[34] In the very celebration of maternal power, she admits its limitations. This gulf between idealism and reality helped prepare the way for suffragists.

At the heart of Johnson's literary inspiration was a faith in women's centrality to a well-ordered world. Like British novelists who employed female characters to critique social conditions in nineteenth-century England, Johnson assigned a key role to women. Her unique contribution was to credit First Nations' women with significance and sensibilities which more than matched those of their European counterparts. No longer sharply differentiated as they were in the racist depictions of the day, both groups of women offered an important perspective by which to reconsider and reorient human society.

Membership in the nation's fledgling community of artists provided Pauline Johnson with an additional vantage point on the failings of modern industrial society. Uncertain of the costs of the rush for development and heightened consumption, Victorians contemplated the materialism of their age with considerable anxiety. Money might bring a comfortable respectability but it was also tainted. Like many of her contemporaries, Johnson was ready to dismiss the newly rich for their vulgarity. It was commonly held that women were responsible for maintaining society's moral foundations, while middle-class men got on with the ethically compromised tasks of accumulation and domination. Good women were not the only potential source of salvation; Victorians also looked to artists and to nature for inspiration. In her person Pauline Johnson was not only highly unusual in linking all three sources of regeneration, but unique in doing so under the banner of 'Indian.'

Artists were key figures, testifying in print, paint, design, and performance to the persistence of transhistorical ideals. Hopes for the revival of traditional virtues such as heroism, generosity, and loyalty underpinned the fascination with both classicism and the primitive in the art of the day. Artists, like women (and they were rarely permitted to be one and the same), could, if true to their higher calling, help restore a moral order threatened by capitalist excesses. Many Canadian writers were among those criticizing the materialism of their time. The role of moral authority could be especially attractive to marginalized cultural critics, such as Pauline Johnson, who, unable to build on the hard-won middle-class status of her parents, had a 'horror of being regarded as "plebian" [which] grew with the years.'[35]

Nature and the uncorrupted Native promised a similar antidote to Victorians' misgivings about modernity. Such faith helped explain the development of tourism into remote places like the northern Ontario bush, not to mention the popularity of nature and animal stories, the spread of children's groups such as the Scouts and Guides, the appeal and recovery of folklore, myth, and archaeology, and the proliferation of White shamans such as Baden-Powell, Ernest Thompson Seton, or, slightly later, Grey Owl. While Pauline Johnson offered access to the wilderness by the very fact of her Aboriginal heritage, her genuine enthusiasm for the outdoors captured the public imagination. This young woman, hailed by one admirer as 'the restless rapid's daughter,'[36] appeared to challenge nature on terms that recalled her primitive ancestors yet was closely attuned to the fitness enthusiasms of urban society. As with her fellow poets Lampman, Roberts, and Duncan Campbell Scott, as well as the painters of the later Group of Seven, outdoors skills provided concrete proof of a special relationship to the land. Although the canoe was widely associated with romantic courtship, Johnson gave it a fresh spin when she aired its potential for liberating women:

> We all have a scrap of the savage, a dash of the primitive man concealed about us somewhere – give it play girls, at least once a year. Be the roving nature-loving, simple-living being that the soul of your ancestors burning yet within you clamors out so loudly at times; just try the old heathen etiquetteless life in a canoe for one summer week, you will be a more womanly woman for the quaffing of nature's wines in the wilderness.[37]

Pauline Johnson also laid early claim to the title of 'Bohemian,' an appellation redolent of artistic non-conformity and a love for the spontaneous and natural – in other words, the antithesis of the age's driven, mercantile spirit. Even before she became famous, she set herself apart from the commonplace of her generation by calling for Bohemian friends. These included Hortense Rhea, a well-known Belgian actress met during Hamilton performances in the 1880s, and the Webling sisters, young recitalists who visited Brantford in 1890–1 and later toured Canada, when life in the theatre was still far from respectable for women. In Johnson's fiction, artist figures – the violinist in 'The Broken String' (1907), the dancer in 'The Potlatch' (1910), and the carver in 'Hoolool of the Totem Poles' – testify to the need for courage and determination.

After she was well established as a performer, Pauline Johnson acknowledged the predicament facing artists in a sketch for an American magazine, the *Rudder*. Sensitive to the single women's need for a suitable chaperone, she transformed her show business partner, Owen Smily, into a more acceptable male companion in this rather fictionalized first-person narrative. 'Barry is my cousin, and quite the nicest boy I know,' she explained. She also distanced herself from her Aboriginal persona in a caricature of her own performance: 'For the last three years we have been owned by a big Lyceum Bureau, that trots us about the country together all winter and half the summer, giving us fairly good salaries to amuse the public, which pays fifty cents per head nightly to hear my cousin perpetrate musical skit work, and to watch me prance about in an uncouth costume while I recite my poems.' In fact, the Grand River recitalist lacked even the legitimacy of a lyceum. Early performances were usually organized by generally unsatisfactory independent managers. While withholding a critical part of her own story, Johnson employed humour to invite readers to acknowledge performers' challenging of convention while espousing their cause: 'By this time the awful truth has doubtless dawned upon you – Barry and I are "show folks." Added to this enormity is a still blacker crime, we are journalists.'[38] In Johnson's hands, one more New Woman had arrived, friendly and familiar enough to reassure all but the most strident of critics.

The era of the New Woman and the promotion of Canadian nature also saw the founding of important artistic and cultural organizations such as the Ontario Society of Artists (1872), the Royal Canadian Academy (1880), the Royal Society of Canada (1882), and the Women's Art Association of Toronto (1890). Even small towns shared in the cultural excitement. In her 1893 article 'The Song My Paddle Sings,' Johnson proudly pointed to the Ontario village of Doon, just up the Grand River from Six Nations and the home of Homer Watson (1855–1936), perhaps the leading Canadian painter of his day: 'amongst bohemians it is a household name, inasmuch as artists have made it a sort of summer breathing spot, where nature and study blend harmoniously.' The hustle and bustle of urban life held little appeal. A river outing, typical of those that Johnson wrote up for eager newspapers and magazines, highlighted an experience of nature that many would envy: 'We are very brown and horribly untidy, but our Bohemian afternoon has surpassed anything that the gaiety of the most brilliant Canadian city could give us.'[39]

Far from her beloved canoe routes, Johnson told much the same story when she toured England in 1894. Like another noted London visitor, Joaquin Miller, the celebrated American 'Poet of the Sierras,' she offered high-society English audiences a vicarious thrill.[40] When Miller, costumed in western boots with spurs, reclined on an animal hide to deliver his lines in the 1870s, or Pauline brought out wampum and uttered war cries in the 1890s, spectators were led to link New World poetic genius with the wild. In London, Johnson depended on the well-to-do to pay the bills but sought out actors, writers, and artists to share sensibilities. An English painter, the lionized creator of pictures of Greek and Roman fantasies, was the subject of a later poem, 'The Art of Alma-Tadema' (1903).

In North America, Johnson attempted to maintain a sense of membership in the artistic avant-garde. Friendship with Charles G.D. Roberts, whom she fondly characterized as a 'genial Bohemian figure'[41] and visits to the publisher of an American magazine, *The Philistine*, affirmed her continuing identification with non-conformity. So did her recurring flirtation with religious scepticism when she flouted convention by condemning churchmen's hypocrisy and praising the 'pagan' Iroquois.[42] Her poem '"Give Us Barabbas"' (1899), with its criticism of official France and support for Emile Zola's defence of Captain Alfred Dreyfus, similarly demonstrates sympathy with the liberal spirits of her time. Later, despite the onset of a desperate illness, she set herself up as an iconoclastic champion of Native virtues at a time when local newspapers encouraged a stock racism that relegated Indians to jails and museums. Acknowledged by a commemorative biography as a 'Bohemian of Bohemians,'[43] Pauline Johnson manipulated a persona that blended the ladylike and the unconventional in a polite but consistent challenge to the age's social and cultural politics.

Breaking Ground as a Woman Writer

Authorship was a difficult business for anyone but, as one British critic has suggested, 'for a sheltered, middle-class, late-Victorian woman, in fact, merely to enter the premises of a newspaper, a publishing house, or a place of business was an alienating and potentially intimidating experience.' Johnson's own publisher, John Lane, was notorious for signing up a 'chorus of lady novelists.' Treating the least sophisticated of his ladies to lunch, he soft-soaped contracts little to their advantage.[44] Johnson's first volume, *The White Wampum* (1895), was a limited edition of poetry, hardly likely to make her fortune. A second volume of verse, *Canadian Born* (1903), did not change matters. If she hoped not to die in poverty, Johnson needed better paying, more popular outlets for her work.

Fortunately, the newspaper world was beginning to recognize that women represented a fruitful market. Dailies and weeklies increasingly sought a mass readership and with it the potential for attracting well-paying advertisers of industrial capitalism's new products. Since wives and mothers were reckoned critical arbiters of family consumption, their patronage was critical. In the last quarter of the nineteenth century, a new mass-circulation press offered unprecedented careers to aspiring female writers who could, it was assumed, better appeal to their sisters.

While assigned a key role in attracting customers, women remained clearly subordinate in the publishing hierarchy. E.E. Sheppard, editor of *Saturday Night*, one of Canada's first magazines with mass circulation ambitions and a significant market for Johnson's work, brutally summed up the situation: 'Our offices are crowded with young women who say and write the most common things. Life is short and we have no time to make a selection ... The majority of the young women who apply desire a situation and a salary. On a daily newspaper this is impossible in the case of an untrained and conventional young lady who expects to be escorted when she goes out and waited upon when she comes in.' He went on to argue, 'I have had the pleasure of introducing more than one bright woman to newspaper work.'[45] Even with this half-apology, he gave notice that the demand for female reporters was limited. With the notable exception of a very few like Sara Jeannette Duncan, who worked her way into political writing, female journalists were largely restricted to the coverage of so-called women's news – social gossip, housekeeping hints, and children's columns. Most tried to avoid such pigeon-holing. Johnson told a familiar story in her plea to another Toronto editor:

Could you make over a *corner*, a *page* in The Weekly News, that I could fill *regularly*, and could you pay me for the stuff, a little at first and more when I make myself valuable to the paper. You know I *never* handle fashions, teas, ball-gowns etc. My work would be – unbeaten trips over unbeaten trails,

corners of the world that other writers have few chances of meeting, outdoor pastimes for women, – an unusual unhackneyed style of journalism
with a verse or poem thrown in now and again.[46]

In a crowded market, Johnson's wish to assert her independence from
the usual backwaters of female journalism fell on deaf ears.

Johnson's fate, like that of the vast majority of writers, was to be constantly in search of publishers who would pay a living wage. The situation for North America's 'raced' writers was still more complicated. On
the one hand, prejudice barred them from a host of experiences and
employments. On the other, a few, while remaining on the margin of
the literary world, could benefit from publishers' desperate hunt for
appealing material. In the United States, Johnson's fruitful last two
decades have been hailed as the Black Woman's era, with the appearance of a talented energetic generation who attempted to address both
race and gender in their writing.[47] A small band of Native women
authors also joined the ranks of those demanding space for a more
inclusive view of North America. For the most part, however, such voices
would fade from popular consciousness after the First World War, only
to be retrieved in the 1980s and 1990s.

Canada too is beginning to recover a lost heritage. Sarah Carter has
recently alerted us to the significance of Amelia McLean Paget, the
Mixed-race author of *The People of the Plains* (1909). Montreal-born
Edith Eaton (Sui Sin Far), who started writing about the problems of
Asian newcomers in the nineteenth century, can now be properly
understood as a pioneer Canadian Mixed-race writer. While invoking
the significance of female friendships and experiences that centred on
domesticity, she questions the moral underpinnings of the imperial
regime and, like Johnson, addresses the costs of racism in relation to the
plight of women.[48] These hard subjects were confronted at both the personal and professional level as each struggled financially. The prejudice
which allowed the son of the editor of Manitoba's *Minnedosa Tribune* to
dismiss Pauline Johnson as 'the Squaw' dogged every move of such talented women.[49]

When Johnson eventually found enthusiastic buyers, namely the mass
circulation American magazines, the *Mother's Magazine*, and the *Boys'
World*, and the weekend magazine of the popular Vancouver daily newspaper, the *Province*, early in the twentieth century, the hard-pressed
writer made the most of her opportunity. Satisfaction with hard effort
and its returns was summed up in a few telling words:

Every morning up at 7:15; breakfast and doing up the rooms over and I at
work at nine o'clock. In all I did 12,500 words, 9,500 for the Elgin people at
$6.00 per M, if it is all accepted and 3,000 for the Province, bring me in
about ten dollars. So, if everything is accepted, as I am pretty confident it
will be, I shall net over sixty dollars for my week's work. My eyes and shoulder played out toward Friday, but I'm at it again this week. The young Chief
[Mathias Capilano] spent all day nearly here yesterday and told me lots of
legends that will make good copy. Today, for a change, I cut out a duck
skirt for myself. I really must get some clothes made so when my arm plays
out I attack the dressmaking problem ... I am fair sick of a pen and the
sight of ink, but I am satisfied with what I accomplished last week.[50]

This schedule was especially impressive as she was suffering acutely from
breast cancer, the cause of the pain in her shoulder.

While Johnson is best remembered as a writer, her reputation in her
own day owed at least as much to her performances. From 1892 to 1909,
she drove herself ruthlessly, maintaining a second life as the author of
almost all her own stage material. While exhaustion and depression
took their toll, she frequently appears to have enjoyed the new experiences and new people, not to mention the fame, which stage life
brought. The travel sketches of the woman nicknamed by Grand River
'Ta-yah-agh-ge-yah-guah' or 'One who travels a great distance away off,
crosses a great deal of land,'[51] conjure up enthusiastic participation in
the beginning of a period of independent travel for women. Even while
mourning the death of her brother Beverly, she could speak positively:
'I am mastering myself – and after all work, and work alone helps me in
these things ... I like it [the life] even though traveling is hard.'[52] When
times were good, Johnson rejoiced in having 'slept like a baby, laughed
like a child, and [eaten] like a lumber-jack.' Her later account of an
enthusiastically received performance before Cariboo miners, ranchers,
farmers, and Natives, followed by a barn dance where she was partnered
by the premier of British Columbia, Richard McBride, evokes her irrepressible bohemianism.[53]

Equally important, touring provided fresh subject matter. When
Grand River grew distant as years passed and visits decreased, Johnson
broadened her scope to include a range of human interest stories.
These frequently centred on the trials of women and children on an
essentially male frontier and sometimes included sympathetic portraits
of the Natives of the regions through which she travelled. Readers were
introduced to such characters as a generous aunt adopting three

orphaned nieces and, on another occasion, 'magnificent types of the Cree.'[54] In describing her response to scenery and inhabitants, Johnson joined a middle-class Victorian sisterhood of tale-telling travellers. Like them she had the privilege of choosing to move on, to gaze at others' lives as an outsider. Yet, if even she could rarely be more than a friendly stranger to the mosaic of Aboriginal nations she encountered, she did not forget their welfare and merits.

When she settled in Vancouver after her retirement from the stage in 1909, Johnson's gaze shifted to coastal First Nations, giving them the close attention previously reserved for the Iroquois. *Legends of Vancouver* brought her writing full circle to its early inspiration in the Indigenous community. Her descriptions are notably more positive than those of such contemporaries as Emily Murphy or Agnes Deans Cameron.[55] In speaking with informants such as Su-á-pu-luck, Johnson was sympathetically allied with an extended Native community. In contrast, her few brief observations on Chinese and Japanese newcomers, comparing them unfavourably with Canadian Indians, suggest that she shared the intolerance of the dominant society. The anti-Oriental sentiments among the western tribes themselves may have further reinforced prejudice.[56]

Travel tales were a logical extension of Johnson's long-standing commitment to physical activity. In the 1880s she began to make her name as an advocate of outdoor activities for women. A sickly child, she had been invigorated by physical exercise. As a teenager and young adult she joined Muskoka's Camp Knock-About for summer holidays. Her happiest days were spent in a canoe, 'manned at the stern, maidened at the bow.' As she regularly attested, 'there is nothing in life that sends me as crazy as a rapid.'[57] Her long-time enthusiasms dovetailed perfectly with the interest in fitness and exercise as a source for physical and moral redemption which swept Europe and North America before World War One.

Such passion helps explain the appeal of the American Canoe Association and its annual regattas. By 1893, when Johnson was an eager member of the Brantford Canoe Club, Ontario's hosting of the North American event in Kingston testified to the fashionable enthusiasm for this means of Native transport. An American reporter was surprised to find that 'the Canadians have this year introduced enervating luxuries that make old-time camp a thing of tradition.' There were now 'a telegraph office, two pianos, a baggage wagon, a Custom House officer and Postmaster, steamboats making seven trips a day, bait and boats to hire for fishing, a dancing platform, a hotel and restaurant, a steamboat landing, a laundry agent, a daily news service and other things.' At least as significantly, there was also an 'unusual number of young women in camp. They are mostly Canadians, and in justice it must be said that they are the handsomest lot ever seen in an American Canoe Association camp. As a rule, the American girls are a little more stylishly dressed than the Canadians, but the fair Canucks have a little more than their share of attention.'[58] The sport which had once been regarded as dangerous and unfeminine had clearly taken on a new character; by the end of the nineteenth century it had become firmly linked to good health and national identity.

By 1893 Pauline Johnson had wedded her new employment as a public performer to her long-standing enthusiasm for the paddle. Respectably accompanied by her mother, 'a dear old English lady who mourns her dead Indian husband as deeply as any woman ever mourned man,' the newly minted 'Indian Princess in full Indian costume,' as she was tagged by an American admirer, was applauded as 'very well educated and highly cultured.' Still better, she combined reminiscence of ancient origins with the right-up-to-date provocation of the New Woman in her sporting guise. Admirers saw her handle 'a canoe like one of her red brethren' and also, albeit not at the same time, recline 'on a cushion,' 'letting some amiable American paddle her canoe in the shade of over-hanging trees along shore.'[59]

In turning to the wilderness for regeneration and inspiration, Johnson took advantage of the slowly dawning recognition that women, like men, had rights to holidays from daily labour. Since anti-feminists regularly cited women's supposed physical inferiority as a justification for male domination, the larger significance of fitness claims was not lost on the self-conscious, if cautious, writer. In one of her few explicitly feminist statements, Johnson observed that

> The whole age is crying out for reform, political, moral, spiritual, and one of the first steps toward that much-needed achievement is *individual reform* ... But we women are brought up with little idea of individual importance. Any boy that is born may be a President, or a railway king, or, at the least, carve out for himself an excellent niche somewhere in life. But the little girl baby? Well, its mother smiles and kisses it, and prays in her heart that the little maid may grow up strong and pure and womanly, and that is all ... There are still plenty of people whose old-fashioned prejudice hints at many sports as too 'masculine' for womankind. To these well-meaning folk I can only reply that all depends upon *how* that sport is played.

At the brink of radical advocacy, Johnson draws back, admitting that 'I have a terrible consciousness that I am wandering outside my province.' Still, she justifies the intervention if 'a single girl' resolves 'that during the coming summer she will not devote her *entire* mental energies to pretty seaside gowns.'[60]

In another article, she assured young women that their investment in physical culture posed no threat to femininity. 'Lady canoeists' are little different in their dexterity with a paddle than 'the mantillaed senora' in fingering 'her fan.'[61] Subsequently, she observed that women's paddles might be strong and their souls fearless, but it was wise to steer with an admiring 'big fellow in the bow' in case rescue was needed.[62] Her portraits of 'the most laughter-loving, unconventional, sunburnt maiden that the physical faddist could desire to see' strongly resemble the all-Canadian girl celebrated by her own admirer, Hector Charlesworth.[63]

Johnson marshalled almost equal enthusiasm for a host of other outdoor activities for women, including snowshoeing, skating, tobogganing, and camping. 'The girl who can weather the wintry gale can command a kingdom of exercise and enjoyment. She may not be able to rove the Northern wilderness with boys and bullets, but she will slay more than bears, bring to her feet rarer game than deer; she and her sisters will hold their own against all rivals, for theirs by right of conquest is that priceless boon to womankind – glorious health.'[64] Citing such respectable authorities as the vice-regal couple, Lord and Lady Lansdowne, as converts to skating, Johnson insisted that the right to sports was part of the legitimate heritage of the modern girl.

Nor was sport's modern marvel on ice in danger of being desexed. In a remarkable rejection of long-standing sentimental investment in a fragile and tiny femininity, Johnson hails the robust heterosexual heroine: 'in another moment she appears, a magnificent, large figure, flying down the lake like a brilliant fugitive bird, and close on her heels her handsome college-boy brother, followed by a heterogeneous assortment of young ladies and gentlemen in hot pursuit. What a splendid thing she was.'[65] Just as with fishing, where the supposedly superior male is humorously saluted for his talent in handling worms,[66] winter's lords of creation are put in their proper place, skating attendance on the modern sportswoman.

Johnson's treatment of young men in her sporting pieces offers a provocative contrast to the age's calls for a renewed masculinity that was seasoned, hardened, even brutalized, in a contest with nature. Many thought that civilization's presumed tendency to produce effeminate,

not to mention homosexual, men could be cured through renewed contact with nature's fierce demands for courage and toughness. Such anxi-
eties seem far from our author's mind. At times she waxes quite cynical
about male leadership. Skilled outdoorswomen are humorously shown
to be courted for reasons beyond their visual attractiveness.

> There are two occasions when you are in demand, the first is, when the lazy
> man of the party wants an outing. It is astonishing with what rapid growth
> his affection for you springs forth into flower, although it apparently was
> not even budding at last night's hop, for he never once came near you. The
> second time your popularity dawns upon you is when a long cruise is on
> the programme and you are sought by every masculine member of the
> camp, and the honor of your company begged, nay, supplicated for ...
> (they always stand by you, those dear, athletic college boys, who admire
> your skinny, muscular arms, and turn up their noses at the plump white-
> ness 'rolled like dough' as they tell you on the arms of the non-paddling
> maidens) ... Yes, they always stand by you unless you have a canoe to pack,
> and then – well![67]

Even when the masculine will is present, skills might be woefully lacking. Such is the case with the comic, if affable and attractive, misfit on a
fantasy canoe trip where the modern heroine imagines herself

> far, far away on a wild inland river, kneeling in the stern ... while a hand-
> some, lazy affair in white flannels decorates the bow. He sings, while you
> shoot through a score of eddies ... With a great deal of floundering and
> bungling he gets the mast up and excavates the sail from under the
> thwarts. You tell him several times just how to fix the whole business and he
> does exactly the opposite way, then you beach the bow and walk up to the
> deck, stepping meanwhile over his big shoes and telling him he is a great
> stupid.

Such a lummox was hardly the rugged embodiment of his sex sought by
critics of Oscar Wilde. Significantly, however, this flirtatious figure performing a conventional female role continued to suggest erotic appeal
both in this sketch and in Johnson's poetry. How else to explain the
next line here, 'He laughs a tantalizingly little laugh.'[68] Such portraits of
masculinity, with their use of a word like 'little,' suggested that the difference between the sexes may not be as clear as anti-feminists would
like.

In her advocacy of sports, Pauline Johnson joined other feminist campaigners.[69] While they rarely attracted the same attention as crusades for equality in education, employment, or marriage, the demands of health reformers and would-be athletes might be similarly subversive in liberating women from the crippling constraints of domestic occupations, not to mention corsets. Outdoor sports in particular offered escape from 'neurasthenia,' or hysteria, the affliction that was believed to have reached near-epidemic proportions among middle-class women bound up in a world of restraints. Potential and actual victims provided a ready audience for Johnson's argument that 'people who live much in the open air are seldom ill; aye! most blessed of all things, they seldom have nerves.'[70] Her celebration of healthy appetites in a marvellous salute to frog's legs can also be interpreted as a rejection of her sex's supposed daintiness: 'it was with vicious satisfaction that I hooked their owner [of 'lumpy eyes'] and dumped him with his fellows into a bag to await the inhuman amputation act ... [later] I passed my plate for a second helping.'[71]

Sports offered benefits beyond exercise itself. Their advocacy was closely linked to the clothing reform movement, which aimed to rid women of restrictive and unhealthy garments. Only then could they play a full role in the new emancipated world. Such unsettling implications underlie Johnson's challenge to wear 'a plain dark serge skirt as short as your daring spirit will permit.'[72] Sensitive to the subversive potential of seemingly innocuous shifts in apparel, she is careful to assure her audience that femininity will not be lost: 'few girls look prettier in evening dress than in [the] blanket suit (the most sensible thing ever devised for weathering a northern climate)' of the snow-shoeing girl.[73] For the author who wished to continue her sales, the threat of the New Woman required careful dissimulation. For sympathizers, those in the know, however, Johnson's doubled-voice message held no mystery. On paper at least she was nothing less than a clothing reformer.

Lovers, Wives, and Mothers

Johnson's exuberant spirit, which made her claim to be 'an ardent canoeist with an ardent appetite, ... in love with my two professions, and strongly addicted to tam o'shanters, animals, camping, Black's novels, and Ottawa at session time,'[74] was far removed from the pale and passive females who haunted the Victorian imagination. Hence the advertisement of her work in the *Mother's Magazine*: 'The subject of mother's health is given considerable space in this issue. In her article, "Mothers of the Great Red Race," E. Pauline Johnson (Tekahionwake), the Iroquois Indian author, tells of many customs and habits by which the Indian mother maintains her health and splendid poise.'[75] If they could model themselves on more natural women, readers might regain a rightful but now compromised heritage of vitality. Such comparisons between Native and settler women were subversive, relying as they did on some suggestion of the former's superiority. Johnson's frequent celebration of 'a certain brown beauty, the birthright of the summer' athlete and equation of health with the 'sun tan of a desert ranger' also helped erode racial difference, and hinted that 'White' was not the only desirable colour.[76]

Reflecting her attachment to active expressions of womanhood, Johnson's female fictional characters, like their author's public performances, are distinguished by passionate sentiments and actions. While seeming traditional in their commitment to family life, her heroines assert their sexual independence. In a manner reminiscent of the biblical Judith, the Mohawk Ojistoh kills her Huron kidnapper while pretending to be seduced. Christie's resolve at the end of 'A Red Girl's Reasoning' not to yield to the temptation of a lover's apology is an extraordinary testament to the ultimate irrelevance of institutional wedlock and to women's right to repudiate unworthy men. Daughters resist fathers and communities to embrace traditional enemies. Others, like Neykia of 'The Quill Worker' (1896), ignore the appeals of 'pale-faced traders' to await 'a young red hunter' while some, as in 'The Legend of the Qu'appelle Valley' (1898) determine to remain loyal to European suitors. As with the Mixed-race girl in 'The Derelict' who surmounts charges of thievery to provide the moral core of the story and the anchor for her weak English lover, women choose the men they deem suitable, just as Iroquois matrons appoint clan leaders. The refusal of Native heroines, such as Yaada in 'The Grey Archway' (1910), to countenance marriages dictated by men's wishes and not by women's will, reminds the careful reader of the rejection of institutional marriage in favour of the natural union of equals found in some New Woman novels such as Joanna Wood's *The Untempered Wind* (1894).

Pauline Johnson occasionally portrayed successful marriages – the Robinsons in 'As It Was in the Beginning,' the Lysles in 'Mother o' the Men' (1909), and the Benningtons in 'The Shagganappi' – but for her, as for fiction writers in general, good marriages were not the stuff of good stories. However, unlike the serious realistic novelists of her era, she seldom analysed marital failure. Only the failed union of Christie and Charlie McDonald in 'A Red Girl's Reasoning' receives sustained attention, and this is more a metaphor for the mutual incomprehensibility of races, not to mention the shortcomings of European men, than a study of the problems of marriage. Like Sara Jeannette Duncan and earlier Canadian writers, Johnson employed the metaphor of marriage to symbolize alliances between countries, or in her particular case, between warring or estranged tribes and races. The heroines' difficulties in resolving these conflicts rather than the demands of individual patriarchs create the basic tension of 'The Tulameen Trail' (1911), 'Dawendine' (1895), and 'The Ballad of Yaada' (1913).

In Johnson's stories, Aboriginal women are significantly more eroticized than Whites. Since sexuality was commonly used to justify exploitation, she courted obvious danger. Nevertheless, she dared to create young women who are much more physically expressive than their Euro-Canadian counterparts. The stories 'A Red Girl's Reasoning' and 'As It Was in the Beginning' conjure up passionate Mixed-race women who physically resemble the author herself. In the former, Christie Robinson, later McDonald, 'looked much the same as her sisters, all Canada through, who are the offspring of red and white parentage – olive-complexioned, grey-eyed, black-haired, with figure slight and delicate, and the wistful, unfathomable expression in her face.'[77] Both she and Esther, heroine of the second tale, form emotionally and physically intense attachments to blue-eyed, blond young men, very like those who figure in some of Johnson's love poetry. These two male characters, despite their contact with Native peoples, prove incapable of fidelity. Punishment by those they betray is inexorable and, from the point of view of the storyteller, well justified. Other stories, such as 'The Pilot of the Plains' (1891) and 'Dawendine,' reward male loyalty with Native women's love beyond the grave. The ultimate triumph of Johnson's Aboriginal lovers in very different scenarios invites an understanding of Indigenous sexuality which is essentially noble, thus striking at the very heart of the colonial attempt to assert superiority by debasing Native women.

In contrast, Johnson's few young White women, Della Kennedy in 'The Envoy Extraordinary' (1909) and Miss Connie in 'The Barnardo Boy' (1910), appear colourless, cold, and ultimately uninteresting. Their essential asexuality might reflect Pauline's accommodation to the passionless ideal of middle-class womanhood current in her time. It might also draw on her experience with her mother. According to her daughter, Emily Howells Johnson confronted sexuality with considerable difficulty. In offering advice to other mothers, Johnson outlined an intense and problematic reserve:

> Innumerable periodicals and papers are crying out for the daughter to learn what concerns her own self, sex, and probability of marriage and motherhood, from her own mother's lips. I cannot possibly imagine my mother imparting to me one iota of information that could not be given in the presence of my father and brothers. Her naturally shrinking nature would have made it a torture and an agony to speak of the essentially untalked-of things, even to her daughters ... so she buried her failure to do so beneath a peculiar training that has served us in place of aural knowledge.[78]

Although life beyond Chiefswood broadened her awareness of female passions, Johnson's White characters reflect lessons learned at her mother's knee.

Like her sporting pieces, Johnson's love poems, which are discussed in more detail in chapter 4, reject the passivity of her White prose heroines. Their female subjects, often presented in the first person, repeatedly demonstrate their capacity for intense feeling and passionate action. Unrepentant women take full responsibility for their choices and their disappointments. In dramatizing and celebrating female passion, Pauline Johnson extended Canadian literature's range of emotional possibilities. Only Joanna Wood, in *The Untempered Wind*, ventured as far. How readers understood her presentations is impossible now to know. Were her portraits taken as proof that women *sua generis* had sexual desires or were they viewed as an expression of the author's Native heritage – in other words, a demonstration of inherent primitivism or even degeneracy? Sexuality was complicated terrain for both New and Native women. Whether it promised liberation or exploitation, female sexuality unsettled the patriarchal status quo.

For all their problems, heterosexual unions largely remain the order of the day in Johnson's stories. Happy spinsters, like congenial Aunt Gertrude of a *Rudder* sketch, seldom appear. Marriage produces children who ultimately, as in 'Catharine of the "Crow's Nest"' (1910) and 'The Envoy Extraordinary,' give meaning and purpose to human existence. Adults', particularly mothers', relations with children, supply an abiding interest in her prose. Because of the significance of *Boys' World* as a market, sons appear in her fiction more frequently. Daughters, however, produce the most sustained reflections on the meaning of children's gender, as in the Aboriginal legend, 'The Lost Salmon Run' (1910). Here the Native storyteller, a grandmother, contrasts and explains the Capilano tribe's preference for 'girl-children': 'first, we not always wish boy-child born just for fight. Your people, they care only for the war-path; our tribe more peaceful. Very good sign first grandchild to be girl. I tell you why: girl-child may be some time mother herself; very grand thing to be a mother.'

Johnson's 'Heroic Indian Mothers' (1908) sets the record straight about the views of her own people: 'Girl babies are always welcome to the Iroquois mother, who knows well how dear the tribesmen hold their womankind, notwithstanding all that has been written and said to the contrary.' Another testament comes from an English-Canadian character in 'Mother O' the Men.' Mrs Lysle, far north with her Mountie husband, struggles with loneliness: 'there are times even in the life of a wife and mother when her soul rebels at cutting herself off from all womankind, and all that environment of social life among women means, even if the act itself is voluntary on her part.' Later on, 'during days when the sight of a woman's face would have been a glimpse of paradise to her,' she 'almost wildly regretted her boy had not been a girl – just a little sweet-voiced girl, a thing of her own sex and kind.' Although not so explicit in its message, 'The Legend of the Ice Babies' (1911), which features two Native mothers surrendering their daughters to the Great Tyee, or god, who alone can protect their innocence and purity, similarly idealizes girls. The repetition of such sentiments suggests resistence to the lesser value commonly attributed to female children in European society and sensitivity to ties binding one generation of women to another.

Whether girls or boys, children in much of Johnson's work further the agenda of the New Woman, proving catalysts in the transformation of the opposite sex into more fully realized human beings or new men. The uncle in the short story 'The King's Coin' (1909), the governors general in 'The Shagganappi' and 'The Saucy Seven' (1906), the fathers in 'The Whistling Swans' (1909), 'The Recluse' (1910), and 'The Siwash Rock' (1910) all reveal capacities to nurture and inspire, talents which Johnson's men seem curiously devoid of in their relations with women. While men help boys to be strong, they also foster virtues which could bring the sexes closer together. In 'The Whistling Swans' a father guides youngsters to take up animal rescue as a project. Animals, which occur infrequently in Johnson's stories, allow children to develop empathy and demonstrate nurture, qualities more regularly associated with women.[79]

Just as critically, fathers could also champion purity. This possibility is explored metaphorically in the legend of 'The Siwash Rock,' where a Native man defies envoys of the Great Tyee. He bars their way into Burrard Inlet as

> he must swim, swim, swim through this hour when his fatherhood was coming upon him. It was the law that he must be clean, spotlessly clean, so that when his child looked out upon the world it would have the chance to live its own life clean. If he did not swim hour upon hour his child would come to an unclean father. He must give his child a chance in life; he must not hamper it by his own uncleanliness at its birth.

Sensitive to the issues of the day, the *Vancouver Province Magazine* subtitled this legend 'a monument to clean fatherhood.' Another father's endurance of ten years of celibate isolation in 'The Recluse' takes up much the same theme, again affirming the superiority of Native values. In Canada, as elsewhere, many feminists, outraged by prostitution and sexual violence, demanded that men equal women's standards of sexual conduct.

Masculinity is also the subject of 'Gun-Shy Billy' (1907), a story in which a young Canadian bugler returns home from the Boer War to conclude, 'there was nothing left of this terrible war but the misery, the mourning, the heartbreak of it all.' Such sentiments not only draw him closer to a friend's widow, but also link the readers of *Boys' World* to all women, assumed by the dominant ideology to be the more peaceful gender. The androgynous quality of that heroic teenager is also reminiscent of the hero in 'The King Georgeman' (1911), who 'blushed like a girl.' Con's merits are not displayed in the traditional masculine proclivity for fighting, although he is a success there as well. Instead, his superiority shows in his care of others. Nursing a scoundrel beset with smallpox, he loses nothing of masculinity and gains something in feminine virtue. In another story for boys, the Cree hero, 'Five Feathers,' whose hands are 'slender and small as a woman's' tends a stricken child.[80] Such male characters not only celebrate more androgynous new men, who triumph in their capacity for sacrifice and empathy, but often place Native men in the vanguard of progress.

In both fiction and non-fiction, Pauline Johnson attended still more closely to women's maternal role. While this focus was to some degree

determined by her connection to the *Mother's Magazine*, it also predomi-
nates in items written for more general periodicals. The feminism of the
day placed a high premium on superior mothering and her account of
her own mother's life lovingly portrays someone devoted to her children. As well, Johnson's attitude was firmly grounded in her First
Nations heritage. As she explains of Native legends: 'To me they are
filled with deepest meaning, especially for womankind; for there is
rarely a tradition among the British Columbia Indians that does not
have as its base womanhood – wifehood, and above all, motherhood.'[81]
Her poems 'The Birds' Lullaby' (1893) and 'Lullaby of the Iroquois'
(1896) lovingly invoke Aboriginal practice as an expression of universal
maternal sentiment.

In her unpublished prose piece, revealingly titled 'The Stings of Civilization,' Johnson makes a case for the satisfactions of women whose
lives centre on work and children. The respect and power of the Native
women in her account of traditional society resemble the qualities
attributed to pre-industrial European women by historically-minded
feminists in the early twentieth century. Capitalism has not yet stripped
either group of their independence and authority, their rights as men's
productive equals. Honoured by their community, Johnson's forest
matrons work as hard as 'American and English women in the same
walk or strata of life,' freely accepting that their 'birthright of labor is to
wash, scrub, split wood, carry coal and bear children while doing it.' In
a damning comparison, Johnson hails the lot of such Natives as infinitely preferable to that of 'Russian women, flaxen haired, creamy
skinned hitched to a plough in bonds like horses,' whom she had spied
in the northwest, where 'the lordly husband father, or relation drives
them – a pitiful sight blotting the freedom of God's virgin plains.' Worse
still, as the author further explains, 'some of these Russian plough
women were Mothers! No Indian man ever asked or permitted his womankind to do such toil.' Unless contaminated by Europeans, Native societies treat women with respect.

Such assessments seem close to what Janet Mancini Billson has argued
in examining the attitudes of Canada's Aboriginal peoples at the end
of the twentieth century: Native women are revered as 'keepers of the
culture.' Their role in maintaining community values means they 'are
appreciated, respected, trusted, and admired.'[82] Few turn-of-the-
century accounts, however, recognized Aboriginal women's power and
status. Johnson's portraits stand out as a remarkable repudiation of the
widespread view of Aboriginal women as promiscuous and dangerous.

At her hands, they exhibit and surpass all the higher virtues commonly credited only to their European sisters as natural women and competent mothers.

Indeed, women's maternalism ultimately provides an important point of connection among the races. An early poem, which commemorates the suffering of the prairie tribes during the Riel Rebellion, initiates this critical theme. In 'A Cry from an Indian Wife' Johnson's narrator describes her desperate agony when her family and nation prepare for war and death. Despite her own suffering and loyalties, she reminds listeners that

> ... my heart is not the only one
> That grieves the loss of husband and of son;
> Think of the mothers o'er the inland seas;
> Think of the pale-faced maiden on her knees[.]

Johnson also hinted that maternal feelings could heal more than racial differences. In 'The Tossing of a Rose' she portrays two European North Americans separated by class. One woman, the young social leader in the home town, 'had married a college-bred lad with a good start in life.' The other, 'the bare-footed child of Old Eliza the laundress,' had wed a foundry worker. Yet if their incomes and their prospects were disparate, 'their children had won them to a certain common interest.' To be sure, 'the social sea would always be there, it had been instituted by stronger hands than theirs, but the oceans of mother love were wider, deeper, older, and more infinite, and greater.' The ability of the two women to negotiate class difference eases life for the poorer family. In this exchange, Johnson suggests, there are no losers: 'The Douglas's had not lost their social prestige by stepping outside their own exclusive circle to entertain obscure strangers. The Kentons had not lost their self-esteem and independence by accepting the unostentatious hospitality of truly interested people beyond their own sphere of life.' The implications of this unpublished story for the class relations of the day are intriguing; Johnson suggests a solution, with maternally minded women helping to mend a society split between rich and poor. Such a response was highly idealistic, a red toryism reminiscent of the paternalistic response of some middle-class families to the problems of some small-town Ontario. In Johnson's day, stress on a beneficent paternalism, or rather maternalism, as a solution to potential class conflict attracted many liberal critics of the status quo, including many feminists.

As with the traditional Iroquois practice of adoption, actual biological relationships are secondary to those constructed socially. Mothering women, both Native and Euro-Canadian, stand out in 'Catharine of the "Crow's Nest,"' 'The Nest Builder,' 'Mother o' the Men,' 'The Tenas Klootchman,' and '"Old Maids" Children.' In the first, an Indian woman, Maarda, embodies generosity in her rescue of a White foundling without thought of reward. The same virtue motivates another woman, this time a prairie settler, in 'The Nest Builder,' cheerfully to ignore her own poverty and adopt three orphaned girls. Indeed adoption of one kind or another is the theme of all five accounts. In the third, Mrs Lysle mothers not only her own son but all the young Mounties entrusted officially to her officer husband's care. The Tenas Klootchman loses one fragile daughter to illness but her goodness to a dying mother is rewarded by the gift of another. In the unpublished story '"Old Maids" Children,' an aunt gets a chance to nurture children and, not incidentally, to become a better woman.

Johnson also affirmed the critical social functions fulfilled by women. In 'How One Resourceful Mother Planned an Inexpensive Outing' (1908), a farm woman teaches her husband and offspring the value of going 'gypsying.' Her ingenuity and sensitivity to her family's emotional and physical needs restore a husband's love and keep her from joining the list of casualties to overwork to whom contemporary farm women activists were drawing attention. Men's difficulty in providing the emotional heart of the household is similarly illustrated in 'The Home Comers' (1907). Burnt out of their old home, a family is forced to resettle in sawmill country north of Lake Superior. The husband can earn the money to start again but his wife, the mother of three daughters, supplies the inspiration and the emotional support that ensure success. Such often sentimentalized female characters create the sense of community that gives life meaning.

In stories written for *Boys' World* between 1906 and 1911, women are no longer the central characters, yet they remain pivotal in civilizing their sons and inspiring them to higher levels of accomplishment. Lads in 'The Shagganappi,' 'Hoolool of the Totem Poles,' 'The Broken String,' and 'The Shadow Trail' (1907) adore their mothers. These in turn gently exercise a moral, nearly spiritual, authority which elevates their offspring. As the husband acknowledges in 'The Shadow Trail,' it is 'mothers who have the real Christmas things in their hearts.' *Legends of Vancouver* similarly credits mothers with critical influence. In 'The Sea-Serpent' (1910), a Native woman helps her son kill the monster, the greedy 'totem' of the White man. Maternal aid and inspiration keep the family, and civilization itself, on the right track. Regardless of nationality, women's tasks remain much the same.

Inspired by their capacity for nurture, Johnson's female characters, both Native and White, emerge as the chief promise of a more just and peaceful world. Native women lead the way in ensuring peace by marrying tribal enemies in poems such as 'Dawendine' and 'The Ballad of Yaada.' The legend of 'The Two Sisters' (1909), where chief's daughters bring an end to warsongs and reconcile ancient enemies, makes the same point. In the story 'The Envoy Extraordinary,' old Billy, himself initially a major obstacle to reconciliation with his son's family, sums up the critical female role: 'these mother-wimmen don't never thrive where there's rough weather, somehow. They're all fer peace. They're worse than King Edward an' Teddy Roosevelt fer patchin' up rows, an' if they can't do it no other way, they jes' hike along with a baby, sort o' treaty of peace like.'

Johnson's sympathy for the female victim, often the sexual prey of a censorious and brutal world, further aligns her with those who condemned the double standard. Her poem 'Easter Lilies' singles out a girl, the casualty of an uncaring city and a secret woe, whose 'lilies, pure as snow' reveal her to be finally 'God's Own.' 'The City and the Sea' (1903) casts another 'body spoiled and spurned of man' as 'image of her God since life began,' an extraordinary revision of biblical exegesis that feminizes an apparently Christian deity. Johnson offered at least two differing explanations of the origin of another poem, 'The Prodigal,' which presents a similar message.[83] The sad and silent urban subjects of all three supply a dramatic contrast to the active nature-loving representative of the New Women who elsewhere in Johnson's writing take charge of their own destinies, and, not so incidentally, often the men in their lives. Like many supporters of women's rights, the poet portrays the plight of the less fortunate of her sex with compassion and anger.

The exact nature of first wave feminism itself remains controversial. Although first accounts emphasized its heroism, scholars at the end of twentieth century stress the narrow class and race interests of a White middle-class crusade.[84] Few White feminists bothered to investigate Aboriginal practices and traditions that empower women, or if they did, fewer still sought alliances. For the most part they collaborated, often enthusiastically, in European domination. In Canada, as elsewhere in the world, it was nearly impossible to be 'a feminist and simultaneously

to have an alternate view of popular imperialism.' Even Pauline
Johnson's friends, such as the thoughtful and sympathetic Nellie
McClung, seem to have lacked a 'vision of liberating politics that connected the struggle against masculinist ideology and power with the
struggle against racist domination in the colonies.'[85]

And yet, at times, glimpses of a more sympathetic response surface.
Rosanna Leprohon and others wrote verse that recognized Native virtues. Some women historians and writers such as Agnes Maule Machar
admired the early contribution of Native peoples to Canada. A few
chroniclers knew them intimately. In 1913 Augusta Gilkison of Brantford, a Johnson family friend, was adopted by both the Mississaugas and
the Cayugas. Nellie McClung occasionally published short stories invoking sympathy for Mixed-race women. A Hamilton writer of Scottish
ancestry, Jean McIlwraith (1859–1938), created a Scottish heroine, servant to English Canadians, who found good reason to marry an
Ojibwa.[86] Evidence of racial understanding is, however, relatively rare
and usually assumes the decline of Native communities. In Canada at
least, the marked absence of attention to Native peoples from White
feminists remains the dominant impression.

Native women were nevertheless not immune to feminism. The American Iroquois champion Minnie Kellogg was a fervent advocate, as was
the Mixed-race writer and activist, S. Alice Callaghan.[87] In Canada, as
yet, we know only of Pauline Johnson whose continuing interest in current events, her sister Evelyn insisted, did not include support for suffrage which she 'thought would cause marital unhappiness.'[88] If that
opposition is true, and we have no other evidence, it may well be
grounded in Johnson's faith in the essential complementarity of male
and female roles. Documenting women's family-based authority in
'Mothers of a Great Red Race' (1908), Johnson argued that 'the contrast is sufficiently glaring to give rise to discussion as to merits of "savagery" or civilization for womankind.' In a volume celebrating the
accomplishments of Canadian women on the occasion of the Paris
Exposition of 1900, published by the National Council of Women of
Canada, she also deftly turned the tables: 'I think the reader will admit
that not ALL civilized races honor their women, as highly as do the
stern old chiefs, warriors and braves of the Six Nations Indians.'[89] What
would suffrage mean to such powerful women? Johnson might well have
regarded the franchise as European women's solution to the problems
of their own community. Moreover, the question of just how the franchise would help or hinder their struggle for equality had long divided

Six Nations. Just what were the benefits and disadvantages of behaving like White men? Enfranchisement with its greater integration into the dominant society could threaten both their land base and their culture. Perhaps Johnson feared the prospect of masculinizing, even diminishing, women by engaging them too deeply in formal politics. Perhaps. At this point we can do no more than speculate.

Although it is often forgotten, there was far more to the woman's rights movement of the day than the franchise. From the espousal of clothing reform to the critique of male sexuality, Johnson shared a good deal with the reform-minded of her sex. She too was not immune to class and racial biases. She readily stereotyped Asian newcomers and expressed horror at 'illiterate and immoral European immigrants.'[90] The range of such views reminds us of both the complicated nature of Johnson's identity and the complicated politics she had to negotiate. She was simultaneously female, middle class, and Mixed-race. She had to make her way as a respectable woman in a world that regarded her as an exotic other.

Perhaps the nature of Johnson's commitment to women's rights is suggested in conclusions about Native women at the end of the twentieth century. Janet Mancini Billson credits a modern generation with

> selectively incorporating the impact of the women's movement into their everyday lives, but participation in movement activities is minimal. While most applaud the new options for women, many also view with suspicion an ideology that appears to pit women against men, to deny the logic of their traditional gender roles, or to devalue the concept of homemaker. The concept of liberation seems to be bound up as much in its perceived impact on the delicate socio-emotional balance in couple relationships as it is in equal opportunities ... They support role equality; few favor role change.[91]

The threads we find in Johnson's work suggest that she would have been at home with such sentiments.

Whatever her response to the suffrage campaign, Johnson had to confront the fact of her sex's special vulnerability in an age which took for granted that women's wages and opportunities were inferior to those of male competitors. As H.G. Wells's fictional character Ann Veronica demonstrated, even well-placed single women were hard put to maintain respectable financial independence. During the course of more than two decades of 'barn-storming[ing] a continent, writing prose as

well as poetry ..., of selling herself as a writer and performer,' Pauline
Johnson often found herself 'with her back to an economic wall.'[92] The
hard work of keeping body and soul together was humorously explained
to her Saskatchewan friend, journalist Kate Simpson-Hayes. Johnson
lamented having to bypass Regina but the city had not turned up a good
contract. 'Now you know you are alluring, your invitation is like – sin,
tempting, insinuating, insistent, and I, in virtuous chase after dollars,
stoically turn my back on it, prayerfully resist it and with bated breath,
locked teeth and averted eyes – dash past, resisting the fascination of it
and thus gaining a crown of glory – composed of many bank notes and
jingling coin of the realm.' In a more serious, or desperate, moment she
also confessed that

> My debts are a continual source of worry to me. That is the reason I could
> not stop to play Winnipeg ... I could never have cleared enough to pay what
> I owe there, and people calling for money daily at a hotel when I have
> none, get me so nervous I am unfit to give performances. My jewelry is not
> yet out of pawn. I have not a ring to my name. I owe six printers and I don't
> know when I can pay them.[93]

Although she worked strenuously in her last touring years to amass
enough funds to set up as a writer in Vancouver, life remained difficult.
Long before her health had worsened to the point that survival
depended upon the public intervention of friends and admirers,
Johnson hit close to bottom. A younger friend remembered a scenario
that would have done justice to Dickens:

> Once when I dropped into her apartment Pauline was ill in bed and the
> gas-man was reading the meter in the kitchen. The range worked on one of
> those diabolical quarter-in-the-slot contrivances and though the apart-
> ments were supposed to be heated they were so cold that Pauline tried to
> get warm by putting extra quarters in the range and leaving oven and grill
> doors open. This morning the gas-man took thirteen dollars and seventy-
> five cents from the range. I had discovered that a new sharp-edged quarter
> would last three times as long as a thin, worn quarter, so the new coins I got
> hold of I always laid on the shelf by the kitchen door, and though we never
> mentioned them I knew they were used as they always disappeared, but
> how needed they were I discovered this morning. 'Have you a quarter,
> Tommy?' she asked. 'Yes John,' I replied. 'Will you give it to the gas-man
> and get back the black quarter?' I did so and handed her the retrieved

money, which was covered with a coat of shoe polish. 'It's the last money
my mother ever gave me,' she explained, then turned her face into the pil-
low and heaved with terrible sobs.[94]

Not surprisingly, the uncertain income of a self-described 'mere doll
of the people and slave to money' forced her into urgent, often undigni-
fied, appeals for hard cash.[95] Clifford Sifton, Laurier's minister of the
interior and the ultimate political authority for Indian Affairs, heard her
confess to being financially embarrassed. She desperately needed his
approval to raise $500 on her future share of the Chiefswood rent. This
successful application she concealed from her sister Evelyn, who had
provided funds on other occasions.[96] Other relatives also knew of
Johnson's plight. Achille Fréchette, husband of her cousin Annie Howells, gave her money. His reflections suggest how her poverty was interpreted by her extended family: 'the poor thing has a hard time of it, I
am afraid, and this life does her no good. She and a young Californian
[an incorrect description of Walter McRaye, the touring partner of
whom the family evidently disapproved] give a third-rate show in the
small towns across the country and don't do much for Art nor for themselves.'[97] From the Maritimes, Laura Wood described Johnson's endeavour to deal with the decreased interest in recitals, which represented
her major source of income. She was, Wood believed, contemplating
vaudeville in New York, which, if true, would have meant a massive loss
in status. In accounting for Johnson's desperate plight, this sympathetic
observer offered a mixture of racial prejudice and romantic guesswork:
'Improvident as all Indians are, she was in difficulty. I have always heard
that she supported an idle and dissipated brother, whom she adored
with all her heart.' Similar sentiments inspired the summary explanation offered by Johnson's first book-length biography: 'It was always
a giving-away feast with her. She was chief of the great Canadian
Potlatch.'[98]

These are other explanations for the artist's difficulties. While her
mother was alive and her brother Allen at home, the costs of assistance
sometimes proved 'more than a poor pen could cope with.'[99] Johnson
was also well-known for generosity to others in distress. As she freely
admitted, if down to her last few dollars, she would gladly purchase
beautiful flowers and a wonderful meal, rather than succumbing to pen-
ury's meaner spirit. Temperament is, however, only one part of the
explanation for recurring hardship. As *Silenced Sextet*, the collective biography of six remarkable Canadian women writers, confirms, women of

very different inclinations were only too likely to confront poverty.[100] Johnson's generation of New Women, like such authors as Susanna Moodie before them, could not readily overcome the socio-economic disabilities under which they laboured.

Women's situation was further complicated by the special problems posed by aging, especially for those without spouses or children. While years could bring a sense of competence and the rewards of good friends, they were also likely to worsen already uncertain budgets. Although for a long time counted youthful, Pauline Johnson was never strong. Her demanding routine of writing and performing increased her vulnerability to illnesses that undermined the exotic good looks which were a critical part of her capital. She made the best of things in describing her encounter with the president of a Ladies' Aid in a small prairie town: 'She had the air of one who has been badly fooled. "Be you the real Pauline Johnson?" she asked, dourly. I said I was the one and only. "Be them your photygraphs?" pointing an accusing finger at my advertising posters! I admitted this also, and foolishly asked "Why?" The President looked grimly from me to the photographs and back again. "Well, I reckon them pictures was took a right smart time ago!" said she, for she was a great believer in speaking the truth in line!'[101] This reception, which the performer could anticipate being repeated, was ultimately more terrifying than comic. As Johnson explained to a sympathetic listener, 'I lose every time people undertake to estimate when I was born. You see when a woman depends upon the public for her bread and butter she *must not get old*.'[102]

Even as she lay dying, she remained sensitive to the way the world judged the value of women. The defences of a lifetime at their weakest, she unburdened herself to the Canadian critic and editor J.D. Logan in requesting a favour:

> If you have in the write-up, quoted any date of my birth will you please have it blue-pencilled ... I have been so long on the stage that I have a woman's and particularly an actress's aversion to my years being made general knowledge ... It hurts a woman's heart to grow old, particularly when the heart itself is in an everlasting April ... Perhaps I shall tell you someday what sorrow came to me just because of those published articles announcing my supposed age. It will be too bitter an experience for me to write of when I am as discouraged and bitter as I am tonight ... Even here, in this delightful home of a hospital, where many strangers come to see me, where incoming patients strive to get me to visit them in their rooms, I feel the old shrink-

ing, and oftentime I grow painfully nervous, and physically upset when strangers plague me by staring, and almost forcing themselves upon me. How dearly and how frequently I wish with my whole being that I have lived and died in obscurity I can never tell you.[103]

Wise in the ways of audiences, Johnson treasured good looks. New Women, not to mention supposed Indian princesses, were most likely to win a hearing when they were beautiful. Enduring a prolonged painful decline must have involved more than one hell for a woman who counted on her body for stamina and charm.

While the Squamish and Iroquois peoples did not forget her, Pauline Johnson died as she had lived, surrounded for the most part by Euro-Canadian admirers and friends. From Brantford to Vancouver, she negotiated a professional life which offered both independence and freedom. In writing and performances she joined other New Women in challenging prejudices constraining her sex. Women were neither men's playthings nor mere domestic ornaments. In her mind's eye, the 'natural' woman, whether the Iroquois matron or the liberated sportswoman or the influential mother, provided the critical moral and productive centre of a superior social order. This vision, with its inspiration in her commitment to the First Nations and to a fair deal for her sex, made Pauline Johnson one of the most remarkable of her generation of Canada's New Women.

CHAPTER THREE

'Unique figure on the borderland':
Literature, Performance, and Reception

Entering the Spotlight

Pauline Johnson grew up in an era of expanding self-awareness for the new Canadian nation. Political and cultural leaders recognized litera-ture as a major cultural agent for establishing national images and val-ues. In 1864, on the eve of Confederation, the Reverend Hartley Dewart compiled *Selections from Canadian Poets*, the first significant anthology of Canadian literature, arguing that 'A national literature is an essential element in the formation of national character.' His motive was more political than aesthetic. 'It may be fairly questioned,' he continued, 'whether the whole range of history presents the spectacle of a people firmly united politically, without the subtle but powerful cement of a patriotic literature.'[1] After Confederation, calls for a distinctively Cana-dian literature echoed from political leaders, magazine and newspaper editors, and authors. In 1884, when the twenty-three-year-old Pauline Johnson began to publish her poetry, the birth of a national literary identity, while warmly debated in the press, was still more wish than real-ity. The fact that Johnson's first verses appeared in *Gems of Poetry*, an American periodical issued in New York, illustrates the embryonic state of Canadian culture in the early 1880s, two features of which were the paucity of publishing venues and the precariousness of authorship as a profession. Yet despite her experience that 'it is a lamentable fact that, because of the refusal of our own papers to pay for poetry, we are driven to the States,'[2] Johnson quickly established herself as a Canadian writer by cultivating a national readership in the pages of established Toronto periodicals, including the *Globe*, *The Week*, and *Saturday Night*. As an accomplished woman poet, she contributed significantly to the remarkable upsurge of Canadian literary activity that occurred during an era of fervent cultural and political nationalism on both sides of the Atlantic. From about 1885 onward, Pauline Johnson joined a critical mass of writers who were constructing a distinct national identity for former colonies struggling towards collective consciousness.

Johnson signed her early work as 'E. Pauline Johnson' and initially drew very lightly on her Native background. Of eleven poems that appeared in *The Week* from 1885 to 1889, just two, 'The Cry of an Indian Wife' and 'A Request,' suggest the ethnicity of their author. And of her more than fifty poems, articles, and stories that appeared in *Saturday Night* from 1888 to 1893, only about a dozen refer overtly to Aboriginal topics. Like her contemporaries Charles G.D. Roberts, Archibald Lampman, William Wilfred Campbell, Bliss Carman, and Duncan Campbell Scott (later labelled the 'Confederation poets'), Pauline Johnson frequently lyricized Canadian life, landscapes, and seasons in a post-Romantic mode that reflects the British orientation of her formal education. Like her now obscure female peers, such as Agnes Maule Machar, Rosanna Mullins Leprohon, and Susan Frances Harrison, she penned drawing-room and domestic verse about love, pets, families, and friendship. As many earlier and contemporary Euro-Canadian poets wrote poems on First Nations subjects, usually expressing considerable sympathy with the plight of a 'fated race,'[3] readers were initially offered little reason to distinguish Johnson as Aboriginal.

The presence of two of Johnson's poems in W.D. Lighthall's 1889 anthology *Songs of the Great Dominion*, quickly recognized as a cornerstone of Canada's new literary identity, signalled her inclusion in the pantheon of the country's significant English-language writers. Lighthall organized his book into nine topical sections, beginning with 'The Imperial Spirit' and 'The New Nationality.' There is also a section titled 'The Indian,' but this is not where Johnson's verses are placed; her canoeing poem, 'In the Shadows,' appears in the section on 'Sports and Free Life,' and her poem about the Grand River, 'At the Ferry,' is in the 'Places' section. To the casual Canadian reader, Johnson probably blended into the Anglo-centric mainstream of English-language Canadian literature. Yet this was not quite where Johnson situated herself. Her original selection of her 'best' verse, that was 'most Canadian in tone and color,' included 'A Cry from an Indian Wife' and 'The Indian Death Cry' (1888), poems that she felt would interest Lighthall on account of her 'nationality.' The recurrence of this word to signal 'Indian' rather than 'Canadian' in her correspondence with the editor of the most noteworthy post-Confederation literary anthology marks her unique self-placement within the country's emergent national literature.[4]

Johnson's still tentative public identification with her Native roots received considerable encouragement from English critic Theodore Watts-Dunton. His review of *Songs of the Great Dominion* in the prestigious London journal *The Athenaeum* drew heavily on Lighthall's biographical notes to focus on Johnson as 'the cultivated daughter of an Indian chief, who is, on account of her descent, the most interesting English poetess now living,' and quoted the entire text of 'In the Shadows.'[5] The imperial metropolis's fascination with the relatively exotic aspects of the former colony would contribute substantially to Johnson's later self-dramatization for her British audiences, for whom she downplayed her English mother in order to highlight her Mohawk father.

Accounts of Johnson's early career have been decisively shaped by the legend of her 1892 debut as a stage recitalist, which in turn have obscured her previous visibility in the general press. Particularly unremarked have been her contributions to *Saturday Night*, which in 1890 printed her portrait along with a laudatory column that had appeared in *The Twentieth Century Review*, characterizing her as 'A Clever Canadian.' A turn-of-the-century path-breaker who both upheld and transgressed cultural codes and structures of a society in transition, Johnson is always highly mediated: by the reportage and vested interests of those who wrote about her, by her own various self-representations on stage and in her writing, and now by feminism, post-colonialism, and developments in First Nations culture. The problem of recognizing both the inevitability and the impact of such mediation imbues later understanding of the now legendary Toronto Canadian Literature Evening of 16 January 1892 organized by Frank Yeigh. His accounts of this event multiplied after Johnson's death:

> Knowing of her promising talent as a writer, an opportunity came to test her elocutionary powers at a Canadian Authors' Evening away back in 1892, arranged by the Young Men's Liberal Club ... In strict truth, the evening was dragging a little and interest lessening when 'the Indian poet-princess' was introduced ... She glided rather than walked to the platform, her dark eyes flashing nervously and her sinewy form, the essence of gracefulness, representing the acme of physical rhythm and motion ... Thrilling was the effect, dramatic the appeal of this dark-hued girl who seemed to personify her race ... Tekahionwake leaped into fame that night twenty-five years ago, as a poet reciter, in declaiming a few verses.[6]

Yeigh embellished this event to highlight his own role as Johnson's discoverer and subsequently her manager. While this recital did indeed initiate a fifteen-year touring career, it was neither Johnson's first public appearance, nor was she quite the 'bashful and frightened Indian Princess-Maiden' of Yeigh's accounts.[7] Rather, E. Pauline Johnson (who did not yet use the name Tekahionwake or ever represent herself as a 'princess') was nearly thirty-one years old, and quite familiar not only in the Toronto press, but also to readers of the *Canadian Magazine*, the *Dominion Illustrated*, and Brantford newspapers. By the spring of 1891 she was being heralded as 'a writer of high promise ... already well-known in literary circles as the author of the most exquisite poetry we possess.'[8] Hector Charlesworth's *Saturday Night* account of the Canadian Literature Evening went still further, pairing Johnson, 'Canada's greatest and most representative poetess,' with William Wilfred Campbell, whom he viewed as Canada's greatest poet.[9] By the early 1890s, canoeing enthusiasts in Canada and the United States knew her as an expert paddler and frequent author of recreation narratives in *Outing*, the *Detroit Free Press*, and other American journals.

Yeigh's so-called discovery of Johnson fits into the colonial paradigm, in which he performs the role of patriarchal European explorer, while she serves as the feminized indigenous 'virgin land' awaiting his intervention and identification of her value. Less appreciated was the way that she asserted control of her own art and performance. During a subsequent appearance, after faltering with her lines, she quickly regained her composure and went on to captivate the Toronto audience. On stage, as her many often humorous accounts illustrate, she was never at a loss. Her command of one-liners to capture and manipulate later audiences put her in the same league with the suffrage campaigner Nellie McClung, whose platform speeches collected in *In Times Like These* (1915) pulse with confidence and good-humoured intelligence.

Because much of the poetry and prose that Johnson published in newspapers and magazines was never collected into her books, it is difficult to establish her textual output. But to focus solely on this aspect of her career overlooks the role of performance in bolstering her textual identity and facilitating her versatility. As Johnson was unique among the major Canadian poets of her era in both her career and her Native heritage, it is important to situate her literary work within the larger field of her disparate activities, and to place these within the cultural attitudes of her time and place.

Johnson on Stage

In small-town Canada of the 1880s and 1890s, young women of good
character frequently appeared publicly in amateur theatricals, which
were a mainstay of community culture in the days before radio and film.
According to Hector Charlesworth, Johnson knew many famous actors
and actresses of her day, 'for it was customary to entertain them at
Chiefswood when they visited Brantford.' However, as he did not meet
Johnson until around 1891, well after her family's 1885 move into Brantford, it is more likely that her friendships and visits with the actresses he
lists – Hortense Rhea, Rosina Vokes, and Belle Archer – developed after
her father's death in 1884.[10] In 1886 and 1887 Johnson's performances
with the Brant Amateurs were lauded in the local press; she also joined
the Hamilton Dramatic Society. But for a genteel young woman to
choose the stage as a full-time career was a different matter. During
Johnson's lifetime, one of the major unwritten tasks faced by the female
stage performer, especially if unmarried, was to maintain social propriety: always to perform as a 'lady,' whether on the stage or off.[11] Few
actresses could command respect, especially in unsophisticated social
circles; Johnson's biographers usually speculate that her identity as an
actress contributed to the demise of her engagement to Charles Drayton. According to Tracy Davis, social attitudes towards actresses were
quite complex. Although the middle classes disapproved of acting as a
female occupation, the social education of Victorian middle-class
women (music and the arts, industriousness, preoccupation with dress
and appearance) had the effect of equipping them with a number of
attributes suited to the stage. Moreover, 'compared to teaching, the civil
service, seamstressing, idleness, marriage, or obscurity, the theatre was a
powerful lure for thousands of women,' especially those who had to
earn a living. While questioning the gathering and analysis of demo-
graphic data, Davis agrees that, to some degree, in England 'the late-
Victorian theatre experienced gentrification.' Although some sectors of
Canadian society found it uncomfortable to socialize with women who
regularly appeared on stage, this development would contribute to
Johnson's acceptability with the social elite when she first toured
England in 1894.[12]

    In Canadian middle-class circles, formal training might provide a
valid route to the legitimate stage but did not eliminate the taint of
greasepaint. Although Margaret Anglin (1876–1958) attended the
Empire Dramatic School in New York in preparation for an interna-

tional career in classical drama, her father refused to watch her perform.[13] More happily, in the *Emily* books, L.M. Montgomery sends irrepressible Ilse Burnley to the fictional School of Literature and Expression in Montreal,[14] from which she emerges as a star elocutionist who is honoured when she glamorously sweeps back home to visit the conservative folk on Prince Edward Island. A concern for respectability underlies one of Johnson's early publicity brochures, which reproduces a testimonial dated 28 November 1892 from J.E. Wetherell, principal of the Strathroy Collegiate Institute, who heartily recommends her as a Canadian poet, an elocutionist and artist, whose 'presence with us last week helped us to clear nearly a hundred dollars for our Library and Reading Room Funds.'[15]

But elocution, as a genre of entertainment that was usually quite serious, genteel, academic, and suitable for presentations in schools and church halls, did not encompass some aspects of Pauline Johnson's style and material. Programs and reviews usual describe her stage appearances as recitals. In her biography of Johnson, Betty Keller uses the terms 'recitalist' and 'platform entertainer' to distinguish Johnson from actors, who often had a reputation for being 'morally lax' if not utterly 'depraved.'[16] Indeed, other than rare references to her early amateur roles in plays, Johnson is never described as an actress. Margaret Atwood has recently reinterpreted her for modern sensibilities by designating her as 'what would now be known as a performance-artist, but was called at that time an elocutionist – that is, she gave public performances in drawing-rooms and theatres, at which she recited her own poetry to great dramatic effect.'[17] While reviews of Johnson's performances from early 1892, when she shared the program with local singers and musicians, do indeed use the term 'elocutionist,' this word slipped from her promoters' vocabulary after she adopted her Indian costume later that year. No single term serves as a ready substitute.

An early broadside designates Johnson as the Mohawk Indian Poet-Reciter; her letterhead from 1899 describes her more generally as 'The Indian Poet-Reciter'; in 1906 she was advertised to Londoners as 'The Iroquois Indian Poet-Entertainer,' and a late poster labels her as 'The Mohawk Author-Entertainer.'[18] Isabel Ecclestone Mackay's memorial tribute cites Johnson's self-description as a 'dramatic reciter.' One newspaper account suggests that she was also a storyteller: '"The White Wampum" ... a legend of the prairies and the northern lights ... was interpreted from a wampum belt, the most precious thing she possesses.'[19] As her recitals evolved into 'entertainments' comprising a mixed program of poems, stories, and comic skits (the latter all now lost except for reviewers' comments), presented in drawing-rooms, theatres, roadhouses, and church halls, reviewers most often sidestepped the problem of terminology by omitting direct references to performance and simply describing her as a poetess (Canadian, Indian, Mohawk, or Iroquois). Occasionally they use the word 'comedienne.'[20] This ongoing difficulty in assigning Johnson a specific niche captures her more generally aberrant position in the historical spectrum of Canadian culture. By blending genres of writing and performance and transcending neat categories of stagecraft, she intrigued and tantalized audiences.

Viewers and reviewers repeatedly called attention to two distinctive aspects of Johnson's recitals. Unlike other entertainers on the platform circuit whose programs consisted of second-hand texts, Johnson recited only original works – a feature regularly highlighted in her publicity material. Even more memorable was her performance style: 'her poems are literary gems, but one cannot thoroughly appreciate them without hearing them read by the authoress.'[21] As a successful presenter of her own work, she was likened to Charles Dickens, who had mesmerized English audiences of an earlier generation with his reading of such scenes as the murder of Nancy in Oliver Twist.[22] Many decades after Johnson's death, an elderly woman, who, at the age of fifteen had seen Johnson perform, vividly recounted her effectiveness: 'I still shudder, it was so real when she recited "When Red Men Die." Of course there was no radio, no TV, and a concert like that was a great event and the whole town was there.'[23] One columnist recalled: 'I heard her in Strathroy in a recital which I have never forgotten. The musical voice which seemed to hold the echoes of both the forest and the river, and the slender, swaying form, made a startling appeal to Canadian audiences, accustomed to the conventional elocution of the young graduate from a school of oratory.'[24]

Johnson's thrilling or forcible manner, in the words of her viewers, was described as the manifestation of a 'great dramatic gift [that] has been allowed to develop without being trammeled and hampered by the conventional elocutionary education.' Such commentary, while lauding her talent, also implicitly primitized her by distinguishing her from the usual trained performer whose skills are honed through dedicated study. In a similar vein, the reviewer for the Carberry News opined that 'As a reciter, Miss Johnson is governed by but few of the principles bowed down to by the professional elocutionist. She throws herself into her work with complete abandon. At times she is terrible in her ferocity and in a few moments will be as winsome as a girl.' Many commentators specifically cited her 'clear, resonant voice' as 'one of [the] richest of her possessions.' A Peterborough fan likened her to one of the greatest tragedians of the English stage: 'There is nothing that can compare with her recitations since the days of Mrs Scott-Siddons.' To a seasoned Charlottetown viewer, Johnson's greatest talent was her versatility: 'It is no easy task for any one single-handed to interest an audience for two hours, but in this Miss Johnson succeeded remarkably well.'[25]

As might be expected, the power of her performance enhanced the intensity of her message:

> Miss Johnson, as an elocutionist, brings out to the last degree and with the greatest effect the meaning of the selections. So natural are the motions to the act that they are scarcely noticed; the listener following only the trend of the play. But more striking even than the elocutionary power is the train of thought that is awakened. The Indian poems themselves tell of the hardships of the Indian at the hands of the white man. They picture in tender words their savage state and how they might be bettered, but that the greed of gain grasps all in exchange for the poor Indian's body and soul. Such is the train of thought that the poems arouse in the minds of the audience, and when the anger of an Indian maiden, feeling from experience the sufferings of her race, is depicted in every line; dull indeed is the man that cannot be aroused by Miss Johnson's recitations.[26]

The *Globe* journalist who wrote as 'Uncle Thomas' devoted his entire column to Johnson following her debut performance, dwelling at length on how her presentation of 'the other side of the story' in 'A Cry from an Indian Wife' induced remorse and 'a shrinkage of the conscience.' The Reverend E. Ryerson Young's obituary essay on Johnson likewise commemorated the powerful effect of this poem: 'the victorious, complaisant intellectual whites were startled and the arrows of conviction flew and awakened thought, if they did not bring penitence.'[27]

In addition to her dramatic power, Johnson possessed a gift for barbed comedy. Her practice of presenting her Indian pieces in the first half of her program, followed by poems and skits that were alternately humorous and patriotic, mitigated her challenge, allowing her audience to return home comforted rather than perturbed. Her quick-witted repartee earned plaudits, as did her ability to 'suit her entertainment to the time,' as with comments on 'the relations of Canada and England [that] were decidedly opportune.'[28] Some of her off-the-cuff remarks, showing 'how intensely sarcastic she can be,'[29] were never intended for the printed record. The captivated reviewer for a Kingston newspaper, citing Johnson verbatim, jotted down an aspect of the North West Mounted Police conspicuously absent from any of Johnson's published adulations of the Force: 'That excellent corps, the Mounted Police, scour the prairies and seize any whiskey they find, and take it to the barracks. They drink it themselves, I am told.'[30] Other jokes hint at her challenge to organized religion and mainstream politics. The assiduous reporter of the St Thomas Times recorded several samples of her repertoire, including 'a droll description of her experience in Nova Scotia, when she had to help her a boy who was particularly stolid, whose father was not an "intelligent man" nor "an idiot," but the boy at last explained that his father was "a Grit," (Roars of laughter).' She also gave an account of 'the deacon of the Presbyterian church north of Winnipeg, who had so much work to do that he could not attend her entertainment. He had to take in cabbages and turnips that night to escape the frost. "Then you must be a vegetarian" she said to him. "I'm nae vegetarian, I'm a Presbyterian," said he with warmth. (Laughter).' Such routines reflected an increasingly seasoned performer's recognition of the taste of regional audiences. Moreover, as she said herself, 'there is enough sadness in life without presenting it from the platform.'[31]

From coast to coast, from 1894 after her return from England to the end of her performing career, Johnson's audiences were delighted with the topical updating of her regular skits. In 'The Success of the Season,' her 'impersonation of a well known C.P.R. man, a western grain man, and a six year old child wonder reciter were capitally given and pleased the audience immensely.' 'Mrs Stewart's Five O'Clock Tea,' according to the Fredericton reviewer of the 1908 Johnson-McRaye tour, 'proved to one of the best numbers on the programme, its humour appealed to the audience very strongly. In this original work Miss Johnson illustrates the manner of the wife of [an] M.P. who, while the House of Commons is in session, goes from her little town to Ottawa and shines in the social life of the capital.'[32] Another skit, 'The Englishman,' combined colonial humour with patriotism. At first 'pictured as the typical Britisher, with his carefully waxed moustache and his eye glasses, "quite the prettiest thing in sight,"' he becomes heroic 'when Her Majesty's troops march out, grasping his sword and driving the enemy back. Her enthusiastic rendering of this so struck the audience that her last words were drowned in tumultuous applause.'[33]

Other than comments from reviewers and friends, little of Johnson's sense of humour survives in the written record. The archives yield one early example in her retort to a columnist from the Toronto *World*, who blandly described her as 'a pleasant-looking Indian maiden' and 'writer of some good verse.' Her acerbic rebuttal appears in a scrapbook:

alas! how damning praise can be!
This man so scared of spoiling me
Shook all the honey from his pen
Dipped it in acid, and scribbled then –
"No compliments on her I'll laden
She's but a *pleasant looking* maiden.["]
E.P.J.[34]

Not surprisingly, Johnson's sense of humour was, in some quarters, more acceptable on the stage than in print. During the winter of 1895 there occurred a small flurry in *The Week* regarding the poetic value of satiric verses included in a light-hearted article by Johnson and her performing partner. These appeared in the *Globe* of 15 December 1894 under the title 'There and Back, by Miss Poetry (E. Pauline Johnson) and Mr. Prose (Owen A. Smily).' 'Malcolm' of the St Thomas *Evening Journal* took particular exception to Johnson's use of slang in two witty squibs. These were 'The Gopher' (who 'dresses like a hypocrite in soft religious grey' and 'monkeys with his conscience, as they're apt to do out west') and 'His Majesty, The West Wind,' Johnson's parody of her own signature poem, 'The Song My Paddle Sings.'[35] Over the course of several weeks, Johnson received more support than condemnation, with one contributor opining, 'There is a sad lack of humour in the present generation, perhaps the real estate agent and the fashionable church may be at the root of it.' When considered in retrospect, especially in light of the popularity of male-authored satire that had sustained Toronto's *Grip* magazine for some twenty years, the issue seems to have been less the definition of poetry than the identity of the poet. In the eyes of a few self-righteous men, Johnson, as a woman performer, could not be acknowledged as 'a leading Canadian poetess' if her poetry bore any taint of the comic stage.[36]

After her first recital season, Johnson decided to emphasize the Indigenous content of her poems by assembling an Indian costume, a decision that associated her presentations, however distinctive, with other Aboriginal performers familiar to many audiences. On 18 September 1892 she wrote to W.D. Lighthall in Montreal, who in her next letter would be dubbed her 'Literary Father' (a reference presumably to his editorship of *Songs of the Great Dominion* but with disturbing echoes of the image of the 'Great White Father'):

> This season I am going to make a feature of costuming for recitals – always an interesting topic with ladies, but I am beset with difficulties on all hands. For my Indian poems I am trying to get an Indian dress to recite in, and it is the most difficult thing in the world. Now I know *you know* what is feminine, so you can tell me if the 'Indian stores' in Montreal are *real* Indian stores, or is their stuff manufactured? I want a pair of moccasins, worked either in colored moose hair, porcupine quills, or very heavily with *fine colored beads*, have you ever seen any such there? I have written to Chief [Jacks?] about getting some bead work done on my dress, and to several N.W. Reserves, for bears teeth necklaces, etc., but if you see anything in Montreal that would assist me in getting up a costume, be it, beads, quills, sashes, shoes, brooches or indeed anything at all, I will be more than obliged to know of it. My season begins Oct 20th, so I must have my costume by that date, but I want one that is made up of *feminine* work.[37]

This request suggests that before 1892, unlike her father and brothers whose photographs in Native dress reside in the National Archives of Canada, Johnson did not possess distinctive Native garments or ornaments of her own. Her performance costume, later promoted as 'correct,'[38] made no effort to replicate the actual clothing of any specific Native group. Her asymmetrical buckskin dress, short enough to reveal her ankles which were usually chastely enclosed in leggings, was embellished with various symbols of Native culture, including fur pelts, Iroquois silver medallions, wampum belts, and her father's hunting knife. From Ernest Thompson Seton she later acquired a necklace of bear claws; one photo shows her with a feather in her hair and a necklace of elks' teeth. In 1895 she was given a Sioux scalp by a Blackfoot chief. According to her sister, the original buckskin fringe serving as the right sleeve came from the north-west, and the 'rest of her Indian costume and silver brooches were copied from a picture which we had of Minnehaha.'[39] That an artist's rendition of Minnehaha, the fictional Indian maiden in Longfellow's *Hiawatha*, underlies Johnson's collage approach to creating a recognizably Indian costume highlights the self-conscious and constructed nature of her stage identity.[40] Whatever Johnson thought of the complexities of her personal situation as a Mixed-race woman, she knew how to play to settler audiences' expectations of stage

Indians by adorning herself with an eclectic combination of tokens of nature that connote the noble savage, and Indigenous cultural artifacts that suggest the primitive warrior. Such objects, many of them valuable (some would be sold to eager collectors when Johnson's finances floundered) and even sacred in their original context, took on different meanings in settings where they served to stimulate the foreign imagination in its process of appropriating Native signs.

Johnson's decision to appear in buckskin indicates that eastern Canadian audiences were well educated to recognize what represented Indianness on stage. Buffalo Bill Cody's Wild West Show, with its troupes of costumed Indians on horseback, had included Brantford in its 1885 tour of forty Canadian and American cities. It went on to entertain English and continental audiences several times before Johnson reached London in 1894, achieving such popularity that the American cowboy, with the accompanying Indian, 'was better known in Europe at century's end than the president of the United States.'[41] Competing troupes abounded; between 1894 and 1903, Show Indians toured the United States, Canada, and parts of Europe in record numbers. In the 1890s ethnological Indian exhibits became popular at American fairs and expositions.

Above the level of the midway and closer to home were several Mohawk performers. These included the three members of the prominent Loft family of Six Nations, whose concerts to raise money for Mohawk translations of the gospels were described by Susanna Moodie in 1852, and John Ojijatekha Brant-Sero, Six Nations-born historian and actor, who preceded Johnson to London where in 1891 he appeared on stage as 'The Only Canadian Mohawk Indian Now Before the English Public.'[42] A decade later Brant-Sero was again in the imperial capital, his competition with Johnson evident in his revised billing as 'the only full-blooded Canadian Mohawk Indian now before the British Public in a Lecture, Concert and Dramatic Tour.'[43] It is unlikely that Johnson was aware of several Ojibwas who had travelled to London considerably earlier. George Henry (Maungwudaus), cousin or brother of Ojibwa Methodist minister Peter Jones, toured England and France with a Native dance troupe from 1845 to 1848, and George Copway, an Ojibwa Methodist minister who donned buckskins to lecture in North America and Europe was also active at mid-century. There were women as well. Catherine Soneegoh Sutton, Jones's niece, protested against illegal takeovers of Indian land in the Port Credit/Owen Sound area with a 1860s lecture tour of Canada, the United States, and ultimately England. Johnson mentions another female champion, Susette La Flesche. A member of the Omaha tribe, she became prominent as 'Bright Eyes' for her appearances in major American cities during the 1870s advocating the land rights of Native Americans. In the late 1880s La Flesche added British venues to her itinerary.[44] In making deliberate mention of this American activist, Johnson reminded readers that she was not alone, and emphasized the cross-border ties that linked North American Natives.

Despite, or more likely because of, the ubiquity of Show Indians, Johnson's promoters and reviewers uniformly took care never to link her with the ilk of Buffalo Bill's Rocky Bear, Red Shirt, and other Wild West stars, and seldom connected her with Native public advocates. In the syntax of her promoters and reviewers, 'Indian,' 'Iroquois,' and 'Mohawk' modify 'poetess,' thereby securing her status in the culturally elevated realm of poetry. Prominent male authors occasionally embarked on local or extended lecture tours; for example, Charles Dickens and Oscar Wilde each visited North America, and the flamboyant Western American poet Joaquin Miller made four promotional trips to England in the 1870s and 1880s. However, it was rare, if not unheard of, for a woman writer to do so. Hence even without reference to race, Johnson occupied a unique niche as 'the only living woman who recites her own poetry.'[45] Less clearly enunciated was her role as mediator between elite and popular culture, especially in bringing Natives, commonly reduced to burlesque figures, into arenas of high culture performance such as drawing-rooms and theatres.

Johnson's careful construction of her costume suggests that, like the narrator of Henry James's story 'The Real Thing,' she recognized that to an audience, the truth of an identity is created in its trappings and performance. On and off stage, she performed both woman (as lady) and Indian. Recent feminist analysis of identity as 'fundamentally dramatic,' and as 'a manner of doing, dramatizing, and reproducing a historical situation,' helps us to see how Johnson's heightened enactment of her gender and race played into contemporary categories of the feminine and the Aboriginal. In the analysis of Judith Butler, race or gender is 'real only to the extent that it is performed.'[46]

As a part-Native woman developing an independent career in a sociopolitical world dominated by powerful White men, Johnson developed several performance strategies to exploit the power structure on her own behalf. One was to address directly Canadian political and cultural leaders in letters seeking introductions and other favours, while mitigating her boldness with flattery and a tone of humility. Another was to manipulate her audience through her use of costume. Towards the end of 1892 she established her practice of appearing for the first half of her program in buckskin, and the second in evening dress.[47] This overt display of both sides of her parentage enabled her to create a unique stage persona, distinguishing the strands of her background in a manner possible only in performance, while maintaining conventions of gender and class.

Johnson expanded her performance visually through her extensive use of publicity photographs, most of which show her in her Indian dress. Unlike full-frontal documentary photographs of historical First Nations male leaders, posed so that their direct stares challenge the observer, Johnson's costumed photos heighten her artfulness as a performer. Full-length portraits are arranged to best display the details of her outfit as well as her feminine figure. Her face is usually turned in full or half-profile – most often to show her right side, which she felt to be more attractive. Her uplifted gaze towards an invisible horizon, often enhanced by a raised arm, signalled her engagement with a story extending beyond the frame of the picture, while eventually concealing a sagging chin as she tried to remain forever youthful.

Over time, the role of stage Indian inflected her public identity, as evidenced in the increase in the Native content and Native commitment of her work, through which she acted as intermediary, explaining and justifying Indian concerns to her White audiences. Thus, to some extent, Johnson was 'a woman who actually became her role.'[48] At the same time, the sequence of her costumes refrained from posing any threat to the prevailing hegemony by showing the 'wild' Indian, sexually alluring with visible ankles and loose long hair, replaced by the cultivated European in chignon and corset. At least one critic regretted this transformation:

She stands an unique figure upon the border-land between the worlds of ancient tradition and modern art ... With true artistic perception she has seized upon the most romantic aspects of Indian life and embodied them in truly poetical and consequently lasting form ... It was unfortunate, to my mind, that the exigences of a popular performance should have necessitated a change from the strikingly picturesque Indian dress in which she appeared during the first part of the evening to modern evening costume, for the effect was destructive of a highly poetical illusion. Various views may be entertained as to Miss Johnson's powers as a reciter, but there can be only one opinion regarding her gifts as a poetess.[49]

This author's choice of the word 'costume' to describe fairly conventional evening dress reminds us that 'her evening gown was as much a costume as her Native outfit.'[50] While her external persona dilated from the visible costume to the realm of the spiritual, such that the earnest member of the Church of England[51] of 1890 appeared to metamorphose into the dramatic 'A Pagan in St. Paul's' of 1906, Johnson's inner self remains closed to us. Her ability to play to her audience resulted in a wide range of characterizations by those who met her, their reportage based in turn on their individual expectations and motivations. Thus their impressions range from seeing Johnson as the embodiment of 'the valkyrie-like wild passion of the traditional Red Indian,' given to thrilling her companions with the occasional Iroquois war-whoop, to presenting her as the patrician who was 'not quite as primitive as she pretended.'[52] To a query about consistency, she reportedly responded, 'Oh *consistency*! ... How can one be consistent until the world ceases to change with the changing days?'[53] A figure of Johnson's complexity, with her ability to conjure up, sometimes simultaneously, a host of cultural images, demonstrates how individual identity is lived as 'a matrix of subject-positions, which may be inconsistent or even in contradiction with one another.'[54] Recent interest in the First Nations artist as trickster – as a shape-shifting humorist with a sharp sense of irony, whose essence is 'doing' rather than 'being' – suggests another way to understand Johnson's complexity.[55]

When she first appeared in print in *Saturday Night* and elsewhere, Johnson was a Canadian writer who, like many inhabitants of the Dominion, happened to be partly Indian and whose work, like that of many Canadian writers, included occasional attention to Native topics. For as long as print remained her primary medium, the term 'poetess' was a more powerful sign of her public identity than were references to the origins of her father. After she turned to the stage, her Nativeness acquired stronger political and cultural dimensions, as her persona enhanced the intensity and frequency of her advocacy of Native issues. By 1896 the Native aspect of her work assumed sufficient priority to produce the term 'poet-advocate.'[56] In print, the effect of a poem such as 'A Cry from an Indian Wife' was confined to those who noticed it in the newspapers in 1885 and 1892,[57] and those who read it again in *The White Wampum*, published in 1895. But in performance, this confrontational dramatic monologue, highlighted in reviews as the climax of the evening, was repeated hundreds of times to thousands of Canadians and others who may have had limited access to Johnson's writings.

This gives rise to the troubling and ultimately unanswerable question as to whether the dramatic effectiveness of Johnson's performance overrode her content, as occurs today in high-end entertainment such as the musical *Rent*, which puts actors into the roles of homeless people who themselves cannot afford to join the audience.[58] If political action had been her primary aim, would she have been taken more seriously if she had lectured in sober dress? But would she then have attracted an audience – moreover, an audience who would pay? While Johnson's newspaper reviewers represent only a small portion of those came to see her, it is their responses which survive. These demonstrate greater comfort in praising her stage skills than in acknowledging her challenge to European hegemony.[59] As well, her position as the most prominent spokesperson for Canadian Natives homogenized many tribal groups into a single race, so that 'listening to Johnson's poetry forestalled the necessity to engage other Native voices.'[60] Similar to the way her prominence encouraged Euro-Canadians to essentialize Aboriginals, she was herself essentialized by many commentators, who read her entire oeuvre through her dramatization of her Native work. For example, at her death, the *Vancouver Province* claimed that 'Through a great many of her works there runs a thread of savagery that betrayed her origin. In spite of her English mother she was Indian to the core.'[61] Yet only eight of the thirty-six poems in *The White Wampum* present explicitly Native subject matter. These are outnumbered by canoeing and nature poems, which strongly resemble similar verse by non-Native Canadian poets of the 1890s but, in the perception of contemporary and later readers, acquire an Indian inflection due to the public identity of their author. In her next volume, *Canadian Born*, published in 1903, just five of the thirty poems directly reflect Native concerns. A similar proportion characterizes the final version of *Flint and Feather*.

Before Johnson publicly asserted her Native identity on stage, her education and social milieu predicted integration through marriage into the dominant Anglo-Canadian culture. When she started to perform in costume, her assumption of a clearly racialized identity intersected with her representation of gender and class such that the 'high-spirited daughter of her warrior sires'[62] was always described in language implicitly drawing on the stereotype of the noble savage. However, while there are frequent references to her elevated First Nations ancestry and to her father's status as chief, Canadians seldom described her as a princess during her lifetime, especially in contrast to the frequency of the term 'poetess.'[63] When the Canadian author Gilbert

Parker wanted to convey the high station of a Native woman character in his novel *The Translation of a Savage*, he coined the term 'chieftain-ess.' Americans, obsessed with popularized images of Pocahontas and Hiawatha's sweetheart Minnehaha, more often labelled Johnson a princess.[64] Despite their fascination with Johnson's self-dramatization, the British press, familiar with real royalty, used the term sparingly. Significantly, it was when writing to an American, the influential editor Edmund Clarence Stedman, that Charles G.D. Roberts in 1895 described Johnson as 'Our Canadian Mohawk Princess' (and coyly added: 'Beware, beware, beware! She is charming; & she is a poet!').[65] More meaningful for imperial audiences was the comparison with Boadicea, Queen of the Iceni, made by some critics. Linkage to the earlier anti-colonial figure, also romanticized by Victorians and Edwardians in search of a heroic heritage, inducted Johnson into a pantheon of admirable British protesters.

On her 1894 trip to London, and on the title page of *The White Wampum*, Johnson acquired an Indian name when she added her grandfather's Tekahionwake to her regular by-line.[66] No evidence survives as to whether she followed proper Mohawk custom to obtain legitimate use of the name. Like Johnson's lack of Native clothes and ornaments, her lack of a Native birth name suggests her family's distance from Iroquois culture where language and ritual are highly valued. Of the four siblings, only Allen Wawanosh, the third child, received an Indian baptismal name; however, this was not a family name but bestowed to honour a Chiefswood visitor present at the time of his birth, the Ojibwa Chief Wawanosh. When Johnson first began to publish, her pseudonyms were entirely English: 'Margaret Rox' for one of her first poems and 'Rollstone,' the family name of her father's Dutch American grandmother, for her first columns of prose.[67] In the practice of New Woman journalism in Canada and the United States, such pseudonymns were not taken in order to disguise the author, but rather to provide her with a professional identity. Readers well knew that 'Garth Grafton' of the *Globe* was Sara Jeannette Duncan, 'Lady Gay' of *Saturday Night* was Grace Denison, and 'Faith Fenton,' a later *Globe* columnist, was Alice Freeman. After 1894, Johnson's publications and publicity usually identified her with both names as 'E. Pauline Johnson, Tekahionwake.' In 1906 she was further exoticized for British readers when stories appeared in the London *Daily Express* by 'Tekahionwake, The Iroquois Poetess' whose English name remained silent.

That Tekahionwake was adopted largely to enhance Johnson's professional status is evident in her personal correspondence, which she usually signed as 'E. Pauline Johnson.' Demonstrating her skill with strategic self-representation, her surviving letters reveal her ability to mould her tone and image to her purpose and audience. Her letters to Lighthall, Yeigh, and Henry O'Brien, are all from 'E. Pauline Johnson.' Those to her sister Evelyn are from 'Paul.' To her friends Lionel Makovski and sister author Kate Simpson-Hayes, she was 'Pauline.' To Sir Wilfrid Laurier she became 'Tekahionwake' only when seeking letters of introduction for Australia and England. A similar 1906 request to railway magnate Sir William Van Horne, for letters for a never-realized trip to the West Indies, was signed with her usual 'E. Pauline Johnson.' Moreover, this is the only name on several letters where a more distinct proclamation of her Native identity might be expected, such as her 1903 request to editor John Willison for a regular newspaper column, and her 1909 appeal to Laurier regarding the appointment of the next superintendant of the Six Nations reserve. As well, references to herself as Indian tend to accompany special requests, apologies, or expressions of gratitude. Thus when apologizing to Kate Simpson-Hayes for her delay in finishing a letter, she wrote, 'Do not think my friend that I am indifferent – far from it, I am too good an Indian for that.' When belatedly repaying a Saskatchewan host for medicine, she jested, 'Whoever it was obtained from will think me a very bad Indian, won't he?' These occasional comments suggest that in her private life, presenting herself as Indian could accommodate and even mitigate embarrassing situations, such as indebtedness, that would otherwise be regarded as transgressive for a lady of her class.[68]

From 1892, Johnson's literary work was almost always received and assessed in relation to her performance. Some reviewers of her books recalled her stage appearances in order to enhance her published texts, while in the eyes of others, Johnson's reputation as a popular public figure detracted from the seriousness of her writings. In addition to linking Euro-Canadian and Native identities, Johnson bridged high and low culture over a deepening chasm that would prove increasingly difficult to span during the decades after her death. Moreover, as no primary documents survive concerning the publication of most of her work, including her first two books, the problem of penetrating the mediations and mythologies that surround Johnson plagues her composition and publishing history. Given that her most visible Canadian peers were issuing their early volumes of poetry in Canada and the United States, we don't know why she believed that her first book had to appear in

London.[69] If her attraction to England was personal or ideological, she did not leave statements to either effect.

The other poets on the program for Johnson's debut of January 1892, at which 'the cream of Toronto's intellectual 400 were present,'[70] identified her literary peers as the major Central Canadian literary figures of the early 1890s: the still familiar names of Archibald Lampman, W.W. Campbell, D.C. Scott, and W.D. Lighthall, along with the now more obscure Susan Frances Harrison, Agnes Maule Machar, and Helen Merrill. Scott, Lampman, and Campbell were about to give their generation a more tangible profile through their 'At the Mermaid Inn' column, which ran in the Toronto *Globe* from February 1892 through July 1893. Their free-ranging discussions of literary, cultural, and intellectual affairs frequently addressed Canadian literature and poetry without, however, ever mentioning Johnson by name. As she indicated in a letter to Lighthall the following October, this was the group with which she cautiously identified:

> I am to go to Ottawa, and am looking forward to seeing our friends and fellow singers there. I say 'our' in a Canadian use of the word, not personally, for it sounds rather saucy, to use no stronger word, for me to leap even in my own estimation into the ranks where you and Lampman, Campbell and Scott have stood so long before I breathed poetic air. Do not think a little success is spoiling me, it is not so. I feel now as I always did, that were it not for my friends and my nationality, I would never stand where I now do. My work would be little without the 'booming' or if it had been written by one without romance of ancestry.[71]

This apparently off-hand reference to 'romance of ancestry' links Johnson to another thread of late nineteenth-century Canadian culture. In 1883, the year before her first poems appeared in print, a manuscript of verse by Emily Martin from Caughnawaga was displayed at a local exhibition. Her work won commendation from John Reade, literary editor of the Montreal *Gazette*, for 'poetic feeling and mastery of language.' The context of his remarks, a formal essay presented to the Royal Society of Canada on 'The Literary Faculty of the Native Races of America,' suggests that Johnson appeared on the scene just when Canada's intellectual climate was prepared to welcome an identifiable First Nations poet. As a current member of Reade's Montreal social circle and future member of the Royal Society, Lighthall may even have been present at the essay's first reading on 21 May 1884.

As well as W.D. Lighthall, Johnson's literary mentors included Charles G.D. Roberts, who, although not present at her literary debut, promoted her work thereafter. While they would not meet in person until she toured New Brunswick in 1895, in the *Globe* of 13 February 1892 Roberts lauded her as 'the aboriginal voice of Canada by blood as well as by taste and the special trend of her gifts.' Three years later he wrote a letter introducing her to Richard Watson Gilder, editor of the *Century*, as 'one of the acknowledged leaders of our Canadian group.'[72]

Johnson's position in the Canadian literary community was further consolidated by her inclusion in J.E. Wetherell's *Later Canadian Poems*. This slim anthology was issued in 1893 for school use because, according to Roberts, Wetherell found Lighthall's *Songs of the Great Dominion* included 'too much trash.'[73] Wetherell's initial selection focused on Roberts, Carman, Lampman, Campbell, D.C. Scott, and F.G. Scott; his addition of women (in a supplement) seems to have occurred through Johnson's intervention.[74] Here she is favoured with a portrait and the greatest number of poems, followed by Ethelwyn Wetherald, Susan Frances Harrison, Isabella Valancy Crawford, Agnes Maule Machar, and Sara Jeannette Duncan. By 1896 Johnson had achieved sufficient prominence to be named first in the New York *Bookman*'s assessment of the 'strong tendency of the literary impulse in Canada to express itself in verse.'[75]

From the surviving historical record, it appears that the first decades of Johnson's career were enhanced by her ability to foster protégée relationships with prominent literary men and other male public figures. Relationships with literary women became more significant in her last years, when she needed comfort and understanding more than promotion. One literary figure who proved disappointing was her mother's cousin, American writer W.D. Howells. The connection at first seemed promising. Sara Jeannette Duncan reported in 1886 that 'the notable novelist spoke in terms of the liveliest interest of his "Indian cousins" when I met him last winter in Washington.'[76] While this interest recurs in the very few references to the Johnson family in the Howells record,[77] all accounts from the Johnson side represent him as embarrassed by the connection and dismissive of her writing.[78]

Of less stature but more enthusiasm was Hector Charlesworth, eleven years Johnson's junior and clearly smitten by her.[79] Before his twentieth birthday, at the very beginning of what would become an illustrious career in Canadian journalism,[80] Charlesworth quickly followed his *Saturday Night* review of the Canadian Literature Evening with a dedicated study for the short-lived *Lake Magazine*. This latter remained for many years the longest serious literary analysis of Johnson's work. Of particular interest is his positioning of Johnson in different literary contexts. As an Indian, she demonstrates that 'each and every red man is innately a poet.' As a North American, she vies with Walt Whitman in her poetic expression: 'who sings with a note so sure as hers the freedom, the grandeur, the wealth of this great continent of America?' As a woman, 'not only is she the greatest living poetess but, were the few of the greatest women-poets of all times to be counted on the fingers of one hand, her name must be included in the number.' And as a Canadian, she offers the emergent national culture its lost early phase: the equivalent of the Homeric/Saphhic era that underpins the culture of ancient Greece.[81] This notion that national identity should be rooted in an Indigenous folk or oral culture was then a recurring theme throughout the Western world, as exemplified in the linking of cultural and political nationalism in Ireland as well as in Walter McRaye's performances of W.H. Drummond's habitant poetry. That Johnson could make such a contribution to the larger development of Canada was argued in 1915 by Professor J.D. Robins of Victoria College, who looked more to 'myths of the soil than of race' for local equivalents to the Classical and Celtic underpinnings of Anglo-European literature.[82]

After the early 1890s, Johnson's position as the foremost Canadian woman poet of her era was boosted by several internationally successful Canadian-born male authors. Sir Gilbert Parker, who had met her on her first trip to England and shared her strong imperialism, introduced her to important London editors and newspapermen on her second trip in 1906, and wrote the introduction to *The Moccasin Maker*. Naturalist painter and author Ernest Thompson Seton, whom she met in the early 1890s, likewise maintained a connection that produced posthumous memorials, including the introduction to *The Shagganappi*. With both men, the public record is coloured by elegaic tributes to a mythologized Mohawk princess, and the private obscured by the scantiness of surviving correspondence.

More veiled is her interaction with Duncan Campbell Scott, with whom her path crossed frequently, due to her dual identity as a poet and as a legal Indian. In his capacity as senior administrator in the Department of Indian Affairs, Scott was well acquainted with the Six Nations and the Johnson family.[83] As a literary figure, he was present at Pauline's debut recital and appeared alongside her in the Lighthall and Wetherell anthologies. Two of Scott's privately printed Christmas poetry broadsides, for 1891 and 1896, can be found in the Johnson papers at Trent University, and another poet remembers Johnson's presence at an 1895 dinner at D.C. Scott's Ottawa home.[84] The obvious reserve on both sides in the archival and the public record – especially when compared with the promotion of Johnson's career by other public men – may derive from the necessary professional reticence of the professional civil servant. As Scott's administration of government policy to 'civilize' the Indians into mainstream Euro-Canadian culture included active discouragement of 'the reproduction of barbaric costumes or custom,' we might well imagine his opinion of Johnson's costumed performances.[85]

At the same time, there arises the vexing question of literary influence. There are a number of occasions when Scott's well-known Indian poems intersect with similar work by Johnson. The triumphant heroine of 'Ojistoh' (1895), characterized as 'white star' and 'pure white star,' echoes in Scott's Keejigo of his 1935 poem, 'At Gull Lake: August 1810.' She is resurrected from her amorous tragedy by association with the rising moon, 'A lovely perfection, snow-pure in the heaven.' In the troubled title character of 'The Half-Breed Girl' (1906) Scott rewrites the Mixed-race heroines of Johnson's stories of the 1890s. While it is customary to attribute Scott's literary representation of Natives to his experiences during his treaty-making ventures into the hinterland, his indebtedness to Johnson has remained unexamined.

Johnson's connections with the literary women and journalists whose companionship and shared experiences created a private network over the years, and who rallied to support her materially in her last illness, have already been described. Unfortunately, writers like Nellie McClung, Kate Simpson-Hayes, Kit Coleman, and Isabel Ecclestone Mackay could do nothing to ensure her place in the Canadian literary canon in the middle years of the twentieth century. They, too, were destined to be discredited as writers of enduring worth.

Johnson's Literary Reputation

An examination of the reception of Johnson's writing over the course of a century provides a rich opportunity to study changing notions of literary value, and the shifting demarcation between high and popular culture. During her lifetime, this line scarcely existed in Canada, where nationalism prevailed as the primary evaluative criterion. The *Vancouver Province* headline on the day of her funeral in March 1913 simply stated, 'Canada's poetess is laid to rest.' What author, before or since, could be perceived as so indubitably a figure of national significance? During the following decade, an elegaic quality often imbued references to Pauline Johnson. To Euro-Canadians, she was the last spokesperson for a people destined to disappear: 'The time must come for us to go down, and when it comes may we have the strength to meet our fate with such fortitude and silent dignity as did the Red Man his.'[86]

However, Johnson's reputation was also fated to go down, due to changes in the literary climate introduced by the fresh (some might say ill) wind of literary modernism, which blasted a chasm between elite and popular culture. This decline began during the 1930s, and peaked in 1961, when centenary celebrations of Johnson's birth aroused the vituperative wit of clever young literary men who were themselves competing to mark the Canadian literary map. At the popular level, Johnson maintained a presence that kept her books in print and preserved her name in schools and schoolbooks, a Vancouver chocolate company, and almost in a major Vancouver theatre.[87] But at the level of elite culture, she experienced a dramatic downward slide. Literary critic David Perkins claims that 'the possible plots of narrative literary history can be reduced to three: rise, decline, and rise and decline.'[88] Although Johnson did indeed experience a decline, this study posits a fourth pattern that has become increasingly familiar in women's literary history – decline and rise – by recuperating Pauline Johnson in light of current critical interests in race, gender, and Native Rights.

Twentieth-century literary canons, as we know from the analysis of critics such as Leslie Fiedler, Barbara Herrnstein Smith, and John Guillory, have for the most part been created and buttressed by institutionalized education, especially at the post-secondary level. The canon of Canadian literature, as transmitted in colleges and universities, was confirmed from the 1950s through the early 1970s by several major projects whose goal was to legitimize Canadian Literature as a distinct scholarly and artistic field. Most influential in this process were Desmond Pacey's *Creative Writing in Canada* (1952; revised 1961), the establishment of McClelland and Stewart's New Canadian Library series (initiated in 1959), the multi-authored *Literary History of Canada* (1964; revised 1976, 1990), Louis Dudek and Michael Gnarowski's *The Making of Modern Poetry in Canada* (1970), and the final edition of Carl Klinck and R.E. Watters's *Canadian Anthology* (1974). The agenda of these various undertakings – to determine the features of Canadian writing that were unique to Canada – was underpinned by the academic high modernism in which their editors and authors (almost exclusively male) had been trained. Scorning romanticism and sentimentality, they valued detachment, alienated individualism, elitism, and formalism over emotion, domesticity, community, and popularity, thereby solidifying a set of oppositional qualities that barred most of Canada's women writers from serious academic consideration.

The literary history that these publishing projects espoused was based not on what the majority of Canadians had written and read in the past, but on the elitist vision that prevailed among Canadian scholars and critics. Applying these principles to the 1920s, for example, Northrop Frye's notion that 'the indifference of nature to human values' was the 'central Canadian tragic theme'[89] elevated A.J.M. Smith's poem 'The Lonely Land' and Frederick Philip Grove's bleak prairie fiction over the much more popular, and therefore arguably more representative, fiction and poetry of L.M. Montgomery, Marshall Saunders, Nellie McClung, and Marjorie Pickthall. While male popular authors such as Robert Service and Ralph Connor received recognition as regional writers in anthologies and reprint series, their female counterparts were usually dismissed. Indeed, the endurance of Frank Scott's 1927 poem, 'The Canadian Authors Meet,' which mocks the female members of the Canadian Authors' Association, demonstrates the extent to which modernist critics treated 'poet' and 'woman' as incompatible concepts. Poetry was thus claimed as a masculine enterprise, with true poets congregating in universities, bars, and smoking rooms, not around the teacups.

When we trace the historical peaks and valleys of Pauline Johnson's posthumous reputation, it becomes evident that the single most powerful contribution to the erasure of women poets like Johnson from Canada's literary canon was Malcolm Ross's slender anthology, *Poets of the Confederation*. Published in the New Canadian Library in 1960, this book not only reduced the complex field of early Canadian lyric poetry to four of Johnson's male peers, but also formalized the subsequently solid quartet of Charles G.D. Roberts, Bliss Carman, Archibald Lampman, and D.C. Scott as 'The Confederation Poets.'[90] All, like Johnson, were born between 1860 and 1862 and achieved recognition in the 1880s and 1890s.

Ross's dismissal contradicted not only an earlier generation of critics but the so-called Confederation poets themselves. In 1933 Roberts, generally regarded as the senior member of this 'School of Canadian Poetry,' identified the 'men & women of the 1860 group (1860–61 & 62)' as 'Carman, Lampman, D.C. Scott, F.G. Scott, W.W. Campbell, Gilbert Parker, Pauline Johnson' and several others.[91] The authors of the spate of serious studies of Canadian literature published during the 1920s situated Johnson likewise. According to W.A. Deacon, she was 'in skill, sentiment and outlook, one of the powerful "Group,"' and wrote 'with a mastery equal at times to the best of them, and seldom much below it.' Professors Logan and French judged her to be 'in some respects ... the most original and engaging singer in the company of the Canadian lyrists who were born in 1860, 1861, and 1862.' Lorne Pierce described her as 'one of the most gifted singers of Canada,' and O.J. Stevenson found her 'in one sense, the most Canadian of all Canadian poets.'[92]

For the next generation of cultural taste-makers, the reception of Pauline Johnson was influenced by representations of the Indian in popular culture. The rise of modernism in Canada coincided with the increasing commercialization of the image of the Indian princess, visually documented in the exhibit on 'Indian Princesses and Cowboys,' mounted in Montreal in 1992 and in Vancouver in 1997. According to curator, Gail Guthrie Valaskasis,

> From about 1915 through the 1940's, the dominant representation of the Indian Princess was the 'red tunic lady,' a maiden draped in a red tunic, wearing the requisite headband and feather, and posed with mountains, waterfalls and moonlit lakes. These romanticized princesses which adorned calendars, advertisements, paintings and postcards – with names like Winona, Minnehaha, Iona and even Hiawatha – worked in consort with their male counterpart, the Indian warrior, to establish the historicized Indian as 'one of the icons of consumer society.' Calendar princesses, gazing wistfully or longingly, appeared in a remarkable range of poses and settings. There are paddling princesses and fishing maidens, sewing princesses and maidens of the feathers or the flowers; but most common are maidens ... merely posed as imaginary Indians amid pristine, romanticized scenery.[93]

Although Johnson was described as a poetess far more often than a princess while she was alive, the term poetess disappears after her death, totally eclipsed by princess. The serious nature of the first full-length study of Johnson and her works, published by Mrs W. Garland Foster in 1931, is belied by its title, *The Mohawk Princess*, which not only describes Johnson's heritage incorrectly, but also plays directly into the prevailing stereotype.

Complicating the reception of Johnson, particularly during the 1930s, when her detractors of the 1960s were avid young readers, was the prominence of Grey Owl, who has been called one of Canada's most successful literary poseurs. English-born Archie Belaney achieved public stature as author, speaker, and conservationist by masquerading as an Indian, replete with braids, buckskins, and cute pet beavers. His performance set him on centre stage as a national figure, with his authenticity apparently confirmed in the 1931 film *The Beaver People* made by the Dominion Parks Branch. Grey Owl's powerful presence displaced Pauline Johnson, no longer alive and now seen in many quarters only as an inauthentic 'princess,' as a national representative of Native Canadians. The revelation of Belaney's real identity after his death in 1938 was greeted with public dismay. Grey Owl's imposture had been preceded by that of Buffalo Child Long Lance (Sylvester Long), who had also created an artifical identity through the media of print and film before his unmasking led to his suicide in 1932. The stories of these two phony Indians, both of whom had been remarkably successful in deceiving audiences eager for 'safe' representatives of oppressed peoples, did little to create confidence in the authenticity of Native authors and performers. At the end of the twentieth century, the lingering taint of the imposters continues to stigmatize Johnson, even in the view of commentators sympathetic to Native peoples.

Grey Owl and Long Lance thus provide the implicit context for the modernist devaluation of Johnson. During the 1930s, while Johnson's admirers continued to praise her work in the pages of the *Canadian Bookman*,[94] the more august *Canadian Forum* presented 'the Pauline Johnson legend' as merely 'a very genteel lady in a bustle who has nice thoughts about Nature and the proper sentiments toward love and yearning, motherhood, and the manly virtues.' Declaring that she 'is no more Indian than Henry Wadsworth Longfellow,' John Ayre was more interested in demolishing Johnson than in taking the courtesy to read her.[95] His article demonstrates that Johnson's dismissal by Canadian modernists was largely due to four features that make her especially interesting today: she was female, she claimed a First Nations identity, she used her literary talents to advance a social cause, and she was amazingly popular.

Canadian modernism's insistence on its own immaculate conception, at McGill University in Montreal in the late 1920s, led its proponents to pillory its female companions and precursors as 'virgins of sixty who still write of passion,' to return to Scott's 'The Canadian Authors Meet.'[96]

The project of reinserting women writers into Canadian literary history directly challenges the self-fashioning of Canadian modernists. For example, could Irving Layton, the most outspoken iconoclast of the next generation of Canadian poets, have posed so effectively as the inventor of eroticism in Canadian poetry if Johnson's 'The Idlers' were better known? Had he been aware of this poem, it might have appeared in his 1962 anthology of Canadian love poetry, *Love Where the Nights Are Long*, in which Johnson's era is represented by several far chaster efforts by the predictable Confederation poets; in the entire volume, women authors account for just six of the fifty poems.[97]

In addition to misogyny, uncertainty about the relation between art and activism characterized high modernism in Canada. Although feminist and post-colonial critics have now dismantled the notion that art is (or ever can be) apolitical, in academic circles there still remain substantial vestiges of Hector Charlesworth's opinion that Johnson's polemics marred her poetry. Despite the political commitment of Dorothy Livesay, who went on to win Governor General's awards for poetry in 1944 and 1947, the modernist vision that eventually triumphed was the aestheticism of A.J.M. Smith, who elevated intellectually difficult 'cosmopolitan' poetry over 'provincial' romantic verse through his influential anthology, *The Book of Canadian Poetry*. The three editions (1943, 1948, and 1957), which begrudgingly allotted Johnson one poem, 'Shadow River,' established the canon of early and mid-century Canadian poetry that still prevails today and underscores the master narrative of Canadian modernism subsequently constructed by Louis Dudek and Michael Gnarowski in *The Making of Modern Poetry in Canada* (1970).

The modernist assessment of cultural value saw little compatibility between poetry on a high creative level and the commercial side of authorship. Canada's most influential modernist poets and critics upheld the ideology that 'resisted the commodity-text' and 'held art and money to be antithetical,'[98] an attitude reinforced by Northrop Frye's discomfort with popular writing, evident throughout his Canadian criticism.[99] During and before the modernist era, popularity – and occasionally even commercial success – were sins frequently committed by women writers, including Johnson, McClung, L.M. Montgomery, Mazo de la Roche, and Edna Jaques. To the elitist mind, poetry presented in costumed performances aimed at audiences of the semi-washed could not possibly inhabit the same realm as poetry published in small university-based magazines. Today it is intriguing to read the page allotted to Johnson in the *Literary History of Canada*, where the inability of modernist criticism to account for her enduring appeal leads Roy Daniells into uncharacteristically tentative phrasing and puzzlement. 'What value her poems will have when the memory of her vigorous personality has faded it is difficult to say,' he prevaricates. He then characterizes her as a 'symbol which satisfies a felt need,' and distances her from both her gender and her First Nations advocacy by identifying that need as a kind of primordial romanticism: 'the continuing secret desire of all Canadians to reach back into an innocent and heroic world of wild woods and waters before the white man came and the guilt of conquests, whether French or English, was incurred.' Johnson's political and erotic charge are thus co-opted into a Euro-Canadian aesthetic based more firmly on the poetics of Northrop Frye than on an analysis of her historical context.[100]

Compounding the picture was the problem of national cultural definition: 'could one be modern *and* Canadian?'[101] Seeking recognition in the larger spectrum of British and American culture, Canadian modernists asserted a sense of national distinction by invoking geography to construct the trope of the empty land, usually anthropomorphized as the 'lonely' land.[102] Frye further mythologized this image into the hostile land, an inflection created by 'an introverted boy who grew up in the relatively harsh climate of New Brunswick, and who in his early student days in Toronto lacked the money to buy warm clothes.'[103] His analysis permeated the influential generation of Canadian critics assembled in *The Literary History of Canada*, who claimed that

> From the beginning, the 'literature' of Canada was stamped by a struggle against the climate and against the land itself. For Northrop Frye, reviewing A.J.M. Smith's *The Book of Canadian Poetry* in the *Canadian Forum*, 'the outstanding achievement of Canadian poetry is the evocation of stark terror. Not a coward's terror, of course; but a controlled vision of the causes of cowardice. The immediate source of this is obviously the frightening loneliness of a huge and thinly settled country.'[104]

Now almost a cliché to most Canadians familiar with the painting of Tom Thomson and the Group of Seven, this view required the erasure of Canada's First Nations, to whom the land was neither empty nor lonely nor terrifying.[105] Whereas pioneer writing attempted to bring order to the wilderness by containing its representation within European conventions, modernist primitivism aimed to decivilize the land by depicting its elemental qualities. To be questioned is the extent to which the notion of Nature as challenging and even hostile is both masculine and urban, in that it elevates the lone male seer/adventurer in his canoe, with his pen or paintbrush, as master of the wilderness.[106] As soon as women glide into view, this picture is disturbed: visually by Emily Carr, whose paintings of Coastal British Columbia are infused with images from First Nations cultures, and in poetry by Pauline Johnson, whose expertise as a solo canoeist was well publicized in her verse and her New Woman recreational journalism of the early 1890s.

Most remarkable about First Nations Canadians in modernist art and writing is their virtual absence. Looking specifically at poetry, we can see that their sparse appearances fall into several categories. The dominant image is the Indian as museum piece, a remnant of the past. This depiction enters Canadian modernism with the transitional figure of Duncan Campbell Scott, whose reticence about Johnson has already been noted. As deputy superintendant of the Department of Indian Affairs, Scott collected West Coast Native art while supervising the repression of the potlatch, and administered the government policy of assimilation while naturalizing the disappearance of Native Canadians in elegiac poetry. Published regularly throughout his career, from the 1890s to the 1930s, were poems focusing on Indian women whose relations with White men poetically enact the absorption desired by government policy.[107] From Scott, it is not far to E.J. Pratt's epic *Brébeuf and His Brethren* (1940), much admired throughout Frye's Canadian criticism for the way the 'Indians who martyred Brébeuf' represent 'the capacity in man that enables him to be deliberately cruel.'[108]

Rarer in mid-century Canada are poems that acknowledge the Indian in the poet's own time. The alienness of Douglas LePan's 'lust-red manitou' teetering at the conclusion of his well-known 1948 poem, 'A Country without a Mythology,' was preceded by a more obscure articulation in Frank Prewett's 'The Red Man' (1924). This poem describes the relation between Native and Euro-Canadian as utter incomprehension and unknowability, concluding: 'His ways are strange, his skin is red / Our ways and skins our own.'[109] A.M. Klein's 'Indian Reservation: Caughnawaga' (1948) may be the only occasion when left-wing modernism's call for social justice extended in poetry to Native Canadians. His description of the reservation as 'a grassy ghetto, and no home' links the dispossession of two ancient minorities. Both Jews and Indians are victims of 'the better hunters,' 'the pious, prosperous ghosts' of those responsible for genocide. Like much of Johnson's verse, Klein's poem is elegiac, infused with regret but positing no viable future for those whose 'past is sold in a shop' and who are themselves 'but fauna in a museum kept.'[110]

Modernism was most comfortable with Indians when they were cast as primitives and studied by anthropologists, whose salvaging of 'original' Native culture furnished materials to corroborate the modernist effort to discover new, more authentic modes of expression.[111] The connection between imagism, one of the first phases of literary modernism, and the recording of Native songs at the beginning of this century has been noted by several critics.[112] Indian poetry became especially visible in 1917 in a special issue of *Poetry* (Chicago), followed the next year by *The Path on the Rainbow*, the first anthology of North American Aboriginal verse. Consisting largely of translations by anthropologists, this book also included poems by several interpreters of Indian culture. Pauline Johnson, the only Native literary author, was admitted on the insistence of the publisher, despite the view of the editor that her poems 'show how far the Indian poet strays from her own primitive tribal songs, when attempting the White Man's mode.' She was singled out in reviews and in subsequent criticism as 'ironically, the most traditionally Western [European] and the least Indian in both content and form,' an attitude still dominant in 1983, when an American critic studying primitivism in modern American poetry faulted Johnson's work as 'excessively romantic,' and having 'little to do with actual Native American modes of life and expression.'[113]

Johnson's appearance in these American studies signals her significant impact on Native writing in the United States, her works transcending the international border that she disliked to cross in person. American scholars now situate her in the context of a generation of Native authors who were probably more aware of her than she was of them: S. Alice Callahan, Charles A. Eastman, Francis La Flesche, Alexander Posey, John Milton Oskison, and Zitkala-Sa. Her importance is visible not only in her inclusion in current reference works to Native American literature, but also in the statements of authors themselves. Maurice Kenny, for example, links Johnson with Robert Frost and Robinson Jeffers as the three poets to whom he clung during the 1940s as he struggled to find his literary identity. To him, Johnson was 'grandmother to Native American poets, a Mohawk who did not renounce the Indian ... She had no fear and possessed much talent. She has remained a flag breathing the same air as the reputable and resilient hawk, and her work survives in a world where poetry is neither read nor respected ... Fortunately, Johnson's literary grandchildren have continued to pay the respect of admiration, and her poems – though often didactic and a touch too purple – have remained stamped in printer's ink.'[114]

The year 1961 was a critical moment in the reception history of
Pauline Johnson, with celebrations of the centennial of her birth accen-
tuating the gulf between elite and popular culture. For the occasion, the
Canadian federal government issued a commemorative stamp, making
her the first woman (other than the Queen), the first author, and the
first Native Canadian to be thus honoured. The Institute of Iroquoian
Studies in Brantford organized a summer pilgrimage of twenty-eight
members of the Six Nations to Vancouver to attend local ceremonies.
Stories about Johnson, including the question of naming the new Vancouver theatre after her, filled the city's newspapers. The Vancouver
press also cited a number of assessments by Canada's literary authori-
ties, most far from laudatory, reflecting the prevailing values of the time.
In his capacity as both poet and professor, Earle Birney disdained
Johnson as not 'at all important in Canadian literature.' R.E. Watters
faulted her verse for lacking 'philosophical or intellectual content.'
Robertson Davies described her poetry as 'elocutionist-fodder' and
Johnson herself as 'not given to reflection,' thereby excusing A.J.M.
Smith's decision to omit her entirely from his 1960 edition of *The Oxford
Book of Canadian Verse.* In a column for *Maclean's Magazine* reprinted in
the *Vancouver Sun*, Mordecai Richler derisively reported on the launch
of McClelland and Stewart's reissue of Johnson's *Legends of Vancouver.*
The same year, in his *Creative Writing in Canada*, Desmond Pacey
scorned her poetry as 'meretricious' and disdained to consider further
a writer whose work he elsewhere described as 'cheap, vulgar, and
almost incredibly bad.'[115]

Birney's dismissal of Johnson includes the comment, 'I don't read her.'
This statement raises the question of whether Johnson's work was actually read by any of her 1961 detractors, given that by this time her image
was so tainted by the category of Indian princess that no self-respecting
mid-century man of letters would likely take her seriously. If we regard
the metonymy literally, we can see that Earle Birney had indeed read
'her' – as person – and that having read Pauline Johnson's identity as the
commodified Indian princess of popular culture, he rejected the notion
that her poetry could deserve his attention. Birney's statement replicates
R.E. Watters's decision to omit Johnson, as author, from his British
Columbia *Centennial Anthology*, and to represent her instead with a 1952
Maclean's article about her, titled 'The Passionate Princess.'

In a 1997 survey of the state of Canadian Native Literature in the
1960s, Hartmut Lutz points to the importance of this decade in establishing the groundswell for the new wave of Native writing that surged in

the 1980s and 1990s. He cites '1967 as the beginning of contemporary writing by Native authors in Canada,' with the publication of George Clutesi's *Son of Raven, Son of Deer.*[116] While his discussion mentions Johnson in passing, his failure to pay attention to the many large public gestures accompanying the 1961 celebration of the Johnson centennial demonstrates the endurance of her placement on the wrong side of the divide between high and popular culture. Ignored, for example, is the special Pauline Johnson Centenary Edition of *The Native Voice*, which includes congratulatory messages from such illuminaries as Prime Minister John Diefenbaker, Ellen Fairclough, the minister of citizenship and immigration, the lieutenant-governor of British Columbia, and Lester B. Pearson, leader of the opposition, as well as commemorative advertisements from British Columbia businesses, municipalities, and labour unions. Also overlooked is the performative appeal of Johnson's life and work that gave rise to two independent Toronto productions of plays inspired by the buoyant cultural nationalism of the early 1970s: Theatre Passe Muraille's *Pauline* in 1972 and Pauline Carey's *Pauline Johnson*, mounted at the Studio Lab in 1975. Both, like Betty Donaldson's script, *Pauline Johnson (Tekahionwake): Proud Poet and Patriot*, produced in Calgary in 1993, served as occasions to return Johnson's own texts to the stage.

Ultimately, however, despite such interest and the groundwork laid by Betty Keller's 1981 biography, *Pauline*, Johnson has received less attention than one might expect. It would not be easy to dislodge the attitudes deeply imprinted on older critics, as evidenced by Charles Lillard's scathing, even misogynous, 1988 dismissal of Johnson's readers as 'tourists, grandmothers ... and the curious.'[117] The 1992 Specialized Catalogue of Canadian Stamps, issued by Canada Post, fell into the familiar trap of misrepresenting her as a 'Mohawk princess.' In 1999 Patrick Watson introduced the History Channel's biography of Johnson by deprecating 'The Song My Paddle Sings.' In the scholarly realm, because consideration of Natives in Canadian literature began with critical analysis of representations of Indians in writing by White authors, Duncan Campbell Scott receives more attention than Johnson in two 1980s influential studies, by Leslie Monkman and Terry Goldie.[118] In a 1985 article, Margaret Harry calls attention to the lack of critical interest in Johnson relative to that accorded Isabella Valancy Crawford, a point restated five years later by George W. Lyon, whose 1990 reconsideration constitutes the first sustained scholarly discussion dedicated to Pauline Johnson since Norman Shrive's 1962 attempt to reconcile her romanticism with his modernism.[119] Over more than a century, the enduring mystique of Crawford's obscure life and early death in 1887, has better satisfied the romantic stereotype of the poetess, created by L.E.L. (Letitia E. Landon) in England and Emily Dickinson in the United States, than has Johnson's more complex and less precedented persona. However, change may be on the horizon, as a new generation of feminist scholars has at last begun to counter the prevailing master narratives of Canadian literary history.[120]

Another brake on revival of interest in Johnson is suggested by Indigenous author and critic Janice Acoose, who points out that until very recently, Native male writers received far more attention than did women. As well, Acoose cites the problem of defining 'literature' as contributing to the marginalization of Indigenous women authors. In so doing, she also implicitly identifies the reason why Johnson appears so briefly in her own recent study of literature about and by First Nations women.[121] Frequent exclusion of the literature of advocacy from modernist definitions of art not only misrepresents Johnson's significance, but has also ensured that her work was more commonly read for its romanticism than for its politics. Hence the version of Pauline Johnson most accessible to Acoose is the 'princess of nature' image whose appearance in Margaret Laurence's story 'The Loons' (1966) she strenuously critiques. Here, the stereotyping of Johnson through the childish eyes of Laurence's fictional character, Vanessa MacLeod, vividly renders the many layers of mediation, through both academic and popular culture, that still distance Johnson from creative authors and cultural analysts who should find her pertinent. Prevailing discomfort with Johnson's connection with the now despised image of the 'Indian Princess' may account for her noticeable absence from recent works that reinscribe Aboriginal women into the history of the Americas.[122]

Editorial selection of Johnson's work for anthologies, which is where readers and students are now most likely to first encounter her, shapes their sense of her poetic range and accomplishment. Atwood's edition of *The New Oxford Book of Canadian Verse in English* (1982), for example, includes only 'Ojistoh' and 'Marshlands,' thus balancing Johnson's Native voice with her more generalized nature verse. Recent anthologies of First Nations writing stress her overtly Native pieces, with different perspectives created by different editorial choices. Focusing on links between past and present, Penny Petrone, in *First People, First Voices*, preferred poems that closely resemble traditional oral culture – 'Lullaby of the Iroquois' and the dramatic narratives 'As Red Men Die' and 'Ojistoh' – none of which refers to Native/White relations or ongoing political issues. First Nations editors, on the other hand, accentuate the more politicized Johnson of 'The Cattle Thief' and 'The Corn Husker.'[123]

While Johnson received obligatory acknowledgment in the cluster of studies and anthologies of First Nations literature that appeared in the early 1990s, Margaret Atwood's 1990 claim that 'she is undergoing reclamation today' optimistically overstates the case. In fact, Johnson receives more deliberate reclamation in Atwood's 1991 Clarendon lectures on the North in Canadian literature than in the books specifically dedicated to Native writing (including the special issue of *Canadian Literature* in which Atwood's comment appeared).[124] Moreover, most of Johnson's titles have been allowed to slide out of print, with the exception of *Legends of Vancouver*, which has appeared in a fresh 1997 illustrated edition, and LaVonne Brown Ruoff's edition of *The Moccasin Maker*, reprinted in 1998. Despite its local referentiality, the former has never attained status parallel to that of Helen Hunt Jackson's *Ramona* (1884), written to create sympathy with the evicted Indians of the American Southwest. Perhaps most revealing is the fact that Joan Crate's fine volume, *Pale as Real Ladies: Poems for Pauline Johnson* (1989, 1991), remains virtually unknown to scholars of Canadian First Nations literature.

Our American neighbours do not show the same disinterest. Their enthusiastic quest for Native American literary history has pulled Pauline Johnson into the United States canon, where she now appears in reference books specifically designated 'American.'[125] The author of the 1903 poem 'Canadian Born,' which proclaims 'The Yankee to the south of us must south of us remain,' would probably not be amused to be included in the *Oxford Companion to Women's Writing in the United States* (1995) nor to have the specifics of her relationship to Canada, Britain, and the United States ignored.

As previously demonstrated, Johnson presents a striking example of the turn-of-the-century New Woman in her successful forging of an independent literary and performing career. Hence it is not surprising that, both outside and inside the community of First Nations writers, interest in Johnson tends to follow gender lines. During the 1920s, Cree recitalist Frances Nickawa performed Johnson's poems. For subsequent Indigenous writers and public speakers, like Bernice Loft Winslow ('Dawendine'), born on the Six Nations Reserve in 1902, Johnson has been more important as an example of public success than for her specific writings.[126] Women from geographical regions associated with Johnson seem particularly aware of her achievements. Vancouver writer

Lee Maracle commended Johnson's handling of the voice of Su-á-pu-luck's (Joe Capilano) in *Legends of Vancouver,* and Beth Brant, a Mohawk writer from the Theyindenaga Reserve on the Bay of Quinte, declares 'It is ... time to recognize Johnson for the revolutionary she was,' whose bequest is to have 'walked the writing path clearing the brush for us to follow.'[127]

Despite all the historical and literary analysis that academics like us can bring to Pauline Johnson, at another level it takes a poet to catch a poet, to capture the larger complexity of a woman whose many published writings took different stances in different situations. Joan Crate's Pauline Johnson is a sister poet, of mixed European and Native descent like herself, who offers a point of identification: 'I no longer know where I end and you begin ... I am half me and half you ... I write poems for you. I re-invent you. It is not your words I want ... It is the sound of your voice, your breath cool on my cheek, your insistent geniality, your travel, your toughness, your pretense. And your loneliness, your stretched-thin days, desolation, illness, suffering.'

Some of Crate's poems draw on Keller's biography, while others imaginatively fill gaps between known events and link Johnson to Crate's own experience. For example, 'The Censored Life of a Lady Poet,' which opens 'My poems are an opaque window,' describes both the elusiveness of Pauline Johnson and the challenge shared by all poets in working with the limited medium of language. Several poems ('The Society Page,' 'Last Words'), create a dialogue between Johnson and Crate.[128] However much we two professors apply our academic training to illuminate Johnson's historical context and argue for her significance as a Canadian cultural figure, the most visceral connection belongs to First Nations women writers: to Beth Brant, for whom 'Pauline Johnson began a movement that has proved unstoppable in its momentum – the movement of First Nations women to write down our stories,'[129] and to Joan Crate, whose meditative quest for Johnson's image in her own reflected face, concludes: 'It is either you or me, Pauline.'

'The most interesting English poetess now living': Reading Pauline Johnson

Johnson as Author

The reader who goes to a general library seeking the writings of Pauline Johnson will likely find four titles, all issued during the last two years of her life. *Flint and Feather*, published in 1912 with the inaccurate subtitle of *The Complete Poems of E. Pauline Johnson*, includes all the verses from her first two volumes, *The White Wampum* (1895) and *Canadian Born* (1903), plus twenty-five later poems.[1] *Legends of Vancouver*, published in 1911, selects fifteen pieces from the dozens of newspaper and magazine stories and articles she penned about First Nations culture from 1908 to 1911. *The Shagganappi*, which appeared posthumously in 1913, includes a score of her many more stories that first appeared in *Boys' World*. And *The Moccasin Maker*, also from 1913, collects a scant dozen of her stories and articles for adult readers, many originally published in the *Mother's Magazine*.

More recently, Johnson's admirers have brought additional texts back into print. In 1965 Brantford writer Marcus Van Steen issued *Pauline Johnson, Her Life and Work*. This compilation of biographical information and literary selections includes a number of poems omitted from *Flint and Feather*, mostly clipped from newspapers and magazines. Designed to interest the general reader, the book lacks the dates and bibliographical citations essential to a more scholarly, contextual understanding of Johnson. Recently, Sheila F. Johnston, who inherited Van Steen's materials, prepared *Buckskin and Broadcloth*, characterized as a celebration of Johnson's life and work. Her book reprints selections from Evelyn Johnson's 'Chiefswood' manuscript now in the Archives of Ontario, as well as Van Steen's collection of clippings, including a number of 'lost' poems, without tracing their original appearances. Johnson's uncollected prose has attracted considerably less interest. Editors of the most recent reprints of *The Moccasin Maker* and *Legends of Vancouver* have rested content with the original selections made for these volumes.

The chronological list of Johnson's writings which appears as an appendix to this volume tells a more complicated story about the trajectory of her writing career. This list is not quite definitive, as Johnson did not keep records of her publications. Others' attempts to catalogue the appearances of her work in the daily press and magazines have been scatter-shot at best, complicated by the general lack of indices to newspapers and the more popular journals.[2] Thus it has not been possible to verify her sister's claim that 'When Pauline was away from home, she often wrote letters which were published in the *Brantford Expositor.*'[3] The fact that one of Evelyn's illustrative examples recounts an anecdote (the possibility of having eaten cat rather than rabbit) that appears in one of Johnson's contributions to the *Rudder* suggests that, like many professional authors, she frequently recycled her work. Even her friends did not know the details of her publishing history. For example, in July 1913, just after Johnson's death, the *Canadian Magazine* closed Isabel Ecclestone MacKay's memorial tribute with Johnson's poem 'Benedictus,' claiming this as its first appearance, yet the *Globe* had printed the same verses nearly twenty years earlier. Indeed, Johnson herself seems to have been less than reliable. In a letter defending herself against the negative criticism of *Canadian Born*, she told Arthur Henry O'Brien that 'half the poems it contained were accepted by Harper's and brought me excellent notice.'[4] But a careful search of both *Harper's Monthly* and *Harper's Weekly* has yielded only two poems, both published in 1896.

The common view that Johnson sacrificed her literary career when she turned to the stage to make a living romanticizes her identity as a poet and overlooks her voluminous production of prose. Instead, our appendix shows that Johnson's literary life falls into three fairly distinct phases. While poetry dominated the first stage of her career, her publication of verse diminished noticeably after her return from London in 1894. For the next ten years, she produced a range of genres: fiction, various sorts of journalism (recreational, juvenile, and general), as well as some poetry, with her output tapering to near silence as the century turned. Reviewers of *Canadian Born* generally concurred that Johnson's second book was weaker than her first. Given the dramatic decline in her poetic output after 1895, this judgment was hardly surprising. C.G.D. Roberts's enthusiastic introduction of Johnson to the editor of the *Century* in 1895 did not result in any of her poems appearing in this major American magazine, which suggests that she had nothing to send. After the appearance of *Canadian Born* in 1903, her publication of poetry virtually ceased. The final phase, 1906 to 1913, is distinguished by an astonishing output of prose for distinct markets, including the armchair travellers who settled down to the *London Express*, the juvenile enthusiasts of *Boys' World*, the female, domestic audience of the *Mother's Magazine*, and the urban readers of the *Vancouver Province*. Over the course of her life, Johnson's writing, like her stage performances, must be situated in relation to the various audiences she consciously addressed, ranging from the sporting subscribers to *Outing* and the *Rudder*, who could be expected to understand her distinctions among various styles of canoes, to readers of the *Province*, for whom she enhanced the local landscape with graceful Native legends.

Johnson's publishing career is fairly typical of Canadian writers of her era, especially women, who sought to survive by their pens. While publication in local periodicals, where payment was meagre (if any) was fairly easy to achieve, the challenge was to move up the scale to the major magazines, and finally to books. Despite the greater prestige attached to poetry, then as now fiction was by far the more marketable genre. And with a potential readership ten times that of Canada, American publication was far more lucrative. Most Canadian poets active during Johnson's lifetime had to subsidize the production of their books, a situation that was usually more difficult for women than for men, whose position as wage-earners and legally sanctioned trustees (and beneficiaries) of family resources gave them better access to funds. Under these circumstances, Johnson's desire to earn her living as a poet was not realistic, and the often repeated (but undocumented) 'fact' that during her lifetime she earned no more than five hundred dollars for her poetry[5] ignores the common situation for poets across the English-speaking world. By the middle of the nineteenth century, poetry had ceased to be profitable, and even a poet of the stature of Robert Browning struggled financially. Among turn-of-the-century authors, editors, and publishers it was generally known that poetry, despite its status as the elite literary genre, did not pay, and that an economically viable literary career could only be founded upon prose, especially popular fiction and journalism. The detailed account books of L.M. Montgomery, who entered the literary marketplace in the 1890s, concretely demonstrate that economic stability depended upon feeding American publishers' desire for fairly predictable, entertaining prose.[6] Of the four so-called Confederation poets, the two Ontario writers (Scott and Lampman) earned their living as civil servants in Ottawa, while the two Maritimers (Roberts and Carman) left Canada for the United States, where they depended on various editorial positions, personal patrons, and, in Roberts's case, a substantial output of saleable fiction. Even the wide and generally hospitable reception of *The White Wampum* in Britain had little direct influence on her ability to sell her poems at home or abroad.[7]

While Johnson's advocates justify her stage career as an economic necessity due to the failure of publishers and readers to buy her poems, another Brantford-born author, Sara Jeannette Duncan, demonstrated that in the 1880s and 1890s, a determined young woman with charm and talent (and family resources) could develop a viable literary career. A year younger than Johnson, Duncan also at first wrote verse, but soon made a calculated switch to journalism and fiction, in 1886 becoming the first regular woman columnist of the Toronto *Globe*. While we do not know if they ever moved in the same social circles, surviving sources indicate that the two young women were well aware of one another. Both were attractive, vivacious, and known for their lively sense of humour, and may well have enjoyed each other's company. In a rare direct reference, Johnson recalled 'Miss Duncan ... always made sport of her poetic flights when speaking of them to me.'[8] When Duncan devoted a *Globe* 'Woman's World' column to Johnson in 1886, under her transparent pseudonym of Garth Grafton, she coyly alluded to their shared history: 'I have had the pleasure of her acquaintance for some time ... I have always thought her beautiful and many agree with me.' Duncan's departure from Brantford in the late 1880s, followed by residence in India and England after her 1891 marriage, provided rich material for her fiction, which earned enough to keep her in steamship tickets. Unfortunately, documentation of subsequent contact with Johnson is lost. Brantford's two turn-of-the-century literary lights may have met again during one of Duncan's family visits to Brantford or Duncan may have been sojourning in England during one of Johnson's London visits but, in the absence of records, we can only speculate. Both writers became childless itinerants, whose papers were to remain scattered and incomplete. However she may have viewed Duncan's temerity in joining the first wave of Canadian women journalists, Johnson would have been advised by her mentor, Charles G.D. Roberts, to follow his own example of living '*for* poetry, *by* prose.'[9]

Johnson's Poetry

Pauline Johnson began as quite a conventional poet. Although some accounts claim that she started to write poetry in her early youth, little evidence remains. Several other Canadian women writers, such as Lucy Maud Montgomery and Margaret Laurence, have, in contrast, left wry accounts of their juvenile literary efforts. Of Johnson's first poems, several (for example, 'Rover' and 'The Sea Queen') ring with the melodrama and sentimentality that would have enraptured the adolescent Anne Shirley of Green Gables. With practice, Pauline gained greater control over emotional tone and formal technique. Evidence of Johnson's conscious interest in poetic structure appears in her writing of four rondeaus, a medieval French form that was revived by late nineteenth-century English poets.[10] It is therefore interesting to note that while many of her lyrics are fairly brief, she wrote no sonnets – a favourite form with both Roberts and Lampman. Sonnets written by Romantic or Victorian poets tend to be contemplative rather than narrative, whereas Johnson's preferred mode of expression is the dramatic monologue. That she could have handled the sonnet is evident in her skill with the iambic pentameter line, basic both to the sonnet and to Shakespearean soliloquy, as demonstrated in some of her most successful performance pieces, including 'Ojistoh', 'A Cry from an Indian Wife,' and 'As Red Men Die.' However, standard nineteenth-century recitation pieces tend to be written in the more regular rhythm of the tetrameter line, as in 'The Cattle Thief,' 'The Song My Paddle Sings,' 'The Pilot of the Plains,' and 'Dawendine.' Her frequent use of variations of this metre renders her verse especially congenial to being set to the standard forms of Euro-Canadian music. While Victorian poets were frequently described as singers in a figurative sense (drawing on classical associations between poetry and song), with Johnson, the term 'song' often led to actual musical settings, thus adding a dimension of performance to her work that reaches beyond her own recitals.[11]

Three concerns of Johnson's poetry which are particularly enriched by discussion from a literary perspective are Native Canadians, nature, and love. Whatever her topic, even when writing in the third person, Johnson can never be read as a neutral voice. Because her full name – E. Pauline Johnson – always visibly attached a female signature to her work as it circulated extensively in newspapers and periodicals, the gender of the speaker/author constantly informs the understanding of her reader, well accustomed to the self-identified verse of nineteenth-century

English women poets. Hence, whatever the reader's knowledge of Johnson's racial origin, her poetic speaking position was firstly that of woman. This gender identity is especially relevant to her love poems, all written in the first person. Johnson's speaking woman is energized and authorized not only as one of the participants in the romance, but also as the more articulate partner, thereby reversing the conventional binary of the vocal, active man and and the silent, objectified woman. Johnson's often erotic love poems comprise her first original contribution to Canadian writing, before she established her position as Native advocate. Yet they have received the least attention, because their very uniqueness has denied them a receptive context.

During the later 1880s and early 1890s, Johnson struck an individual, radical note in a series of romantic poems whose sexual explicitness enhances the bohemian identity she also claims in her articles about her canoe and camping trips. When read in the order of their publication, they present a narrative that invites a biographical interpretation. The story of her ill-fated engagement to Charles Drayton in 1898 was common knowledge. Betty Keller's detective work has unearthed Johnson's subsequent relationship with her manager, Charles Wuerz, around 1900–1.[12] But the romances of her younger years, that gave rise to her most strikingly erotic verse, have remained a mystery. In 1947 Walter McRaye offered a tantalizing reference to a 'an old friend of Pauline's,' a 'gray haired gentleman,' with whom he had recently reminisced about 'the old days when [he and Pauline] were both young and sweethearts and paddled on the Grand River,' and whom he described as the addressee of her 1891 poem, 'Re-Voyage.'[13] This might be the long-lived Henry O'Brien (1865–1957), who wrote the foreword to Walter McRaye's *Pauline Johnson and Her Friends*, were it not for O'Brien's own statement that he first met her in 1892 at the annual gathering of the American Canoe Association on the St Lawrence River. Might McRaye's visitor have been the unidentified blond canoeist whose photograph appears in the scrapbook at Chiefswood? And is either man also the unnamed 'young boy' whose photo, in a gold locket, Johnson requested to have placed around her neck before her body was cremated?[14] Might James Tucker, who in March 1894 wrote a poem to Johnson, have been of special significance?[15] Or James Watt (who eventually married Josephine Webling), or Frank Russell, to cite two identified canoing partners?[16] According to the archives of the Canadian Women's Press Club, which handled Johnson's funeral arrangements,

Collecting the cards from [the funeral] wreaths for Miss Eva Johnson (Pauline's sister), Miss Edna Brown found one on a large and very beautiful wreath which read, 'To his dearest from her dearest.' In the face of a sister's grief, no questions were asked, and would probably not have been answered. But those who saw the card and the flowers are still asking themselves if it was a confirmation of an oft repeated story of Pauline's great love for a suitor who had loved her as dearly, but was steadfastly rejected since his family had once objected to the union because of her mixed blood. It may well have been true, for she was very proud of her Indian blood. We shall probably never know now, but the Press Club girls who saw it in 1913 will always remember it, just as they will always remember Pauline herself.[17]

There seem, in fact, to be two discernible chapters to the romantic story presented in Johnson's early love poems. As dates of publication may not reliably reflect dates of composition, the following interpretation must be regarded as entirely speculative. The first narrative involves a lover who may have left her in 1887 or early 1888. Evidence appears in 'The Firs' (1886), 'Fasting' (1887), and 'Unguessed' (1888), which all present failed love from the woman's point of view. In 'Fasting,' she is willing to sacrifice healing Sleep if her self-denial will benefit her distant lover. But after being commanded to comfort the grieving man, Sleep never returns to the woman who is left standing bereft at the window: 'The long, long night has bitter been and lone.' 'The Firs' concludes with a request to the man to 'unclasp your fair warm hand' if he cannot offer love. 'Unguessed' takes the situation a step further. The first of Johnson's erotic canoeing poems to reverse traditional male and female roles, it portrays the woman as watcher over the supine man, whom she likens to young Apollo as she enumerates his features while he dozes on 'the settled couch ... that softly floats and sways.'

> Did young Apollo wear
> A face than yours more fair,
> More purely blonde, in beauty more complete?
> Beloved, will not you
> Unclose those eyes of blue
> That hold my world and bless and curse the life they render sweet?

Over the course of the poem her passion, which she has been trying to repress because he desires only friendship, transforms into such anger that she spurns him in a dramatic finale:

For I have drunk the wine
Distilled from Love's wild vine,
And reeling with its subtle fumes I strike our friendship dead.

This group is followed by a set of poems from the following year of 1889. 'Close By,' 'Ungranted' (later titled 'Overlooked'), 'Rondeau' ('Some bittersweet ...'), 'Nocturne,' and 'Day Dawn' (1890) all mourn the separation of lovers and express 'hunger for the one I may not see.'[18]

Linking these two groups of poems is 'My English Letter' (1888), which suggests the destination of the absent beloved. While good critical practice avoids identifying the fictional 'I' of a poem with the historical person of the poet, we may nonetheless hypothesize that a lover from the late 1880s may have left Johnson for England. That a personal rationale underpinned her determination to get to London, ostensibly to publish her first book of poems, is plausible in view of the actual publishing situation of the 1890s. To further complicate the picture, there is another set of love poems that point to a second romantic encounter (or a renewal of the previous relationship), this one occurring during the summer of 1890 and acutely remembered the following year when 'the dear and distant one' is 'unrelenting leagues' away ('Outlooking'). The pivotal poem for this episode is 'The Last Page,' a New Year's verse that appeared in *Saturday Night* on 3 January 1891. Using the ancient extended metaphor of the book of life, the speaker contemplates the previous year and speculates about the one to come. She wonders whether it will be as sweet and as bitter as the one just ended; whether it will contain chapters 'writ in the warmth of the summer sun ... [e]ntrancing, subtle, sweet as this,' or whether she will experience again the misery of 'empty words, or a careless kiss.'

The passion of the summer of 1890 throbs through several of Johnson's most explicitly sexual poems. In 'The Idlers' and 'Re-Voyage,' the woman's erotic gaze combines with her physical prowess as canoeist to create powerful assertions of female desire which equal the statements of better known New Woman prose writers like Olive Schreiner and 'George Egerton' (Mary Chavelita Dunne), author of *Keynotes*. The bodily details of 'The Idlers' focus on the man as sexual object: his 'muscle' and his pulsing 'splendid sunburnt throat,' his 'arm superb' and 'tumbled hair,' which lead to 'ardour,' a 'perfect ... kiss,' and, between the final two stanzas, consummation. Indeed, the post-coital tone of the last stanza, referring to what 'you and I have lost,' suggests that the woman's passion is her downfall.[19] It is not surprising that in other poems Johnson treats the errant woman with compassion.

Certainly it is the absence of the lover, combined with the woman's hunger to retrieve the past, which motivates the poems of late 1890 and 1891. '"Through Time and Bitter Distance"' (1890) finds her on the 'cheerless shore' seeking 'in the blue / Of these sea depths, some shadow of your eyes.' In the winter poem 'Outlooking' (1891), she asks, 'can you / Not feel the frozen world throb, melt, and beat, / Warmed by my heart's great heat?' The speaker of 'In Days to Come' (1891) begs the absent lover for some sign that, 'in some homesick moment,' he shares her memories. 'Re-Voyage' invites the lover to return to relive 'that sunkissed July,' and implies that his absence is not of his choosing:

Oh! well I know that you
Would toss the world away to be but lying
Again in my canoe,
In listless indolence entranced and lost,
Wave-rocked and passion-tossed.

Further support for this biographical hypothesis lies in the fact that Johnson's general output of poetry diminished abruptly upon her return from London; after 1894 her publication of love poems virtually ceased. We will never know how many love poems remain unpublished, other than the two that survive in manuscript at McMaster University, which Betty Keller has identified as having been written to Charles Wuerz: 'Morrow Land' (dated Holy Saturday 1901) and 'To C.H.W.' Johnson's two later trips to England in 1906 and 1907 were followed by her last dateable love poem, published in 1908. The suite of verses titled 'Autumn's Orchestra,' inscribed to 'one beyond seas,' bids a final farewell to a violin-playing lover with whom the speaker once dallied 'beneath the English pines beyond the sea.' Characterized by 'a lonely minor chord,' the music of the Canadian forest bids a mournful 'Goodnight, Good-night,' in an accomplished poetic adaptation of classical musical form. 'Song,' (1913) which appeared in print after her death, also links the beloved with music. To add to this tissue of conjecture, through which runs the recurring figure of the Anglo-Saxon lover, we might ask whether the reiterated 'blue' of the lover's eyes carries racial significance, encoding the reason for the breakdown of the relationship.

This is indeed the case in Johnson's 1893 story 'A Red Girl's Reasoning,' when the Mixed-race Christine relinquishes her own love when she takes revenge on her blond English husband after he questions the integrity of her parents' marriage. The now familiar figure of the treacherous 'tall, slender young man ... with laughing blue eyes, and always those yellow curls about his temples' makes his final appearance in her 1899 story 'As It Was in the Beginning,' when the betrayed part-Indian woman, rejected because she is '*one of them*,' fatally poisons her fickle lover.

In 1894 and 1895, when Johnson finally succeeded in placing her poems with a London publisher, her selection of John Lane at the Bodley Head was entirely appropriate. This firm created its image as the producer of avant-garde literature by cultivating 'unknowns and rebels' who had 'manuscripts that had already been rejected on the grounds of risqué subject matter.' Lane's motives were both economic, in that such authors were likely to accept modest financial terms, and aesthetic, as the firm established its 'reputation for breaking conventions.' From 1892 on, the Bodley Head specialized in '"New Woman" fiction, naturalistic short stories, and "decadent" poetry and art.' One of its most lucrative productions was the controversial 1895 novel *The Woman Who Did* (whose author, Grant Allen, hailed from Kingston, Ontario). Concerned with the physical design of his books, Lane created artistic volumes 'that were marketed both as status objects and as sex objects.'[20] Aubrey Beardsley designed many of Lane's covers and title pages; Oscar Wilde was one of Lane's authors. Although a vast ideological chasm separates 1890s decadence from 1890s feminism, the one feature they do have in common is what has been called 'inappropriate sexual knowledge.'[21]

Recognition of Pauline Johnson as one of the 'Daughters of Decadence,' women writers who 'rescue female sexuality from the [male] decadents' image of romantically doomed prostitutes or devouring Venus flytraps, and represent female desire as a creative force in artistic imagination as well as in biological reproduction,'[22] has been hampered by subsequent literary criticism at home and abroad. In Canada, our puritanical national identity as 'the true North strong and free' so abhors the notion of local Wildes and Beardsleys that we acknowledge only nature as a distinctive feature of Canadian poetry at the turn of the century. The native son closest in artistic temperament to the English aesthetes was probably Bliss Carman, whose elegant and erotic *Sappho: One Hundred Lyrics* (1905) remains highly under-rated. Needless to say, recognition of a female Canadian decadent would have been inconceivable. Available accounts of the acceptance of Johnson's book by John Lane are marked by inconsistency, and date from long after the Wilde scandal, suggesting that they may have been shaped by Johnson's need to distance herself from any hint of notoriety.[23] In the larger English-speaking literary world, women poets of the 1890s have generally been left in the shadows. While recent feminist literary criticism has recuperated a substantial group of turn-of-the-century British and American women authors, interest has focused almost exclusively on prose, largely because the 'woman question' was more publicly and vociferously argued in fiction and journalism (genres that were economically rewarding) than in verse. Thus the recent canonization of Kate Chopin's 1899 novel *The Awakening* as a 'frank exploration of a late-nineteenth-century woman's growth toward sexual and emotional independence'[24] has not been matched by attention to the equally frank and somewhat earlier poetry penned by Pauline Johnson. The 1924 opinion of Logan and French that 'Pauline Johnson has yet, by other Canadian poets, to be equalled as a lyrist of the passion and pathos of romantic love'[25] carried little weight in a national culture that omitted romantic love from its self-definition.

Whereas readers of Johnson's love poems who encountered them individually in periodicals had little reason to link them with the ethnicity of their author, few reviewers of *The White Wampum* were able to separate these verses from the emphatically Indian flavour of the book as whole. The Indian motifs on the title page designed by E.H. New, along with the addition of Tekahionwake to the author's name and the opening placement of seven Indian poems, cast an exotic glow over the entire volume. The anthropologist Horatio Hale drew on his personal acquaintance with the Johnson family when he shrewdly observed that 'Her compositions will be judged as those of a "wild Indian girl," and not as those of a well-bred and accomplished young Canadian lady with a dash of Indian blood, such as she really is.'[26] This prediction is quickly borne out by a survey of Johnson's reviews. Few echo the *Manchester Guardian*'s compliment that 'The love poems, such as "The Idlers" and "Re-Voyage," inform their Swinburnian style with something like true passion.'[27] Instead, Johnson's reviewers almost uniformly constructed her as the erotic Other, the passionate poetess[28] whose non-European heritage accounts for the unabashed sexuality of poems which are not, in themselves, explicity Indian. In fact, her poems about romantic love among identifiable Indians, such as 'The Pilot of the Plains' and 'Dawendine,' are relatively restrained, in line with her description of the chastity of Indian women in her article 'A Strong Race Opinion' (1892). The latter's denunciation of White writers' practice of stereotyping romantic Indian maidens fell on deaf ears. Instead, obituaries of Pauline Johnson reveal that it was her fate to be turned into the artificially noble, passionate, self-sacrificing Indian maiden she deplored.[29] When passion does find expression in her Indian poems it is not in relation to romantic love, but in relation to vengeance and justice. Only in 'Ojistoh,' with its first-person account of a woman using her sexuality to achieve retribution (in the tradition of such Judeo-Christian heroines as the biblical Esther and the apocryphal Judith), is there an overt link between the erotic and the Indigenous. Significantly, the Native woman assumes the role of the moral and physical superior in this encounter. Unlike the Indian and White victims and temptresses that populate literary and legal accounts of the day, Ojistoh is not a woman for the taking.

To try to read this poem through the lens of 1980s feminism, as George Lyon does, is to miss its political deployment of erotic agency. Ojistoh's accomplishment must be understood in the context of the power relations of turn-of-the-century settler Canada, where women were regarded as inferior, as when the enemy Hurons' 'hearts grew weak as women' at the name of the great Mohawk. Ojistoh's strategy, in declaring love to her captor in order to kill him, demonstrates a clever woman's ability to overcome physical weakness through tactical strength. In addition, the Hurons' decision to attack the Mohawk chief by abducting his wife – to 'strike him where / His pride was highest, and his fame most fair' – reminds audiences of the status of Iroquois matrons. More subtle is Johnson's poetic manipulation of her characters' names, and thereby their narrative value. While we are told that the very name of the Mohawk chief inspires terror in his enemies, we never hear it; he remains the invisible, unnamed husband who, in effect, simply provides the occasion for Ojistoh's courageous action. Her name, however, appears first as the title and is then reiterated six times in a poem of seventy lines. As with Johnson's love poems, this poem inverts conventional gender roles by highlighting the action and subjectivity of a woman, while diminishing masculine presence and power. Contrary to Lyon's claim that 'Johnson cannot attack patriarchy at its source,'[30] she very aptly tackles the linguistic and narrative structures that support the social patriarchy responsible for both Ojistoh's self-definition as wife and her need to use sexuality as weapon.

As has been mentioned, only a small proportion of Johnson's poems concern First Nations material or issues. Several of her earliest verses on

Native topics take a careful stance, arguing for acceptance and reconciliation. In October 1884 Johnson wrote 'The Re-interment of Red Jacket,' her first identifiably Indian poem, to commemorate the ceremonial re-burial of the Seneca orator in Buffalo, New York. Speaking as a First Nations participant in the local historical moment, she proclaims pride in her ancestry and requests mutual forgiveness between settlers and 'red-skins.' In 'Brant,' written for the 1886 unveiling of the monument to Chief Joseph Brant erected in the city named after him, she describes two peoples blending into 'one common Brotherhood,' to build a 'Young Canada' guided by 'the loving hand of England's Noble Queen.' From the same year, 'A Request' seeks to repair the violence of the 1885 Northwest rebellion through the actions of missionaries: 'The jewels in your crown will be the Indian souls you've saved.'

Following the composition of these poems, which attempt to soothe inter-racial relations, Johnson wrote dramatic narratives of Native-to-Native strife and vengeance, some published in Christmas issues of *Saturday Night*. 'The Death Cry,' 'As Red Men Die,' 'The Avenger,' and 'Ojistoh,' are all set in pre-contact times. They celebrate the Indigenous values of courage and justice, endorsing the notion that vengeance is a primary principle of Native society, a concept quite recognizable to the educated Euro-Canadian reader familiar with the motives underlying most classical Greek and French tragedy. The power of these poems arises from their present-tense, moment-by-moment enactment of scenes of stalking, chase, torture, and death. Although only 'Ojistoh' is explicitly recounted in the first person, the narrative voice of the others builds detail as if the events are seen through the eyes of an attentive witness. The distinctive style of Johnson's dramatic monologues becomes especially evident when they are compared with other Indian poems of this era, such as D.C. Scott's sonnet portraits of Native women and Charles G.D. Roberts's accounts of Malecite legends. Although Roberts occasionally replicates the oral style of First Nations narrative, the detachment of his and Scott's narrators heightens, by contrast, Johnson's dramatic engagement with her reader/listener that earned her commendation as Canada's outstanding 'story-telling balladist.'[31] Whether due to their author's stage career or to the oral culture of her Indigenous heritage, the poems are performance pieces: scripts as much as texts, written for herself by 'an accomplished actress with a presence and a power of sincerity that made one believe that she was indeed a disinherited princess and gave an epic touch to her slightest verse as she recited with Siddons-like majesty.'[32]

A change in Johnson's poetic presentation of Native/settler relations becomes evident late in 1893, with the appearance of 'Wolverine' in the Christmas issue of *Saturday Night*, followed the next winter by 'Silhouette' in the *Globe* and 'The Cattle Thief' in *The Week*, and, in 1896, 'The Corn Husker' in *Harper's Weekly*. No longer calling for reconciliation as in her verses dedicated to Brant and Red Jacket, her poems 'Wolverine' and 'The Cattle Thief' now present a politicized awareness of not only the utter disempowerment of Indians, but also the starvation resulting from destruction of their traditional economies. In 'The Cattle Thief' she even subverts her usual Anglophilia to accuse the 'English settlers' of consciously participating in genocide. This accusation is modified in 'The Corn Husker' which cites the abstract phrase 'might's injustice' as the cause of the decimation of Canada's First Nations. At least one critic noted this shift in her verse, evident as well in the way she altered the ending of her 1885 poem 'A Cry from an Indian Wife' for publication in *The White Wampum*. It is unfortunate that 'His Sister's Son,' a poem about residential schools that frequently appeared on Johnson's recital programs during the mid-1890s, seems never to have been published. The one verse preserved by an assiduous journalist suggests that it presents a strenuous critique:

For they [killed] the best that there was in me
When they said I must not return
To my father's lodge, to my mother's arms;
When my heart would burn – and burn!
For when dead is a daughter's womanhood
There is nothing left that is grand and good.[33]

Hector Charlesworth's unconditional praise in his 1892 study, where he distinguishes Johnson as one of the 'greatest women-poets of all times,' shifts into discomfort three years later in his review of *The White Wampum*, where he finds that 'she has marred works that are in essence poetic and strong with mere polemics. She has reversed the settler's joke, and with her it would appear that a good pale face is a dead pale face.'[34]

English reviewers of *The White Wampum* were likewise troubled by the problem of evaluating her poems which 'give a voice to the wrongs of the Indian, driven back and back as the white man filches more and more of the land his fathers owned.' One anonymous commentator found them intriguing for giving 'expression to the mind and moods of

Wedding portrait, Chief George Johnson and Emily Howells Johnson, 1853.

Iroquois Chiefs from the Six Nations Reserve reading wampum belts, 14 September 1871. L to R: Joseph Snow, Onondaga; George Henry Martin Johnson, father of Pauline Johnson, Mohawk; John Buck, Onondaga; John Smoke Johnson, grandfather of Pauline Johnson, Mohawk; Isaac Hill, Onondaga; John Seneca Johnson, Seneca.

Pauline, Beverly, Allen, and Evelyn Johnson, January 1878.

Chiefswood during the Johnsons' residence. This view depicts the front entrance that faces the Grand River.

Pauline Johnson in her canoe, the 'Wild Cat,' on the Grand River near Brantford, early 1890s.

MISS E. PAULINE JOHNSON, THE INDIAN POET RECITER.

This array of photos appeared in the *Globe*, 23 September 1893.

Pauline Johnson in evening dress, 1897.

Pauline Johnson in Native dress, c. 1902.

Tekahionwake,

(MISS E. PAULINE JOHNSON)

THE IROQUOIS INDIAN POET - ENTERTAINER,

In Native Indian Buckskin Costume, presenting her own poems of Red Indian Life and Legends, from her own Book

"THE WHITE WAMPUM."

THE TIMES,

LONDON, JULY 17TH, 1906.

Miss Pauline Johnson, whose native name is Tekahionwake, is descended from the chiefs of the Iroquois' race of American Indians, and comes before the London public as a reciter of the stories and legends of her race. She dresses in native costume, and she has herself written her pieces in clever and effective verse, which, when spoken in the vivid manner, which is characteristic of her, is dramatic and moving. At her entertainment at Steinway Hall yesterday, she gave "Ojistoh" and "A Legend of Qu' Appelle," and each in its way was a fine piece of declamation. "As it was in the beginning" is no less effective, though its mixture of bitterness and savagery makes it less pleasant. Mr. Walter McRaye gave recitations and sketches in the quaint French-Canadian dialect and was successful in all, though perhaps he was at his best in the little poem "Bord a Plouffe."

Mr. Walter McRaye, ❧ Humorist,

In Selections from Dr. Drummond's "Habitant" Folk Lore Stories of French Canada.

QUAINT, HUMOROUS, AND PATHETIC.

Agents—KEITH PROWSE & Co., 167 New Bond Street, London, W., and Branches.

Publicity material produced during Johnson's second trip to England, 1906.
The photo was taken c. 1893.

a strange, interesting race,' but ultimately 'not her best; indeed in certain ways, they are hardly poetry at all.'[35] Claiming that 'her talent is better suited to reflective poetry, partly because, as yet, she has not mastered the art of writing ballads,' another reviewer cited a portion of 'The Cattle Thief' as evidence of her lack of skill.[36] But Johnson's use of popular narrative forms (sometimes in ballad metre) for her overtly Indian poems was a calculated choice. Not only did she select a medium well-suited to performance, but the resulting accessibility of these poems guaranteed that, like the verses of Robert Burns, Robert Service, W.H. Drummond, and similar poets grounded in oral traditions, they would engrave themselves in public memory.

Particularly deserving of detailed attention, for both its subtle analysis and its changed ending, is 'A Cry from an Indian Wife.' It gains further significance when we consider that it appeared in *The Week*, the country's most prestigious intellectual periodical, on 18 June 1885, during the course of the Northwest Rebellion, between the surrender of Poundmaker (26 May) and the surrender of Big Bear (2 July). For the previous two months, the Canadian press had been filled with speculation about the fate of Mrs Delaney and Mrs Gowanlock captured by Big Bear at Frog Lake on April 2. By 8 June, news of their safe return to Fort Pitt had reached the outside world. However, different versions of their story then began to circulate, some quite sensational. These were shaped by political expediency and by the conventions of the captivity narrative, according to which White women were hapless victims of Indian savagery, and Aboriginal women were either degraded or complicit. Johnson's poem, articulating sympathy for the dispossessed Aboriginal population, represented a radically different view of both women and Indians.

'A Cry from an Indian Wife' marks Johnson's first public positioning of herself as woman/Native/other. As well, it is one of her few overt textual engagements with her own hybridity, thereby anticipating the Mixed-race heroines of several later stories. However, in this case the hybrid is the nation rather than a person, in that Canada is presented as a site of conflict between two founding peoples: European and Aboriginal. This dramatic monologue's self-interrogating and self-interrupting voice, as the speaker alternates between advocating the cause of the dispossessed Natives and expressing sympathy with the Euro-Canadian perspective, rendered it one of her most successful performance pieces. Yet, by not explicitly recognizing the Métis as a major element in the Northwest Rebellion, as well as Canada's most visible Mixed-race community, it seems to present an unconventional slant on this critical moment in Canadian history. On the one hand, their absence can be seen as typical of Johnson's general indifference to the French-speaking portion of Canada. But reading the poem in relation to its original context suggests that the Métis are implicitly acknowledged when the narrator states the fundamental issues that fuelled their anger: ownership of the land and the integrity of their 'nation.' Johnson's tactic of blending the Métis cause with that of the Indians deepens the poem's dramatic conflict as it oscillates across an unresolvable either/or, White/Native dichotomy, its tension underscored by an additional opposition of female and male that represents women as powerless to intervene in masculine warfare.

In giving voice to the unnamed 'Indian Wife,' Johnson demands recognition for the silenced figures of colonial history, a position reinforced by her revision of the ending for publication in *The White Wampum*. The original 1885 version simply yields to divine and national destiny, concluding:

> O! heart o'erfraught – O! nation lying low –
> God, and fair Canada have willed it so.

The word 'fair,' carrying at least three meanings (just, light-skinned, and favourable), demands an ironic reading that could, however, be missed by the unaware reader. Johnson subsequently altered this ending to clarify her political position. She inserted three penultimate lines which assert Native rights by reiterating original ownership of the land and identity as a nation, followed by a challenge to the white man's God that locates the speaker outside European Christianity:

> Go forth, nor bend to greet of white man's hands,
> By right, by birth we Indians own these lands,
> Though starved, crushed, plundered, lies our nation low ...
> Perhaps the white man's God has willed it so.

In 1885 the need for Johnson to clarify her argument was quickly demonstrated when one reader of *The Week* responded with a 'Sonnet in Reply to an Indian Wife,' which, while sympathetic, rather missed the political nature of Johnson's argument by generalizing that sorrow is the lot of her sex, whether 'white woman or squaw.' Subsequent poetry in *The Week* celebrated the victory of 'our brave Canadian soldiers,'[37] likewise defusing the impact of Johnson's poem. In addition to the questions posed within 'Cry' by its speaker, there is also at issue the larger social role assumed by the poet in that her description of a plains warrior as a 'Forest Brave,' armed with knife and tomahawk, suggests her adoption of a pan-Indian identity. In other words, while writing as a woman seems to have been a clearly defined position for Johnson in 1885, writing as a Native appears to have been complicated by a need to speak for all Natives – a need that grew over the years between the poem's two endings.

Similar to the way 'A Cry from an Indian Wife' presents an internal dialogue between forces within Canadian history, 'The Corn Husker' (1896) creates a dialogue within Canadian literature because of its implicit challenge to Duncan Campbell Scott's better-known pair of sonnets, 'The Onandaga Madonna' (1894) and 'Watkewenies' (1898). All three poems focus on a single woman as the embodiment of a people thought to be in decline. Like Scott, Johnson presents Indians as a people of the past; the woman is thinking only of 'the days gone by.' But she also calls attention to the present: her people 'to-day unheeded lie.' Whereas Scott's verses place responsiblity for the decline of Indigenous culture on its own weaknesses (promiscuity in 'The Onandaga Madonna' and violence in 'Watkewenies'), Johnson cites the cause as 'might's injustice.' This carefully crafted phrase allows her to use the powerful word 'injustice,' here making its sole appearance in her verse, while attributing its origins only to the abstract noun 'might.'

After the publication of 'The Corn Husker,' poetry yielded to prose as Johnson's preferred genre for Native advocacy. With the exception of 'The Train Dogs' (1904), which suggests that the apparent docility of 'wild red blood' may be illusive, her few later Indian poems, like those from the 1880s, seem to reincorporate First Nations into normalizing Euro-Canadian conventions. At the same time, however, the poems contain subtle reminders of difference. Nekyia, the courted maiden of 'The Quill Worker,' sits at her doorway absorbed in her embroidery, in a picturesque sunlit tableau. Yet, to recall the less than pastoral events of recent history, the setting is described as north of the Cypress Hills and Nekyia is identified as the daughter of the Sioux chief, both references which recall imperial barbarism and betrayal.[38] Such troubling reminders do not haunt the more overt reconciliation which imbues 'The Indian Corn Planter' (1897), whose scene and language directly echo Charles G.D. Roberts's well-known sonnet 'The Sower,' which in turn is based on Millais's painting of the same name. In Johnson's hands, the

Indian man represents a culture in the process of adjusting from dependence on 'the trapping and the chase' to an agricultural economy (in line with government policy). However, she injects a reminder of First Nations and feminist values by showing the presiding capitalized and therefore presumably Christian God partnered with a feminized 'honest sod' that 'mothers every grain.'

Johnson's poems that describe the Canadian landscape without direct reference to its Aboriginal inhabitants demonstrate that, as a poet of nature, she was well in tune with the canonical poets of her generation. So successful was she at sharing their ethos that many of her lyrics could masquerade as verses by Lampman or Roberts. 'Reclaimed Lands' and 'Aftermath,' two poems published posthumously and therefore undated, specifically echo Roberts's Tantramar poems, which describe the protective dykes that shelter farmland. In 'Joe: An Etching' (1888), an early poem which first appeared in *The Week*, the influential periodical which published or republished many Canadian poets of the 1880s and 1890s, some phrases directly echo or forecast phrases by Lampman or Roberts. Moreover, its ending, 'The axe of pioneer, the settler's plough,' unquestioningly sanctions the historical process that Johnson would later dramatically challenge. In poems such as 'In the Shadows' (1885), she, like Lampman, uses imagery of dreaming to describe the poet's healing or mystical relationship with the landscape. 'Shadow River' (1889), can be compared to Lampman's 'Morning on the Lièvre,' as Johnson suspends the canoeing speaker 'midway 'twixt earth and heaven,' in a moment of idealized understanding. Like Roberts, in descriptive poems such as 'At Husking Time' (1891), 'Marshlands' (1895), and 'Low Tide at St Andrews' (1896), she captures specific moments in the cycles of nature which serve as metaphors for larger human experience. Her poem 'Bass Lake: (Muskoka)' (1889) celebrates wilderness itself as poetry: 'The littleness of language seems the flower, /The firs are silence, grandeur, soul and power.'

Because nature poetry accounts for a small portion of her oeuvre, her range seems narrower than that of her male peers. And because representations of the dominance of nature came to be viewed as the distinctive feature of Canadian literature, critics in this tradition, finding that most of Johnson's work did not accord with their analysis, have had little to say about her. Northrop Frye's argument that 'the indifference of nature to human values [is] the central Canadian tragic theme,' and that Canadian poets of Johnson's era 'seem most deeply convincing when they are darkest in tone, most preoccupied with pain, loss, loneliness, or waste,'[39] leaves little room for a poet who sees the destruction of First Nations as Canada's major tragic theme, and does not present nature as hostile. For example, Johnson wrote few poems about the coming of winter, a topic that Canadian poets like William Wilfred Campbell exploited as an occasion to link personal melancholy with the bleakness of the season. Her poetry usually depicts the relation between the natural world and its human inhabitants as harmonious, with nature giving pleasure to those who respect it. This relationship appears most concretely in her references to the canoe, a fragile craft that requires cooperation with nature and close reading of its signs.

Hence, Johnson's distinctive contribution to Canadian nature poetry lies in her identity as female, a presence usually also associated with her mastery as a canoeist. Consider, for example, 'Under Canvas' (1888), where the campers' 'joy of living' is tempered in the last line by the eerie sounds of 'The owl's uncanny cry, the wild loon's laugh.' Because the speaker refers to 'we,' the reader knows that this trip involves more than one person. In 'In the Wilds,' a somewhat similar poem by Archibald Lampman, based on his canoe trips with his good friend, D.C. Scott, the 'we' whose strenuous exercise and camping restore them with 'the savage vigor of the forest' are most likely male. But who is camping in the wilderness in Johnson's poem: a couple, a group of women, or a mixed group of friends? To what extent should gender enter our understanding of this poem's ominous conclusion? Might its invocation of a kind of natural madness hint of the danger of freedom for women who are bold enough, bohemian enough, to leave civilization's urban moorings?

'The Song My Paddle Sings,' probably Johnson's best-known poem, is, like much of her verse, articulated in a first-person voice that accentuates the oral and performative presence of the speaker. As an expression of female agency, it celebrates the physical prowess of a solo woman canoeist fearlessly making her way through a sensual, wild landscape that hums with its own vitality, but whose challenges invite collaboration (the paddler and her canoe become 'we') rather than the confrontation that colours the rhetoric of conquest typical of men's poetry. The title metaphor of 'song' suggests a harmonious relationship between paddler and river: the rapids that 'seethe, and boil, and bound, and splash' are overcome by being 'raced' rather than conquered or raped. Here the canoe supplies a Canadian iconographic counterpart to the New Woman's bicycle as a physical symbol of freedom of movement and general independence. Moreover, the canoe (unlike the bicycle) can provide a site of sexual liberation,[40] as in 'The Idlers' and similar canoeing poems of such erotic power that one critic concluded that the paddler of 'Re-Voyage' was presumably masculine.[41] In many of Johnson's romantic canoeing poems, it is clearly the woman who is in joyful control of the vessel, either on her own or as the commanding paddler in the stern ('Thistledown').[42]

While the canoe is the scene of sexual encounters when occupied by a heterosexual couple, 'The Song My Paddle Sings' offers a different erotic relationship, in which nature is the woman's lover. This tryst, described in strongly sensual language, opens with the canoeist 'wooing' the wind to fill her sail. When there is no response, it is up to her to initiate the encounter, by caressing the stream with her paddle: 'soft is the song my paddle sings.' The physical intensity increases from stanza to stanza, from the teasing, drifting motion of the third, to the more deliberate thrusts through the foaming 'breast' of the waves in the fourth, to enthusiastically negotiating the swirling eddies of the fifth. The climactic sixth and seventh stanzas, in which the canoe 'reels' and 'trembles' as it fearlessly plunges through the 'reckless waves' of the roaring rapid, are followed by the post-coital peace of the last two verses. At the end, 'The river slips through its silent bed,' with nature restored to the comforting metaphor of 'A fir tree rocking its lullaby.' In this account of nature as lover, Johnson retains the mythic identity of nature as female, from 'the prairie nest' of the first stanza, to the swimming lullaby of the last. Unlike the men in Johnson's poems, nature does not betray those who love her.[43]

The sporadic poems from the last phase of Johnson's career lack the passion of her love poetry, the advocacy of her Indian poetry, and the vigour of her nature poetry. Many are occasional verses written for the inhabitants of the towns and cities she visited while on tour. The desire of some critics to trace a clear line of development in Johnson's verse, beginning with concerns that were primarily Indian and local, and eventually broadening to 'cosmopolitanism, pure humanity, and mysticism,' founders in light of the chronology established in our appendix. Other critics trying to identify a progressive evolution in her work look to her use of poetic form rather than her choice of content, citing her 'increasing strength and surer touch and finer sensitiveness to musical cadence.'[44] In truth, as a poet Johnson peaked early. Whether her reasons were romantic, political, or economic, after she returned from her 1894 trip to England she diverted her literary energy to prose, a genre which proved more congenial to Native advocacy and economic survival. But because poetry was regarded as the highest literary genre, both Johnson and her critics insisted on interpreting her career as that of a poet rather than that of the multi-generic author-performer she really was. However, regardless of the pattern of her career, the foregoing discussion makes a case for Johnson as a subtle and self-conscious poet, contradicting the modernist critics of 1961 who declared that her verse lacked 'philosophical or intellectual content' and that Johnson herself was 'not given to reflection.'[45] We also rescue her from the primitivism of her earlier admirers who gave her little credit for intellectual acuity and conscious crafting when they praised her verse for 'its naiveté of thought, its simplicity of structure, its lovely color images, its winning music, its passion, pathos, and womanly tenderness.'[46]

The irony underlying both the canonical and economic fortunes of writers of Johnson's generation is that the high cultural capital of poetry as the elite literary genre was undercut by its low economic power to generate support for its producers. Until very recently, the only genres in which she wrote that received serious attention were poetry and recounted Indian legends; collections of these two genres constituted the only books that were reviewed seriously during her lifetime, and that enjoyed regular reprinting subsequently. Criticism of Johnson to date has suffered from the view that she herself expressed, in moments of self-doubt and self-justification, that only her poetry can be considered art, and that most of her prose was merely utilitarian commodity-production.[47] Moreover, the bias of small-town, Protestant Canada in favour of poetry while suspicious of fiction and theatre, reinforced Johnson's decision to present herself to the public primarily as a poet. Yet it is the more ephemeral prose – the recreation journalism, travel writing, sentimental stories, and informative articles – that deepens our insight into the mindset of Johnson and her era, in part because forms of writing that are at once spontaneous and formulaic often reveal the implicit assumptions and conventions of their social context more directly than do highly polished poetic lyrics.

In order to describe the way they fit into or, more often, feel alienated from their society, writers in the European tradition frequently transpose their personal situations onto fictional figures of the writer or artist. Major works by L.M. Montgomery, Margaret Laurence, and Alice Munro centre on characters whose experiences as writers partially mirror those of their creators. The relative rarity of artist figures in Johnson's writing may be due to the patronizing idea that 'each and every red Indian is innately a poet.' If she bought into the notion that her talent was merely 'the fulfilment and expression of a latent national poetry which has hitherto lacked the nourishing hand of civilization for its development,'[48] she may not have felt the confidence that led other writers of her era to examine, within their own artistic creations, the issue of creativity. However, gender rather than ethnicity may have imposed the greater limitation. During her lifetime, the figure of the female artist was at least as problematic as the figure of any other woman breaking with traditional gender roles, as evidenced in Sara Jeannette Duncan's 1894 novel, *A Daughter of Today*. Despite Duncan's own literary success, the ambitions of the novel's titular heroine, Elfrida Bell, are presented as egotistical and are therefore disparaged.

Johnson's only artist character who is a full-fledged adult creator is indeed male – the painter Lawrence Alma-Tadema, whom she met in England in 1894. Her poem 'The Art of Alma-Tadema' celebrates his work as a re-creator: his paintings of ancient classical carvings that make 'the marbles leap / To life.' If this poem contains a philosophy of art, it is an echo of Walter Pater's notion that 'all art constantly aspires to the condition of music.' The poem opens by describing Tadema's paintings in terms of music – 'There is no song his colours cannot sing' – and concludes with his power to create not only life ('copper-coloured leopards') but the supernatural ('A goddess with a wealth of tawny hair'). The need to create for the sake of self-expression is an infrequent theme in Johnson's work. It appears in the robin of 'The Songster' (1896) who sings because 'his breast was born for song,' which metaphorically describes the compulsion of the poet much like Duncan Campbell Scott's 1905 poem, 'The Wood Peewee': 'Not as he would but as he must / He sings.' More frequently, reality intervenes. When the artist character is an adult, art finds justification on economic grounds, especially the need to support family. In her story 'The Broken String' the musical talent and generous personality of the main character are eventually rewarded with a high salaried orchestra position which allows him to repay his impoverished mother. Similarly the titular character of 'Hoolool of the Totem Poles' becomes 'the best carver of Totem Poles on the North Coast' in order to secure a future for her son and her people's culture. Only Ta-la-pus, the boy dancer of 'The Potlatch,' engages in his art with no motive other than to express his creativity, although in the process he brings honour to his family too, in an act of performance that may mirror dynamics between Johnson's own stage persona and her constructed identity.[49] These artists are far from the isolated, alienated rebels favoured by many male writers, but stand firmly within a social system of mutual obligation and affection. In the end, their artistry benefits real people.

From Poetry to Prose

During the early 1890s, while developing her poetic voice and her stage persona, Johnson expanded her public presence by writing recreation articles. In contrast to the decadent eroticism of the romantic canoeing poems, the dominant note in these pieces is the promotion of outdoor exercise in the interest of both personal and national health. Here, as in her other writings, her modes of address and self-identification vary according to her audience and place of publication. In essays covering various outdoor activities, including lacrosse and snowshoeing, she speaks in a personal voice, frequently citing her own experience, as in her description of hurtling down the toboggan slide on Mount Royal in Montreal.[50] Canoeing and camping predominate, beginning with her first prose articles in Brantford and Toronto newspapers, in which she establishes her characteristically active style. In most instances the opening is immediate, the tone is jaunty, and the setting is specified in crisp detail by a first-person narrator who cheerfully characterizes her social group as bohemian as they savour an escape from urban proprieties.[51] While her companions' actual names are always disguised, there is a strong sense of transparency, suggesting that her canoeing community relished seeing themselves in print. The excursions Johnson describes in the early 1890s range from one-day paddles on the Grand River that winds through Brantford and past Chiefswood, to three-week forays into the Muskoka region. Of particular interest are Johnson's characterization of the 'lady canoeist,' her advocacy of Canada in articles written for American publications, and her occasional references to herself as Iroquois, while in company that clearly is not.

In her series of articles on 'Outdoor Pastimes for Women,' published in *Outing* (New York) in 1892 and 1893, Johnson's persona is no longer the vivacious adventurer of her canoe narratives, but the mature counsellor offering advice to younger women, a stance which seems to acknowledge her own passing years. This is a role that she assumes only when addressing White readers or hearers. With Aboriginals, she always assumes the position of listener and recipient of information and advice, whether from the family servant, old A'bram, or from Chief Su-á-pu-luck (Joe Capilano). In *Outing*, addressing 'my girl readers,' she advocates outdoor exercise in all weather, not only for better health, but for improved sex appeal and mating opportunities: 'The girl who can weather the wintry gale ... will slay more than bears, will bring to her feet rarer game than deer.'[52] In these articles, copious positive references to Canada (especially in relation to canoeing, skating, snow-shoeing, and women's hockey) implicitly convey Johnson's nationality and Canadian patriotism, with no reference at all to her Mohawk heritage.

None of Johnson's recreation articles and stories appeared under the name Tekahionwake, even those published after 1894, a gesture that separates this writing from most of her other work. Thus, in these pieces, there seems to be little direct linking of her prowess as a canoeist with her identity as an Indian, even after she began to recite 'The Song My Paddle Sings' in Native costume, and despite abundant popular awareness of 'vital and continuing dimensions of the Native relationship to recreational canoe use.'[53] In most of her recreation pieces, such as those for *Outing* and the *Rudder*, Johnson presents herself as a lively, middle-class New Woman, much like the readers of these American journals. During the same period, she wrote several articles about the Six Nations in which the narrator, while arguing for justice, assumes different positions in relation to her own ethnicity. In May of 1891 the *Dominion Illustrated* published 'Our Iroquois Compatriots,' an essay whose narrator describes Johnson's home community, and even Chiefs-wood, entirely in the third person. Her use of possessive pronominal adjectives to distinguish between 'their [i.e. Indian] churches' and 'our Canadian cities' archly situates herself as an impersonal observer, a position reiterated nine months later in 'A Glimpse at the Grand River Indians.' Several subsequent articles in both American and Canadian serials ('The Iroquois of the Grand River' and 'The Six Nations') retain this peculiar voice, in which the narrator argues on behalf of Iroquois accomplishments, rights, and rituals, while declining to identify explicitly with the people under discussion.

On the other hand, in articles written for a local Brantford audience, she sometimes assumes that her readers know her and her family. One such piece, 'Forty-Five Miles on the Grand,' published in the Christmas 1892 issue of the *Brantford Expositor*, is particularly interesting for its attention to both recreation and the Six Nations, expressed through the shifting positions of its narrator in relation to race and gender. At first glance an apparently rambling light essay, it creates considerable impact as a political statement about the place of women and Aboriginals in Canadian society. The beginning differs from Johnson's usual practice of commencing her canoeing articles with a first-person on-the-spot opening by using instead a third-person narrator. This impersonal, authoritative voice not only recalls that the previous inhabitants of the area were 'that most powerful of North American nations, the Iroquois,' but also reminds the reader that large tracts initially granted to the Iroquois have been reduced to 'only a few thousand acres.' Then ensues reference to a generalized masculine figure of 'the canoeist,' followed at last by a more personal 'we.' By thus deferring her own specific appearance in the article, Johnson adroitly accomplishes several goals. Having represented the common canoeist as male, her subsequent account of running the rapids near Galt (with a male partner) highlights her implicitly feminist feat as a woman 'of the pliant wrist and mighty muscle.'

Even more politically subtle is the way she slips between situating the Indian as Other when she refers to 'the red man and his traditions,' and identifying as that Other when she tells how 'my father' spoke Mohawk into Alexander Graham Bell's experimental telephone. This anecdote, which recurs in both her writing and her sister's memoirs, describes an occasion when Bell invited a group of distinguished dinner guests to each talk to the telegraph operator two and a half miles away, at the other end of the wire. The man recognized the voices until George Johnson's turn came around. Speaking in Mohawk, he so confused his hearer that after several unsuccessful repetitions, the unaware listener finally suspected that Bell's party had over-indulged and asked 'how many cases did you open?' Not found in standard history books, this incident symbolizes the larger disruption to paradigms of Euro-Canadian history and culture occasioned by acknowledgment of the Native presence. With Johnson, this disruption occurs across the field of Canadian literary history, where she challenges the relative values of different genres of writing, requires us to read her written work in light of her performance and public identity, and insists that attention be paid to advocacy as well as to literary concerns. In the context of 'Forty-five Miles on the Grand,' the incident is framed by reference to the Tutela, a 'now extinct Indian tribe' overtaken by 'the redman's doom.' While the article ends by focusing on the festivities of the canoeists of the Brantford Canoe Club, its final lines circle back to its opening description of the original inhabitants of the area in that its last human reference is to 'the lonely reserve of the Iroquois.'

According to this reading, imbedded within this apparently casual piece of journalism lies a double-barrelled political statement. It is fairly obvious that Johnson's female canoeist represents the New Woman.

More subtle, and probably less deliberate, is the way her alternation between depicting the Indian as doomed Other and identifying herself as Mohawk shows First Nations in transition. No longer the romantic red man, the Native who now articulates the injustice of the past (the depletion of the land reserve) and dines with the prophets of the future (Alexander Graham Bell) implicitly asserts a place in the present, most locally in such mainstream institutions as the Brantford Canoe Club and the *Brantford Expositor.* This aspect of Johnson, 'the modern red man's cheerful attempt to voice the meaning of this country in an age of progress,'[54] was rarely acknowledged in her lifetime.

Johnson's articles published in American newspapers and magazines during the same period contain little direct acknowledgment of her Native identity, beyond a wry passing reference to 'the ghosts of all my Iroquois ancestors,'[55] and few comments on the political aspects of Native concerns. For example, her article on lacrosse as Canada's national game merely credits the appeal of lacrosse, canoeing, and snowshoeing, all 'born of Indian brain and bone,' to the superiority of their originating culture.[56] In her six articles for the *Detroit Free Press,* when she turns from sports to the 1869 visit of the Duke of Connaught to Six Nations, she refrains from acknowledging that the venerable chief on whom she lavishes so much praise is her own grandfather.[57] Hence readers may have been startled by a paragraph in the last article in this series, 'The Song My Paddle Sings,' which appeared in 1893, a year after publication of her poem of the same title. Digressing from the details of the canoe trip, she questions again the reduction of the original tract given to the Six Nations (without positioning herself as a member thereof): 'What have the Six Nations now? A scrap of reserve embracing 53,000 acres of uninteresting, timberless and in many places marshy land, while the garden lands of the river are again in the white man's possession.'

After her return from her first trip to London, Johnson ceased this vein of recreational writing, with the exception of two series of canoeing stories that appeared in the *Rudder,* the first in 1895 and the second in 1896. In the first series, the narrative voice is now more mature, and the tone more elegaic and ironic. Lacking specific comments about Native advocacy or the desirability of canoeing as a sport for women, the first four 'Canoe and Canvas' episodes are polished pieces of adventure journalism in which Indians appear only as 'two splendid Chippewas' who serve as guides when needed. Although set in Canada, the country is scarcely named except as 'the Northland,' giving the articles a peculiar sense of displacement and even anonymity.[58] This vagueness is replaced with more specific promotion of Canada in the second series, which takes the American reader on a grand armchair tour. Beginning in the east, in 'The Land of Evangeline,' the series then travels north to 'the great unknown – almost unexplored – region that lies between the Ottawa river and Hudson's Bay,' west to the South Saskatchewan with a glimpse of 'Canada's national emblem, the beaver, in his own haunts,' and returns to Johnson's home turf in central Canada, 'Ontario's Old Grand River.' Titled 'With Barry in the Bow,' this series seems more overtly fictionalized than Johnson's other canoeing stories. Its tone and the adventures are less innocent, with the women sharing the contents of men's flasks on several occasions. As in most of her writing for American readers, the position of the narrator is complicated by a dual identity. While she makes one allusion to 'the superstitions of my red ancestors,' and describes learning to paddle during her 'old baby-days on the Indian reserve,' she refrains from any present identification with the Indians hired as guides or encountered en route. Especially surprising is Johnson's utter silence, in the concluding episode set on her own Grand River, about the presence or displacement of the Six Nations. While this final series is characterized by wit, as when she speculates how she may have unwittingly eaten a cat, it is also marked by a sense of fatigue, as in her lengthy retelling of the story of Ojistoh, with the major characters altered to 'a French Gentleman and his little Indian wife.'[59] Although the printer of the *Rudder* set the words 'To be Continued' after the final instalment, Johnson published no further adventures with Barry, nor, indeed, any additional articles about canoeing. The termination of the series marks the end of this phase of her writing.

More conducive to Johnson's career than these self-concealing recreation articles, in which names of others are couched in pseudonyms, were the self-promoting travel articles that appeared sporadically from 1894 until 1914. Travel was a hospitable subject for New Women journalists, as evidenced by the early career of Sara Jeannette Duncan. In Johnson's first two ventures into this genre, written with Owen Smily for the *Globe*, 'Miss Poetry and Mr Prose' indulged their sense of humour, almost to the peril of her poetic reputation. Later articles frequently situate Johnson on a 'trail' in the West, the adventurous New Woman of the canoeing narratives transposed to the intrepid older trouper bouncing along rough tracks across awe-inspiring scenery.[60] Indeed, scenery dominates as we learn far more about what Johnson sees than what she does. Perhaps the most enthusiastic of these articles is the one that is also the most questionable. 'Coaching on the Cariboo Trail,' published posthumously nearly a year after Johnson's death, casts a nostalgic glow over a trip that was initially described with considerably less zest in 1906.

As prose overtook poetry in Johnson's writing, she tried her hand at different saleable genres. In the later 1890s she occasionally told reporters that she soon hoped to bring out a book of stories, and made direct overtures to the Harper publishing house.[61] While this turn to fiction recognized the reality of the literary marketplace, Johnson's focus on a book of stories was as impractical as was her earlier hope to survive on her poetry. Then, as now, novels were the dominant literary commodity and were often serialized in newspapers or magazines before appearing in separate volumes. With stories, the pattern was different. The burgeoning of popular magazines from the 1880s through the 1920s, with a parallel increase in discrete readerships, supported hundreds of creative writers whose short works were seldom collected into volume format. Around the turn of the century, the only saleable Canadian books of stories represented two distinct genres, neither of which attracted Johnson: the realistic animal story, more or less invented by Johnson's friends Charles G.D. Roberts and Ernest Thompson Seton, and the local colour tale of French Canada, whose practitioners included her acquaintances E.W. Thomson and Duncan Campbell Scott. Magazine stories of domestic life, even when penned by as successful an author as L.M. Montgomery, usually remained uncollected. For many Canadian, American, and English women of Johnson's generation, newspaper journalism, along with placing stories, articles, and occasional poems in periodicals, was a career in itself.

During the 1890s Johnson's sporadic forays into short fiction can best be described as a quest for a comfortable genre. Whereas the bulk of her journalism readily fits into several distinct categories (recreation writing, informative promotions of the Six Nations, and travel memoirs), her creative stories from the same period are less easily grouped. *Saturday Night*, the customer for much of her early verse, also published several samples of her commodity fiction. As literary efforts, her first two stories, 'Prone on the Earth' (1891) and 'A Story of a Boy and a Dog' (1892), are undistinguishable from the bulk of contemporary sentimental anecdotes which end with tears for a deceased hero, whose self-sacrificing nobility of soul is revealed only to the reader. More deftly narrated is her only known attempt at the saleable genre of the mystery story, 'The De Lisle Affair' (1897). These pieces could have come from any of the hundreds of writers who supplied material to the periodical press and pale in comparison to the stories that draw directly on Johnson's Aboriginal interests and experience.

When Johnson published her 1892 article, 'A Strong Race Opinion, on the Indian Girl in Modern Fiction,' in the Toronto *Sunday Globe*, she set a major challenge not only to Canadian novelists, but also to herself. Although there is no evidence that the article attracted attention at the time,[62] it is now recognized as a prescient assault on the prevailing stereotype of the Indian maiden in nineteenth-century Canadian fiction. Deriding the representation of the generic Indian heroine, who, despite her unseemly eroticism, seems only too eager to sacrifice herself on behalf of her inaccessible settler lover and his inevitable White bride, Johnson calls upon authors to 'create a new kind of Indian girl, or better still portray a "real live" Indian girl' with a distinctive personality and a recognizable tribal identity. Johnson's first retort occurs implicitly in her literary representations of herself, not only in her poetry and journalism, but also in two personal memoirs. In both 'A'bram' and 'Indian Medicine Men and Their Magic,' Johnson speaks as a modern woman recounting her personal knowledge of characters and practices from her Six Nations heritage. She takes the position of both participant and informant as she respectfully presents material that is Other to the reader, using the conventions of cultivated literary discourse. Thus the Indian Girl as enacted by E. Pauline Johnson in her capacity as author-narrator, fulfills the request of Pauline Johnson the critic for realistic representations of 'the quiet, sweet womanly woman she is, if wild, or the everyday, natural, laughing girl she is, if cultivated and educated.'

Within the genre of fiction, Johnson rose to her own challenge on just three occasions, each the story of a Mixed-blood woman and her White lover. These stories are all set in what Mary Louise Pratt calls the 'contact zone,' which she defines as 'the space of colonial encounters, the space in which peoples geographically and historically separated come into contact with each other and establish ongoing relations, usually involving conditions of coercion, radical inequality, and intractable conflict.' Unlike the notion of the frontier, which 'is grounded in a European expansionist perspective,' the term 'contact zone' allows some reciprocity by foregrounding 'the interactive, improvisational dimensions of colonial encounters.'[63]

The primary geographical contact zone of Johnson's fiction is the Canadian wilderness, whether Penetanguishene ('The Derelict') or an indeterminate Northwest associated with the Hudson's Bay Company

('A Red Girl's Reasoning,' 'As It Was in the Beginning'), where the co-
habitation of European men with Native women gives rise to Johnson's
Mixed-race fictional heroines. However, the site of each story's major
conflict is the secondary contact zone of the Canadian village or city
where the Native or Mixed-race woman, removed from her original
home, must negotiate her lonely way through White prejudices and
expectations. Both stories recount the failure of inter-racial heterosexual relationships from the perspective of the non-White woman. In
these examples of 'writing back,' the woman refuses the role of com-
pliant Indian maiden despite the emotional agony caused by her self-
assertion. While each story relates the same basic plot, in which a handsome but weak White man yields easily to social pressure and rejects his
beloved, both the narrative perspective and the final resolution sharpen
acutely from the first telling to the second. The earlier story, 'A Red
Girl's Reasoning,' narrated in the third person, concludes with the two
lovers painfully going their separate ways. The later version, 'As It Was in
the Beginning,' is narrated by the woman herself and climaxes as a
revenge tragedy when Esther poisons the man who has spurned her.
Between these two catastrophic tellings, Johnson published a version
with a happy ending, accompanied by a trenchant critique of the nar-
row-mindedness of the church. In 'The Derelict' the conflict is resolved
with the lover choosing the woman over his career as a clergyman.
Lydia's love, more redemptive than 'the service of God,' provides 'the
world's most sheltered harbour' for her erstwhile derelict lover. It seems
hardly a coincidence that Johnson later chose the same name, Lydia, as
a pseudonym for her mother in 'My Mother,' which recounts the long,
happy marriage of her parents.

   'As It Was in the Beginning' proved a major fulcrum in Johnson's
writing career – as important a transitional moment as was her public
recital of January 1892. Granting subjectivity and agency to a First
Nations woman, the story continues in the direction initiated by her
early poem, 'A Cry from an Indian Wife.' But rather than setting
Johnson on the path followed by fin-de-siècle authors of serious New
Woman fiction, the story served as a point of closure. Fiction subsequently disappeared from her oeuvre until 1906, when she began her
production of juvenile stories for *Boys' World.* Her use of fiction to illuminate contemporary social problems during the 1890s muted into the
relative conventionality of her later magazine stories, none of which
recaptures the powerful resistance of Christine or Esther. As with
Johnson's romantic poetry, one cannot help wondering if the heroines'

stories, which finally close with the death of the unreliable lover, originate in Johnson's personal experience. At the same time, we must not
forget that these stories are not historical documents but literary constructs. It is more appropriate to query the relation between Johnson's
fiction and Gilbert Parker's novel on the same theme of intermarriage,
The Translation of a Savage, which was first published in 1893 and
reissued in a longer version in 1898. Parker transfers the contact zone to
the heart of the Empire (as did Johnson herself by visiting London)
when a petulant Hudson's Bay trader sends his half-Native wife to
England to live with his family. Lali not only rises to the occasion,
becoming the perfect English lady, but, due to her dual heritage from 'a
noble if dispossessed race' and 'good white blood, Scotch blood,'[64] she
demonstrates greater integrity than many of the Europeans she encounters. The first version of this novel preceded Johnson's 1894 visit to
England and her initial meeting with Parker. However, its appearance
just when Johnson was making her first heady public impact in Ontario
seems hardly coincidental. Parker was after all a transplanted Canadian
with ready access to the Canadian press.

The Last Phase

As the century turned, Johnson published little poetry and less prose. We
can only guess that she was particularly preoccupied at this time with her
stage career and, perhaps, the disappointments of her romantic life. By
1906 she was ready to commence the final phase of her writing life with
a fresh surge of publications that would peak in 1910, during which year
she issued more than forty separate items. This last phase was initiated by
four articles published during her 1906 visit to England, for which the
London *Daily Express* paid her two guineas apiece.[65] 'A Pagan in St Paul's,'
which she reportedly described as 'the best piece of prose I ever wrote,'[66]
is a dramatic tour-de-force, playing up to the British taste for exotic, primitive spectacles from the far corners of the Empire. Discarding her
English mother as well as her Chiefswood home and her later residence
in the bustling town of Brantford, she creates the persona of an innocent
moccasin-shod 'Red Indian' fresh from 'the far Saskatchewan' – a place
name probably chosen for its alien sound. Counting on her readers' lack
of geographic knowledge, the narrator glides from the present reality of
attending a service in St Paul's Cathedral to a sequence of enticing,
euphonious associations that arise in her own mind, from 'the far-off
cadences of the Sault Ste Marie rapids,' to the 'Onondaga "long-house"'

with the celebration of the feast of the white dog.[67] If there were no more to it, we could simply enjoy this essay as a bravura performance. But, as with so much of Johnson's writing, we soon discover another dimension. St Paul's Cathedral represents the headquarters of the powerful Anglican church, which sent squads of missionaries to Canada, and to which her own parents belonged. The end of this essay does not depict the paganism of the Onondaga yielding to the Church of England, but rather asserts the equality of First Nations spirituality with European religion, and of 'the weird monotonous tones' of the Iroquois celebrants with 'the clear boy-voices' of the St. Paul's choir. The other three London *Express* essays, depicting features of traditional Iroquois culture, more directly anticipate the work Johnson would soon publish in the *Mother's Magazine* and *Boys' World*. In 'The Lodge of the Law-Makers,' she scored a point on behalf of her people by indicating that Iroquois women have long enjoyed a degree of political power denied to English women, an interesting observation to come from someone who was not an avowed suffragist.

When she settled in to the last stage of her writing career, which became her major means of support, Johnson addressed three distinct readerships of three different periodicals. While she continued to reach a general audience with occasional appearances in *Saturday Night* and the *Canadian Magazine*, the bulk of her work was explicitly tailored to either the juvenile readers of *Boys' World*, the women readers of the *Mother's Magazine*, or the Vancouver readers of the *Province*. Johnson's meagre surviving financial records reveal that in 1907 *Boys' World* and *Mother's Magazine*, both published by the religious press of David Cook of Elgin, Illinois, paid six dollars per thousand words. Payment for individual stories ranged from $13.95 for 'The Winter Indoor Life of the Indian Mother and Child' to $23.23 for 'A Night with "North Eagle,"' both published in 1908.[68]

Although Johnson's *Boys' World* stories only began to appear in the summer of 1906, after her return from England, she had already established a connection with the magazine the previous autumn. From 1906 to 1913 she published over thirty stories of which six were serialized in two or more instalments, resulting in an overall total of forty-four contributions. Much of Johnson's fiction appeared as the lead story on the title page, thus highlighting her prominence as a continuing presence in the magazine. With occasional blending and variation, her pieces follow three discernible patterns: tales of Euro-Canadian adventure or urban daily life that promote responsibility, bravery, manliness, and fair play; stories set in the Native/White contact zone that show the innate virtues of First Nations life; and informative articles about Canada, England, and, above all, aspects of Mohawk culture. The magazine's audience is presumed to be pre-adolescent American boys in need of literary entertainment that inculcates education about wholesome masculinity, Canada, and Indians. Thus the narrative voice is that of a nationalistic Canadian adult – never explictly female – possessing considerable knowledge of recreation, an affinity for Native history and culture, and strong allegiance to the British Empire. Given the blindness of late twentieth-century American popular culture to anything beyond its own borders, a surprising feature of these stories is their overtly Canadian content and pro-British stance. Elizabeth Ansley, the editor of *Boys' World*, found Canadian nationalism not only acceptable but desirable, the promotion of patriotism per se being one of her goals: 'What we are in need of is good Canadian stories. We have experienced considerable difficulty in procuring Canadian stories with the real patriotic ring – stories where the loyalty does not seem forced. We have many Canadian subscribers, and we wish to give them of our best, and what will appeal to the best in them, and the love of country is part of every boy whether of Canada or the United States.'[69]

Stories both with and without explicit First Nations content display Johnson's mastery of the conventions of turn-of-the-century moralistic juvenile fiction, whose basic plot line shows a young male successfully overcoming challenges by drawing on his courage, intelligence, and integrity. Didacticism frequently takes the upper hand as she takes pains to establish veracity, thus blurring the line between fiction and nonfiction. The factual basis of the story is sometimes invoked to justify its moral value and to intensify its example of manly behaviour for incipient young men, whether the heroic youth is Euro-Canadian (as in 'The Broken Barrels' and 'The Whistling Swans') or First Nations (as in 'The Little Red Messenger' and 'The Delaware Idol'). No story in *Boys' World* departs from the conventional happy ending. They do, however, often offer the unexpected. Native youth emerge, far from the savage or depraved Other, as comparable in feelings and aspirations to young settlers. Conventional notions of masculinity are further interrogated in 'Gun-shy Billy,' a tale of the South African War. Although the first part seems to equate virility with the glory of the battlefield, it concludes with a strongly pacifist statement about 'the misery, the mourning, the heartbreak of it all.' Equally provocative was her picture, in another story, of a unusual group of moral equals: 'the king and queen of England in their

coronation robes, Edward Hanlon [presumably Ted Hanlan] the oars-
man, Edison, Sir Henry Irving, Sitting Bull, Napoleon Bonaparte.' Each
had a particular role to play as models for young readers: 'Their Majes-
ties stand for culture and kindness and the purity of the Court. Hanlon
stands for upright sportsmanship. Edison for study and perserverance.
Irving for art and the actions of a gentleman. Sitting Bull for grit and
fighting for even a lost cause when he thought it right, and Napoleon
for putting his shoulder to the wheel and never budging until that
wheel turned.'[70] This extraordinary linkage of monarch, inventor, athlete, Indian, and French emperor, like an earlier essay, 'Some People I
Have Met' (1899), encourages sensitive readers to examine prevailing
assumptions about relative worth. Natives and performers are particular
beneficiaries of such reappraisal.

As with Johnson's adult fiction, the more innovative of her boys'
stories are set in the contact zone, where settler/Native interactions
counter negative stereotypes of Indians. When the protagonist is fully or
partially Native, he proves his mettle by overcoming White villainy,
sometimes in alliance with the North-West Mounted Police.[71] When the
young hero is a settler, the plot centres on encounters that educate him
about Aboriginal culture, traditional skills, and knowledge of the natural world.[72] The notion of the contact zone takes on a broader dimension when we consider the magazine as whole. In addition to directly
addressing imperial relations within many stories, Johnson used the
Boys' World as an opportunity to endorse several First Nations' cultural
practices which were highly controversial, while deftly avoiding explicit
reference to the current political context. By creating direct identification between her boy protagonists and her youthful readers, both of
whom embody the possibility of a more tolerant and inclusive future,
she presents both the white dog feast of the Onondaga and the potlatch
of the Squamish as not only normal within the social and religious practices of the Indian nations, but also meriting the respect of non-Native
readers peering in from the outside.

'We-hro's Sacrifice' in which an Onondaga boy earns the praise of
'the great Anglican bishop' for relinquishing his beloved pet to provide
a pure white dog for his people's ritual sacrifice, shatters several important tenets of the Edwardian middle class. Towards the end of the nineteenth century, the tremendous popularity of horse and dog stories, like
Anna Sewell's *Black Beauty* and (Margaret) Marshall Saunders's *Beautiful
Joe*, enhanced the rapid growth of humane societies and similar organizations aiming to teach children to be kind to animals. Johnson herself

contributed two examples of the genre to *Boys' World* with the Animal Rescue Club of 'The Whistling Swans' and the saving of the old horse in 'Jack O' Lantern.' These stories, which appeared two years after 'We-hro's Sacrifice,' may well have been written to atone for the latter's uncritical presentation of the killing of a pet dog to satisfy pagan ritual. The white dog feast, which she herself had witnessed, fascinated Johnson. It recurs in her adult prose, at first as a matter of regret, then as a subject of celebration.[73] But to endorse both the strangling of a pet and the practice of paganism, in a magazine for children produced by a religious press, was a remarkable gesture. Yet the story presumably passed muster with the editors who continued to buy Johnson's work. The political significance of 'The Potlatch,' one of her last stories for *Boys' World*, is more subtle. This account of Ta-la-pus's creation of his own dance implicitly endorses the practice of the potlatch during the period when the Canadian government was determined to eliminate a tradition that was essential to the social economy of West Coast Indigenous culture. While Johnson remains silent about the relation between her story and Canadian government policy, readers with any awareness of current events could hardly avoid making the connection.

In January 1910 Johnson was seeking a publisher for a book of short stories for boys, which she wanted 'put into every School Library possible in Canada' as 'the Schools and the Sunday Schools are all crying loudly for boys books.'[74] No such volume appeared until after her death, during the summer of 1913, when a selection of her stories from *Boys' World* appeared as *The Shagganappi*, dedicated to the Boy Scouts. Details of the book's selection process, publication, and profits remain sparse.[75] Omitted entirely were six articles on 'The Silver Craft of the Mohawks' which appeared in *Boys' World* in 1910. This set of informative discussions, illustrated with Johnson's own sketches, displays a distinct anthropological bent, emphasizing the craftsmanship and ingenious symbolism of Mohawk silver brooches, along with the lofty principles they embody. A fortunate editorial decision for the 1913 volume was the inclusion of the title story, for which there is no evidence of previous publication. Indeed, the survival of a fair copy of 'The Shagganappi' in the Brant County Museum suggests that the manuscript, if ever sent out, had been returned to the author. One of Johnson's most outspoken attacks on social discrimination against those of mixed European and First Nations heritage, like her unpublished essay 'The Stings of Civilization,' the story may have been rejected for its unreserved political message.

As with *The Shagganappi*, details of the compilation and publication of *The Moccasin Maker*, also issued shortly after Johnson's death, remain undocumented.[76] Seven of its twelve stories originally appeared in the *Mother's Magazine*, the others coming from an assortment of sources. The book thus represents only a small portion of Johnson's twenty-nine contributions to the *Mother's Magazine*. Produced by the same publisher and editor as *Boys' World*, this periodical was the latter's counterpart in the specialized field of popular women's magazines. Johnson's involvement began at the invitation of editor Elizabeth Ansley, whose specification of the kind of material she wanted would shape the stories that the Canadian wrote. Ansley's first letter, referring to Johnson's previous contributions to *Outing*, suggested that 'you might have something very good to offer the mothers in the way of Outdoor Sports, Mother and Child out-of-doors, Health Exercises, Picnics, Camping, etc., all written especially for the mother, and her family.' A subsequent letter expands:

> The Indian stories and legends that you have sent us for the Boys' World have all been extremely interesting, and it has occurred to us that you might have something equally pleasing suitable for The Mother's Magazine ... We are endeavoring to lighten the tone of The Mother's Magazine somewhat, and are looking for matter along popular lines. We want to picture only the best and highest; but we do want the good attractively presented. We want some humor and bright, happy stories that will serve as a recreation for the mother when she picks up the Magazine.[77]

Quite obviously, the *Mother's Magazine*, with a mandate to 'better the conditions of the mothers and children and strengthen the home as the mainstay of the nation,'[78] would not welcome critical statements on social and religious hypocrisy. As age and fatigue compelled Johnson to retire from public performance, her periodical writing would provide a much-needed steady income, as long as she produced the required bright prose and happy endings. Her notes on the back of one of Ansley's letters indicate her familiarity with the rhetoric of decorous popular discourse:

> 1. Mothers of the Iroquois Indian Race, the habits & customs which fit them to bear warrior sons & gentle daughters, their training of their children in the refinements of native religion, morals, etiquette and food getting
> 2. The simplicity, purity, activity & outdoor occupations which native cus-

toms demand of the Red Indian mother in her uncivilized but rare & beautiful life ...

5. Three *authentic* instances stories of heroic but not dramatic motherhood.

6. Healthful pursuits in the open air that have proved profitable as brain & body builders to both mothers & children.[79]

The *Mother's Magazine* stories, like those written for *Boys' World*, are divided between conventional instructive tales of Euro-Canadian life and selections explicitly concerned with First Nations content. For mothers, as for boys, Johnson made a strong case for Canada, her first substantial story focusing on the Confederation of 1867. Perhaps surprisingly, the proportion of her work on First Nations topics is greater for mothers than for sons.

Johnson's rendition of Aboriginal life for the *Mother's Magazine* demonstrates the same political acuity that underscored her stage performances. Although she voiced her anti-Americanism on other occasions, here it was firmly under control. Carefully assessing her audience, she plays to their expectations while at the same time using her hold on their attention in order to stress the intrinsic merits of Native culture. This tour-de-force is well illustrated by comparing similar articles written for different readerships. Her description of 'Iroquois Women of Canada,' appearing in several mainstream Canadian publications between 1895 and 1900, stresses the progress of Six Nations homemakers. However, her later articles on Indian mothers, which emphasize how the Iroquois woman 'has not yet joined the ranks of the "new woman,"' fulfil the *Mother's Magazine* ideal of 'old-fashioned womanliness.'[80] When placed in this context, her articles, while on the surface quite romantic and essentialist, can also be seen as strategically crafted interventions in the ideological battle to legitimitize the claims of First Nations (and also of women) for respect and civil rights.

This series opens with brief sketches of the Iroquois version of two familiar North American holidays, Thanksgiving and the New Year. At the outset, Johnson creates a comfortable cultural bridge for her non-Native readers, while establishing her position as both qualified informant and partisan supporter: 'Who shall say that, with her point of view, the pagan Indian mother has not done as great and noble a thing as she of fairer skin and more modern civilization?'[81] Following this carefully prepared introduction, Johnson then celebrates the Indian mother in four separate articles about traditional Native life, placing the Iroquois in wigwams in isolated forest surroundings where there is no school for the children during the winter, thereby virtually obliterating two centuries of contact. At the same time, her phrase 'the mothers of the great Iroquois Nation of Canada' denies any separation between the two nations. Echoing her earlier London *Express* description of the traditional political privileges of the Iroquois matriarch, she then implicitly links idealized maternity with the exercise of matronly power.[82]

Like her 'Silver Craft' series for *Boys' World,* Johnson's articles for the *Mother's Magazine* detail traditional ways of life. Here the focus is on work performed by women, such as the cultivation and use of corn, and cultural practices relating to courtship and child-rearing. Johnson worked comfortably within the uplifting ideology of the *Mother's Magazine,* which allowed her to idealize pre-contact times as free from worry, theft, and any notion of want or warfare. The idyll of the 'kindred of the forest' is disrupted only when the white man introduces 'extravagance, social rivalry, whisky, love of display.'[83] Her stories about non-Native family life, for example 'The Envoy Extraordinary' and 'The Nest Builder,' share the same sentimental outlook, which simplifies social conflicts and their solutions in order to advocate a specific moral and ameliorative vision. Critics revisiting nineteenth-century American women's writing now argue that its sentimental vision 'created a sacred space dedicated to women' that was hospitable to women's concerns for affiliation 'on the planes of emotion, sympathy, nurturance, or like-minded moral or spiritual inclination.' The 'heightened feeling' of sentimental discourse was appropriate to the seriousness of the social issues being addressed.[84] Moreover, American authors such as Harriet Beecher Stowe and Frances Harper provided cogent examples of the power of sentimental language as a political tool, a power exploited in Canada by Johnson's contemporaries such as Nellie McClung and L.M. Montgomery.

After Johnson's 1908 focus on Indian women, we can trace two significant subsequent preoccupations in her adult writing. The first is the pair of less than trustworthy memoirs, 'My Mother' (1909) and 'From the Child's Viewpoint' (1910). In the absence of personal sources other than scattered letters, these are the only pieces of sustained self-reflection available to her biographers. Like all her contributions to *Mother's Magazine,* they are motivated by her need to supply commodity writing that plays into the magazine's ideology of the sanctity of motherhood, the romance of the happy family, and the importance of good mothering to the future well-being of the nation. At the same time, she now realizes that her mother's inculcation of tight-lipped, 'aristocratic' self-repression may have damaged her children's emotional well-being, especially their ability to marry into stable domesticity. While the first article (reprinted in *The Moccasin Maker*) is a tribute to Emily Howells Johnson, the second admits criticism through a clever doubling of the narrative voice. Speaking for herself, Johnson states that 'it was almost sacrilege to think of mother at fault in anything.' She then attributes to her now-deceased brother Beverly a statement that challenges their mother's values: 'I wish she had not regarded talking of love and sweethearts as "foolish." We should all have probably married, which is far the better thing for men and women in this world.'

The second development, which established her final phase as a writer, was her series of recounted West Coast legends arising from her acquaintance with Chief Su-á-pu-luck (Joe Capilano) of the Squamish Nation. The project was first broached in January 1909 in the *Mother's Magazine* with 'The Legend of the Two Sisters.' Not until the summer of 1910, however, after Su-á-pu-luck's death that March, did Johnson embark on an extensive series of West Coast First Nations 'legends,' many of which came from the chief and his wife, Líxwelut (Mary Agnes). The final versions of most of the stories in *Legends of Vancouver* are presented as being told by the Squamish chief to Pauline, who in turn transmits them to the general Canadian reader. While this tactic creates unity, it discredits the status originally granted to Líxwelut as a storyteller in her own right. In its initial *Mother's Magazine* version, 'The Legend of the Two Sisters,' a tale of women as peacemakers, is entirely a female production, narrated by 'a quaint old Indian mother' who speaks woman-to-woman of 'the secret that is held in the mountains, the secret of the Indian mother's heart.' Similarly, 'The Legend of the Squamish Twins' (1910), originally related by 'both of you,' is later attributed solely to the chief when it reappears as 'The Recluse.' Most of the subsequent legends in the *Mother's Magazine* likewise originate with an old 'klootchman' (probably Líxwelut) and concern relations between parents and children, with a recurring stress on the value of female children in First Nations society. Johnson frequently makes the point that 'there is rarely a tradition among the British Columbia Indians that does not have as its base womanhood – wifehood, and above all, motherhood.'[85] The latter iteration, from her final contribution to the *Mother's Magazine*, was added for the occasion to 'The Great Deep Water' (1912), a legend previously published in the *Vancouver Province Magazine*. The words are also absent from the version that was authorized by its appearance in *Legends of Vancouver*, thus depriving Johnson's general reader of greater recognition of the difference between the Amerindian world view, based on the 'great circle of relations,' and their own linear patriarchy.[86]

This discussion of Johnson's honing of First Nations legends to suit her specific audiences requires us to confront an issue that has been hovering over our consideration of all her performed and written work – namely the role of traditional First Nations oral culture in shaping her creativity. The question is most directly pertinent to two areas: her narrative poems, in which her practice of first-person dramatization may owe some inspiration to Native oral traditions, and her recounting of stories which she originally received orally – the material that became 'My Mother' as well as the First Nations tales from her final writing period.

The upsurge of First Nations literary activity in the 1980s and 1990s has encouraged both writers and scholars to study the oral traditions of Aboriginal culture and to contemplate the complex relationships between traditional oral performance and its textual transmission, whether in the preservative recording of linguists and anthropologists, or in the engagement with oral forms of discourse by creative writers like Tom King.[87] Margery Fee notes that in current creative literature, Indigenous writers who necessarily work in English deliberately adopt a differentiating style in which 'textual markers of orality substitute for near-extinct Aborginal language and the writer takes on the mantle of the oral story-teller.' Differences arising from contrasting discourse traditions require considerable alertness on the part of the non-Aboriginal reader. For example, Fee says, 'In Indigenous writing, what looks like failures or gaps to a Western reader may simply mark a reluctance to impose interpretation.' Arnold Krupat argues that literary critics need to develop a new approach that he terms ethnocriticism, which pays careful attention to 'Native constructions of the category of knowledge.'[88] Just as literary scholars are becoming more aware of how the work of anthropologists, linguists, and folklorists contributes to our understanding of First Nations 'oral literature,'[89] so the latter have become more sensitive to the artistic elements in the material that they transcribe.

With regard to Pauline Johnson, the important concern is the traces of First Nations oral culture in her work. What evidence survives of her direct knowledge of Mohawk oratorical traditions? Do her use of oral forms and her conscious orientation of written texts to different audiences derive from her Six Nations upbringing, or from Euro-Canadian modes of social entertainment and the culture of the professional platform circuit? As a child, she spent considerable time with her grandfather, Chief Smoke Johnson, a famous orator known as the 'Mohawk Warbler,' yet there is no reliable evidence that Johnson herself understood (or retained) much Mohawk, a significant limitation in her claims to Iroquois nationality.[90] Her father was fluent in English and her mother never learned more than 'half-a-dozen words of Mohawk.'[91] Surviving vocabulary lists in her papers suggest that her knowledge was at best elementary, consisting of a few words that appear in her stories and poems.[92] Moreover, her published memories of witnessing Aboriginal ceremonies are limited to one encounter with a 'Medicine Man'[93] and the oft-mentioned white dog feast of the Onondaga. Textual evidence of her lack of direct acquaintance with Six Nations oral culture is even stronger, in that few of her narratives, prose or poetry, originate in Six Nations traditions. That Johnson had not created an identity as an author of Iroquois-based stories is evident in Marjorie Pickthall's 1903 suggestion that Johnson turn her attention to fiction as 'the wide field of Indian lore and legend remains practically untouched, at any rate in Canada.'[94]

Until she met Su-á-pu-luck, Johnson's experiences with the oral practices of Euro-Canadian stage culture exceeded those of First Nations tradition. With the Squamish, her position became that of a privileged outsider. Implicitly tuned into the rhythms of Indigenous culture (she frequently describes herself as patiently waiting in silence for the story to begin), she represents herself as taking on the role of interpreter, validating Su-á-pu-luck by translating his 'quaint' speech into discourse conventions that non-Native readers recognize as literary. The stories usually begin and end with a First Nations primary speaker who opens with an *incipit* (literally 'it begins') phrase typical of oral discourse.[95] Johnson draws attention to this feature of storytelling in 'The Siwash Rock' when she quotes her friend beginning 'It was "thousands of years ago"' and adds '(all Indian legends begin in extremely remote times).' After she picks up the narrative thread in her own romantic style, she frequently interrupts herself with parenthetical comments, like the one just cited, that remind the reader of the original source. The result is a highly sophisticated double-voicing, which shifts between features of oral and literary discourse. By the time most of the Capilano stories were published, the primary informant had died, thereby reducing any challenge to Johnson's authority to speak on behalf of a nation that was not her own. Her position somewhat resembles that of the anthropologists, notably Horatio Hale, with whom she had been acquainted since childhood. In response to a question about why 'she alone of her

father's race had translated its beauty of thought into verse,' she reportedly responded, 'Writing was never the Indian's mode of expression. It
was the speech, the oration of which was his great achievement. And
that, like all the old customs, is dying out.'[96] Her role was to capture the
oral medium on the page, to preserve a culture apparently doomed to
extinction on behalf of those who appeared unable to do so themselves.
The poignancy of this situation is that she recorded Su-á-pu-luck's stories as he was dying of tuberculosis, the White man's disease that
destroyed so many First Nations people, while she herself was dying of
cancer.

Johnson's divergence from systematic ethnography, as founded by
Franz Boas and pursued by Charles Hill-Tout, was noted by her contemporaries in Vancouver. In 1929 J.N.J. Brown, who had been superintendant of the Capilano Reserve and who claimed Johnson as one of his
staunch and admired friends, argued that communication difficulties
between Johnson and Chief Joe Capilano rendered her versions inauthentic: '"The Legends of Vancouver" will live as emollient, romantic stories with beautiful flow of language – but their mythology is
not historical, as carved out by the Indians themselves.'[97] But another
local pundit argued that Johnson's major cultural contribution lay
elsewhere:

> This book represents the beginning of a new literature on the Pacific
> Coast: the imaginative treatment of Indian folklore ... The legends have
> revealed unsuspected fields of work for the creative imagination close at
> hand, challenging, as it were, the young culture of our own country, and
> lighting up with living interest a moribund race that has been regarded as
> somewhat dull and stupid. I have not overlooked the valuable work done in
> Indian folk-lore by Charles Hill-Tout ... But it has always been done in the
> interests of exact science. His object has rightly been accuracy first and last
> ... Miss Johnson's object was different and British Columbia is fortunate in
> having a mind whose congenital sympathy and poetic endowment could
> supplement so effectively the scientific work of a pioneer anthropologist.[98]

This view is now supported by current reassessments of anthropological
methodology. According to Christine Marshall, Johnson's entertaining
and dramatic style approximates the experience of a live rendition: 'In
the light of post-Boasian ethnography ... it is clear that Pauline's handling of the legends includes contextual elements now considered
essential to an oral storytelling.' Those elements include 'her detailed

descriptions of her relationship to the storyteller, of the occasion of the storytelling, [and] of the language and gestures used.'[99]

While the texts of Johnson's legends play an important role in validating West Coast Aboriginal culture, an examination of the original contexts of their publication in the *Vancouver Province Magazine* in 1910–11, and subsequently in book form, shows that they also performed significant cultural work regarding local White/Native relations. During the period 1907–9 Su-á-pu-luck was characterized by the *Province* as an activist and agitator, and was regularly blamed for inciting a series of conflicts and rebellions, most notably those in the Nass and Skeena Valleys in Northern British Columbia.[100] The *Province*'s coverage of his 1906 visit to London to appeal to the King, the occasion of his first meeting with Johnson, was dismissive and mocking, as was its account of his visit to Prime Minister Laurier two years later.

What should we make of the fact that Johnson's versions of Su-á-pu-luck's stories appeared in the weekend magazine of a newspaper that was distinctly hostile to the Aboriginal cause? We know that their publication was due to her friendship with its editor, Lionel Makovski. On 26 March 1910, several weeks before the appearance of the first of her pieces, the magazine respectfully acknowledged Capilano's recent death with photographs on the cover and a two-page tribute, written by Makovski, citing the deceased chief's opinions about his own experiences and the future of his people. Johnson's accounts of her friend's tales continued that tribute, in her ongoing participation in a complex conversation with European Canada. On the one hand, if read in conjunction with the slanted reporting of news about First Nations, Johnson can be seen to be participating in the colonial project of appropriation – of using the Squamish stories to create a usable past for the White community. This is certainly the perspective of Johnson's early audience. Bernard McEvoy's preface to the 1911 edition of *Legends of Vancouver* celebrates how 'a poet has arisen to cast over the shoulders of our grey mountains, our trail-threaded forests, our tide-swept waters, and the streets and sky-scrapers of our hurrying city, a gracious mantle of romance.'[101] But we should remember that Johnson wanted her book to be titled *Legends of the Capilano.* It is therefore also possible to read Johnson as countering the dominant discourse – as once again exploiting her friendship with a powerful White man, this time to immortalize her friend and fellow advocate, Su-á-pu-luck, in the very pages that had tried so hard to discredit him.

CHAPTER FIVE

'Canadian Born':
Imagining the Nation

Loyalties

From her birth in Six Nations in 1861 to her death in Vancouver in
1913, Pauline Johnson tested and expanded the meaning of Canada.
Her respectable middle-class Mohawk-English family embodied the
hopes of a Mixed-race community on North America's imperial frontier.
She too attempted to embrace an enlarged view of the British Empire
and the Canadian nation. Her efforts unfolded in the midst of widespread soul-searching about the future of the new confederation. Just
what was the relationship of former colonies to the imperial centre?
What justified a separate existence in face of the American behemoth?
What was the relationship among the different peoples who called Canada home? Like other Canadian writers of her generation and later,
Johnson grappled with such questions. That task was far from easy, even
for the privileged. For a Mixed-race, unmarried woman, handicapped
by failing health and uncertain finances, the effort to force European
Canada to acknowledge the centrality of Native people and the value of
her sex to the new nation was courageous, albeit sometimes uncertain
and contradictory.

In this light, Johnson's 'Canadian Born,' first performed around 1897
and published in 1903 as the title poem of her second book, deserves scrutiny. Like Sara Jeannette Duncan's 1904 novel *The Imperialist*, it contributes to debates about Canada's future within the British Empire, debates
sharpened by controversies surrounding Canada's participation in the
South African War. The poem's jaunty rhythm and jingoist tone fall far
short of today's literary standards. Nonetheless, careful reading reveals
that its perspective offers an important departure from the racism that

imbues most Canadian patriotic verse, such as Alexander McLachlan's 1874 poem 'The Anglo-Saxon,' which opens 'The Anglo-Saxon leads the van,/And never lags behind,/For was he not ordain'd to be/The leader of mankind?' and Robert Stead's 1908 poem 'The Mixer,' whose chorus repeats 'I turn 'em out Canadians/All but the yellow and the brown.' Johnson, in contrast, defines Canadian according to place of birth. Her chorus, 'we were born in Canada, beneath the British flag,' asserts an identity that not only implicitly denies racial distinction, but, given that according to Indigenous belief Canada's First Nations 'have lived here since the world began,' also celebrates Natives as more authentically Canadian than any immigrant. As Johnson bluntly points out in 'The Duke of Connaught as Chief of the Iroquois,' 'it would be difficult to find a man more Canadian than any one of the fifty chiefs who compose the parliament of the ancient Iroquois nation.' At the end of the twentieth century, a Cree songwriter-singer's words in 'Proud Indian' would carry the same message: 'I'm proud to be a Canadian but more proud to be an Indian. Under god's golden sun I am the true native-son.'[1]

Yet if primogeniture favoured the Dominion's Native offspring, Johnson's ideal nation included other partners, adopted siblings as it were in the greater Canadian family. The original 1903 edition of *Canadian Born* bears the inscription: 'Let him who is Canadian born regard these poems as written to himself – whether he be my paleface compatriot who has given to me his right hand of good fellowship, in the years I have appealed to him by pen and platform, or whether he be that dear Red brother of whatsoever tribe or Province, it matters not – White Race and Red are one if they are but Canadian born.' In short, the young Dominion could be a home and native land not only to the First Nations but to all those of European origin who repudiate a racist past.

The question of loyalties had been basic to Johnson's earliest upbringing. Acutely conscious of her role in an elite Mohawk family with close ties to settler society, her mother intended her children 'to grow up nationalists, and they did, every mother's son and daughter of them ... Indians in spirit and patriotism, and in loyalty to their father's race.'[2] These sympathies were reinforced by a daughter's love for a charismatic father who died at the hands of the Whites. They survived Pauline Johnson's integration into the dominant society, first as a member of the extended Howells clan and then as a writer and entertainer with congenial ties to Non-Native women and men in North America and Britain.

However far from the Iroquois territory she strayed, Johnson's origins were never forgotten, nor 'the latent germs of nationality' early inspired

by her grandfather, 'a veritable Indian Ruskin.' In an age when authority, credibility, and, in her case, a professional career, depended heavily
on racial identification, she intensified the First Nations components of
her persona and writing. Fame and income, as well as sentiment,
required that until the end of her life Pauline Johnson would demand:
'Never let anyone call me a white woman. There are those who think
they pay me a compliment in saying that I am just like a white woman.
My aim, my joy, my pride is to sing the glories of my own people.'[3] Like
the prodigal in her poem of the same name, she would always 'through
a wilderness of thorn and rue' return to her first loyalties to Canada's
First Nations.

Members of First Nations sometimes insist that Pauline Johnson
belonged to the Mohawks. Understandable as such claims are, and cog-
nizant as Whites must be of the dangers of appropriation, confining
Johnson to her Mohawk, or even Aboriginal, identity ultimately under-
states her significance. As feminist and post-colonial theorists at the end
of the twentieth century are quick to remind us, the 'I' is not unitary.
The 'Other,' however distinguished, embodies multiple identities which
slip, slide, and overlap as each is called into being over a lifetime. This
natural multiplicity, membership in humanity's many communities,
questions any simple relationship of subordination or dominance. In
the transatlantic world at the turn of the last century, Pauline Johnson
became expert in invoking the unsettling potential of simultaneity.
Whatever her own wishes in the matter, and she herself could be ambiv-
alent, she encompasses the Native storyteller and the European artist,
the middle-class lady and the bohemian spirit. While critics of her own
time and later often tried to locate her inspiration solely in either 'her
white or red blood,' the combination itself helps explain why, as Walter
McRaye emphasized, 'she loved Canada.'[4] Like the nation she
attempted to call into being, she is complex and contradictory, participating in an identity that is always a process of discussion rather than a
stable definition.

An intellectual and an entertainer addressing both elites and masses,
Pauline Johnson develops what Mikhail Bakhtin later termed 'dialogic
or double-voiced discourse' which offers the possibility of remarking
'convention by incorporating the word of another within it.'[5] She
reminds audiences of alternatives to, or enlarged versions of, the nation
fabricated by the White male politicians of the day, the singularly unpre-
possessing lot featured in her 1907 short story, 'Her Dominion – A Story

of 1867 and Canada's Confederation.' Just as her poetry and prose restore Natives to the land's historic and moral landscape, this story insists that we recognize the unacknowledged 'mothers of Confederation' along with the publicly celebrated 'Fathers.' In her mind's eye, Natives and women constitute essential elements in the forging of the new nationality. In contrast, although Walter McRaye performed William Henry Drummond's dialect poems of French-Canadian habitant life, thereby including Quebec in the duo's staging of Canada, Johnson's writings reveal very little consciousness of the French fact as a distinct component of Canadian identity.

Johnson's person, like her performed and written texts, ultimately obscured the lines between insider and outsider. Indeed this blurring was critical to her mystique and her authority. First in Six Nations and Brantford and then in the wider world, Johnson acted as a highly visible bicultural mediator between contending national groups. In London in 1906, when she was called upon to translate the Chinook of Su-á-pu-luck and other British Columbia chiefs who sought the King's assistance with their land claims, she was reprising a familiar role, broadened to reflect her growing pan-Indian sensibility. Her uncertain command of Chinook and, for that matter, Mohawk, nevertheless underscores a long-standing difficulty in inter-cultural communication. In the reverse of her father's experience, when his Mohawk was incomprehensible to a White listener during his experiment with the new technology of his neighbour and friend Alexander Graham Bell, his daughter later lacked a language, other than English, which she could readily speak and understand in her exchanges with Native peoples. Issues of language joined those of gender, class, and race to render Pauline Johnson simultaneously an insider and outsider to both Native and settler communities.

Marginality, twinned with persistence, recurs as a major theme through a wide range of Johnson's poetry and prose. The speaker of the poem 'Christmastide,' after initially finding herself excluded from conventional observation of the holy occasion, nevertheless ensures participation when she 'may kneel without.' Triumph is clearer still in 'Lady Lorgnette.' Here an actor, a 'mimic king 'mid his mimic lords,' recognizes and wins true love while rejecting worldly alternatives. However, the common fate of many who speak from the periphery is invoked in poems such as 'The Mariner,' where seas are 'portless' and 'shelterless,' in '"Thro' Time and Bitter Distance"' with its 'cheerless shore,' and 'Overlooked,' where love is denied. For all her vitality and essential optimism, Pauline Johnson consistently recognized the disempowerment of those occupying the margins as Native and female, along with their inability to determine the outcome of events.

The impotence and disinheritance of Aboriginal peoples runs as a dark thread through much post-Confederation writing. Indians are routinely presented as remnants of an irrevocably lost, if sometimes, noble past. Johnson herself could not always escape the same conclusion, as in an 1894 London interview where she mourned the dying out of the Iroquois. A 1919 volume, *The Birthright* by Arthur Hawkes, captures the prevailing vision. Subtitled in part 'A Search for a Canadian Canadian,' it surveys a range of groups for inspiration and notably, if negatively, includes the Chinese, the Japanese, and the Sikhs. In sharp contrast, Indians fail to merit even the courtesy of a dismissal. And yet, for all such rejections and her own recurring fatalism, Johnson built a career and a life on the willingness of some observers to suspend the dominant racism. She courted a favourable response from White audiences while retaining her Native loyalties. To her admirers, she could be 'the quintessential Canadian speaker, as important to Canada as Mark Twain was to the United States,' an ironical comparison itself, since that American dismissed Indians as vermin.[6]

Pauline Johnson's attention to the origins and fate of the new Dominion was far from unique. She joined most of the literary community of her time, including the male writers singled out in Carl Berger's critical study of Canadian imperialism, *The Sense of Power*. For all that they shared her nationalist sympathies, however, few of these men took much time to consider the fate of the land's original inhabitants. The Canada Firster Charles Mair, author of a lengthy poem on Tecumseh and an admirer of Pauline Johnson, was willing to agree that 'the Indian's history is the background of our own.' In leaving 'behind him a halo of romance which is imperishable,' however, Mair's Native could only haunt the modern landscape.[7] History went on without him. Even Mair's limited concession did not always prevail. Sara Jeannette Duncan, in *The Imperialist*, introduced First Nations characters only as a device to further her plot, at the expense of their honesty and dignity. By 1941 Stephen Leacock asserted with little fear of contradiction that

> the continent remained, as it had been for uncounted centuries, empty. We think of prehistoric North America as inhabited by the Indians, and have based on this a sort of recognition of ownership on their part. But this atti-

tude is hardly warranted. The Indians were too few to count. Their use of
the resources of the continent was scarcely more than that by crows and
wolves, their development of it nothing.[8]

Ultimately, as this comment suggests, Canadian imperialists other than
Pauline Johnson paid sustained attention to Native peoples only as a
romantic backdrop. The nation they cared to imagine existed to serve
Whites, and most often, White males at that.

Central to the emerging Canadian identity was a distinct view of the
past. Writers of fiction, poetry, and prose mined history for clues to Canada's future. While male contributors have received closest attention,
they were not alone. Inspired by Confederation and the Loyalist Centennial of 1884, a generation of women took up the cause of constructing a lineage for the young nation. Passionate local historians like
Evelyn Johnson were always part of the social and literary circles in
which Pauline moved and upon which she depended. Heroic stories of
exploration, settlement, and warfare, related in both fiction and non-fiction by writers like Janet Carnochan, Sarah Anne Curzon, Agnes Maule
Machar, and Constance Lindsay Skinner, outlined a critical genealogy.[9]
The emerging patriotic pantheon sometimes included Native founders
such as Joseph Brant and Tecumseh and heroines such as Madeleine de
Verchères and Laura Secord. Such figures remained the stock-in-trade
of history's popularizers but as the discipline became increasingly pro-
fessionalized they and their advocates won little interest from academic
scholars. After World War One the canon of Canada's history, like that
of its literature, settled down to a long preoccupation with the achievements of White men. In Johnson's time, however, the past sometimes
seemed ripe with possibility. Her reminders of the Dominion's Native
history and the significance of women secured a place in the popular
imagination.

As a New Woman of her age, Johnson also bears comparison with the
somewhat younger Nellie McClung, the feminist activist and writer who
became a staunch friend. Both Ontario-born women ultimately
anchored their hopes in the West. Although they differed substantially
in their awareness of Aboriginal suffering, both women sought to
enshrine justice as the cornerstone of the new nationality. Distinct from
old Britain and the nouveau-riche United States, Canada could combine
the best of both continents. While she was never entirely one of them,
Johnson shared the idealism of a significant group of female intellectuals who sought to place their mark on the national imaginary.

In Canada, as with the other offspring of the British Empire, the study of nationalism provides an opportunity to confront the meaning of the imperial relationship. Indeed, Canadian nationalism sometimes constituted itself as both heir to and critic of British imperialism. Pauline Johnson participated directly in this tradition. Steeped deeply in British literature and history, like the Mixed-race Mohawk president of the Independent Order of Foresters, Oronhyateka, who used 'mainstream values to further specifically Iroquoian interests,'[10] she found much to admire. That very admiration, however, set a high standard by which she judged failings in Britain, Canada, and the United States. Part of an educated Aboriginal elite within the outposts of empire, she could, as Salman Rushdie put it so memorably, sometimes 'write back with a vengeance.' In her defence of Native traditions, Pauline Johnson constructed an image for herself and her country which demanded respect for the Aboriginal Other. She was someone who, as the Mohawk lawyer Patricia Monture-Angus observed more generally, 'learned to use a language that was forced upon us to create powerful messages that convey to you our experiences.'[11]

Nonetheless, in her efforts to recast the Canadian nation to include acknowledgment of Aboriginal peoples and women, Pauline Johnson did not escape nationalism's snares. Her imagination was inevitably caught within the confines of the racial thinking of her age. Neither Europeans nor First Nations were all equal; Canadians of Asian or African origin were still more suspect. Even as the Native female Other, she readily sustained a particular nationalist narrative that left some less worthy or even less human than others. Like even the more progressive of her Euro-Canadian contemporaries such as J.S. Woodsworth, the social gospeller and later founder of the Co-operative Commonwealth Federation, she too sometimes designated others as 'the strangers within our gates.'

Yet however flawed, deferential, and incomplete her formulation, Johnson challenged a prevailing view of Canada, which, like that of the other dominions, granted superior privileges to European settlers. For the majority of her contemporaries, the Native provided no more than 'the ground on which the national figure is delineated, the buried foundation on which its structure of power is erected.'[12] Ongoing Native-settler partnerships were no part of the dominant agenda. Ultimately, Johnson and other Indigenous critics in the colonial world lost ground because their credentials, however aligned with imperial culture, were never regarded as a match for Europeans and the urgency of their self-interest. Consigned to remain only a 'mimic' of her 'betters,' Pauline Johnson is finally a 'contradictory figure,' simultaneously reinforcing and disturbing colonial authority.[13] Like Walter Scott in his tales of the Scottish highlands, she makes poetic the plight of the loser. The still harder task for another generation is to make loss the inspiration for redress.

In her effort to communicate equality, Pauline Johnson struggled to retrieve a Native past distorted and destroyed by colonialism. The commonsensical view of the day, held by Johnson's contemporaries such as J.E. Logan, took for granted, albeit sometimes rather regretfully, the irrelevance of human history prior to European arrival:

> We have had no barbarous infancy moulded by the natural features of our land. No divinities have sanctified to us our mountains and streams. No fabled heroes have left us immortal memories. We have not amalgamated with the native and woven the woof of our refinement in the strong sinuous web of an aboriginal tradition and religion. In our civilized arrogance we swept away that coarser fabric, knowing not that we destroyed that we would now, as a garment, be proud to wear.[14]

Far rarer were voices like that of anthropologist Horatio Hale, who insisted on the value of the Iroquois in the modern world:

> the annals of this portion of the continent need no longer begin with the landing of the first colonists, but can go back, like those of Mexico, Yucatan and Peru, to a storied past of singular interest ... The love of peace, the sentiment of human brotherhood, the strong social and domestic affections, the respect for law, and the reverence for ancestral greatness ... are apparent in this Indian record and in the historical events which illustrate it ... The sentiment of universal brotherhood which directed their polity has never been so fully developed in any branch of the Aryan race, unless it may be found incorporated in the religious quietism of Buddha and his followers.[15]

Yet, for all its commonplace hostility and ignorance, settler society's intense desire for a sense of place required some recognition of Indians. Seeking to come to terms with their loss of old lands elsewhere, newcomers endeavoured to endow the North American landscape with comparable meaning and sentiment. Updated mental maps were essential if Europeans were ever to feel at home. Romanticized Indians, whether they appeared in poems or parades, provided a communal focus for diverse groups of newcomers as they struggled to construct a new nationality.[16]

Native History and Nation-Building

The recovery of Aboriginal history, like the turn-of-the century enthusiasm for Native nomenclature, could, ironically enough, contribute to ultimate Europeanization. Duncan Campell Scott's 1905 poem, 'Indian Place Names,' presents 'the wild names' of Canadian geography as remnants of a 'race [that] has waned and left but tales of ghosts.' While the poem claims that 'the land is murmurous' with the musicality of polysyllabic words like Miramichi and Wagamac, the words themselves serve as empty signs. Untranslated and therefore bereft of their Indigenous meaning, to the Euro-Canadian the names are merely romantic rhythmic reminders of displaced Others. The popularity of wilderness tourism during this period, with its induction of Whites into selected, often sanitized, mysteries under the tutelage of Native guides, is another aspect of the same phenomenon. Anxious to make intellectual land claims, Whites sifted through the detritus of the conquered. Just as their turn-of-the-century counterparts in northern Europe turned to romantic tales of the Aryan and Celtic peoples, White Canadians readily fancied themselves heirs to 'superior' Natives. The Six Nations Confederacy, with its loyalism and links to Longfellow's hero Hiawatha, was a particularly attractive antecedent.

Pauline Johnson drew on this long-standing appeal with her characterization of the 'Grand River, with its romantic forests, its legend-thronged hills, its wide and storied flats, its tradition-fraught valleys ... the great domain of the most powerful of the North American nations, the Iroquois.'[17] Unlike most other enthusiasts, however, her commitment was far more than antiquarian. At least from 1884, the year that heard the public recital of her earliest known Indian poem, 'The Re-interment of Red Jacket,' Johnson attempted to knit a new nationalist narrative. In non-fiction, short stories, and poems, she points not only to a substantial set of Native traditions but also to their continuing value as signposts to the possibility of a common future. *Legends of Vancouver* brings the story she attempted to tell full circle in its celebration of the culture of the Squamish people and its critical observations on the Euro-Canadian world that was engulfing them. However, unflattering comparisons were rarely appreciated by White commentators such as Bernard McEvoy, whose preface to the 1911 volume appropriated the stories as confirming possession of '*our* grey mountains, *our* trail-threaded forests, *our* tide-swept waters' (our emphasis).

Like her sister Evelyn, Pauline Johnson took up the cause of history. By turns educating, charming, and denouncing those who saw nothing but Native savagery, she highlights the 'dignity, glory and solemnity' to be found in the exploits of the Iroquois, the Cree, the Sioux, the Haida, and the Squamish. She proposed myths and artifacts to connect a Native past to an inclusive future. Indians such as the Onondaga, whom she identifies as the most traditional of the Six Nations, present 'a history that would be envied by any white native of the earth.'[18] A full century before Ronald Wright's *Stolen Continents* (1993), she required audiences to contemplate alternative perspectives on the European settlement of North America. Why, she asks, do 'they always call an Indian victory a "terrible and bloody massacre," and a white victory a glorious defeat of the rebels?'[19] Whereas the Aboriginal past, like that of the land itself, as she suggests in her poem on Thunder Bay, 'The Sleeping Giant,' might be deliberately locked against intruders, she, the Indigenous poet, offers the key to those who would repudiate White dominion and share an inheritance.

As important as historical misrepresentation, and perhaps more difficult to counteract, were the distortions of romanticism, an ideology which mythologized the Indian in the interests of a dominant European nationalism. Johnson's own investment in this tradition as a means of offsetting the prevailing insistence on Native degradation and degeneracy, not to mention her pragmatic dependence on romanticism's celebration of Indian stereotypes, substantially complicated her stance as a Native advocate. Not surprisingly perhaps, the strongest denunciation of the romantic perspective, with a passionate reminder of historical fact, came when the poet was just starting out, freshly idealistic and least dependent on mainstream conventions and expectations. In May 1892 the Toronto *Globe* published her extraordinary essay, 'A Strong Race Opinion on the Indian Girl in Modern Fiction.' A testament to early daring and confidence, it did not foresee the author having to make a lonely living in life's hard markets.

The general run of authors are, Johnson states quite categorically, abysmally ignorant. Taking particular aim at a contemporary novel, *An Algonquin Maiden* by G. Mercer Adam and A. Ethelwyn Wetherald, she mounts a blistering attack on its 'dwarfed, erroneous and delusive' and, unfortunately, far from unusual plot and characters. In 'A Strong Race Opinion' she ridicules the prevailing assumption that one Indian, or one Indian tribe, is much like another. However indistinguishable to the uncaring author, Natives are in fact as diverse and as individual as Europeans themselves. In face of persisting misrepresentation and prejudice, she scoffs at claims of real interest in North American Aboriginals. It is only too likely, she bluntly observes, that the Indian is 'introduced into literature but to lend a dash of vivid coloring to an otherwise tame and somber picture of colonial life.' Why else 'should the Indian always get beaten in the battles of romances, or the Indian girl get inevitably the cold shoulder in the wars of love?' Such self-serving depictions had nothing to do with reality. Real Indians have won 'many combats ... in history from the extinction of the Jesuit Fathers at Lake Simcoe to Cut Knife Creek.'

Nor is the Native girl always the loser. Johnson points out that many have 'placed dainty red feet figuratively upon the white man's neck.' 'Surely,' she asks, 'the Redman has lost enough, has suffered enough without additional losses and sorrows being heaped upon him in romance.' The time is long overdue when Native victories should be acknowledged: 'Let us not only hear, but read something of the North American Indian "besting" some one at least once in a decade, and above all things let the Indian girl in fiction develop from the "dog-like," "fawn-like," "deer-footed," "fire-eyed," "crouching," "submissive" book heroine into something of the quiet, sweet womanly woman she is if wild, or the everyday, natural, laughing girl she is if cultivated and educated; let her be natural even if the author is not competent to give her tribal characteristics.' While she curbs her criticism in acknowledging the merits of a few writers, including Charles Mair and Helen Hunt Jackson, the American author of the bestseller *Ramona*, North Americans were so unaccustomed to such frankness from an Aboriginal writer in a leading daily newspaper that their response was silence. Some months later, practising what she preached, the outspoken Johnson captured the *Dominion Illustrated*'s prize for fiction with her short story 'A Red Girl's Reasoning.' Its strong-minded heroine is no man's pawn and, like her author, speaks to the condition of women and Natives.

Johnson continued this forceful championship when she was finally able to raise the funds to take her case and her first manuscript to the imperial heartland. Interrogated by an inquisitive London reporter in 1894, she makes her intentions plain: 'I have come here because my Indian people are very much misunderstood among you English. You do not believe them to be poetic, artistic, and as beautifully moral in their religion as they are. You have a poor idea of the grandeur of the Red Man's nature, and you do him an injustice.'

Her interviewer counters by referring to Canada's reputation for fair play. Conscious of the dangers of offence and the need for allies, Johnson prevaricates and dissembles:

> Yes, the Canadian government treats us with the greatest consideration, while the United States government does not study the Indians at all. We of the Six Nations tribes ... have our own government. We are, of course, under white law, but the Canadian government never does a thing without asking the chiefs of the Iroquois in council, and when the chiefs pass a bill in our council it is submitted to the Canadian parliament. But there is never any dissension. They do not impose on us, and we do not impose on them. But then, we are one reserve out of hundreds.

Later on in the same interview, she goes on to say that Indians had cause for grievance during the time of the Northwest Rebellion but not now.

Such misrepresentation on her part, which could only have been expedient given her need for good social references, may have been intended to suggest the superior level at which relations should be maintained. Yet this ideal is far too often, as the last sentence indicates, betrayed in reality. Indeed, she used the London opportunity to insist that Indians in general suffer because of the perpetuation of distorted portrayals by self-centred Europeans. While a few writers were fair-handed, she points out, others, even the popular historian Francis Parkman, are far from just in their characterization of Native peoples.

Admitting her own loyalties – 'I am an Iroquois, and, of course, I think the Iroquois are the best Indians in civilization and birth, just as you English think you are better than the Turks' – she invites her audience to shed conceit and recognize equals: 'Do you know that the Iroquois have done more in the last hundred years than it took the native Britons all their time to do? Indian families who fifty years ago were worshipping the Great Spirit, in the old Indian way, have turned into professional men and finely-educated women who hold responsible positions ... the Red Man ... is no savage if only given a chance.' Flaunting her own command of the oppressors' history, she celebrates the Iroquois Confederacy and its constitution as one of the most marvellous in the world. So equipped, the Iroquois were able 'to sweep the continent of America as Napoleon swept Europe' and to consult 'as Disraeli gathered the Berlin Conference together.' The apparently inevitable disappearance of the Indian, like that of 'the Pole and the Jew,' is a serious loss. Revealingly, she singles out not her own nation, the Mohawk, with

its long history of coexistence, but the traditional Onondagas for special mention. The most conservative of the Confederacy, they were
'blue-blooded – not a drop of any other blood in them ... I know an
Onondaga family which can count back nine hundred years in direct
line, and a great many Crees and Sioux Indians are the same.' All this
heroism and talent went, however, for naught because of the malfea-
sance of 'the awful class of white people near our reserves.' Here is the
dark side of empire. Making the most of her own favourable reception,
she claims that 'when I was a child I was never allowed to have any white
friends except those of the missionary's family. They drag the Indian
down.' London and Ottawa, the two national capitals where this interview was published, are asked to contemplate the underside of their
own civilization.

Johnson goes on to hammer home responsibility by turning the tables
on her imperial host. 'Suppose,' she asks, 'we came over to England as a
powerful people. Suppose you gave us welcome to English soil, worshipped us as gods, as we worshipped you white people when you first
came to Canada; and suppose we encroached upon your homeland and
drove you back and back, and then said, "Oh, well, we will present you
with a few acres – a few acres of your own dear land." What would you
think of it all? ... The whole continent belongs to us by right of lineage.
We welcomed you as friends, we worshipped you, and you drove us into
a little corner.'

Clearly taken aback by the passion he had unleashed, the London
journalist struggled to put a brighter face on matters by observing that
Pauline Johnson herself 'could hardly be leading your present life of
culture had it not been for the white man's invasion.' She was not, however, to be waylaid. Her response captures her predicament perfectly.
She would not, she admitted, be the same person 'but there are two of
me.' And then, in a claim which seems now extraordinarily revealing
and all the more powerful to readers familiar with the heroic tales of
Walter Scott and the poetry of Robbie Burns, she concludes, 'sometimes
I feel I must get away to the Highlands among a people who seem somehow akin to mine.'[20] In that moment, she creates a powerful link
between the experience of two conquered peoples across the breadth of
empire, uniting the romance of two lost causes. She also reminds attentive readers that Scott characterized the Highlanders as the 'aboriginal
race' of Scotland.[21] Her conclusion that 'We are without a country. I
cannot say America is my country' bluntly sets the record straight. Her
choice to name not Canada but the generic 'America' as not hers is also

suggestive. North America has been lost. The United States is beyond redemption. Perhaps an unnamed country can offer salvation? In a series of interviews that asked 'where would your British America have been had he [the Iroquois] helped the French as he helped you long years ago,' Pauline Johnson let her audience know that colonialism often represents a travesty of justice.[22] By the early 1890s it was clear that an articulate champion had emerged to bring Indians to the attention of the country and the Empire. Here is far more than the voice of 'sentimental regret' seen by some critics.[23]

The temptation of at least one British newspaper critic to label Johnson an 'Indian Boadicea' also suggests that her championship of the Native and her criticism of colonialism evoked, at least in some imperial circles, a certain identification. While the complete story still remains shrouded in national mythology, British patriots, including feminists, have been fascinated by Boadicea, a Celtic queen who led her tribe, the Iceni, in the first major revolt against the Roman conquerors of Britain. A comparison could be made between two communities of Indigenous peoples, the Celtic Iceni and Johnson's Iroquois, both allied to powerful empires which ultimately betray them. The unnatural – from the perspective of Victorian and Edwardian traditionalists – public advocacy of the two Native women, Boadicea and Pauline Johnson, simultaneously highlighted injustice, admitted female authority, and eroticized the relationship between the imperial power and those it ruled. This revealing comparison with an early British heroine supplied a complicated and contradictory iconography which yet again interpreted the poet-performer as simultaneously self and Other.

Although Canadian commentators have sometimes liked to believe that they witnessed her inevitable evolution from an angry Native critic to a less disturbing champion of the Dominion, Johnson's commitment to the defence of Aboriginal peoples and women, and her enthusiasm for a perfected Canadian confederation, persisted throughout her life. Her poetic salutes to the Iroquois leaders Red Jacket and Joseph Brant in the mid-1880s, presented to mixed crowds in Buffalo and Brantford, initiated her public effort to associate Natives with a higher form of nationalism. Red Jacket (1758–1830), a Seneca chief who advocated independence for the Confederacy, is characterized as a 'gifted son,' a 'superhuman,' and a 'master mind' whose thought was 'so vast, and liberal, and strong.' Even so, he could not stem the waning of his race. Instead his foes have 'made America [their] rightful home.' The need some half-century after Red Jacket's death is for mutual forgiveness and dialogue: 'Forgive the wrongs my children did to you,/And we, the red-skins, will forgive you too.'

In 1886, at the unveiling of a statue of the Mohawk chief Joseph Brant, Pauline Johnson addressed Canada directly. The indictment is also more severe: as 'Indian graves, and Indian memories ... will fade as night comes on, so fades the race/That unto Might and therefore Right gives place.' Brant, whom the sharp-eyed and sharp-tongued Sara Jeannette Duncan summed up on the same occasion as his nation's great betrayer,[24] is noticeably less personalized and heroicized than the Seneca chieftain. Johnson chooses to concentrate on the meaning of the alliance he had espoused. The young Dominion is reminded of the debt to and 'allegiance from thy Indian son.' It is time to embrace 'one common Brotherhood.' Under the rule of 'England's Noble Queen,' Indian allies, when properly treated, have 'no fear of wrong' and 'no cause for us to rise/To seek protection under other skies.' Both odes emphasize unpaid claims for justice and reconciliation but the later poem is the more passionate. Johnson's argument that the future for Native and newcomer depends on addressing the past contrasts starkly with Charles G. D. Roberts's patriotic odes from the same period, which completely erase the Native presence.[25]

The Brant poem introduces another theme of special significance for Aboriginal peoples living within the British Empire. Queen Victoria, like her successor, Edward VII, and their representatives, the governors general, presides as the ultimate guarantor of good faith. Appeals to the monarch, over the heads of recalcitrant and oppressive local authorities, were a regular feature of nationwide Aboriginal efforts at resistance and redress throughout the nineteenth and twentieth centuries. According to this perspective, the British Crown, to which Natives such as the Iroquois were linked as allies, not victims of conquest, enshrines much of the best of western civilization. Its symbolic and sometimes actual power is called upon to check abuse and require settler societies to live up to their own ideals. In a short story for boys, 'A Night with "North Eagle"' (1908), Johnson creates an authoritative professor from the University of Toronto to reaffirm the source of fair play within the Empire: 'These Indians *look* savage, in their paint and feathers, but King Edward of England has no better subjects; and I guess it is all the same to His Majesty whether a good subject dresses in buckskin or broadcloth.'

In Johnson's view, Natives had remained true to their alliances and treaties. Their good faith, in stark contrast to White betrayal, confirmed their moral superiority and, with this, their claim to better treatment. In

the 1890s, during the build-up to the South African War, Johnson highlighted ongoing loyalty in her reminder that the Six Nations, in keeping
with their martial traditions, had 'recruited a corps of militiamen and
an exceedingly good military brass band. They hold annual drill, and, in
all probability, if the country required their services, they would be
among the first to go into action.'[26] Her later salute to a Sioux chief, 'a
greater Britisher,' who gave her a much-desired scalp trophy only
because her forefathers had fought for the Crown, extended the theme
of faithfulness into the prairies.[27] When in 1910 she arranged for the
new Squamish leader, Mathias Capilano, to meet Prime Minister Laurier
during the latter's visit to Vancouver, her introduction recalls her testament to Ontario's Brant. Chief Capilano also combined an 'admirable
character, and extraordinary devotion to his own people' with the 'most
unswerving friendliness to the White man and loyalty to the Crown.'[28]
As a regular visitor to the Squamish Reserve, Johnson also knew of the
'energy and enterprise,' 'kindly hospitality,' and patriotism of Líxwelut
or Mary Agnes Capilano, 'the Grand Old Woman' of British Columbia.
Despite the confirmation of the ongoing tragedy of Aboriginal Canada's
contact with European imperialism in the untimely deaths of twelve of
her fifteen children, she preserved an honoured place for the portraits
of King Edward and Queen Alexandra given to her husband, Su-á-pu-
luck, during his 1906 London visit.[29] Such well-tested loyalty called on
Canada and the British Empire to keep faith with Aboriginal peoples.

   Servility was out of the question; quite the contrary, as Johnson made
clear in the Mohawk hero of her poem 'As Red Men Die,' who 'bends to
death but *never* to disgrace.' He may be 'Captive! But *never* conquered;
Mohawk brave/Stoops not to be to *any* man a slave.' Unlike 'the white
or black man you happen to tip,' the contemporary Indian is not readily
reduced to 'servility and urbane oilyness.'[30] Aboriginal peoples may
have met a 'great all-conquering race,' but, having 'fought, and bled,
and died to hold the western continent against an incoming eastern
power, as England's sons would battle and fall to-day, were their own
mother country threatened with a power that would eventually annihi-
late, subject – then alas! absorb their blood, their traditions, their
nation, until naught promises to remain save a memory,' they are in no
way diminished. In face of the terrible threat to their survival, fierce
resistance to 'French and English invaders' is entirely justified. 'The Iroquois got a bad name for ferocity and blood thirstiness in the early days
of American history, but I can tell you reader, that those Indian warriors
were savage with a righteous patriotism, and that they won the respect of

the whole world by the way they contended and wrestled to retain their forest home, their game, their gods.'[31] Johnson's poems 'The Cattle Thief' and 'A Cry from an Indian Wife,' with their insistence on the legitimacy of resisting the theft of 'our land and our country,' ring with the same passion. The British commitment to freedom and justice which her friend Charles Mair celebrates in 'Tecumseh' is shown to be utterly delinquent in poems which speak back to the foreign intruders.

Despite growing evidence to the contrary, Pauline Johnson hoped for better times. In her role as conciliator, she represents the two peoples who constitute her own mixed heritage as having much to learn from one another. The Iroquois, with the 'bluest blood in their veins that America boasts ... no imported nobility but a native American aristocracy that counted itself ancient at Hiawatha's time,' were always inspirational.[32] Whenever she ranked the Native cultures of the New World, her ascription of superiority to her own tribe revealed her imprinting with the notions of racial hierarchies that infected the thinking of both Europeans and First Nations in her day. At the same time, Johnson credits Natives in general as having much to offer fair-minded newcomers. For many decades there had been a 'brotherly exchange of many things,' sometimes including shots but more often corn, lacrosse, and canoeing.[33] Benefits, however, went far beyond the land and its products. Native society above all constituted a moral resource offering redemption to a European civilization compromised by capitalist excess.[34]

Whatever the meaning of her intermittent adherence to the Anglican faith in which she eventually died, Johnson frequently highlights the virtues of Aboriginal religion. As is often the case when it comes to issues of morality, she cites the Iroquois traditionalists, the Onondaga, as the model: 'Their standard of morality is much higher than that of the whites in a similar state of life.' These outstanding, high-minded pagans of the Grand River Territory are, to forge a comparison her White listeners might appreciate, 'Unitarians with a dread of their God, without revolting practices or repugnant sacrifice.'[35] In a similar spirit, and in an unusual departure from turn-of-the-century women writers' tendency to sentimentalize and anthropomorphize animals, Johnson rehabilitates the Iroquois tradition of the white dog sacrifice. Far from barbaric, it embodies Native gratitude to '"The Great Spirit," a kind and loving God' for those who 'live good, honest, upright lives.'[36] Such faith, flourishing as it did long before Christianity came to North America, provides an enduring wellspring of Aboriginal superiority. In contrast, Christianity frequently fares badly at her hands. The furious woman of 'The Cattle Thief' denounces *a book* brought by the English settlers 'to save our souls from the sins *you* brought in your other hand,' while the villain of 'As It Was in the Beginning' is a 'Blackcoat' named Father Paul. But her critique of churches was destined to fall on deaf ears. The Reverend Egerton Ryerson Young, for example, eulogized her at length for voicing 'the thoughts of the Indian' and ignored her repeated criticism of his faith.[37]

In Johnson's idealized vision, courage, endurance, and generosity, as well as respect for women, distinguish and animate traditional North American societies. The old Iroquois game of lacrosse typically embodies Native potential: 'How thin and bloodless seem the Whiteman's sports in comparison with that splendid display of mental and bodily combat between these tawny throngs of Redskins.'[38] Hence in 1892 she enlarges upon the national significance of the growing popularity of the game:

> Canada has done wisely in appropriating this as her national sport. Her sons are hardy, muscular, active, three essentials in this wildest of all wild games, her climate favors it, her people are enthusiastic over it, it was born within her borders, and to-day boasts at least half a dozen teams that can defeat anything in the world that assays to meet them fair and square in the grand old game of lacrosse.[39]

Johnson's Native heroes and heroines further embody unmatched mental toughness which allows them, even in supposed defeat, to triumph over enemies, including European invaders. Her ironically titled prose account, 'Sons of Savages. Life-Training of the Redskin Boy-Child' sums up ideal manliness. Above all, the Native boy is taught 'the primitive courage that must absolutely despise fear,' instruction reinforced by training in religion, the hunt, medicine, and etiquette. The result is 'a brave, capable, well-educated gentleman, though some yet call him an uncivilized savage.' By echoing the familiar language of British social values, she claims equality for First Nations men.

Native customs offered other moral resources. Johnson is especially adamant about the significance of generosity. The west coast potlatch, outlawed by the federal government in 1885, is singled out for praise. Far from the waste and savagery chronicled by ignorant settlers, the potlatch demonstrates Aboriginal society's capacity to redistribute wealth from rich to poor, and the responsibility of those in power to those in need.[40] In sharp contrast to a dominant community obsessed with money, Native communities are idealized for their 'particular socialism ... they are taught that possession of means is nothing short of a crime if any known being is without such possessions ... There are consequently no Indian Carnegies or Rockefellers.'[41] As in the legend of 'The Deep Waters,' Native peoples willingly sacrifice for the greater good, in this case for the children of their community, who survive a great flood in the mythic past. Johnson's repeated reminders that the elderly receive respect and care similarly confirm Native virtue and contrast markedly with the brutal picture conveyed by such Euro-Canadian writers as Duncan Campbell Scott in his famous 1903 poem, 'The Forsaken.' She agrees with Su-á-pu-luck's appraisal of the newcomers: 'Their love of the gold was a curse.'[42] Such assessments highlight the imperfections of European capitalism that were worrying and energizing Canadian reformers like J.S. Woodsworth in the same years.

Another mark of superiority was the place of women in Indigenous culture. Johnson regularly repudiates the dominant European notion of Native women's oppression and ascribes gender equality to First Nations in general. From birth, whether in Squamish or Iroquois society, girls are portrayed as welcome. They grow up in a community of their own sex, secure in the knowledge of their importance as future mothers and producers. Unless Native men have been contaminated by European vices, women need not fear abuse since 'Indian marriages, particularly in the "uncivilized state,"' are reckoned 'proverbially happy.' Only when the 'white man's ways enter into the forest lodge, [do] domestic difficulties arise. Extravagance, social rivalry, whisky, love of display – these are what strike at the roots of Indian family felicity.' White women had reason to envy the power and authority wielded by their Native sisters. As Johnson emphasizes, in an observation that typically highlighted Iroquois superiority: 'In all the trails I have traveled to the White man's camping grounds I do not see that his women have the importance either in his council or in his camp, that we have long given to our womankind these many centuries.'[43]

In her humorous skits, whose contents probably owe more to mainstream critiques of social posturing than to a specifically First Nations' perspective, Pauline Johnson ridiculed pretensions to superiority. She was also alert to the exploitation of First Nations culture by profiteers. Natives knew full well that 'there are few who meet the North American Indians disinterestedly; if native life is studied at all it is generally for gain.' To be sure, Johnson is prepared to acknowledge welcome exceptions who 'show the world how the good old Indian character when unsullied by contamination with the vices of their white brethren, breathes nobility, romance and beauty, as forest pines in their native grandeur exhale a wild stimulating perfume.'[44] Intelligent good will is, however, more often wanting than practised in the imperial enterprise.

Culture, the first line of defence, needed special protection, for 'strip the Indian nation of its heredity, its romance, its legendary lore, its faith, and indeed all its mental and sentimental acquirements, and what is there left of man and manhood to work upon?'[45] At issue often was the education offered and, increasingly, imposed upon, Native children. Both Johnson's brothers had unhappily attended the Mohawk Institute, the residential school run by the Church of England. On her travels Johnson occasionally visited other such facilities including the Qu'Appelle Industrial School in Saskatchewan. Her short stories featuring Native pupils, such as 'As It Was in the Beginning,' 'The Shagganappi,' and 'Little Wolf-Willow,' condemn the prejudice and intolerance commonly found in Canada's classrooms. The Cree hero, 'Little Wolf-Willow,' refuses to assimilate, while admitting the usefulness of imperial knowledge in the modern world. His speech before a determined, if ultimately sympathetic, principal of a residential school puts the case simply and powerfully: 'I speak. I keep hair, good. I keep name Wolf-willow, good. I keep skin Indian color. I not white man's skin. English skin no good. My skin best, good ... I keep skin, better skin than white man. I keep skin, me.' In time, this integrity wins him the post of government interpreter on the reserve (a position held by Johnson's own father at Six Nations) trusted alike by White traders and the North-West Mounted Police. Most important of all, he is pictured as standing 'fast in the affection of his own Indian people. They never forgot the fact that, had he wished, he could have stayed with the white people altogether, that he was equal to them in English education, but he did not choose to do so – he was one of their own for all time.'

In contrast to the stories about the betrayal of Native women by White men, several later stories feature young male characters who cooperate with sympathetic Whites in linking Aboriginal and European cultures. The displacement in much of Johnson's twentieth-century work of religious by secular authorities, notably the North-West Mounted Police and governors general, testifies both to her growing anti-clericalism and to her recognition of the evolution of the new state. 'Good' White men, 'Indian loving' men, like the new Indian superintendent she urged Prime Minister Laurier to appoint at Six Nations in 1909, would work generously with Aboriginal leaders. Desirable public administrators shared Governor General Lord Dufferin's recognition of the 'distinct nationality' he found in the Iroquois Confederacy in 1874 and his 'trust

that the Indian subjects of her majesty will always take a similar pride
in preserving intact, from generation to generation, the distinctive
attributes of their national circumstances.'[46]

By the time she moved to Vancouver, however, Johnson had good reason to be disheartened by Canada's Indian policies. As the poem '"And
He Said, Fight On"' testifies, she did not readily surrender to despair.
While its defiance of death is usually regarded as a personal proclamation, akin to Dylan Thomas's 'Do Not Go Gentle into That Good Night,'
its emphatic militarism, much like the earlier 'As Red Men Die,' also
invites a political reading. Even as the speaker is left to 'fight alone, and
fall, and die,' her final words proclaim resistence: 'Capitulate? Not I.'
There are nations, such as those she cites in words remembered in 1913
by Ernest Thompson Seton, that death cannot defeat:

> Ours was the race that gave the world its measure of heroism, its standard
> of physical prowess. Ours was the race that taught the world that avarice
> veiled by any name is crime. Ours were the people of the blue air and the
> green woods, and ours the faith that taught men to live without greed and
> to die without fear. Ours were the fighting men that man to man - yes, one
> to three - could meet and win against the world. But for our few numbers,
> our simple faith that others were as true as we to keep their honor bright
> and hold as bond inviolable their plighted word, we should have owned
> America to-day.[47]

From her vantage point during the decades after Confederation,
Johnson feared that Native North America was dying. Mixed-race peoples might be its only heirs. In turning to this community, she confronted her own idealization of the unhyphenated Native, her
ambivalence about her own 'washed-out' skin.[48] The perfect Indian,
often the Iroquois matron or the chief with his 'purer pedigree, a
"bluer" blood, than any hand, British or French, that ever planted the
Red, White and Blue within his territory' haunts the narratives of this
Mixed-race author. Despite a career that depended on her ability to pass
back and forth across the colour line, Johnson knew the dangers of intimate race relations. At the end of the twentieth century one of her
admirers captured the continuing dilemma: 'New People are the survivors of five hundred years of colonial rule. Our grandmothers' bodies
were appropriated by the conquerors.'[49] While the female body in the
case of Emily Howells was White, Pauline Johnson knew that she too
represented the triumph of the European conqueror.

Occasionally, however, the daughter of Emily Howells and George

Johnson voiced hopes for the thousands like her in North America. Her short story 'The Shagganappi,' apparently written toward the end of her life, makes the case for those whom Louis Riel, the most famous Mixed-race Canadian of the nineteenth century, called 'the new nation.' It tells of the Métis boy, Fire-Flint Larocque, who 'was born to be a thing apart, with no nationality in all the world to claim as a blood heritage.' Alienation and loneliness end, significantly, with the blessing of the governor general. This superior British aristocrat, the best of his own people, hates the word '"breed" applied to human beings. It is a term for cattle and not men.' The 'loyal young heart reached out towards this great man' who redeems him with the words,

> 'you have blood in your veins that the world might envy,' he said slowly. 'The blood of old France and the blood of a great aboriginal race that is the offshoot of no other race in the world. The Indian blood is a thing of itself, unmixed for thousands of years, a blood that is distinct and exclusive. Few white people can claim such a lineage. Boy, try and remember that as you come of Red Indian blood, dashed with that of the first great soldiers, settlers and pioneers in this vast Dominion, that you have one of the proudest places and heritages in the world; you are a Canadian in the greatest sense of that great word ... Most of the people on the continent of America are of mixed nationality – how few are pure English or Scotch or Irish – or indeed of any particular race?'

Unusual in its explicit optimism towards the future of racial amalgamation, this passage lies at the heart of Pauline Johnson's ultimate aspirations for Canada. Both the Dominion and the Empire, like Britain before them, were great because of, not despite, their mixture of races.

A more recent generation of Native advocates argues that Mixed-race individuals enjoy the advantage of occupying 'the middle ... the place between two cultures, where any bridges of understanding will be constructed.' In the words of writer Kateri Damm, 'Mixed-bloods see with two sets of eyes, hear with two sets of ears,' and can therefore function as "bilingual" interpreters.' Paul Seesequasis takes the image one step further when he argues playfully that the 'no-man's land between Indian and white,' is the realm of the trickster. 'We are not victims. We are survivors' becomes the motto of those who can use humour to subvert the system.[50]

The Empire

Primary as it might have been, Johnson's dedication to Native people was never her only loyalty. Her hopes for the future rested with a more inclusive British Empire. Indians and Mixed-race peoples may be the worthy first daughters and sons of the North American landscape but Britain too had much to offer. In ways that would be difficult to imagine for subsequent generations of Native champions, she could be celebrated as both 'a great daughter of the flag' and 'Indian to the core.' This dual loyalty, profoundly debilitating as it may often have been for the private person, informed almost all her life.

As a child Johnson knew Britain first as the birthplace of her beloved mother and subsequently through immersion in the works of Woodsworth, Byron, Shelley, Swinburne, and the great popular authors of the nineteenth century. For her, as for many others, 'the English literary text functioned as a surrogate Englishman in his highest and most perfect state.'[51] Her early poem 'My English Letter' articulates the strong sense of familial attachment that characterized much of her response to the country whose designation as 'Motherland' was, for her, more than a figure of speech.

Naught would I care to live in quaint old Britain,
These wilder shores are dearer far to me,
Yet when I read the words that hand has written,
The parent sod more precious seems to be ...

Although I never knew the blessed favour
That surely lies in breathing English air.

Imagination's brush before me fleeing,
Paints English pictures, though my longing eyes
Have never known the blessedness of seeing
The blue that lines the arch of English skies.

While at least one British reviewer found it 'strange' that Johnson 'sings of England just as sincerely as some English colonist might do,' such sentiments resonate with all her mother's influence.[52] They were also rooted in the practical realities of someone trying to make a living as a Canadian writer. The Dominion's small markets, not to mention its colonial attitudes, demanded success in either London or New York. For the heir of United Empire Loyalists, the former would always be far more congenial. Her unrealized dreams of tours to Jamaica and Australia similarly testify to the romantic lure of an empire upon which the sun never set.

In 1894, aided by a gold purse from Brantford fans, the thirty-three-year-old poet tested her worth in the London salons. Like Ida Wells (1862–1931), a leading Mixed-race American abolitionist who remembered visiting England in the 1890s as 'being born again in a new condition. Everywhere I was received on a perfect equality with the ladies who did so much for me and my cause,'[53] Johnson discovered welcome sympathy and support. London, far from the day-to-day race politics of the United States or its own empire, and informed by a strong anti-slavery and Aboriginal protectionist community, embraced her. In *Set in Authority*, Sara Jeannette Duncan satirized the London welcome lavished on a controversial Indian judge, who is adopted by society as a kind of Asiatic Prince.[54] She questions the sincerity of a liberal-minded capital found that it cost little to be generous with exotics, whose presence satisfied a sense of imperial voyeurism.

Johnson was moved and intimidated in ways that many a literary aspirant from the colonies would have found familiar. While her upbringing as a member of Six Nations' Native aristocracy helped her cope with the British class system, she was vulnerable to the pretensions of other forms of rank. As she explained in a letter to a friend:

> I have met all sorts of Lords and things, and found them for the most interesting but I much prefer *Thinking* London to *Aristocratic* London. Tho' I feel more at my ease in the latter, Thinking London is so very clever, so far beyond me, so great, so penetrating that I seek refuge in my own blood and the land of my birth, and they are good enough to be blinded by my posings and mistake my fads, my love of [my] race, my Indian politics for exceeding brightness and the outcry of extreme originality and talent. Bah! and without enough education to pad my intellect, let alone form the substance ... But the great minds make me feel so illiterate ... They do not mean to do so but they do, not so with my Lord and My Lady. They invite me to their houses as a great American Indian authoress, an astoundingly clever poet, a 'marvelous new interpreter of verse,' etc., and I go and am looked up to and dined and wined and I amount to a little tin God, for the titled people pretend not to literature. Therefore am I great. Ah! I feel quite a Giant, a King in the nobleman's drawing room, I feel a worm, a veritable *nothing* in the critic's den or the author's library.[55]

Even her beloved canoe played a role in imperial one-upmanship. To her consternation, she lost a bet that a Peterboro' canoe could not be found in London's Whiteley department store.

Not surprisingly, Johnson cherished every mark of regard. When the

British critic Theodore Watts-Dunton complimented two poems in *Songs of the Great Dominion*, he became, rather to his surprise, a lifetime hero. Long interested in Gypsies, he may have singled out Johnson in part because he saw her as similarly exotic. This imperialist advocate of a Greater Britain hailed her contributions as a confirmation of his belief 'that the great romance of the twentieth century would be the growth of the mighty world-power of Canada.'[56] The Dominion's poetry, he argued, especially that of its Aboriginal daughters and sons, had the potential to make English verse the envy of other languages. While the British Empire could not rival the muse of nations like Italy and Greece in terms of human history, the colonies and, more particularly Canada, offered privileged access to 'Nature's face.' Represented as this is in *Songs of the Great Dominion* by a daughter of 'The Mohawks of Brantford! that splendid race,' Watts-Dunton's accompanying observation that Canadian inspiration is 'uncoloured by associations of history and tradition' is markedly unsettling. And yet, for all this Englishman's cavalier disregard for the Aboriginal history she insisted upon, Pauline Johnson remained sufficiently in thrall to 'London Centre,' the capital of English language culture for colonials like herself, to honour him with a request that he introduce *Flint and Feather.*

This fascination, shared by many who work on the margins of empire, also surfaced when Johnson succumbed to the lure of British aristocracy. Monarchs, lords, and ladies were celebrated by her pen and, in her search for official mentors, often received appeals for patronage. This courting owed much to the continuing uncertainty of the performer's finances but something as well to her preoccupation with morality and station. As with the blue-blooded Iroquois, she characterized British aristocrats as likely to be endowed with a certain inner nobility that gave them special insight into the human character and, more particularly, appreciation of the intrinsic merits of Native North Americans. Such is the case of the British governor general who repudiates the epithet 'breed' in 'The Shagganappi.' Another vice-regal character, Lord Dunbridge in 'The Saucy Seven,' displays the same kind sensibility and wins the allegiance of a Euro-Canadian boy. Lord Aberdeen, the real-life governor general of Canada in the 1890s, is similarly saluted as a kind and wise man.[57] The affinity between Natives and British aristocrats were reiterated when Queen Victoria's son, Prince Arthur of Connaught, a future governor general himself, was installed as an Iroquois chief by Pauline's father and the Six Nations Confederacy in 1869.

The kinship invoked by an honorary chieftainship, or adoption, suggested Johnson's optimistic view of empire as an essentially familial relationship. Just as other Canadian imperialists presented Canada as Britain's eldest daughter, Johnson interpreted ties between the periphery and centre as essentially those of kin and she anticipated tangible family benefits. In particular, she imagined a future union with Newfoundland, which she hailed as 'Our Sister of the Seas' (1902). Surveying its resources while on a money-losing tour in 1901, she advocated that the island join Canada's constellation of former colonies. For islanders who fearfully contemplate mainland designs, she offers reassurance. The scenario invokes all the naturalness of a family reunion: 'You loyal little sea-girt sister of ours, we in Canada don't see you half as often as we should, but the ties are being daily more closely woven. Modern enterprise and capital have placed you nearer to us now; we can lean towards each other, clasp hands, and some day perhaps our fingers will forget to loose their clinging, and we will walk hand in hand throughout the years.' Here, as elsewhere, the Empire promises ambitious colonials the prospect of an enlarged future.

The Empire's chiefs are not merely high-ranking but, like nature's aristocrats at Grand River, are essentially benevolent matriarchs and patriarchs, far above the lesser mortals thrown up by democratic vagaries. Not surprisingly, George the Fifth, 'England's Sailor King' is, from Pauline's perspective, both heroic and modest, a natural leader and deserving father of his people. His mother, Queen Victoria, emerges as a potent symbol for a woman raised in, but not legitimated by, matrilineal Iroquois society. An enthusiastic imperialist, Johnson joined in Britain's 'invention of tradition' in the late nineteenth century with its 'growth in popular veneration for the monarchy.'[58] In her hands the aging British monarch appears as the supreme mother figure, 'a monument to perfect womanhood.' Under Victoria's banner of purity and honour, the Empire conferred the 'benediction of vast liberties' on its offspring. Superior morality, rather than armed might, secures 'empires in the heart,' a 'nobler kingdom' for this 'Sweet English mother on old England's throne!'[59] Johnson's idealization and domestication of the Crown including other references to Edward VII as the 'Great White Father,'[60] reveal something of sentimental chauvinism and something of naive wistfulness. If monarchs were indeed good parents, the Empire should provide a safe home for all its children. If there were Aboriginal victims, then British royalty had failed, something which Johnson was not prepared, at least publicly, to contemplate. A Euro-Canadian contributor to *Songs of the Great Dominion*, Frederick George Scott, was not so

careful. His poem 'Wahonomin: The Indian's Jubilee Hymn to the
Queen' quickly summed up the reign of the Great Mother as a disaster
for the First Nations who 'bow our heads in silence. We must die.'[61] Out-
right condemnation of the monarch was more difficult, however, for
someone, who, like many at Six Nations, made historic loyalty a critical
justification for fair treatment. It was safer to imply that the intentions of
a queen or a king were being circumvented by inferior lieutenants, notably Canada's White settlers, administrators, and politicians. This faith
allowed Johnson to remain an imperialist while excoriating individual
acts of empire.

Nevertheless, she did not escape the disenchantment that dogged
many Canadian imperialists. In 1906, while on a London tour, she was
reported as bitterly deploring 'England's seeming indifference to her
colonies' and prophecying 'a day, not far hence, when all too late she
will learn to regret her aloofness.'[62] Such sentiments reflected the hard
experience of a colonial performer who no longer found ready audiences at the centre of Empire, and the growing disillusionment of a
Native champion and imperialist.

Canadian Born

Ultimately, Pauline Johnson turned to the 'Young Canada' she celebrated in her poem 'Brant. A Memorial Ode' to realize her aspirations
for a better world. With this land, not the old, rested her greatest hopes
for the future. While Natives always stood near the heart of the nation
she tried to call into being, she also made room for superior newcomers
who likewise would elevate Canada above both Britain and the United
States. No group won praise more the Mounties. She highlighted their
virtues and contributed to the forging of the powerful mythology that
quickly surrounded the North-West Mounted Police after its creation in
1873 to secure the prairies from the Americans, safeguard White settlement, and control the Native population.[63] The 'Riders of the Plains,'
she emphasized, bore the critical responsibility to sustain imperial traditions of justice and fair play. Although she occasionally made jokes at
their expense, she never questioned, as far as we know, the significance
of the Mounties in guaranteeing Aboriginal submission to imperial Canada. Like the Iroquois, they too are portrayed as nature's aristocrats and
upholders of manly ideals. Even-handed and heroic, they defend the
weak: the Indian against the White man, the Canadian against the
American. Two short stories, 'The Little Red Messenger' and 'Little
Wolf-Willow' suggest a natural alliance between His Majesty's Indian

subjects and their red-coated champions, a pact without equal in the massacre-blooded land to the south where, ironically, these stories were first published.

A model fraternity, the NWMP is shown to honour superior woman-hood. Mrs Lysle, modelled on the wife of an actual Mountie officer, wins respect and affection as the 'Mother o' the Men' in the short story of the same name. Her high-minded example inspires young recruits to resist alcohol and meet her elevated moral standards. Idealized as sons and brothers, thus desexualized and rendered safe (certainly in compar-ison with the American forces of law and order), the Mounties keep the 'the peace of our people and the honour of British law.' Women and Natives alike rest safe under their protection.

Johnson similarly celebrates the perfected Englishman, the imperial hero of her imagination in the short story 'The King Georgeman' (1911). Constantine, soon comfortably shortened to Con, the androgy-nous protagonist of the title, surmounts early suspicions about his effeminacy and readily settles into life on a British Columbia ranch. In the course of a few short pages, he wins approval for physical pluck and the 'quick flashing English temper that was always aroused at the sight of injustice, of unmanliness, or of underhand dealings.' Such virtues command Indians' respect and reform villains. Con and his Canadian cousin Banty demonstrate what Johnson identified as 'one of the great secrets of England's success with savage races ... her consideration, her respect, her almost reverence of native customs, ceremonies, and poten-tates ... she freely accords like honour to her subjects, it matters not whether they be white, black, or red.' The Lillooet hunter, 'The Eena,' Banty's confidant, is employed to inspire and legitimate a higher man-hood and, with it, the claims of the British born to be true sons of the new land.

Con and his brethren might well have been among the British regu-lars and the Canadian militia – 'all are young and beautiful and good' – who suppressed the prairie rebellions in 1885, a campaign that Pauline Johnson recalled with considerable bitterness. She attempted to recon-cile her dual loyalties by suggesting that repression of the tribes and Métis came not from design but from forgetfulness and ignorance. As the poem 'A Cry from an Indian Wife' explains with a discernible tinge of irony,

... their new rule and council is well meant.
They but forget we Indians owned the land
From ocean unto ocean; that they stand

Upon a soil that centuries ago
Was our sole kingdom and our right alone.
They never think how they would feel to-day, ·
If some great nation came from far away,
Wresting their country from their hapless braves,
Giving what they gave us – but wars and graves.

In a lesser-known poem, 'A Request,' addressed to 'the noble society known as "The Woman's Auxiliary of Missions of the Church of England in Canada," who are doing their utmost in the good work of sending Missionaries to the Crees and Blackfoot,' Johnson tells the same story from a somewhat different perspective. The rebellions and their repression are explicitly identified as a civil war, an attack on 'fellow-country-men,' without honour. The winners' 'laurel wreath,' fragrant with 'Indian blood, its glory Indian lives,' can only be remedied by 'another band of men,' missionaries who will not treat Canada's 'Indian wards as foes.'

This trust in churches did not much outlast the decade. Johnson's powerful portraits of the starvation of the plains tribes in the poems 'The Cattle Thief,' 'The Corn Husker,' and 'Silhouette' and in her short story 'Little Wolf-Willow,' link death unequivocally to 'might's injustice.' The conquest of North America testifies ultimately only to European ignorance and arrogance. Revealingly, it is the Cree chief in 'The Cattle Thief' who becomes the lion, the symbol of imperial rule, while the British settlers are reduced to a 'pack of demons.' By such reversals of the expected, Pauline Johnson suggests that Natives, not newcomers, embody the imperial ideal.

Johnson's admiration for the martial qualities of her Mohawk ancestors, not to mention her hopes for imperial justice, help explain early enthusiasm for imperial conflicts, first in the Crimea and then in South Africa. The first is treated solely as a heroic venture in the poem 'What the Soldier Said.' Later, however, recital pieces such as 'The Riders of the Plains' and 'Canadian-born,' which she used in Boer War fundraisers, reminded audiences that responsibilities accompanied dominion. Like the Iroquois warriors she defended in London in 1894, Canadian combattants needed to show that justice was on their side. According to the conventions of her era, Johnson credited her sex with a special responsibility for peace, but men too could come to see the terrible costs of conflict. In the short story 'Gun-shy Billy,' she uses a heroic veteran to question the jingoism of the South African campaign. In 'The

Brotherhood,' a White admirer admits that Natives offer a lesson: 'some of us are always at war. If we are not fighting here, we are fighting beyond the great salt seas. I wish we had more of your ways, Queetah – your Indian ways. I wish we could link a silver chain around the world; we think we are the ones to teach, but I believe you could teach us much.'

Like many observers in her own time and in ours, Johnson manifested considerable ambivalence about armed conflict. On some occasions it was abhorred, on others it appeared legitimate. Valid causes, like the prairie tribes' defence of their land in 1885 and the redress of the injured, like Ojistoh in the poem of the same name, required action. In her views, Pauline Johnson seems close to Nellie McClung, who opposed war on principle but who came to support World War One on the basis of the brutal conduct of the German enemy. Canada could in good conscience participate in a 'just war.'[64]

Johnson's complicated response to military matters was further displayed when she looked beyond Britain and Canada. Taking imperial France to task for its anti-semitism in the infamous Dreyfus Affair, she associates the European military with the moral failure of the 'vampire-like' French army in '"Give Us Barabbas."' Another poem, 'The Man in Chrysanthemum Land,' written in response to Japan's defeat of Russia in 1904–5, appears at first glance a ditty only too reminiscent of Rudyard Kipling's jingoism. Read more closely, its lines prove more frankly iconoclastic: 'the brave little Jap,' 'the Brownie,' has beaten the White man. On the sidelines at last, Uncle Sam and John Bull can no longer take superiority for granted. Such verse hints at unusual identification with others encountering European imperialism. Unfortunately, little more is known about Johnson's interest in the global politics of racism.

Similarly difficult to reconstruct, if somewhat more obvious, is Johnson's awareness that poverty and despair are not the preserve of any race. The greed and ignorance that condemn some to starvation on reserves count other victims as well. Like many another social critic of her day, including red tory imperialists, she views large cities with deep suspicion.[65] Little more than 'swarming human hives' they deal death with 'their fetid airs, their reeking streets, their dwarfed and poisoned lives.' Two poems focus on generic women, one a prostitute, another old and poor, who embody the mercilessness of the new industrial order. In 'The City and the Sea,' a young girl lies drowned, 'her broken body spoiled and spurned of man.' In 'Workworn,' a humble figure 'has no rest, no joy to call her own.' In a more sentimentalized and melodramatic vein, the 1892 'Story of a Boy and a Dog' fictionalizes the desperate plight of Toronto's 'ragged, dirty Fresh Air Fund youngsters.' Homeless, starving boys are only temporarily rescued by the city's leading children's charity. While 'sweet-faced women' volunteers are depicted sympathetically, Johnson pillories 'an elderly jovial clergyman, who would teasingly pretend that he was going to keep all the cake for himself, just to see the horror in the wide hungry eyes of those poor children from the slums, whose thin little lips had never know what it was to close over anything but a crust. She saves her greatest irony for the conclusion: a thoughtless middle-class young man rallies from the pneumonia he contracted saving a street child's dog, while the child, after donating his last pitiful meal to his benefactor, succumbs to cold and starvation.

Outrage at the plight of society's outcasts was sharpened by Johnson's visits to her beloved London. She could never forget the violence, the abuse, and the poverty of the most terrible slums in the world. While such pest holes thrived, she wondered how British bishops 'dare to send missionaries to our Indians in Canada.'[66] Like many Anglo-Canadians, she harboured mixed feelings about the arrival of the Empire's poor. In 'The Barnardo Boy,' Buck, whose name offers a suggestive hint of a common indigeneity, is saved from London's harsh streets to find full redemption in the comfortable home of a Canadian doctor and his saintly daughter. Rescuing his benefactors from thieves, he is readily transformed from lowly Cockney servant to worthy son of the house. In this adoption, Buck is effectively born again as a far better Canadian.

Not all prospects are so rosy, however. On a visit to Muskoka with a missionary friend, Johnson was outraged at free lands taken up by 'the most illiterate and immoral European immigrants.' Here at home in the Canadian forests, she claims to realize 'for the first time the awfulness of suffering in the "lower classes,"' a class of 'city savages.' However, she seems more impressed by the 'thieves, murderers, bigamists, law breakers of every color and shade of crime, who had fled from detection in the Northern land to bury their past and themselves in this wilderness.' Former London slum-dwellers overturn notions of European superiority. 'Talk of your heathen in Africa! He is nearer the light of civilization than those wretched Whitechapelites, that poison the airs of the great clean forest lands, and rot the morals of the simple but blameless Indian.' She admonished the 'Bishops' and the government for permitting 'Europe's criminals [to] settle our wastes and people our wilds.'[67]

If contact with Great Britain is far from an unmixed blessing, the other empire to which many Canadians, characterized as 'continental-ists,' gravitated in these years is yet more problematic. The United States provided an increasingly crucial market for Canada's writers, home as it was to major publishers and lively lecture circuits. The *Mother's Magazine*, one of the most receptive outlets for Johnson's work, reported a circulation of some six hundred thousand in 1909. By the time she died four years later, such opportunities had made Johnson one of the most widely read Indian authors in the United States. What current American critics eager to adopt an Indigenous author largely fail to note, however, are her substantial reservations about the ancient foe who had driven the Iroquois United Empire Loyalists out of their original territories in the Mohawk Valley and whose Indian wars routinely captured headlines while Johnson grew up. Uncertain relations with William D. Howells, the most prominent of her mother's American kin, coupled with U.S. audiences whom she dismissed as 'very uncultured, very ignorant, very illiterate,' also counted against the southern giant. After one unfortu-nate American tour, she angrily wrote that 'daily I grow to be more and more of a "Canuck" and Mr. McRaye is quite rabid as a Canadian patriot now.'[68]

Like many Canadian authors, both before her time and after, Johnson could not escape the temptation to credit the Dominion with a better record in its treatment of Indians and with better manners generally. The United States, stripped in the Revolution of the moral inspiration provided by the British monarchy with its traditions of justice and ser-vice, and rejecting sources of Indigenous moral authority, has some-times been regarded by critical Canadians as morally bankrupt. In such suspicions, Johnson shared the attitude of Conservative imperialists such as Stephen Leacock. Both believed that 'southward' always lurked 'a rival's stealth.'[69] The massive influx of Americans into the Canadian west before World War One occasioned real worry to such nationalist observers. While travelling across Saskatchewan, Johnson recorded meeting one Yankee who bragged that the stars and stripes would soon follow. The Native United Empire Loyalist immediately responded with a threat to shoot it down. In Canada, Indians were loyal, she reminded her readers, as they had no cause to be in the United States. She con-cluded with a warning: 'The Doukhobors will never harm us – but one shudders to think what this American element we are taking into the veins of our Territories, will some day develop into.'[70]

The same feelings flared when Johnson witnessed American arrogance at one Boston dinner. When told the NWMP were 'the pride of Canada's

fighting men,' her interrogator 'sneered and replied, "Ah! then they are
only some of British Lion's whelps. *We are not afraid of them..*"' Johnson's
rifle-ready response was her poem 'The Riders of the Plains':

> ... whelps in the Lion's lair?
> But we of the North will answer, while life in the North remains,
> Let the curs beware lest the whelps they dare are the Riders of the Plains;
> For these are the kind whose muscle make the power of the Lion's jaw,
> And they keep the peace of our people and the honour of British law.[71]

Subsequently, many a Canadian child, including one of this volume's
authors, happily grew up to counter American cousins by reciting
Johnson's verse, especially the memorable line from 'Canadian Born,'
'The Yankee to the south of us must south of us remain.'

Loyalist traditions, alongside a history which included opposition to
American Fenian raids in the 1860s, helped keep the Johnson family
sympathetic to the Conservative party. This partisanship, although badly
shaken by John A. Macdonald's suppression of western resistance in
1885, was never completely surrendered. While Pauline Johnson sought
mentors from all sides of the political spectrum as she plied her career
in North America and England, she voiced early support for the Conservatives' National Policy of trains, tariffs, and immigrants. Brantford
industrialists, eager to market products, supplied enthusiastic listeners
at the Canadian Manufacturers' Association's banquet in 1903. Here
their local poetess summed up their hopes in light after-dinner verse,
entitled 'Made in Canada.' 'We of the north,' she declaimed, are motivated neither by the 'cry for power,' nor 'the greed of gold.' We are but
ordinary men desiring only 'beef and bread, and a blanket, a pipe, a
mug and a fire.' We favour the home-grown and the home-made, rejecting alike 'the marts of Europe,' 'the trade of the eastern isles,' 'the
Yankee's corn and wine,' and the 'Asiatic's smiles.' And if we face opponents (presumably Liberal free traders but also possibly Uncle Sam)
well, 'we are the young and the strong, and who so fit for the fight as
we?' Such a faith leaves little room for the non-believer, for 'Canada for
Canadians is the creed that we call our own.'

A similar rhyme, entitled 'The Good Old N.[ational] P.[olicy]' (1896)
won Johnson first prize from the Industrial League for the best Conservative campaign song in 1896. To the tune of the suitably martial 'The
Red, White and Blue,' it assembles a highly unusual combination of
advocates:

And shoulder-to-shoulder we'll stand,
We may differ in creed and in colour,
French, and English and Red men are we,
But we're one for our cause and our country,
We are one for the good old N.P.

While its benefits were admitted to be spreading slowly, they would in time guarantee plenty to sons of 'city' and 'soil,' and good wages for the toiling workman. These lines are significant in suggesting how Indians, not to mention workers to whom Johnson normally pays little attention, could be incorporated in the construction of a nationalist ideology. Native peoples form a third founding partner, alongside French and English, in the nation's future prosperity.

Connections among the three peoples went beyond mere expediency, to the heart of the land itself. Like many imperialists of her day, Pauline Johnson shared a faith in northern climes. But she neglected Quebec within this paradigm. Barred by language from much of French Canada, her performances found ready audiences only in the English-dominated Eastern Townships. Winter visits to her brother Beverly in Montreal during the 1880s resulted in descriptions of the city's Victoria Rink and the toboggan slide on Mount Royal, but contact with the Québécois intelligentsia through her cousin Annie Howells's marriage into the Fréchette family seems to have translated into no further connection.

Yet if Quebec remained largely unknown to her, Johnson's espousal of a gospel of northernness provided a further way of linking the British and the Native peoples. In her eyes, the 'northern climate imparted a high degree of energy, vigour, and strenuousness' to Canadian as well as European 'tribes.'[72] In battles between northern and southern peoples, she asserted, 'the warrior blood of the North will always conquer. They are stronger, bolder, more alert, more keen.' Fortunately for pan-Indian, not to mention pan-Canadian, sentiments, north is a relative position. Everyone on the loyal side of the border is ultimately a member of 'the nation of the north' with its own natural flag, a Canadian 'ensign,' the 'blood-hued maple, straight and strong.' All need to guard against the 'craft and the strategy of the southern tribes,' which remain 'hard things to battle against.'[73]

Her cumulative experience of Britain, the United States, and especially the many regions of Canada, did much to encourage Johnson's identification with the Dominion. On her first trip west in the fall of 1894 following her visit to London she rhapsodized: 'This "great lone

land" of course is so absorbing, so lovely, so magnificent, that my eyes
forget the beauties of the older land. Ah! There are no such airs as these
in England, no such skies, no such forest scents and wild sweet per-
fumes.' Her emotions were all the more engaged when she came face to
face with the substantial Native presence in the west; in Ontario, Natives
were less commonly seen off reserve lands. Continuing her letter to an
Anglo-Canadian friend, she could only hint about the connection she
was making between an abundance of Natives and her love of the country as a whole: 'I cannot tell you how I love my Canada or how infinitely
dearer my native soil is to me since I started on this long trip. We are get-
ting into the Indian country now. Every town is full of splendid com-
plexioned Ojibawas, whose copper coloring makes me ashamed of my
washed out Mohawk skin, thinned with European blood, I look yellow
and "Chinesy" beside these Indians.'[74] Her encounter with tribes previously barely known to her was an important revelation, challenging any
Iroquois nationalism that did not readily encompass the diversity she
increasingly encountered. In the years before pan-Native movements
offered other alternatives and when the United States seemed so threatening to Indian hopes of any kind, a more inclusive Canada seemed full
of promise.

Pauline Johnson imagined a new nationality in which differences
would thrive. Just as the Manitoba historian W.L. Morton would later
argue in his powerful defence of the national character, *The Canadian
Identity*, unity does not require homogeneity at its base, as in the American melting pot, but rather fidelity to the British connection. The jingo-
istic title poem to Johnson's second volume of verse, 'Canadian Born,'
emphasizes common allegiance rather than common identity:

> Few of us have the blood of kings, few are of courtly birth,
> But few are vagabonds or rogues of doubtful name and worth;
> And all have one credential that entitles us to brag –
> That we were born in Canada beneath the British flag.
>
> We've yet to make our money, we've yet to make our fame,
> But we have gold and glory in our clean colonial name;
> And every man's a millionaire if only he can brag
> That he was born in Canada beneath the British flag.

Revealingly, she introduced one public recital of this poem by noting
that if there were 'unpatriotic citizens in Canada ... they are certainly

not the Iroquois Indians.'[75] In the Dominion, character counts, at least
for Europeans and Native peoples. Others, however, remain excluded.
Blacks and Asians only momentarily attract Johnson's gaze, where,
reduced to stereotypes, they receive no serious attention. Her imagined
Canada is more inclusive than most European imperialists were willing
to contemplate but, like its mistress, far from colour-blind.

Renewed alliances among those favoured groups who resisted incor-
poration and disappearance in the American experiment were essential
to Canada's future. In the concluding words of 'The Brotherhood,' 'The
Mohawks and the palefaces are brothers, under one law ... It is Canadian history.'[76] Many of Johnson's later short stories for youthful readers
involve young Euro-Canadians who envision a world beyond old prejudices, a world in which Aboriginal peoples have a respected place. In
turn, young Natives like Wolf-Willow and young Delorme in 'Maurice of
His Majesty's Mails' must find strategies to live and work with the newcomers. Their old world has changed forever and different solutions are
required. Noteworthy in this regard is Wolf-Willow's rescue of his starving Cree grandfather, who strongly resembles the murdered chief in the
poem 'The Cattle Thief.' The earlier unhappy ending is changed by the
intervention of another generation skilled in European ways but preserving the best qualities of their ancestors, including respect for the
elderly.

If Canada is to realize its potential, tolerance and understanding are
critical. In her short story 'The Lieutenant Governor's Prize,' Johnson's
boy hero, nicknamed Can, standing far from subtly for Canada, painfully learns important lessons in self-control and generosity. His triumph, symbolically that of the young nation itself, emerges only in the
mastery of his own desires for domination. His sacrifice and sensitivity
mean that his best friend, the son of the town's washerwoman, also gets
his chance in life. Significantly too, Can's maturation is confirmed when
the lieutenant-governor awards the prize to the poorer child and when
the nation's namesake is promised a much-desired canoe, a potent symbol in Johnson's personal iconography.

The setting for Johnson's most optimistic accounts is the west. While
she was initially 'a little afraid of the reception which a civilized Indian
would receive,' she soon found 'all that fear had been swept away ... as
the treatment accorded her had been one long service of kindnesses
both professional and social.'[77] As Walter McRaye remembered,
Johnson always loved the old western spirit of freedom and democracy;
'her lineage and love of the unconventional' made her 'a very part of

this west' and she was 'never happier than when touring these provinces.'[78] Her decision to establish headquarters in Winnipeg in the 1890s and in Vancouver in 1909 echoed the choices of many other easterners. For a Mixed-race woman, the region offered the additional appeal of highly visible Native populations, living off as well as on reserves. The two decades before World War One were boom times for the prairies and the coast. Their streets, crowded with newcomers and plentiful with dollars, embodied change and opportunity. Not surprisingly, Manitoba's capital provided the setting for Johnson's engagement to a businessman from a prominent eastern family, just the match which had eluded her back home.

Well before her first trip west of Ontario, Johnson, in 'The Happy Hunting Grounds' (1889), extended a revealing metaphor, discovering 'prairie billows' in the 'gold westland,' 'world of the bison's freedom, home of the Indian's soul.' In the excitement of escaping a conventional fate as an unmarried, aging daughter of a former hero and an impoverished widow, the Grand River migrant joined in the general exuberance of new beginnings. Perhaps on her frequent trips on the trains she styled 'Prairie Greyhounds' (1903), she too became one of 'the brave and the bold' who left a past that was 'dead' to reach out to 'a world of promise and hope and gain,/The world of gold, and the world of grain.' For Pauline Johnson, as for many Canadians, the territory beyond Superior's shores became the imagined country, 'the "Land to Be."' While she did not forget the hunger of the Plains tribes, when like 'The Indian Corn Planter' they tried to wrest 'some promise from the dormant soil,' she imagined seeds pledging 'large increase.' Perhaps at long last, Natives could share in the bounty unleashed by European technologies. Canada's fertile lands promised to realize the 'dream of the hungry millions, dawn of the food-filled age,' and an end to 'the starving tale of want.' This broad territory held room enough for both the cowboy, that 'unpolished, brilliant diamond,' and the Blackfoot, 'richly garmented' in 'a wardrobe that would represent a small fortune in New York or London.'[79]

As the century matured, however, the romance and freedom which Walter McRaye believed he and Johnson could find in the west seemed in retreat. The growing misery of the prairie tribes in the face of surging settlement and miserly government support of Native agriculture sadly echoed in the fading of her own hopes for a personal intercultural partnership. In the last years of her life, Johnson moved again farther westward to construct fresh hopes.

In expeditions like her five-hundred-mile coach ride to Barkerville,

British Columbia, in 1904, she discovered a new love. Feeling better than ever, seconded by an eager McRaye, and the toast of the Cariboo miners, ranchers, and Natives, Johnson saluted 'God's Country of the west,' and the province that was to become her home. In 'The Trail to Lilloet' the association of a 'placid English August' with 'God's copper-coloured sunshine' implies possible reconciliation of her dual loyalties. In British Columbia, where the tribes remained coherent forces, capable of acting in unison, she might find succour for both parts of her heritage. Hopes for tolerance infuse her otherwise unremarkable 1903 poetic celebration of Vancouver, 'my western queen.'[80] That very royal designation signalled how the former imperial periphery of Canada had moved to the centre of Johnson's aspirations for the new world. Her efforts to continue her family's role as conciliators between Natives and newcomers in her *Legends of Vancouver* and in her mentorship of Chief Mathias Capilano, whom she trained in public speaking, suggested a woman whose hopes of a more inclusive nation had not yet died. When her death occasioned a civic day of mourning, with Indians and newcomers lining the streets to convey last farewells, Johnson would have welcomed the promise of that symbolism.

In some ways, Pauline Johnson resembles the imperialists considered by Carl Berger in *The Sense of Power.* Her Canada is likewise the heir of British virtues. Reminiscent of the Canadian red tory tradition, she is haunted by the misery and materialism of modern industrial society. Intensely idealistic, she also counts on the awakening of friendship and mutual respect, rather than the overthrow of institutions, to secure justice. Virtuous elites, notably great men – British aristocrats and nature's nobles among the First Nations – and motherly women, she suggests, best inspire and lead a new nation facing the dangers of a powerful and corrupt rebel state to the south. Ordinary people would naturally follow such leaders. In obvious ways, as with her uneasiness about certain Europeans, Asians, and Blacks, this nationalist vision is intensely conservative. And yet, for all its very real shortcomings, her legacy remains unique among the Confederation generation of literary figures. No one else tried to take Canada and the Empire to task for their treatment of Native peoples, nor advocated an ongoing role for the original bicultural partnership between Native and European. More than the vast majority of her leading contemporaries, she envisioned the possibility of such fair play and inclusion.

Aboriginal attempts to find a place alongside White North America were of course not restricted to Pauline Johnson. Some Native women journalists in the United States championed inclusion and endeavoured to 'dismantle opposition between Native and white societies.'[81] In the years during which she wrote and performed, other representatives of Canadian tribes were also endeavouring to forge solutions to sharing a northern half of a continent. The Ojibwa leader Shingwaukonse developed an inclusive understanding of Canada. The Six Nations Mohawk John Brant-Sero returned from attempts to enlist in the South African campaigns to condemn racism in both South Africa and the United States and to claim 'a footing of perfect equality in Canada.'[82] Squamish Chief Su-á-pu-luck joined a generation and more of Native leaders in efforts to negotiate with Ottawa and the provincial capitals. Since Aboriginal peoples have never been of one voice in their confrontation with settler society, advocates envisioned many different courses and outcomes.[83] In the long interval between the defeat of Louis Riel, Big Bear, and Crowfoot, and the rise of the modern Indian movement in the mid-twentieth century, only one spokesperson found a national platform. While chiefs in her two home provinces, British Columbia and Ontario, slowly started to weave the beginnings of a pan-Indian response to the legacy of Confederation, Pauline Johnson stood almost alone in helping to keep mainstream Canadians from forgetting entirely the presence of a Native 'Other' in their midst.

Many Euro-Canadian sympathizers welcomed Pauline Johnson's association of their new land with an older history, for romantically linking newcomers and Natives. Some admirers, particularly feminists, also enthusiastically embraced her insistence on women's value. Canada, like the Iroquois and like women, has had to struggle for recognition. The survival of a marginal culture on the periphery of two powerful empires has often appeared uncertain. The few common myths of Euro-Canadians, including those about a relationship with First Nations that is different from and better than that of the Americans, gain resonance when articulated by a New Woman who also dared to envision fair treatment for her sex. Such hopes have kept Johnson and her writing popular long after other imperialists and most writers of her day have been largely forgotten.

For all such admiration, not many of Pauline Johnson's advocates, either during her lifeline or after, cared to contemplate egalitarian partnerships between settler and Native nations or between women and men. That message would have to be delivered many more times by her heirs. Some, like Beatrice Culleton, in her novel *In Search of April Raintree*, have taken up that task. Cheryl, her Métisse heroine, is asked by a naive White woman – 'Oh, I've read about Indians. Beautiful people they are. But you're not exactly Indians are you? What is the proper word for people like you?' Cheryl's reply reminds Canadians yet again of their many identities: '"Women," Cheryl replied instantly. "No, no, I mean nationality?" "Oh, I'm sorry. We're Canadians," Cheryl smiled sweetly.'[84] This ironic and matter-of-fact commentary on the inclusion of Natives and women in the nation recalls the long battle waged by Pauline Johnson. Today her modest monument in Stanley Park still looks westward, a reminder of that fairer future which the paddler from Six Nations wished for Canada.

Chronological List of
Pauline Johnson's Writings

Because Johnson kept few records, and published in many newspapers
and magazines that remain unindexed (if they have indeed survived),
the contents of this appendix can only be described as provisional.[1] This
list begins with dated publications, followed by undated publications,
unpublished writings, and untraced writings. Verse items are identified
as **v**.

DATED PUBLICATIONS

This list cites the first known publication of individual texts, as well as first
appearance in one of Johnson's books. Multiple appearances in periodicals are
occasionally noted as well. Because *Flint and Feather* (*FF*) reproduces both *The
White Wampum* (*WW*) and *Canadian Born* (*CB*), poems which appeared in either
of Johnson's first two books are not also marked *FF*.

WW: *The White Wampum.* London: John Lane, 1895
CB: *Canadian Born.* Toronto: Morang, 1903
LV: *Legends of Vancouver.* Vancouver: privately printed, 1911
FF: *Flint and Feather.* Toronto: Musson, 1912 (and later editions)
MM: *The Moccasin Maker.* Toronto: Briggs, 1913
Sh: *The Shagganappi.* Toronto: Briggs, 1913

1883
'My Little Jean,' reportedly *Gems of Poetry.*[2] **v**

1884
Gems of Poetry
'The Rift. By Margaret Rox,' Aug., 127. **v**

'Rover,' Dec., 190. **v**

Transactions of the Buffalo Historic Society
'The Re-interment of Red Jacket.' **v**

1885

Gems of Poetry

'Iris to Floretta,' June, 90 [later titled 'To Florette Maracle'[3]]. **v**
'The Sea Queen,' June, 95. **v**

The Week
'The Sea Queen,' 16 Apr., 315. **v**
'A Cry from an Indian Wife,' 18 June, 457; *WW.* **v**
'In the Shadows,' 17 Sept., 664; Lighthall, *Songs of the Great Dominion*, 1889; *WW.* **v**

1886

Souvenir pamphlet, 8 Oct.
'"Brant," A Memorial Ode,' **v**

The Week
'The Firs,' 21 Jan., 117. **v**
'Easter Lilies,' 22 Apr., 337. **v**
'At the Ferry,' 16 Sept., 670; Lighthall, *Songs of the Great Dominion*, 1889. **v**
'A Request,' 18 Nov., 821. **v**

1887

Musical Journal (Toronto)
'Life' (music by Arthur E. Fisher), 15 July, 108–9. **v**

The Week
'The Vigil of St Basil,' 7 Apr., 301; retitled 'Fasting,' *WW.* **v**

1888

Saturday Night
'My English Letter,' 17 Mar., 6; *WW.* **v**
'Easter, 1888' 31 Mar., 6; retitled 'Easter,' *WW.* **v**
'Unguessed,' 16 June, 6. **v**
'The Death-Cry,' 1 Sept., 6. **v**
'Keepsakes,' 29 Sept., 6. **v**
'The Flight of the Crows,' 13 Oct., 6; *WW.* **v**
'Under Canvas,' 17 Nov., 6; *WW.* **v**
'Workworn,' 8 Dec., 7; *WW.* **v**

'A Backwoods Christmas,' Christmas no., 12; retitled 'The Lumberman's Christmas.'[4] v

The Week
'Joe (A Sketch from Memory),' 24 May, 413; retitled 'Joe: An Etching,' *WW.* v
'Our Brotherhood,' 26 July, 559. v

1889

Globe
'Evergreens,' Dec., Xmas no., 6. v

Saturday Night
'The Happy Hunting Grounds,' 12 Jan., 6 [also 1891, Sept. 5, 6]; *WW.* v
'Close By,' 2 Feb., 6; *WW.* v
'Ungranted,' 27 Apr., 6; retitled 'Overlooked,' *WW.* v
'Old Erie,' 25 May, 7; retitled 'Erie Waters,' *WW.* v
'Shadow River,' 20 July, 6; *WW.* v
'Bass Lake (Muskoka),' 2 Aug., 7. v
'Temptation,' 24 Aug., 6.[5] v
'Fortune's Favors,' 14 Sept., 6. v
'Rondeau' ['Some bittersweet ...'], 16 Nov., 6. v
'Christmastide,' 21 Dec., 4; *WW.* v

The Week
'Nocturne,' 26 July, 534; *WW.* v

1890

Brantford Courier
'Charming Word Pictures. Etchings by an Idler of Muskoka and the Beautiful North,' signed Rollstone, 15 Aug., 4.
'Charming Word Pictures. Etchings by a Muskoka Idler,' signed Rollstone, 23 Aug., 2.
'Charming Word Pictures. Etchings by a Muskoka Idler,' signed Rollstone, 4 Sept., 2.

Saturday Night
'We Three,' 12 Apr., 7; retitled 'Beyond the Blue,' *CB.* v
'In April,' 26 Apr., 6. v
'For Queen and Country,' 24 May, 6. v
'Back Number [Chief of the Six Nations],' 14 June, 7.
'The Idlers,' 28 June, 18; *WW.* v
'With Paddle and Peterboro',' 28 June, 6.

'Depths,' 19 July, 6. **v**
'Day Dawn,' 9 Aug., 6; *FF.* **v**
' "Held by the Enemy," ' 23 Aug., 6. **v**
'With Canvas Overhead,' 30 Aug., 6.
'Two Women,' 20 Sept., 6. **v**
'A Day's Frog Fishing,' 27 Sept., 7.
'In October,' 11 Oct., 6; retitled 'October in Canada,' *Public Opinion*, 28 Sept.
  1894; *Living Age*, 23 Feb. 1895; *Massey's Illustrated*, Oct. 1895. **v**
' "Thro' Time and Bitter Distance," ' 13 Dec., 6; retitled ' "Through Time and
  Bitter Distance," ' *CB.* **v**
'As Red Men Die,' Christmas no., 32; *WW.* **v**

1891

Brantford Expositor
'A'bram,' Christmas no., 13, 16.

Dominion Illustrated
'Our Iroquois Compatriots,' May, 484.

Independent
'Re-Voyage,' 2 July, 1 [also 18 July, *Brantford Expositor*]; *WW.* **v**
'At Husking Time,' 24 Sept., 30 [also 31 Oct., *Saturday Night*, 6]; *WW.* **v**

Outing
'The Camper,' Sept., 480; *WW.* **v**
'Ripples and Paddle Plashes: A Canoe Story,' Oct., 48–52.

Saturday Night
'The Last Page,' 3 Jan., 6. **v**
'The Showshoer,' 7 Feb., 7. **v**
'Outlooking,' 28 Feb., 6. **v**
'The Seventh Day,' 21 Mar., 6. **v**
'The Vagabonds,' 9 May, 6; *WW.* **v**
'Prone on the Earth,' 6 June, 9.
'In Days to Come,' 25 July, 6.[6] **v**
'Striking Camp,' 29 Aug., 7.
'The Pilot of the Plains,' Christmas no., 36; *WW.* **v**

Weekly Detroit Free Press
'Canoeing,' 2 July, 1.

Young Canadian (Montreal)
'Star Lake,' 22 Apr., 198. **v**

1892

Belford's Magazine
'Wave-Won,' Aug., 415–16; *WW*

Brantford Expositor
'Forty-Five Miles on the Grand,' Christmas no., 17, 20.

Dominion Illustrated
'Indian Medicine Men and their Magic,' Apr., 140–3.

Lake Magazine
'Penseroso,' Aug., 16; *WW*.[7] **v**

Outing
'Outdoor Pastimes for Women,' columns in the 'Monthly Record' supplement.[8]

Saturday Night
'A Story of a Boy and a Dog,' 9 Jan., 3.
'Rondeau. The Skater,' 23 Jan., 6. **v**
'Glimpse at the Grand River Indians,' 20 Feb., 7.
'The Song My Paddle Sings,' 27 Feb., 7; *WW*.[9] **v**
'At Sunset,' 7 May, 6; *WW*. **v**
'Rainfall,' 6 Aug., 6; *WW*. **v**
'Sail and Paddle,' 20 Aug., 7.
'The Avenger,' Christmas no., 15. **v**

Sunday Globe
'A Strong Race Opinion: on the Indian Girl in Modern Fiction,' 22 May, 1.

Weekly Detroit Free Press
'On Wings of Steel,' 4 Feb., 1.
'A Brother Chief,' 12 May, 1.
'The Game of Lacrosse,' 14 July, 1.
'Reckless Young Canada,' 22 Dec.

1893

American Canoe Club Yearbook
'The Portage.' **v**

Canadian Magazine
'The Birds' Lullaby,' Mar., 72; *WW*. **v**

Dominion Illustrated
'A Red Girl's Reasoning,' Feb., 19–28; retitled 'A Sweet Wild Flower,' *Evening Star* (Toronto), 18 Feb.; *MM*.

Illustrated Buffalo Express
'Sail and Paddle. The Annual Meeting of the Canoe Association,' Aug. or Sept.

Outing
'Outdoor Pastimes for Women,' columns in the 'Monthly Record' supplement.[10]
'A Week in the "Wild Cat,"' Oct., 45–8.

Saturday Night
'The Mariner,' 25 Mar., 12; *CB.* v
'Brier,' 1 Apr., 8; *WW.* v
'Canoe and Canvas,' 2 Sept., 6.
'Princes of the Paddle,' 9 Sept., 6.
'Wolverine,' Christmas no., 24; *WW.* v

Weekly Detroit Free Press
'The Song My Paddle Sings,' 15 June, 1; abbreviated version, retitled 'Canoeing in Canada,' n.p., n.d. (clipping, Trent University).

1894

Acta Victoriana
'In Freshet Time,' Feb., 148.[11] v

Art Calendar, illus. Robert Holmes.
'Thistledown,' *CB.*[12] v

Globe
'There and Back, by Miss Poetry (E. Pauline Johnson), and Mr Prose (Owen A. Smily),' 15 Dec., 3–4. Includes: 'Benedictus' [reprinted in *Canadian Magazine,* July 1913, 278], 'Curtain,' 'Fire Flowers' [*CB*], 'The Gopher,' His Majesty the West Wind,' 'Kicking Horse River,' 'The Leap of the St Marie' [retitled 'Where Leaps the St Marie,' *CB*], 'Little Vancouver,' 'The Prairie,' 'Rondeau: Crow's Nest Pass' [retitled 'At Crow's Nest Pass,' *CB*], 'Silhouetted' [retitled 'Silhouette,' *CB*], 'Summer' [retitled 'Harvest Time,' *CB*], 'The Wolf' [*FF*]. v

Harper's Weekly
'The Iroquois of the Grand River,' 23 June, 587–9.

Ladies' Journal
'In Gray Days,' Feb., 7; *FF.* v

Outing
'Moon-Set,' Oct., 43; *WW.*[13] v

The Varsity
'Marsh-Lands,' 17 Dec., 99; as 'Marshlands,' *WW.* v

The Week
'The Cattle Thief,' 7 Dec., 34; *WW.* **v**

1895

Black and White
'The Lifting of the Mist,' 28 Dec., 839; *FF.* **v**

Brantford Expositor
'The Six Nations.' souvenir no.

Globe
'The Races in Prose and Verse, by Miss Poetry and Mr Prose,' 1 June, 11.
   Includes: 'Boots and Saddles,' 'The Favorite,' 'In the Boxes,' 'The Last
   Hurdle,' 'Perspective.' **v**

Halifax Herald
'Iroquois Women of Canada,' 1 Oct. [also *Brantford Expositor,* 8 Oct.].

Our Animal Friends
'From the Country of the Cree,' Sept., 14.

The Rudder
'Sou'wester,' Jan., 5. **v**
'Canoe and Canvas. I,' Feb., 34.
'Canoe and Canvas. II,' Mar., 87–8.
'Canoe and Canvas. III,' Aug., 184.
'Canoe and Canvas. IV,' Oct., 241–2.
'Becalmed,' Oct., 242. **v**

The Year Book
'The White and the Green.'[14] **v**

The White Wampum
Previous publication unknown: 'Dawendine,' 'Ojistoh.' **v**

1896

Black and White
'Low Tide at St Andrews,' 5 Sept., 298; *CB.* **v**
'The Quill Worker,' 31 Oct., 558; *CB.* **v**

Daily Mail and Empire
'The Good Old N.P.,' 4 June, 6. **v**

Harper's Weekly
'Lullaby of the Iroquois,' 11 July, 686; *CB.* **v**
'The Corn Husker,' 5 Sept., 868; *CB.* **v**

Massey's Magazine
'The Singer of Tantramar,' Jan., 15–16.
'The Songster,' May, 296; *CB*. v
'The Derelict,' Dec., 414–17; *MM*

Our Animal Friends
'A Glimpse of the Prairie Wolf,' Apr., 181.

The Rudder
'With Barry in the Bow. Act I. Scene: The Land of Evangeline,' Sept., 268–70.
'With Barry in the Bow. Act II. Scene: The Great North Land,' Oct., 296–8.
'With Barry in the Bow. Interlude between Acts II and III,' Nov., 315–16.
'The American Canoe Association at Grindstone Island,' Dec., 355–8.

1897

Ludgate Magazine
'Gambling among the Iroquois,' Jan., 295–8.

Massey's Magazine
'The Indian Corn Planter,' June, 397; *FF*. v

Our Animal Friends
'In Gopher-Land,' Feb.

The Rudder
'With Barry in the Bow. Act III. Scene: The Land of the Setting Sun,' Jan.,
    31–3.
'With Barry in the Bow. Act IV,' May, 158–60.
'With Barry in the Bow. Act V,' Sept., 270–2.

Saturday Night
'The De Lisle Affair,' Xmas no., 7–9 [also *Evening News Bulletin*, Winnipeg, 18
    Dec., 6].

1898

Canada
'Organization of the Iroquois.'

Town Topics
'The Indian Legend of Qu'Appelle Valley,' 1 Oct.; retitled 'The Legend of
    Qu'Appelle Valley,' *CB*. v

1899

Free Press Home Journal (Winnipeg)
'"Give Us Barabbas,"' 28 Sept., *CB*. v

Globe
'H.M.S.,' Christmas no., 22. **v**

Saturday Night
'As It Was in the Beginning,' Christmas no., 15–18; *MM.*

Town Topics
'Some People I Have Met,' 4 Feb., 1.

1900

Halifax Herald[15]
'Canadian Born,' 9 June, 15; *CB.* **v**

1901

'His Majesty the King,' n.p.[16] **v**

1902

Evening News (Toronto)
'Letter to the Editor' [about *Wacousta*], 25 Mar. [1]

Globe
'Our Sister of the Seas,' 18 Jan., 14.
'Among the Blackfoots,' 2 Aug., 14.

Smart Set
'The Prodigal,' Apr., 149; as 'A Prodigal,' *CB.* **v**

1903

Canadian Born[17]
Previous publication unknown: 'The Art of Alma-Tadema,' 'At Half-Mast,' 'The
City and The Sea,' 'Golden – Of the Selkirks,' 'Good-Bye,' 'Guard of the East-
ern Gate,' 'Lady Icicle,' 'Lady Lorgnette,' 'Prairie Greyhounds,'[18] 'The Riders
of the Plains [performed 1899],' 'The Sleeping Giant,' 'A Toast,' 'Your Mirror
Frame.' **v**

Saturday Night
'Made in Canada,' 28 Feb., 3. **v**

1904

Rod and Gun
'The Train Dogs, Dec., *FF.* **v**

1906

Black and White
'When George Was King,' Christmas issue, 15; *FF.* v

Boys' World
'Maurice of His Majesty's Mails,' 23 July, 1–2, 7; *Sh.*
'The Saucy Seven,' 11 Aug., 1, 7; *Sh.*
'Dick Dines with his "Dad,"' 24 Nov., 1–2.

Daily Express (London)
'A Pagan in St. Paul's,' 3 Aug., 4; retitled 'A Pagan in St. Paul's Cathedral,' *MM*
'The Lodge of the Law Makers,' 14 Aug., 4.
'The Silent News Carriers' 25 Aug., 4.
'Sons of Savages,' 20 Nov., 4; *Sh.*

Over-Seas
'The Traffic of the Trail,' 1 Nov., 188–91.
'Newfoundland,'[19] 1 Nov., 185–8.

Saturday Night
'The Cariboo Trail,' 13 Oct., 11.

Standard (Montreal)
'Chance of Newfoundland Joining Canada Switches Interest to Britain's Oldest
   Colony,' 3 Mar., 5.

1907

Boys' World
'We-eho's Sacrifice,' 19 Jan., 1, 7; retitled 'We-hro's Sacrifice,' *Sh.*
'Gun-shy Billy,' 23 Mar., 1–2; *Sh.*
'The Broken String,' 27 July, 1–2, 8; *Sh.*
'Little Wolf-Willow,' 7 Dec., 1–2, 6; *Sh.*
'The Shadow Trail,' 21 Dec., 1–2; *Sh.*

Calgary Daily News[20]
'The Man in Chrysanthemum Land,' first stanza, 18 June, 1. *FF.* v

Canada (London)
'Longboat of the Onondagas,' 1 June, 250.

Canadian Magazine
'The Cattle Country,' Jan., 240; [also *Saturday Night*, 26 Jan. 1907; retitled 'The
   Foothill Country,' *Saturday Night*, 2 May 1908]; *FF.* v
'The Haunting Thaw,' May, 20–2.

'The Trail to Lillooet,' June, 128; *FF.* **v**

Mother's Magazine
'The Little Red Indian's Day,' Jan., 34.
'Her Dominion – A Story of 1867, and Canada's Confederation,' July, 10–11, 40.
'The Home Comers,' Sept., 4–6.
'The Prayers of the Pagan,' Nov., 10.

1908

Boys' World
'A Night With "North Eagle",' 18 Jan., 1–2, 7; *Sh.*
'The Tribe of Tom Longboat,' 23 May, 6.
'The Lieutenant Governor's Prize,' 20 June, 1, 7.
'Canada's Lacrosse,' 20 June, 6.
'The Scarlet Eye,' 1 Aug., 1–2, 8; *Sh.*
'The Cruise of the "Brown Owl",' 12 Sept., 1–2, 8 [reprinted 14 Nov. 1914, 1, 5, 7].

Brantford Daily Expositor
'Canada,' 22 Feb.; *FF.* **v**

Mother's Magazine
'Mothers of a Great Red Race,' Jan., 5, 14.
'Winter Indoor Life of the Indian Mother and Child,' Feb., 5, 54.
'How One Resourceful Mother Planned an Inexpensive Outing,' June, 19, 63.
'Outdoor Occupations of the Indian Mother and her Children,' July, 22–3.
'Heroic Indian Mothers,' Sept., 23–4.
'Mother of the Motherless,' Nov., 13, 50.

Saturday Night
'The Foothill Country' [previously 'The Cattle Country'], 2 May, 9. **v**
'The Southward Trail,' 24 Oct., 11.

When George Was King, and Other Poems. Brockville: Brockville Times.
'Autumn's Orchestra,' 4–6; *FF.* **v**

1909

Boys' World
'The Broken Barrels I,' 20 Mar., 4.
'The Broken Barrels II,' 27 Mar., 4–5.
'The Whistling Swans,' 3 Apr., 1, 3, 5, 8; *Sh.*
'The Delaware Idol,' 1 May, 1–2; *Sh.*
'The King's Coin (Chapter One),' 29 May, 4; *Sh.*

'The King's Coin (Chapter Two),' 5 June, 4; *Sh.*
'The King's Coin (Chapter Three),' 12 June, 4; *Sh.*
'The King's Coin (Chapter Four),' 19 June, 4; *Sh.*
'The King's Coin (Chapter Five),' 26 June, 4; *Sh.*
'Jack O' Lantern I,' 30 Oct., 4; *Sh.*
'Jack O' Lantern II,' 6 Nov., 4; *Sh.*

Mother's Magazine
'The Legend of the Two Sisters,' Jan., 12–13; as 'The True Legend of Vancouver's
   Lions,' *Daily Province Magazine*, 16 Apr. 1910; retitled 'The Two Sisters,' *LV.*
'Mother o' the Men,' Feb., 14–16, 56; *MM.*
'The Envoy Extraordinary,' Mar., 11–13; *MM.*
'My Mother,' Apr., 9–11; May, 7–9, 14; June, 10–12; July, 15–18; *MM.*
'The Christmas Heart,' Dec., 13, 30.

Saturday Night
'The Chinook Wind,' 24 Apr., 11.

1910

Boys' World
'The Brotherhood,' 1 Jan., 1–2, 6; *Sh.*
'The Wolf-Brothers,' 5 Feb., 1, 6; *Sh.*
'The Silver Craft of the Mohawks: The Protective Totem,' 2 Apr., 3.
'The Silver Craft of the Mohawks: The Brooch of Brotherhood,' 21 May, 3.
'The Silver Craft of the Mohawks: The Brooch of Dreams,' 18 June, 3.
'The Silver Craft of the Mohawks: The Hunter's Heart,' 25 June, 3.
'The Signal Code,' 16 July, 1–2, 8; *Sh.*
'England's Sailor King,' 30 July, 3.
'The Barnardo Boy,' 13 Aug., 1, 8; *Sh.*
'A Chieftain Prince,' 1 Oct., 3.
'The Potlatch,' 8 Oct., 1–3; *Sh.*
'The Story of the First Telephone,' 22 Oct., 3.
'The Silver Craft of the Mohawks: The Traitor's Hearts,' 12 Nov., 3.
'The Silver Craft of the Mohawks: The Sun of Friendship,' 17 Dec., 3.
'On My Honor,' 17 Dec., 6.

Canadian Magazine
'The Homing Bee,' Jan., 272; *FF.* v

Daily Province Magazine
'The True Legend of Vancouver's Lions,' 16 Apr., 2; retitled 'The Two Sisters,'
   LV.

'The Duke of Connaught as Chief of the Iroquois,' 2 July, 4; retitled 'A Royal Mohawk Chief,' *LV.*

'A Legend of the Squamish,' 9 July, 2; retitled 'The Lost Island,' *LV.*

'A True Legend of Siwash Rock: a Monument to Clean Fatherhood,' 16 July, 4; retitled 'The Siwash Rock,' *LV.*

'The Recluse of the Capilano Canyon,' 23 July, 11–12; retitled 'The Recluse,' *LV.*

'A Legend of Deer Lake,' 30 July, 11; retitled 'Deer Lake,' *LV.*

'The "Lure" in Stanley Park,' 20 Aug., 2; *LV.*

'The Deep Waters: A Rare Squamish Legend,' 24 Sept., 7; retitled 'The Great Deep Water: A Legend of "The Flood,"' *Mother's Magazine,* Feb. 1912; retitled 'The Deep Waters,' *LV.*

'The Legend of the Lost Salmon Run,' 1 Oct., 2; retitled 'The Lost Salmon Run,' *LV.*

'The Sea Serpent of Brockton Point,' 8 Oct., 9; retitled 'The Sea Serpent,' *LV.*

'The Legend of the Seven White Swans,' 15 Oct., 2; also *Mother's Magazine,* Sept. 1911.

'The True Legend of Deadman's Island,' 22 Oct., 6; retitled 'Deadman's Island,' *LV.*

'The Lost Lagoon,' 22 Oct., 6; *FF.* v

'A Squamish Legend of Napoleon,' 29 Oct., 11; *LV.*

'The Orchard of Evangeline's Land,' 12 Nov., 4–5.

'The Call of the Old Qu' Appelle Valley,' 19 Nov., 6, 11.

'Prairie and Foothill Animals That Despise the Southward Trail,' 26 Nov., 5.

'Where the Horse is King,' 3 Dec.

'A Legend of Point Grey,' 10 Dec., 5; retitled 'Point Grey,' *LV.*

'The Great Heights above the Tulameen,' 17 Dec., 4; retitled 'The Tulameen Trail,' *LV.*

'Trails of the Old Tillicums,' 31 Dec., 4.

Mother's Magazine

'The Nest Builder,' Mar., 11, 32; *MM.*

'The Call of the Skookum Chuck,' Apr., 14–17.

'From the Child's Viewpoint,' May, 30–1; June, 60–2.

'The Grey Archway: A Legend of the Charlotte Islands,' June, 10–11; also in *Daily Province Magazine,* 7 Jan. 1911; *LV.*

'The Legend of the Squamish Twins,' July, 16–17; retitled 'The Recluse of Capilano Canyon,' *Daily Province Magazine,* 23 July; retitled 'The Recluse,' *LV.*

'The Lost Salmon Run: A Legend of the Pacific Coast,' Aug., 13–14; retitled 'The Legend of the Lost Salmon Run,' *Daily Province Magazine,* 1 Oct.; retitled 'The Lost Salmon Run,' *LV.*

'The Legend of Siwash Rock,' Oct., 10–11; as 'A True Legend of Siwash
   Rock: A Monument to Clean Fatherhood,' *Daily Province Magazine*,
   16 July, 4; *LV.*
'Catharine of the "Crow's Nest,"' Dec., 12–13; *MM.*

What to Do
'A Lost Luncheon,' 26 Nov., 1.
'The Building Beaver,' 3 Dec., 4.

1911

Legends of Vancouver: all contents previously published

Boys' World
'The King Georgeman [I],' 5 Aug., 4. *Sh.*
'The King Georgeman [II],' 12 Aug., 4. *Sh.*

Daily Province Magazine
'The Grey Archway: A Legend of the Coast,' 7 Jan., 7; retitled 'The Grey
   Archway,' *LV.*
'The Great New Year White Dog: Sacrifice of the Onondagas,' 14 Jan., 16.

Daily Province
'La Crosse,' 10 June, 10. **v**

Mother's Magazine
'Hoolool of the Totem Poles,' Feb., 12–13, 71; *Sh.*
'The Tenas Klootchman,' Aug., 12–14; *MM.*
'The Legend of the Seven Swans,' Sept., 17–18, 32; [reprinted from *Province*,
   Oct. 1910]
'The Legend of the Ice Babies,' Nov., 23–4.

1912

Flint and Feather
Previous publication unknown: 'The Archers,' 'Brandon,' 'The King's
   Consort.'[21] **v**

Mother's Magazine
'The Legend of Lillooet Falls,' Jan., 19, 45; *MM.*
'The Great Deep Water: A Legend of "The Flood,"' Feb., 35; [reprint of
   'The Deep Waters,' *Province*, Sept. 1910]; *LV.*

Sun (Vancouver)
'The Unfailing Lamp,' 20 Mar., 5.

1913

The Moccasin Maker
Previous publication unknown: 'Her Majesty's Guest.'

The Shagganappi
Previous publication unknown: 'The Shagganappi.'

Boys' World
'The Little Red Messenger [I],' 21 June, 4.
'The Little Red Messenger [II],' 28 June, 4.

Calgary Herald
'Calgary of the Plains,' 19 Apr.; *FF* (later editions). **v**

Canadian Magazine
'Song,' Oct., 548. **v**
'In Heidleberg,' Nov., 53.[22] **v**
'Aftermath,' Dec., 183. **v**

Saturday Night
'The Ballad of Yaada,' 23 Aug., 29; *FF* (later editions). **v**
Pamphlet (Toronto: Musson), 20 Nov.
'And He Said, Fight On'; *FF* (later editions). **v**

1914

Canadian Magazine
'Reclaimed Lands,' Jan., 17. **v**
'Coaching on the Cariboo Trail,' Feb., 399–400.

Daily Province
'Coaching on the Cariboo Trail,' Feb. 1914 (dup. of *Canadian Magazine*).

1916

Flint and Feather (new edition)
Previous full publication unverified: 'The Man from Chrysanthemum Land'
   ('Written for "The Spectator"').[23] **v**

1929

'To Walter McRaye,' in McRaye, *Town Hall Tonight*, 62. **v**

1947

'The Ballad of Laloo,' in McRaye, *Pauline Johnson and Her Friends*, 131–2. **v**

UNDATED PUBLICATIONS

Poems in the Chiefswood Scrapbook: *c.* 1884–94[24]

'Both Sides.' *New York Life*, 1888, **v**
'Comrades, we are serving.' n.p., n.d.[25] **v**
'Disillusioned' [second part 'Both Sides'] *Judge*, n.d.[26] **v**
'Lent,' signed Woeful Jack. n.p., n.d. **v**
'What the Soldier Said.' *Brant Churchman*, n.d.[27] **v**

Undated Poems: Clippings at McMaster University

'In the Shadows. My Version. By the Pasha.' n.p., n.d.[28] **v**
'Traverse Bay.' n.p., n.d. **v**
'Winnipeg – At Sunset.' *Free Press*, n.d. **v**

Undated Prose: Clippings at McMaster University

'Interesting Description, by a Descendant of the Mohawks, of Tutela Heights,
Ontario.' *Boston Evening Transcript*, n.d.[29]

UNPUBLISHED WRITINGS

Dated Manuscripts

1876
'The Fourth Act.'[30] **v**

1878
'Think of Me,' 14 Feb.[31] **v**

1879
'My Jeanie,' 17 June.[32] **v**

1890
'Dear little girl from far / Beyond the seas.' [33] **v**

1901
'Morrowland,' dated Holy Saturday.[34] **v**

1906

'Witchcraft and the Winner.'[35]

Undated Manuscripts

Early fragment, 'alas how damning praise can be.'[36] **v**
Epigraph, 'But all the poem was soul of me.'[37] **v**
'The Battleford Trail,' c. 1902–3.[38]
'If Only I Could Know' (published as 'In Days to Come').[39] **v**
'The Mouse's Message.'[40] **v**
'"Old Maids"' Children.'[41]
'The Stings of Civilization.'[42]
'Tillicum Talks.'[43]
'To C.H.W.'[44] **v**
'The Tossing of a Rose.'[45]

UNTRACED WRITINGS

On List of Titles, c. 1908[46]

'Britain's First Born C.'
'The Flying Sun.'
'God's Laughter.'
'Indian Church Workers.'
'The Missing Miss Orme.'
'The Rain.'
'The Silent Speakers.'

Untraced Titles[47] from Concert Programs and Reviews

'At the Ball' (1902–3).
'Beneath the British Flag' (1906).
'The Captive' (1892).
'A Case of Flirtation' (1899).
'The Chief's Daughter' (1898).
'The Convict's Wife' (1892).
'Fashionable Intelligence' (1906).
'The Englishman' (1902–3). **v**
'Half Mast' (1897).
'Her Majesty's Troops' (1900); 'His Majesty's Troops' (1904). **v**

'His Sister's Son' (1895–7). **v**
'Legend of the Lover's Leap' (1892). **v**
'Mrs Stewart's Five O'Clock Tea' (1894–1906).
'My Girls' (1897).
'People I Have Met' (1902). **v**
'A Plea for the Northwest' (1892–3).
'Redwing' (1892–3).
'Stepping Stones'[48] (1897). **v**
'The Success of the Season' (1894–1906).
'The White Wampum' (1896–7).

Other Untraced Titles

'Canada for the Canadians'[49] (1902). **v**

Notes

Abbreviations

AIQ	*American Indian Quarterly*
AO	Archives of Ontario
BE	*Brantford Expositor*
BMA	Brant County Museum and Archives
BW	*Boys' World* (Elgin, Illinois)
CB	*Canadian Bookman*
CL	*Canadian Literature/Littérature canadienne*
CM	*Canadian Magazine* (Toronto)
DCB	*Dictionary of Canadian Biography/Dictionnaire de biographie canadienne*
DIM	*Dominion Illustrated Monthly* (Montreal)
IJCS	*International Journal of Canadian Studies/Revue internationale d'études canadiennes*
JCS	*Journal of Canadian Studies/Revue d'études canadiennes*
MM	*Mother's Magazine* (Elgin, Illinois)
MUL	McMaster University Library, William Ready Division of Archives and Research Collections
MURBSC	McGill University Library, Rare Books and Special Collections
NAC	National Archives of Canada/Archives nationaux du Canada
SAB	Saskatchewan Archives Board
SCL	*Studies in Canadian Literature*
SH	*Histoire sociale/Social History*
SN	*Saturday Night Magazine* (Toronto)
TG	*Toronto Globe*

TRSC   *Transactions of the Royal Society of Canada*
TUA   Trent University Archives
TW   *The Week* (Toronto)
UTFRBR University of Toronto, Thomas Fisher Rare Book Room
VCA   Vancouver City Archives
VP   *Vancouver Province*
VS   *Vancouver Sun*
VW   *Vancouver World*

Introduction

1 E. LaRocque, 'The Colonization of a Native Woman Scholar' in Miller et al., eds., *Women of the First Nations*, 12.
2 'Shadow River' (1889).
3 B. Godard, 'The Politics of Representation: Some Native Canadian Women Writers' in New, ed., *Native Writers and Canadian Writing*, 221–2.
4 Quoted in E.T. Seton, 'Tekahionwake (Pauline Johnson)' in Johnson, *The Shagganappi*, 5.
5 Quoted in McRaye, *Pauline Johnson and Her Friends*, 163. For a perspective from the other side, see D.H. Taylor, *Funny, You Don't Look Like One.*
6 See Verna Kirkness, former director of the First Nations House of Learning, University of British Columbial, quoted in C. Haig-Brown, 'Choosing Border Work,' *Canadian Journal of Native Education* 19, no. 1 (1992), 96, and J. Armstrong, 'Writing from a Native Woman's Perspective' in Dybikowski et al., eds., *In the Feminine.* See also the useful discussion of the issues in B. Godard, 'The Politics of Representation: Some Native Canadian Women Writers' in New, ed., *Native Writers and Canadian Writing.*
7 K. Donovan, *Feminist Readings of Native American Literature*, 7.
8 C. St. Peter, 'Feminist Afterwords: Revisiting *Copper Woman*' in Greenhill and Tye, eds., *Undisciplined Women*, 71; she cites Lee Maracle.
9 Haig-Brown, 'Choosing Border Work,' 97.
10 Trinh T. Minh-ha, *Framer Framed*, 96, 105.
11 *Maclean's Magazine* (1 July 1998).
12 We remain aware that some scholars, like Devon A. Mihesuah, consider interviews to be essential. See her 'Voices, Interpretations, and the "New American History": Comment on the *American Indian Quarterly*'s Special Issue on Writing About American Indians,' *AIQ* 20, no. 1 (Winter 1996), 102.
13 Campbell, *Halfbreed*, 2.

14 See the essay of this title in Taylor, *Funny, You Don't Look Like One.*
15 Quoted in I.E. Mackay, 'Pauline Johnson,' 274.
16 'Fate of the Red Man,' *Ottawa Free Press*, 21 June 1894.
17 *VP* (10 March 1913), 1.
18 K. Neuenfeldt, 'First Nations and Métis Songs as Identity Narratives,' 208.
19 'B,' 'Sonnet in Reply to an Indian Wife,' *TW* (25 June 1885), 474. See also the impetus Johnson provided for Euro-Canadian self-criticism about the treatment of Natives in the response by another observer, 'Uncle Thomas,' in 'Impressions,' *TG* (18 January 1892).
20 'A Poem to Brantford's Elocutionist,' TUA, unidentified clipping.
21 McRaye, *Town Hall Tonight*, 42.
22 Quoted in Benidickson, *Idleness, Water, and a Canoe*, 168.
23 E. Wilson, 'The Princess,' *CL* 12 (Summer 1961), 60.
24 Perrault and Vance, eds., *Writing the Circle*, 122.

1: 'One of Them'

The quotation in the chapter title comes from the byline used by Pauline Johnson for 'Iroquois Women of Canada,' *Women of Canada* (1900), 400–2.
1 See, for example, Francis, *The Imaginary Indian*, Monkman, *A Native Heritage*, and Goldie, *Fear and Temptation.*
2 Sir Gilbert Parker, 'Introduction' in Pauline Johnson, *The Moccasin Maker*, 8.
3 See Anderson, *Vancouver's Chinatown* for a useful introduction to Canadian racial discourse of the late nineteenth and early twentieth centuries.
4 There are many examples of this literature but to take only a few, see 'Only Half Civilized,' *DIM* (29 October 1888), 242–3; Maclean, *Canadian Savage Folk*, MacMullen, *The History of Canada from Its Discovery to the Present Time*, and McGaffey, 'The Red Men of Vancouver Island,' *CM* (September 1910).
5 For a useful introduction to official policies, see Miller, *Canada and the Aboriginal Peoples 1867–1927.*
6 See Barman, 'Taming Aboriginal Sexuality: Gender, Power and Race in British Columbia, 1850–1900,' 237, Carter, *Capturing Women*, Van Kirk, *'Many Tender Ties,'* and Brown, *Strangers in Blood.*
7 See McKay, *The Quest of the Folk.*
8 See D.A. Wright, 'W.D. Lighthall and David Ross McCord: Anti-modernism and English-Canadian Imperialism, 1880s–1918,' 134–53.

9 The founder was Arthur O'Meara, a former lawyer and Anglican missionary. Significantly, his father was an Anglican missionary known to the Six Nations. See Tennant, *Aboriginal Peoples and Politics*, 87–8 on this organization. On O'Meara's father, see R. Millman, 'O'Meara, Frederick Augustus' *DCB* XI: 653–5. Another supporter was Canon Tucker, rector of Christ Church, Vancouver, who would later officiate at Pauline's burial. See 'The British Columbia Indian Situation' (Conference of Friends of the Indians of British Columbia, *c.* 1912, University of British Columbia Library, Special Collections).

10 'A Clever Canadian,' *SN* (26 April 1890), 6.

11 AO, E.H.C. Johnson, 'Chiefswood,' unpublished typescript.

12 Young, *Colonial Desire*, 4, 6. See also Stoler, *Race and the Education of Desire.*

13 Wilson, *Prehistoric Man*, 290.

14 See Knowles, *Inventing the Loyalists*, especially chapter 6, for its discussion of the Iroquois.

15 'An Appreciation,' in E. Pauline Johnson, *The Moccasin Maker*, 11.

16 Wilson, *Prehistoric Man.* II: 252–3, 254, 259.

17 See E. Smith, '"Gentlemen, This Is No Ordinary Trial": Sexual Narratives in the Trial of the Reverend Corbett, Red River, 1863' in Brown and Vibert, eds., *Reading beyond Words.*

18 On Traill's family, see Ballstadt, Hopkins, and Peterman, eds., *I Bless You in My Heart.* See also Gerson, 'Nobler Savages: Representatives of Native Women in the Writings of Susanna Moodie and Catharine Parr Traill,' 5–21.

19 This unity is also stressed by the University of McGill professor, J. William Dawson, in his *Fossil Men* (1880). Even the supporters of a single human origin, 'monogenism,' stereotyped Native peoples to their disadvantage. See the views of Lewis Henry Morgan (1818–81), 'the father of American anthropology' in Bieder, *Science Encounters the Indian*, chapter 6.

20 Reade, 'The Half Breed,' 10. Reade was also known to have 'consistently advocated the conciliation of race and religion in Canada, Canadian Confederation and the unity of the Empire,' *Canadian Who's Who* (1910), 190. For similar views, see also Maclean, *Canadian Savage Folk*, 298.

21 As quoted in Salem, '"Her Blood Is Mingled with Her Ancient Foes": The Concepts of Blood, Race, and "Miscegenation" in the Poetry and Short Fiction of Duncan Campbell Scott,' 100.

22 McRaye, *Pauline Johnson and Her Friends*, x.

23 On the response of the country-born, see F. Pannekoek, 'The Anglican Church and the Disintegration of Red River Society, 1818–1870' in Berger

and Cook, eds., *The West and the Nation*. For a moving expression of the dilemmas of belonging for a 'country-born' at the end of the twentieth century, see G. Young-Ing, 'I Am Mixed Blood' in Hodgson, ed. and comp., *Seventh Generation: Contemporary Native Writing*, 48–9.

24 Barman, 'Taming Aboriginal Sexuality,' and Carter, *Capturing Women*.

25 See the assessment of the marital prospects of a lower-class English woman in Van Kirk, '*Many Tender Ties*,' 202.

26 'Bogus Indians,' *Toronto News*, quoted in *BE* (27 November 1885).

27 See Van Kirk, 'Tracing the Fortunes of Five Founding Families of Victoria,' 148–79.

28 See, for example, B. Cameron, 'The North-West Red-Man and His Future,' *CM* (January 1900), 216.

29 Stoler, *Race and the Education of Desire*, 46. See also Barman, 'Taming Aboriginal Sexuality,' 252, and Carter, *Capturing Women*, 15, 191–2, for their attention to the role of these children in Canada.

30 See Bremer, *Indian Agent and Wilderness Scholar*, in particular 75, 93, 97, 119, 256, and 310, for the account of one father whose dealings with his Mixed-race children seem to have exhibited a fair degree of racism.

31 British Columbia, *Yearbook* (1911), 164.

32 On American policies, see Dippie, *The Vanishing American* and Gibson, *The American Indian*. On the explicit American comparison, see H. Coulthard, 'They Shall Covet Their Neighbor's Indians,' *The Young Canadian* (8 April 1891), 163–5.

33 The enfranchisement issues of the nineteenth and twentieth century are complicated, varying from one group to another. Unfortunately, no study has yet made critical comparisons. John A. Macdonald's short-lived 1885 franchise experiment, which enfranchised Native men without loss of Indian status, provided a provocative alternative to the tendency to integrate new voters into the political system without any admission of difference.

34 Quoted in Mackay, 'A Romance of Yesterday,' *TG* (30 November 1912).

35 Quoted in Petrone, *Native Literature in Canada*, 67.

36 'The Indian Conference,' *The Canadian Indian* (June 1891).

37 On women's resort to the law, see Backhouse, *Petticoats and Prejudices*. On Natives in British Columbia, see Tennant, *Aboriginal Peoples and Politics*, especially chapters 5 and 6. On Ontario, see Montgomery, 'The Legal Status of the Six Nations Indians in Canada,' 92–105.

38 Preface to Perreault and Vance, comp. and eds., *Writing the Circle*, xxvi.

39 See, for example, the account by a Tuscarora, NY, chief in Graymont, ed., *Fighting Tuscarora*.

40 R.E. Gosnell, 'Indians and Indian Affairs in Canada,' *CM* (March 1921), 381.
41 See R. Fisher, 'Su-á-pu-luck,' *DCB* XIII: 998–9. For a useful summary of
   Su-á-pu-luck's reputation as a Native agitator we thank Sarah Parry, 'Specula-
   tions on AlterNative Historiography and Colonial Semiotics in Pauline
   Johnson's Legends of Vancouver,' English 804 Paper, Simon Fraser University, 1998. According to Major J.S. Mathews, Vancouver's first archivist, 'He
   was "Capilano Joe" before he went [to London]. After he came back he was
   Chief Joe Capilano.' Handwritten note on clipping headed 'Fifty Years Ago,'
   Joe Capilano file, VCA.
42 'Indian Chiefs Greet Poetess,' *VW* (12 July 1908).
43 On the politics of deference with respect to women, see G.G. Campbell,
   'Disfranchised but not Quiescent: Women Petitioners in New Brunswick in
   the Mid-19th Century,' *Acadiensis* 18, no. 2 (Spring 1989), 22–54. See the
   discussion of how the traditional tory politics of reciprocal deference and
   respect were used by female Loyalists after the American Revolution in
   Potter-Mackinnon, *While the Women Only Wept: Loyalist Refugee Women in
   Eastern Ontario*. See also Johnson's short story, 'A Royal Mohawk Chief'
   (1910) for its description of the adoption of Arthur, Duke of Connaught
   and son of Queen Victoria.
44 This critique surfaces regularly in Native responses from Johnson's time to
   the present. For a good introduction to this perspective, see Petrone, *Native
   Literature in Canada*, and Strong-Boag, 'Claiming a Place in the Nation.'
45 For an important study which begins this difficult task of recovery, see D.P.
   Payment, '"La vie en rose"? Métis Women at Batoche, 1870–1920' in Miller
   et al., eds., *Women of the First Nations*.
46 Paget, *The People of the Plains*, 18.
47 For the recovery of Paget and her sisters, see Carter, *Capturing Women*,
   116–23.
48 D. Mihesuah, 'Commonality of Difference: American Indian Women and
   History,' 16. For a more positive view which stresses the psychological rich-
   ness of operating in two cultures, see J.E. Clark and M.E. Webb, 'Susette and
   Susan La Flesche: Reformer and Missionary' in Clifton, ed., *Being and Becoming Indian*.
49 Quoted in Barman, 'Lost Okanagan: In Search of the First Settler Families,'
   18. See also Turnbull, 'Recollections of Marie Houghton Brent,' 21–2.
50 C. Batker, '"Overcoming All Obstacles:" The Assimilation Debate in Native
   American Women's Journalism of the Dawes Era' in Jaskoski ed., *Early Native
   American Writing*, 191.
51 Van Kirk, 'Tracing the Fortunes of Five Founding Families of Victoria.'

52 Quoted in Foster, *The Mohawk Princess*, 40.

53 Weaver, 'The Iroquois: The Consolidation of the Grand River Reserve in the Mid-Nineteenth Century, 1847–1875,' in Rogers and Smith, eds., *Aboriginal Ontario*, 183 and 132.

54 TUA, Johnson Collection, E. Johnson, handwritten note (undated and unidentified).

55 W. Smith, *Indian Songs of Peace* (1752) as quoted in Shields, *Oracles of Empire*, 211.

56 C. Colden, *History of the Five Indian Nations* (174?), in ibid., 210.

57 See Bieder, *Science Encounters the Indian*, chapters 5 and 6.

58 Hale, *The Iroquois Book of Rites*, 111.

59 Jenness, *The Indians of Canada*, 139, 147. For similar views of a historian of the period, see Dunham, *Grand River*, 3.

60 R. E. Gosnell, 'Indians and Indian Affairs in Canada,' *CM* (March 1921), 383. For confirmation of this sense of superiority to other Natives as well as Europeans, see Shimony, *Conservatism among the Iroquois at the Six Nations Reserve*, xxiv. Of course, such self-confidence did not distinguish the Iroquois from many other Indian nations or, for that matter, most peoples of the globe who regularly harbour notions of group superiority.

61 See the fascinating interpretation of nineteenth- and twentieth-century scholarship by Foster, 'Lost Women of the Matriarchy: Iroquois Women in the Historical Literature,' 121–40. See also the useful discussion of 'relative' and 'absolute' equality in Van Kirk, 'Toward a Feminist Perspective in Native History,' 379–81.

62 Wilson, *Prehistoric Man*, 290, 292.

63 McLean, *The Indians: Their Manners and Customs*, 163. The original 1784 Loyalist land grant 'was specifically granted to the Mohawks and "such others of the Six Nations Indians"' who sought continued protection of the Crown. See Weaver, 'Seth Newhouse and the Grand River Confederacy at Mid-Nineteenth Century' in Foster, Campisi, and Mithun, eds., *Extending the Rafters*, 169.

64 Lord Dufferin, as quoted in J.T. Gilkison, comp., *Narrative Visit of the Governor-General and the Countess of Dufferin to the Six Nations Indians August 25, 1874* (1875).

65 See Johnson, 'Chief John Smoke Johnson: Sakayengwaraton – "Disappearing of the Indian Summer Mist,"' 102–13.

66 Duncan, *A Social Departure*, 27. Note that all non-Anglo-Saxons are treated with equal witty contempt.

67 Smith, 'Land Tenure in Brant County,' 42.

68 Noon, *Law and Government of the Grand River Iroquois*, 121.
69 On these men, see Petrone, 'Brant-Sero, John Ojijatekha,' *DCB* XIV: 150–2;
   G. Comeau-Vasilopoulos, 'Oronhyatekha,' *DCB* XIII: 791–4; T. Nicks, 'Dr.
   Oronhyatekha's History Lessons: Reading Museum Collections as Texts'
   in Brown and Vibert, *Reading Beyond Words*; Monture, *Canadian Portraits*;
   Morgan, 'Aboriginal Travellers and Colonial Subjects? Pauline Johnson and
   John Brant-Sero in Imperial London, 1890s–1900s.'
70 Tennant, *Aboriginal Peoples and Politics*, 84.
71 Ashcroft, Griffiths, and Tiffin, 'Introduction to Part Three, Representation
   and Resistance,' *Post-Colonial Studies Reader*, 86.
72 Sharpe, "Figures of Colonial Resistance," in ibid., 101, 100.
73 On Mohawk dominance and opposition to it, see Snow, *The Iroquois*, especially chapter 11; see also Weaver, 'The Iroquois: The Grand River Reserve in
   the Late Nineteenth and Early Twentieth Centuries, 1875–1945' and 'Seth
   Newhouse and the Grand River Confederacy at Mid-Nineteenth Century.'
74 'Six Nations,' 'Who Is Kah-ke-wa-quo-naby?' *BE* (26 June 1885). See also
   'Bogus Indians' (*Toronto News*), *BE* (27 November 1885) and the different
   opinions of the Indian superintendent, J. Gilkison, and the Liberal MPP, A.S.
   Hardy, regarding intermarriage in their testimony before an Ontario Select
   Committee on Indian Affairs in 1874, cited in W.C. Trimble, *Illustrated Historical Atlas of Brant County, Ontario* (1875, rpt 1972), 9.
75 'Important Notice,' *BE* (23 January 1874). The 'Upper' and 'Lower' Indians
   refers to the location, first of the majority of the progressive and Mohawk
   group and then the traditionalist and Onondaga, on the reserve. See also a
   'holograph fragment' by Emily Johnson which indicates opposition in the
   Confederacy Council as well, cited by A.L.B. Ruoff, 'Notes to Text' in
   Johnson, *The Moccasin Maker*, 235; and Trimble, *Illustrated Historical Atlas of
   Brant County, Ontario*, 9, which notes that restrictions on timber sales contributed to the 'starvation' of families on the reserve.
76 Maracle, *Back on the Rez*, 5. On these conflicts, see Weaver, 'Seth Newhouse
   and the Grand River Confederacy at Mid-Nineteenth Century,' Shimony,
   Conservatism among the Iroquois, and Noon, *Law and Government*, 48–9.
77 See Canada, Department of Indian Affairs, *Annual Report* (1883), 1, for the
   observation that the reserve's population was growing in part because of the
   'intermarriage of Indians of the Six Nations with white women and Indian
   women belonging to other bands.'
78 See Brant-Sero, 'Some Descendants of Joseph Brant,' 116, and Smith, 'Fred
   Loft,' in *The Encyclopedia of North American Indians*, 344–5.
79 See, for example, Weaver, 'The Iroquois: The Grand River Reserve in the
   Late Nineteenth and Early Twentieth Centuries, 1875–1945,' 224–7.

80 For a provocative study of the class, racial, and gender tensions surrounding this endeavour, see Mihesuah, *Cultivating the Rosebuds*. Most of its pupils, whose tribal membership derived through mothers, would not have been considered Indians in Canada. The highly organized Cherokee make an interesting comparison with the Six Nations. Like the Iroquois, they too tended to be Loyalists during the American Revolution and early on had close cultural contacts and high levels of intermarriage with Europeans. Unlike the Iroquois, however, the Cherokee, concentrated in the southern colonies, did not escape to the north but attempted to make their accommodation with the new American nation. Despite treaties and land agreements, the Cherokee were hounded relentlessly west, ending with the 'Trail of Tears' march of 1838–9 to Oklahoma Indian Territory.

81 Montour, *The Feathered U.E.L.'s*, 74.

82 Mackenzie, *The Six Nations Indians in Canada*, 80.

83 As quoted in Smith, *Sacred Feathers*, 175.

84 See a later Six Nations writer's defence of oral history as equally valid to written, in Beaver, 'Early Iroquoian History in Ontario,' 226–7.

85 Cole, 'The Origins of Canadian Anthropology,' 38.

86 On the collectors and anthropologists, see Fenton, ed., *Parker on the Iroquois*; Killan, *David Boyle*, and Snow, *The Iroquois*. On issues for First Nations, see R. Ignace, G. Speck, and R. Taylor, 'Some Native Perspectives on Anthropology and Public Policy' in Dyck and Waldram, eds. *Anthropology, Public Policy and Native Peoples in Canada*.

87 See Weaver, 'Seth Newhouse and the Grand River Confederacy at Mid-Nineteenth Century.'

88 Shimony, *Conservatism among the Iroquois*, n 1, 71.

89 See Killan, *David Boyle*, 186. See also James Bovell Mackenzie's complaint in his *The Six Nations Indians in Canada* (p. 61) of being the target of critical humour from the Six Nations. Since this volume, while not without sympathy for the Iroquois, characterized the marriages of the Longhouse people as 'sexual alliance' and 'fleshly pact' (p. 65) and sees 'indolence' as an outstanding trait of the community (p. 67), such a response seems hardly surprising.

90 E. Johnson, 'Chief John Smoke Johnson: Sakayengwaraton – "Disappearing of the Indian Summer Mist,"' 112.

91 Quoted in Killan, *Preserving Ontario's Heritage*, 44.

92 C. Morgan, 'Wampum and Waffle-Irons: Gender and National Identities in the Writing of Canadian Popular History, 1880s–1930s,' paper presented to the annual meetings of the Canadian Historical Association (1996), 12.

93 Monture, *Canadian Portraits*, 146. For similar anti-Black sentiments, see also

TUA, Johnson Collection, file 1/19, clipping 'Facts about Pauline Johnson' (identified *BE*, 10 April 1916) for a letter from Evelyn Johnson which suggested that the contention of a Grand River 'mulatto' that he was a descendant of Tecumseh constituted an 'aspersion' on the latter's 'name and memory.'

94 Horatio Hale as quoted in Johnson, 'The Iroquois of the Grand River' (1894).

95 For a good statement of this argument by the secretary of the Six Nations' Council, see Hill, 'The Historical Position of the Six Nations.'

96 See McLaren, *The Trials of Masculinity*, and Strong-Boag, 'Independent Women and Problematic Men,' 1–22.

97 J. Brant-Sero, 'A Canadian Indian and the War,' *London Times* (2 January 1901), 10.

98 MacDonald, *Sons of the Empire*, 5. See also Wadland, *Ernest Thompson Seton*, and Keller, *Black Wolf*. On the anti-modern critique embodied in such adoptions see Wright, 'W.D. Lighthall and David Ross McCord.'

99 See, for example, E. Pauline Johnson, 'Mothers of a Great Red Race' (1908), and Brant-Sero, 'The Six-Nations Indians in the Province of Ontario, Canada.'

100 See Tooker, 'Women in Iroquois Society.' For a collection whose contributors take a largely positive view of women's role in North American Native societies, see Klein and Ackerman, eds., *Women and Power in Native North America*.

101 On Handsome Lake's views on women, including his persecution of so-called witches, see Snow, *The Iroquois*, 159–62, and Foster, 'Lost Women of the Matriarchy: Iroquois,' 128–31.

102 See, for example, T. Corrs, 'The Iroquois,' *CM* (May 1874), 403. On feminist sympathies, see Landsman, 'The "Other" as Political Symbol: Images of Indians in the Woman Suffrage Movement,' 247–84.

103 F. Brooke, *The History of Emily Montague* (1769, repr. Ottawa: Carleton University Press, 1985), 49, and Leprohon, *The Poetical Works of Mrs. Leprohon*, 69, first published in the *Saturday Reader* (Montreal) (23 December 1865).

104 See, inter alia, G. Green, 'Molly Brant, Catharine Brant, and Their Daughters: A Study in Colonial Acculturation,' 235–50, and Jean Johnston, 'Molly Brant: Mohawk Matron,' 105–23.

105 On their activity in legal life, see the cases in Noon, *Law and Government*, passim.

106 See Graymont, *Fighting Tuscarora*, 99, and Hauptman, 'Designing Woman.'

107 See Cooper, 'Native Women of the Northern Pacific Coast: An Historical Perspective, 1830–1900,' 44–75.

108 This evocative term is used by Natives; see Green, 'The Tribe Called Wannabee: Playing Indian in America and Europe,' 48. See Smith, *Long Lance*, 'From Sylvester Long to Chief Long Lance' in *Being and Becoming Indian*, and *From the Land of Shadows*. On the tradition of White impostors, see Francis, *The Imaginary Indian*.

109 Murray Porter as quoted in Neuenfeldt, 'First Nations and Métis Songs as Identity Narratives,' 216.

110 Wilson, *Prehistoric Man*, 274.

111 Rollston was variously spelled, including Rallston and Rollstone, the latter a pen name used briefly by Johnson. See also E.H.C. Johnson, 'The Martin Settlement,' 56.

112 Johnson, 'Chief John Smoke Johnson: Sakayengwaraton,' 102 and 106, and Leighton, 'Johnson, John,' *DCB* XI:453–4.

113 For the persistence of this rumour, see VCA, Johnson Papers, Clayton W. McCall, 'Fresh Light on Pauline Johnson' (unpublished ms, n.d.).

114 On G.H.M. Johnson's religious faith, see AO, Evelyn H.C. Johnson 'Chiefswood,' unpublished typescript, chapter 3. See also the fictional account by Johnson, 'The Delaware Idol' (1909), and W. Stevenson, 'The Journals and Voices of Church of England Native Catechist: Askenootow (Charles Pratt), 1851–1884' in Brown and Vibert, *Reading beyond Words* for its critical reflections on the complex meanings of Christianity for a Native churchman.

115 TUA, Johnson Collection, E. Johnson handwritten note (undated and unidentified).

116 On her father's dress and the response to the marriage, see the account by Pauline Johnson, 'My Mother' (1909).

117 Hale, ed., *The Iroquois Book of Rites* 44–5, and 'Chief George H.M. Johnson – Onwanonsyshon,' *Magazine of American History* (February 1885), 142.

118 Horatio Hale, 'An Iroquois Condoling Council. A Study of Aboriginal American Society and Government,' *TRSC*, Second Series (1895–6), vol. I, section 2, 46.

119 See the mock battle involving George Johnson and British troops staged in Toronto in 1867 in Ruoff, 'Notes to Text,' Johnson, *The Moccasin Maker*, 236.

120 In her short story 'My Mother,' Pauline indicates that the controversy occurred with the Confederacy Council, but anthropologist Sally Weaver suggests the struggle occurred within the clan meeting which also represented different tribes. See Ruoff, 'Notes to Text,' *The Moccasin Maker*, 230. See also Smith, *Sacred Feathers*, 158, for a discussion of how Peter Jones

encountered serious resistance from Mississaugas who judged him 'too much like a white man.'

121 The only mention of her period as a teacher, a profession that was just beginning to open up to middle-class women before Confederation, is found in AO, E. Johnson Papers, 'Chiefswood,' unpublished typescript, chapter 4.

122 BMA, Johnson Family Papers, Emily Howells to George Johnson, Kingston August 28, 1850, 13 August 1855 (emphasis in original). See also the similar distress of Eliza Field when subject to the racist rumour mill because of her marriage to Peter Jones, in Smith, *Sacred Feathers*, 40–3.

123 On the relationship and Chiefswood, see Johnson, 'My Mother.' On the Black servants, see BMA, Johnson Family Papers, Emily Howells Johnson to George Johnson, 13 August 1855.

124 Luke, 'White Women in Interracial Families: Reflections on Hybridization, Feminine Identities, and Racialized Othering,' 51. See also Namias, *White Captives*, and Ebersole, *Captured by Texts*.

125 'My Mother' (1909).

126 TUA, Johnson Collection, file 1/13, E. Johnson, undated handwritten note.

127 Randle, 'Iroquois Women, Then and Now' in Fenton, ed., *Symposium on Local Diversity in Iroquois Culture*, 176.

128 'Miss E. Pauline Johnson,' *The Critic* (NY) (4 January 1896).

129 'From the Child's Viewpoint' (1910).

130 Ibid.

131 TUA, Johnson Collection, file 1/13, E. Johnson, undated handwritten note.

132 Ibid. Some of the difficulties of a Mixed-race boy at a private school are conveyed, albeit with a romantic ending, in Johnson's short story 'The Shagganappi' (1913), which was said to be based on Beverley's experience.

133 H. Coulthard, 'They Shall Covet Their Neighbor's Indians,' *The Young Canadian* (8 April 1891), 164.

134 Foster, *The Mohawk Princess*, 42.

135 AO, E. Johnson, 'Chiefswood,' unpublished typescript, chapters 5, 7. TUA, Johnson Collection, E. Johnson, file 1/13, E. Johnson, undated handwritten note.

136 'From the Child's Viewpoint' (1910).

137 See, for example, Keller, *Pauline*, 261–2; NAC, Frank Yeigh Papers, Jean Stevinson to Frank Yeigh (21 April 1931).

138 'Pauline Johnson's Sister Sits in Sun,' *VP* (14 March 1936).

139 T.S.H. Shearman, 'Pauline Johnson's Shy Sister Devoted Life to Her,' *VP, Saturday Magazine* (25 November 1939).

140 TUA, Johnson Collection, E. Johnson, folder 1/13, undated handwritten note.
141 Ibid.
142 See AO, E. Johnson, 'Chiefswood,' chapters 6 and 8. On Converse, see Landsman, 'The "Other" as Political Symbol.'
143 TUA, Johnson Collection, E. Johnson, undated handwritten note, 'My Mother.'
144 'The Martin Settlement,' 63–4.
145 Thanks to Trudy Nicks of the Royal Ontario Museum for a copy of this letter from the Southwest Museum Library and Museum, Evelyn Johnson to 'Chief, dear old chief,' New York (18 February 1914, emphasis in original).
146 TUA, Johnson Collection, file 1/2, copy of E. Johnson to Chief Josiah Hill (20 July 1914).
147 Ibid., copy of E. Johnson to Robert Borden (New York, 18 March 1915).
148 Ibid., file 1/13, E. Johnson, copy of E. Johnson to 'Chiefs,' [Six Nations Council] (New York, December 1919).
149 Ibid., file 1/24, 'Rapacity of the Whites Feared by Six Nations,' *Globe and Mail* (identified 23 April 1921).
150 Ibid., clipping file, 'The Mohawk Institute,' *Hamilton Spectator* (17 November 1923).
151 D. Johnston, 'Evelyn Johnson Remembers Her Sister ... the famous Pauline,' *Early Canadian Life* (April 1980), B6.
152 BMA, Johnson Family Papers, Evelyn Johnson, Final Will.
153 TUA, Johnson Collection, E. Johnson, undated handwritten note.

2: 'I am a woman'

The chapter title is a quotation from Johnson's short story, 'As It Was in the Beginning.' Esther's full statement, 'They account for it by the fact that I am a Redskin. They seem to have forgotten I am a woman,' targets Europeans' failure to acknowledge distinctions among Native peoples.
1 'My Mother' (1909).
2 Quoted in Keen and McKeon, 'The Story of Pauline Johnson, Canada's Passionate Poet,' 96.
3 See 'Fidelis' [Agnes Maule Machar], 'The New Ideal of Womanhood,' *Rose-Belford's Weekly* (June 1879), 659–76. On the role of women journalists generally, see Lang, *Women Who Made the News,* and Lang and Hale, 'Women of *The World* and Other Dailies,' 3–23.

4 See Doyle, 'Sui Sin Far and Onoto Watanna: Two Early Chinese-Canadian Authors,' 50–8; Ling and White-Parks, eds., *Mrs. Spring Fragrance and Other Writings*, and White-Parks, *Sui Sin Far/Edith Maude Eaton*.
5 Cunningham, *The New Woman and the Victorian Novel*, 1.
6 McLaren, *The Trials of Masculinity*, 31, 32.
7 J.L. Payne, 'The Displacement of Young Men,' *CM* (August 1893), 469–70.
8 H. Charlesworth, 'The Canadian Girl: An Appreciative Medley,' *CM* (March 1893), 187, 189–90. For a wonderful satire on the romantic heroine, see Kate Westlake Yeigh, 'The Heroine of Romance,' *CM* (November 1898), 69.
9 Charlesworth, 'Miss Pauline Johnson's Poems,' *CM* (September 1895), 480.
10 'Old Maid' letter from 'Evy,' *BE* (26 December 1873), 2.
11 See Waldie, *Brant County* 103–4.
12 'With Barry in the Bow ... Act II. Scene: The Great North Land' (1896).
13 See Doyle, *Annie Howells and Achille Fréchette*, 89.
14 TUA, Johnson Collection, Evelyn Johnson, undated handwritten note.
15 Quoted in Reville, *History of the County of Brant* 632.
16 M. Conrad, '"Sundays Always Make Me Think of Home": Time and Place in Canadian Women's History' in Strong-Boag and Fellman, eds., *Rethinking Canada*, and her 'Recording Angels: The Private Chronicles of Women from the Maritimes Provinces of Canada, 1750–1950' in Prentice and Trofimen-koff, eds., *The Neglected Majority*.
17 Waldie, 'The Iroquois Poetess, Pauline Johnson,' 72.
18 McClung, *The Stream Runs Fast*, 29.
19 SAB, Simpson-Hayes Papers, Johnson to Simpson-Hayes, June 1902 [?].
20 MUL, Johnson to Alice Fenton Freeman [Faith Fenton], Oct. 17, 1893. See also Downie, *Passionate Pen*, and Freeman, *Kit's Kingdom*. On Pauline's friend-ships with Flora M. Denison and Coleman, see McRaye, *Pauline Johnson and Her Friends*, 92.
21 VCA, Papers of the CWPC, clipping VP (24 November 1910).
22 NAC, Frank Yeigh Papers, Jean Stevinson to Frank Yeigh, 21 April 1931. As Bertha Jean Thompson, before her marriage, she wrote a 1904 sketch of Johnson for the *McMaster University Monthly*.
23 Quoted in J. Stevinson, 'Friends Pay Tribute to Indian Poetess on Anniver-sary of Death,' *Calgary Herald* (5 March 1932).
24 MUL, Johnson Papers, McClung to Johnson, 5 August [1912].
25 McRaye, *Town Hall Tonight*, 62, and MUL, Johnson Papers, Johnson to Mrs Campbell, 5 October 1912, cited by Johnston, *Buckskin and Broadcloth*, 217.

26 These complicated stories are well told in Keller, *Pauline.*

27 Queen's University Archives, Wilfred Campbell Papers, Johnson to Mrs Campbell, 29 June 1895.

28 On the racism of the first Canadian feminists, see Bacchi, *Liberation Deferred?* and Valverde, *The Age of Light, Soap, and Water.*

29 *SN* (3 December 1892), 8; 'Points about People,' ibid. (7 July 1906), 10.

30 E.T. Seton, Introduction, *The Shagganappi* (1913), 5.

31 Stringer, 'Wild Poets I've Known,' 29.

32 'With Barry in the Bow ... Act III: The Land of the Setting Sun' (1897).

33 Rasporich, 'Native Women Writing: Tracing the Patterns,' 43.

34 Our thanks to Wendy Smith for her essay, 'Nationalism and Motherhood/ Domestic Spaces in a Selection of E. Pauline Johnson's Articles Published in *The Mother's Magazine*, 1907–1912.' Paper for English 804, Simon Fraser University (6 January 1997).

35 'From the Child's Viewpoint' (1910).

36 Charles Edward Dedrick, 'To E. Pauline Johnson,' *CM* (September 1893), 549.

37 'Outdoor Pastimes for Women' (July 1893).

38 'With Barry in the Bow. Act I – Scene: The Land of Evangeline' (1896).

39 'With Paddle and Peterboro' (1890).

40 This was Cincinnatus Hiner or Heine Miller (1841?–1913), an American poet, famous in the latter half of the nineteenth century for his rhetorical poems of the West, in which he claimed to have lived with the Indians for a time and served variously as a pony-express rider, Indian fighter, and horse-thief. He was particularly popular among the English, who called him 'the Byron of Oregon.'

41 'The Singer of Tantramar' (1896).

42 Foster, *The Mohawk Princess*, 145.

43 Ibid., 143.

44 M.D. Stetz, 'New Grub Street and the Woman Writer of the 1890s' in Manos and Rochelson, eds., *Transforming Genres*, 34–5.

45 'Around Town,' *SN* (6 September 1890).

46 NAC, John Willison Papers, Johnson to John Willison, 21 January 1903.

47 H.L. Gates, Jr., Foreword to Graham, ed., *Complete Poems of Frances E.W. Harper*, xvi.

48 Doyle, 'Sui Sin Far and Onoto Watanna: Two Early Chinese-Canadian Authors,' 53.

49 P.L. Neufeld, 'Pauline Johnson, The Poet,' *The Native People* (18 August 1978), 4.

50 Quoted in J. Stevinson, 'Indian Poetess' Birthday Is Commemorated Today by Many Lovers of Her Verse,' *Calgary Herald* (March 1934?).
51 TUA, Johnson Collection, E. Johnson, undated handwritten note.
52 AO, Johnson Papers, Johnson to O'Brien, 21 September 1894.
53 'Coaching on the Cariboo Trail' (1914).
54 'With Barry in the Bow. Act IV. Scene: The Same' (1897).
55 See, for example, Cameron, *The New North*, and Murphy, *Janey Canuck in the West*.
56 See, for example, 'Among the Blackfoots' (1902) and, with Owen Smiley, 'There and Back' (1894). Bad feelings between B.C. Natives and Asians owed much to their competition in the fisheries. See Newell, *Tangled Webs of History* and Muszynski, *Cheap Wage Labour.*
57 'The Song My Paddle Sings' (1893).
58 'Around the Pine Camp Fire,' *New York Times* (20 August 1893).
59 Ibid. See also Johnson, 'Sail and Paddle' (c. 1893).'
60 'Outdoor Pastimes for Women' (May 1893; emphasis in original).
61 'Canoeing' (1891).
62 'Outdoor Pastimes for Women' (May 1892).
63 'Canoe and Canvas' (1893).
64 'Outdoor Pastimes for Women' (December 1892).
65 'On Wings of Steel' (1892).
66 'Outdoor Pastimes for Women' (June 1892).
67 'Striking Camp' (1891).
68 'Outdoor Pastimes for Women' (October 1892).
69 See Lenskyj, 'Femininity First: Sport and Physical Education for Ontario Girls,' 4–17 and 'Training for "True Womanhood": Physical Education for Girls in Ontario Schools,' 205–23.
70 'Outdoor Pastimes for Women' (May 1893) and M.J. Smith, 'Graceful Athleticism or Robust Womanhood,' 120–37.
71 'A Day's Frog Fishing' (1890).
72 'Outdoor Pastimes for Women' (July 1893).
73 Ibid. (February 1892). See also 'Canoe and Canvas' (1893).
74 'With Barry in the Bow. Act I' (1896). The reference is to popular Scottish novelist William Black (1841–98).
75 'Announcement,' *MM* (January 1908). See also her 'Winter Indoor Life of the Indian Mother and Children' with its 'charming picture of how the Indian mother and children partake of mental and physical recreations during the winter months' (ibid., February 1908).
76 'Outdoor Pastimes for Women' (October 1892, July 1893). See also her

favourable references to darker skin in the poems 'Harvest Time' (1894), 'Lady Lorgnette' (1903), and 'The King's Consort' (1912). Compare these with the wonderfully ironic commentary, 'Natural Tan,' by the Ojibwa singer-songwriter Shingoose (Curtis Johnny) in Neuenfeldt, 'First Nations and Métis Songs as Identity Narratives,' 215.

77 'A Red Girl's Reasoning' (1893).

78 'From the Child's Viewpoint,' Part II (1910).

79 See also 'A Lost Luncheon' (1910), 'A Story of a Boy and His Dog' (1892), 'We'hro's Sacrifice' (1907), and 'Jack O'Lantern' (1909).

80 'The Scarlet Eye' (1908).

81 'The Great Deep Water. A Legend of "The Flood"' (1912).

82 Billson, 'Keepers of the Culture: Attitudes towards Women's Liberation and the Women's Movement in Canada,' 3, 10.

83 See Johnston, *Buckskin and Broadcloth*, 128–9. She cites an unidentified interview, where Johnson suggests the subject is a young nun she met in St Boniface. Foster, in *The Mohawk Princess*, indicates that the tale of a young unmarried mother buried in the graveyard, told by a nun, provided the inspiration. In either case, the message in its sympathies is much the same.

84 For this perspective see Bacchi, *Liberation Deferred?* and Valverde, *The Age of Light, Soap, and Water.* For an introduction to the controversies among historians, see Strong-Boag, '"Ever a Crusader,"' in *Rethinking Canada.*

85 Burton, *Burdens of History*, 1–2; Ware, *Beyond the Pale*, 163.

86 Leprohon, 'The White Maiden and the Indian Girl,' *The Poetical Writing of Mrs. Leprohon*; Kathleen F.M. Sullivan, 'The Nepigon Indians to Canada,' *CM* (October 1896), 510; D.M. Hallman, 'Cultivating a Love of Canada through History: Agnes Maule Machar, 1837–1927' in Boutilier and Prentice, eds., *Creating Historical Memory*; C. Morgan, 'Wampum and Waffle-Irons: Gender and National Identities in the Writing of Canadian Popular History, 1880s–1930s,' paper presented at the Canadian Historical Association conference, 1996; McClung, 'Babette' (1907) and 'Red and White' (1921) in Davis, ed., *Stories Subversive*; Jean N. McIlwraith, 'The Assimilation of Christina' in Campbell and McMullen, eds., *New Women.*

87 See L. Hauptman, 'Designing Woman: Minnie Kellogg, Iroquois Leader' in Moses and Wilson, eds., *Indian Lives*, and S. Alice Callahan, *Wynema*, edited and introduced by A. LaVonne Brown Ruoff.

88 TUA, Johnson Collection, Evelyn Johnson, handwritten note (unsigned and unidentified).

89 'Iroquois Women of Canada,' (1900).

90 'With Barry in the Bow ... Interlude between Acts II and III' (1896).

91 Billson, 'Keepers of the Culture,' 10.

92 E. Loosley, 'Pauline Johnson 1861–1913' in Innis, ed., *The Clear Spirit*, 89.

93 SAB, Simpson-Hayes Papers, Johnson to Kate Simpson-Hayes, 3 February 1899, 4 July 1902.

94 J. Stevinson, 'Canada's Famous Indian Poetess,' *Lethbridge Herald* (21 March 1931), 3.

95 AO, Johnson Papers, Johnson to O'Brien, 21 September 1894.

96 NAC, Clifford Sifton Papers, Johnson to Clifford Sifton, 9 February 1900.

97 Doyle, *Annie Howells and Achille Fréchette*, 89.

98 Public Archives of New Brunswick, Wood Papers, Laura Wood, 'Reminiscences of 1900'; Foster, *The Mohawk Princess*, 155.

99 MURBSC, W.D. Lighthall Papers, Johnson to W. D. Lighthall, 18 September 1892.

100 See MacMillan, McMullen, and Waterston, *Silenced Sextet*.

101 Isabel Ecclestone McKay, 'Pauline Johnson: A Reminiscence,' *CM* (July 1913), 277.

102 UTFRBR, James E. Wetherell Papers, Johnson to J.E. Wetherell, 20 February 1895

103 Johnson to J.D. Logan, 5 December 1912, reproduced in 'Appendix 1,' John C. Adams, 'English-Canadian Poetry and the Critics,' MA thesis, Acadia University, 1955.

3: 'Unique figure on the borderland'

The chapter title is a quotation from an article by Touchstone (Hector Charlesworth), 'Baton and Buskin,' in the *Vancouver Province* of 6 October 1894.

1 Dewart, 'Introductory Essay,' *Selections from Canadian Poets*, ix.

2 *The Young Canadian* (22 April 1891), 200.

3 Jameson, *Winter Studies and Summer Rambles in Canada* (London: Saunders and Oatley, 1838), 2: 35. For examples of sympathetic poems see M.E. Sawtell, 'The Indian's Refusal' (1840), and A.M. Machar, 'Quebec to Ontario, A Plea for the Life of Riel, September 1885' (1885), both in Gerson and Davies, eds., *Canadian Poetry*, R. Leprohon, 'The White Maiden and the Indian Girl' in *The Poetical Works of Mrs. Leprohon*, and Van, 'The Red and the White,' *SN* (20 July 1889), 6.

4 MURBSC, W.D. Lighthall Papers, Johnson to Lighthall (30 August 1888 and 2 October 1892). 'The Indian Death Cry' is presumably 'The Death Cry,' published in *SN* (1 September 1888), 6.

5 *The Athenaeum* (28 September 1889), 412. Johnson responded to him in the

same idiom with reference to her 'brave wild ancestors,' MURBSC, Johnson to 'Watts' (7 April 1890), Lighthall Papers. Watts-Dunton was so enamoured of his initial assessment of Johnson's contribution to Canadian literature that he cited it at length twenty-four years later, in his memorial introduction to *Flint and Feather* that appears in all editions of that book published after Johnson's death in 1913.

6 Yeigh, 'E. Pauline Johnson: An Appreciation and A Memory,' *Everywoman's World* (February 1918), 11.

7 Yeigh, 'Memories of Pauline Johnson,' *Family Herald and Weekly Star* (23 March 1927). Versions of this article, under the same title, appeared in the *Ottawa Journal* (5 June 1926) and *CB* (October 1929); the latter was reprinted in several newspapers, including the *BE*.

8 H. Coulthard, 'They Shall Covet Their Neighbor's Indians,' *The Young Canadian* 1, no. 11 (April 1891), 164.

9 Touchstone [Hector Charlesworth], 'A Canadian Literature Evening,' *SN* (23 January 1892), 7.

10 Charlesworth, *Candid Chronicles*, 100. He also claims that 'whenever any one of these celebrities was playing in Toronto, Pauline Johnson was usually asked to come and stay with them.' Of this list, only Rhea is named in Saddlemeyer, *Early Stages*.

11 Elfrida Bell, in Sara Jeannette Duncan's 1894 novel *A Daughter of Today*, is shunned by her respectable London friends after flouting propriety by joining a burlesque group in order to research her novel about showgirls.

12 Davis, *Actresses as Working Women*, 14–16.

13 S. Morgan-Powell, 'Margaret Anglin: Star of Canada' in Rubin, ed., *Canadian Theatre History*, 31. Her father, Timothy Anglin, was Speaker of the House of Commons when she was born.

14 L.M. Montgomery, *Emily's Quest* (Toronto: Seal Books, 1983), 6.

15 UTFRBR, Wetherell Papers, flyer.

16 Keller, *Pauline*, 61.

17 Atwood, *Strange Things*, 91–2.

18 UTFRBR, Wetherell Papers, 'Miss E. Pauline Johnson, The Mohawk Indian Poet-Reciter,' n.d.; see also NAC, Clifford Sifton Papers, reel C503; NAC, William Van Horne Papers, Johnson to Sir William Van Horne, 12 November 1906, v. 87; and MUL, Johnson Papers.

19 MUL, Johnson Papers, *Democrat* (Grand Rapids, Michigan) (18 November 1896), clipping.

20 A flyer for her 1900–1 tour of the Maritimes describes her as 'Canada's Foremost Comedienne and Poetess,' MUL, Johnson Papers; 'Miss Johnson's Success,' *Daily Gleaner* (Fredericton) (19 November 1900), 8.

21 MUL, Johnson Papers, *Toronto Junction Tribune* (23 March 1892) clipping.

22 Toronto Public Library, Canadian Literature Scrapbook, 'A Pictorial Poem and a Picture,' *Canadian Club* (12 December 1912), 75.

23 E. Loosley, 'Pauline Johnson' in Innis, ed., *The Clear Spirit*, 79.

24 Toronto Public Library, Canadian Literature scrapbooks, 'The Passing of a Poet,' *Canadian Club* (n.d.), 71.

25 MUL, Johnson Papers, 'Pretty Indian Poetess,' *Evening Press* (Grand Rapids, Michigan) (18 November 1896) and unidentified clippings; 'Johnson-Smily Entertainment,' *Carberry News* (1897), clipping; 'Pauline Johnson, Walter McRaye,' *St. Thomas Times*, n.d.; 'Canadian,' 'A Good Performance' (21 May 1903), clipping; 'Miss Pauline Johnson,' *Charlottetown Daily Examiner* (17 August 1900), clipping.

26 Ibid., 'Elocutionary Entertainment. By Miss E. Pauline Johnson,' *Emerson Journal* (17 December 1897), clipping. Also the *Carberry News* (1897): 'These poems, while possessing considerable poetic merit, are remarkable chiefly as presenting the claims of the red race in a new light.'

27 'Uncle Thomas,' 'Impressions,' *TG* (18 January 1892), 4; E.R. Young, 'E. Pauline Johnson, Indian Poetess and Princess,' *Onward* (19 April 1913), 122.

28 MUL, Johnson Papers, *VW*, undated clipping.

29 Ibid., Kit Coleman, *Toronto Mail*, undated clipping cited by Johnston, *Buckskin and Broadcloth*, 139.

30 MUL, Johnson Papers, *Evening Times* (Kingston), undated clipping. There was considerable truth in this quip: see Carter, *Capturing Women*, 168–79.

31 Johnson Papers, *St. Thomas Times*, undated clipping; ibid. *VW*, undated clipping.

32 Ibid., undated clipping (Winnipeg?); 'Johnson-McRaye at the Opera House Monday Night,' *Daily Gleaner* (18 April 1908). Thanks to Patricia Belier of the New Brunswick Archives for this reference.

33 MUL, Johnson Papers, unidentified and undated clipping.

34 Ibid., 1886–8, Blue scrapbook, Box 6.

35 Her enjoyment of parody appeared as well in 'In the Shadows: My Version,' by 'The Pasha,' not proven to be of her authorship but saved in her scrapbook, and in the playing with audience expectations in her poem 'Held by the Enemy.'

36 'Malcolm' is quoted in 'Personal and Literary,' *TW* (18 January 1895), 186. Frank Yeigh rebutted in a 'Letter to the Editor' (1 February 1895), 228. This was contested by W.A. McLean (22 February 1895), 299, who was in turn answered by Yeigh, A.H. Morrison, and Thomas O'Hagan (1 March 1895), 325–6.

37 MURBSC, Lighthall Papers, Johnson to Lighthall (18 September and
2 October 1892, emphasis in original).

38 The adjective appeared on her letterhead when she was managed by Thomas
Cornyn (SAB, Simpson-Hayes Papers, Johnson to Kate Simpson Hayes, 3
February 1899) and by Charles Wuerz (NAC, Wilfrid Laurier Papers,
Johnson to Laurier, 27 July 1900). Her 1906 publicity materials use the
phrase 'Native Indian Buckskin Costume' and quote Kit Coleman of the *Mail
and Empire* [Toronto]: 'Her Indian costume, which must have cost an
immensity, was accurate in every detail, and most becoming to the wearer'
(Public Archives of British Columbia, Ad Mss 2753, Johnson Papers, pamphlet). I.E. Mackay's term, 'historical Indian buckskins,' also implies authenticity. 'Pauline Johnson: A Reminiscence,' *CM* 41 (July 1913), 277.

39 AO, E. Johnson, 'Chiefswood.' Another interesting example of Longfellow's
influence occurred on the Garden River reserve near Sault St Marie in
August 1900; see Yeigh, 'The Drama of Hiawatha, or Mana-bozho, as Played
by a Band of Canadian Ojibway Indians,' *CM* 17 (July 1901), 208–12.

40 The men in her family were also interested in costume. The account of her
father's wedding outfit in 'My Mother,' whether factual or fictionalized,
points to the importance of dress in creating social value. Her brother
Allen, while an insurance clerk in Hamilton, reportedly partied in his buckskins.

41 Billington, *Land of Savagery, Land of Promise*, 50.

42 Petrone, *Native Literature in Canada*, 75–7. The poster from the William Kirby
Papers, AO, is inserted between pages 70 and 71.

43 VCA, Johnson Papers, flyer for 'The Brant-Sero Concert, Lecture and Dramatic Tour,' May 1902. While preservation of this flyer in the Johnson papers
in Vancouver documents her awareness of him, no evidence survives of personal acquaintance. The Johnson Papers at Trent contain a 1905 clipping
from a Winnipeg newspaper, citing a translation by Brant-Sero, on which
Pauline or Evelyn (their handwriting is similar) disparagingly refers to him
as 'His Nibs.'

44 'A Strong Race Opinion' (1892); B. Wescott, 'Indian Princesses on Parade,'
The Runner 1 (1994), 4–11, 54–5. For later examples of Aboriginal women as
stage performers, see McBride, *Molly Spotted Elk*, and Livingston, *American
Indian Ballerinas*.

45 MUL, Johnson Papers, *Terre Haute Gazette* (1900), undated clipping.

46 J. Butler, 'Performative Acts and Gender Constitution: An Essay in Phenomenology and Feminist Theory' in Case, ed., *Performing Feminisms*, 271. An
interesting comparison is the Canadian-Chinese author Winifred Eaton, who
authenticated her 'Japanese' pseudonym of Onoto Watanna with frontispiece photographs of herself in Japanese dress.

47 There is some inconsistency in reports of the order of Johnson's costumes: according to Walter McRaye (and confirmed by all surviving reviews, e.g. *VP*, 6 October 1894), the Indian costume preceded the evening gown, but Nellie McClung's memoir cites the reverse. See McClung, *The Stream Runs Fast*, 33–4.

48 Evans, *Frontier Theatre*, 184.

49 Touchstone [Hector Charlesworth], 'Baton and Buckskin,' *VP* (6 October 1894) 486.

50 M.E. Leighton, 'Performing Pauline Johnson,' *Essays on Canadian Writing* 65 (Fall 1998), 149.

51 *SN* (26 April 1890).

52 Forster, *Under the Studio Light*, 234; A. Stringer, 'Wild Poets I've Known,' *SN* (11 October 1941), 29. In general, the more moderate descriptions come from those who knew her closely; after her death their elegaic memoirs become more romantic and essentialist. According to Charlesworth, 'I never met any native-born Canadian who gave a more complete sense of aristocracy than Pauline Johnson.' *Candid Chronicles*, 96.

53 Mackay, 'Pauline Johnson: A Reminiscence,' 274. Although discussing writing, the remark extends to her persona.

54 Belsey, *Critical Practice*, 61.

55 See Ryan, *The Trickster Shift*, p. 5.

56 MacLean, *Canadian Savage Folk*, 474.

57 After its first appearance in *TW* in 1885, 'A Cry from an Indian Wife' was reprinted in reviews of the Canadian Literature evening of 16 January 1892 which appeared in both the *TG* and the *BE* on January 18.

58 F. O'Reilly, 'Musical's Departure Leaves Sidewalks for Rent,' *Globe and Mail* (25 July 1998), C1, C8.

59 For example, her essay 'A Strong Race Opinion,' although published in a major newspaper, goes unmentioned in contemporary commentary on Johnson.

60 Leighton, 'Performing Pauline Johnson,' 143.

61 'Pauline Johnson,' editorial *VP* (8 March 1913).

62 *SN* (3 December 1892), 8.

63 On her death, headlines written by newspaper staff frequently paired 'poetess' with 'princess,' testifying to the power of the image of the Indian princess in the popular mind. But it is noteworthy that obituaries written by those who knew her (e.g., Charlesworth in *SN*, Charles Mair in *CM* and in his introduction to *The Moccasin Maker*, Isabel Ecclestone Mackay in *CM*) eschew both 'princess' and 'Tekahionwake,' referring to her as 'Miss Johnson.'

64 Princess references include 'Star Lake (Muskoka)' in *The Young Canadian* (22 August 1891) which is given the by-line 'By E. Pauline Johnson, Brant-

ford, (An Indian Princess),' a passing comment in the *Hamilton Herald*
(1 March 1892), and a fuller description in the *New York Times* (20 August
1893). The *New York Bookman* called her 'the American Indian princess' (July
1895, p. 376), then 'an Indian princess of a proud and ancient tribe' (January 1896, p. 377). The *Democrat* of Grand Rapids, Michigan, described her as
a Mohawk princess 'as lovely as Minnehaha,' MUL, Johnson Papers (18
November 1896), clipping. We have found no evidence to support Keller's
claim that Frank Yeigh billed her as 'The Mohawk Princess,' *Pauline*, 69; see
TG (20 February 1892) for an account of Yeigh's introduction. See also Stedman's chapter on 'La Belle Sauvage' in his *Shadows of the Indian*, Acoose, *Neither Indian Princesses Nor Easy Squaws*, 43, and Canfield, *Sarah Winnemucca of
the Northern Paiutes.*
65 C.G.D. Roberts to E.C. Stedman (8 November 1895), in Boone, ed., *Collected
Letters of Charles G.D. Roberts*, 214.
66 The name belonged to her great-grandfather, then her grandfather. She
once used it shortly after the latter's death, when she signed one of her first
poems, '"Brant," A Memorial Ode' as 'E. Pauline Johnson, Te-ka-hion-wa-ke,'
in the souvenir pamphlet for the unveiling of the Brant Memorial (Chiefswood collection, Johnson Scrapbook). Despite his close acquaintance, Charlesworth was quite mystified when 'Tekahionwake' appeared on the title
page of *White Wampum* ('Miss Pauline Johnson's Poems,' *CM* 5, September
1895, p. 478). As well, the name does not appear on her 1908 booklet, *When
George Was King.*
67 The author of 'The Rift' (*Gems of Poetry*, 1884, p. 127) is identified as Margaret Rox, and the author of 'Charming Word Pictures' *Brantford Courier*
(15 August, 23 August, 4 September, 1890) is 'Rollstone.'
68 SAB, Simpson-Hayes Papers, Johnson to Kate Simpson-Hayes, n.d. second
letter; VPL NW 921, J 664, Johnson to Mrs (?) Higginbotham (4 October
1897). See also MURBSC, Lighthall Papers, Johnson to W.D. Lighthall
(2 October 1892); NAC, Yeigh Papers, E. Pauline Johnson to Frank Yeigh,
(1 April 1901); NAC, Gertrude O'Hara Papers, cited in Keller, *Pauline*, 157;
PABC, Johnson Papers, Johnson to L. Makovski, Christmas 1911; UTFRBR,
E. Pauline Johnson to J. Wetherell (1893); NAC, Laurier Papers, Johnson to
Wilfrid Laurier (28 March 1906) (signed 'one of your Indian wards'). See
also her letters to Seton: her first (2 August 1905), requesting his assistance
in selling a wampum belt, is signed 'Faithfully yours, E.P.J. "Tekahionwake"';
the second (17 August), thanking him for having done so, ends 'Thine in
the brotherhood, Tekahionwake.' NAC, E.T. Seton Papers, vol. 16.
69 Roberts's first book of poetry, *Orion and Other Poems*, appeared in Philadelphia in 1880; his second, *In Divers Tones* (1887), was co-published by Dawson

in Montreal and Lothrop in Boston. Of his eleven books published in the 1809s, only one, *Songs of the Common Day* (1893), had a co-publisher (Longman of London) who was not American. Lampman's poetry was all published in Canada with the exception of *Lyrics of Earth* (1895), which was issued by the Boston firm of Copeland & Day. Publishers in Canada, New York, and Boston likewise predominate for W.W. Campbell and Duncan Campbell Scott.

70 MUL, Johnson Papers, 'An Evening with Canadian Poets,' unidentified clipping, probably 18 January 1892.

71 MURBSC, Lighthall Papers, Johnson to Lighthall, 2 October 1892.

72 *TG* (13 February 1892), 20. See Boone, ed., *Collected Letters of Charles G.D. Roberts*, 157, 160, 161, 209, 214; Keller, *Pauline*, 73, 108–9. As Roberts's letter introducing Johnson to Gilder is dated 12 October 1895, Gilder and Johnson had not met in London in 1894 as is claimed by Keller. Also erroneous is McRaye's assertion that Roberts was responsible for publishing Johnson's poems in *The Week*. See his *Pauline Johnson and Her Friends*, 27. Roberts resigned his editorship in the spring of 1884, a year before her first poem appeared.

73 Roberts to B. Carman (20 November 1892) in Boone, ed., *Collected Letters of Charles G.D. Roberts*, 160.

74 Gerson, 'Some Notes Concerning Pauline Johnson,' *Canadian Notes & Queries* 34 (Autumn 1985), 16–19. UTFRBR, Wetherell Papers, Johnson to Wetherell, 28 April 1893.

75 *Bookman* (New York) (January 1896), 377.

76 Duncan, 'Woman's World,' *TG* (14 October 1886). It is interesting that Mackay's 'Pauline Johnson: A Reminiscence' mentions the Howells family without naming its most famous literary member.

77 According to Polly Howells, great-granddaughter of W.D., there are no extant letters from the Johnsons in the Howells papers. References to the Johnsons in Howells's biography derive from an interview in the *New York Times* on the occasion of his seventy-fifth birthday in 1912, which refers romantically to the Johnsons without any awareness that Pauline was then suffering from cancer and poverty in Vancouver.

78 B.J. Thompson (later J. Stevinson), 'Pauline Johnson: Tekahionwake,' *McMaster University Monthly* (December 1904), 106; Charlesworth, *Candid Chronicles*, 98.

79 The Chiefswood collection at contains two books Charlesworth gave to Johnson in 1892. On the flyleaf of the first, Ernest Rhys's edition of *Malory's History of King Arthur and the Quest of the Holy Grail*, appears a poem addressed to Miss E. Pauline Johnson from H.W. Charlesworth dated 10 March 1892

(Johnson's thirty-first birthday). The simpler prose dedication of the second (*Canadian Songs and Poems*, actually the 1892 London edition of Lighthall's *Songs of the Great Dominion*), a Christmas gift, addresses her as Pauline and is signed Hector. Charlesworth met her through his editorial apprenticeship at *SN* (see his *Candid Chronicles*, 96); there is also an undated exchange of verses in the Chiefswood scrapbook, reprinted in Johnston, *Buckskin and Broadcloth*, 139. Whatever their relationship, his ardour seems to have cooled by 1893, as his reference to her in his article, 'The Canadian Girl' (*CM* 1 [1893], 186–93), is surprisingly perfunctory, while his review of *The White Wampum* (*CM* [September 1895], 478–80) faults her Indian poems for their polemics.

80 He would become editor of *SN* (1926–32) and then in 1932 first head of the Canadian Radio Broadcasting Commission, precursor of the CBC.

81 Charlesworth, 'The Indian Poetess: A Study,' *Lake Magazine* (September 1892), 81–7.

82 J.D. Robins, 'Backgrounds of Future Canadian Poetry,' *Acta Victoriana* 29 (March 1915); reprinted in Ballstadt, ed., *The Search for English-Canadian Literature*, 141. Concerning recent notions of finding Canadian identity in soil-based Native mythology, see J. Newlove's poem, 'The Pride' (1968) and Goldie's critique of 'indigenization' in *Fear and Temptation*.

83 McRaye tried to collect material from Scott for *Pauline Johnson and her Friends*; however, nothing came of Scott's response that he would 'try to write something about Pauline Johnson & her work,' and 'knew all the family & was able to do something for Evelyn.' MUL, McRaye Papers, D.C. Scott to McRaye, 7 April 1943.

84 McRaye cites the reminiscences of F.G. Scott (no relation), *Pauline Johnson and Her Friends*, 56–7. As well, D.C. Scott's published articles on Canada's Indians share Johnson's elevation of the Mohawks and Iroquois above other Aboriginals (e.g., his comments on Brant, in 'Indian Affairs, 1763–1841,' *Canada and Its Provinces* [1913], IV: 700, 713).

85 D.C. Scott to J. Thomson, 8 April 1920, cited by P. Geller, '"Hudson's Bay Company Indians": Images of Native People and the Red River Pageant' in Bird, ed., *Dressing in Feathers*, 65–77.

86 Seton, Introduction to Johnson, *The Shagganappi*, 6–7.

87 'Poet's Name Suggested for Theatre,' *VP* (13 April 1961), 3. Other suggestions included Princess Margaret and Princess Anne; with great imagination, it was eventually christened the Vancouver Playhouse.

88 Perkins, *Is Literary History Possible?* 39.

89 Frye, 'Preface to an Uncollected Anthology,' 1956; reprinted in *The Bush Garden*, 171.

90 Our thanks to Janet Friskney for references to Malcolm Ross's correspondence which indicate that the term 'Confederation Poets' was his own coinage, beginning in 1954 when the volume was first contemplated, and confirmed in response to an inquiry in 1982. See Rare Books and Special Collections, Mills Memorial Library, McMaster University, McClelland and Stewart Papers, series A, box 54, file 15, S.J. Totten to Malcolm Ross, 14 April 1954, and UTFRBR, Malcolm Ross Papers, MS 277, file 6, Ross to William Toye, 24 March 1982, note.

91 Roberts to H.A. Kennedy (27 May 1933) in Boone, ed., *The Collected Letters of Charles G.D. Roberts*, 449.

92 Deacon, *Poteen*, 164–6; Logan and French, *Highways of Canadian Literature*, 195; Pierce, *An Outline of Canadian Literature*, 79; Stevenson, *A People's Best*, 148. Her omission from MacMechan's *Headwaters of Canadian Literature* may be attributable to MacMechan's strongly Atlantic perspective. McRaye is echoing received opinion when he firmly links her with the 'little group of the "60's … The Golden Age" of Canadian literature,' in company with Lampman, Campbell, Carman, Parker, and Roberts, *Pauline Johnson and Her Friends*, 148.

93 Valaskasis, 'Sacajawea and Her Sisters: Images and Indians,' *Indian Princesses and Cowboys*, 27, 31. The interior quotation is from Daniel, *The Imaginary Indian*, 175.

94 See M.A. Walker, review of *The Mohawk Princess* in *CB* (February 1932), 25; Mrs W. Garland Foster, 'The Lyric Beauty of Pauline Johnson's Poetry,' *CB* (March 1934), 37, 43; Foster, 'Pauline Johnson's Gift to Vancouver,' *CB* (June 1936), 6–7. See also J. Mulvihill, 'The "Canadian Bookman" and Literary Nationalism,' 48–59.

95 J. Ayre, 'Canadian Writers of the Past. IX. Pauline Johnson,' 17. The reference to Longfellow connects Johnson to the image of the commodified Indian princess; some of the postcards in the Indian Princesses and Cowgirls exhibit cite a few lines of poetry, all from American poets (they were produced in the United States), and mostly from Longfellow.

96 Scott, 'The Canadian Authors Meet,' *New Provinces* (1936; reprinted Toronto, 1976), 55.

97 Irving Layton, ed., *Love Where the Nights Are Long* (Toronto: McClelland and Stewart, 1962). Two poems by Bliss Carman, one by Charles G.D. Roberts, and one by D.C. Scott represent Johnson's era.

98 Victor Li, 'Selling Modernism: Resisting Commodification, Commodifying Resistance, 38; Wexler, *Who Paid for Modernism?* xii.

99 Despite his rejection of evaluative criticism in his international writing, evaluation was a consistent thread in Frye's Canadian criticism, from his

annual reviews of 'Letters in Canada' in the *University of Toronto Quarterly* in the 1950s, to his two influential conclusions in the *Literary History of Canada,* to his last speech before his death. See L. Hutcheon, 'Frye Recoded: Post-modernity and the Conclusions' in Lee and Denham, eds., *The Legacy of Northrop Frye,* 110–21.

100　Daniells, 'Minor Poets, 1880–1920' in Klinck, ed., *Literary History of Canada,* 425–6.

101　S. Djwa, '"Who Is This Man Smith": Second and Third Thoughts on Canadian Modernism' in W.H. New, ed., *Inside the Poem* (1992), 206.

102　The word 'lonely' recurs frequently in Djwa, '"A New Soil and a Sharp Sun": The Landscape of a Modern Canadian Poetry,' 3–17. On the emptying of the land in the work of the Group of Seven, see J. Bordo, 'Jack Pine: Wilderness Sublime or the Erasure of the Aboriginal Presence for the Landscape,' 98–128.

103　A.C. Hamilton, 'Northrop Frye as a Canadian Critic' in Lee, Chung, and Shin, eds., *Canadian Literature,* 9.

104　D. Galloway, 'The Voyageurs' in Klinck, ed., *Literary History of Canada,* 6.

105　A feat that Scott Watson argues was underpinned by a development agenda, and that Graham Carr suggests may have been assisted by the American-oriented continentalism of the major Canadian modernists. See Watson, 'Race, Wilderness, Territory and the Origins of Modern Canadian Landscape Painting'; G. Carr, '"All We North Americans": Literary Culture and the Continentalist Ideal,' *American Review of Canadian Studies* 17, no. 2 (1987), 145–57.

106　On the artificiality of the Group of Seven's representation of the wilderness, see Frank Underhill, 'False Hair on the Chest,' *SN* (3 October 1936), 1, 3, and Tippett, *Making Culture,* 84.

107　See L. Salem-Wiseman, ' "Verily the White Man's Ways Were the Best": Duncan Campbell Scott, Native Culture, and Assimilation,' 120–42.

108　Frye, Conclusion in Klinck, ed., *Literary History of Canada,* 845–6.

109　*Collected Poems of Frank Prewett* (1964), 5. Ironically, Prewett gained an entrée into elite English Georgian cultural circles by occasionally representing himself as Indian: see Meyer, 'Frank Prewett,' *Profiles in Canadian Literature,* 57.

110　A. Klein, 'Indian Reservation: Caughnawaga,' in Pollock, Mayne, and Caplan, eds., *Selected Poems* (Toronto: University of Toronto Press, 1997), 113–14. A more recent connection between the persecution of Jews and Indians appears in Schneider and Gottfriedson, *In Honour of Our Grandmothers.*

111 'Modernists, in America as elsewhere, drew on "primitive" art as a critique of bourgeois philistine modernity. Native Americans were now seen not as an "immature race" but as inheritors of ancient wisdom. Primitivism was reborn.' Carr, *Inventing the American Primitive*, 200.

112 See Colombo, *Songs of the Indians*, vol. 1: 103–4, and Carr, *Inventing the American Primitive*, 222–9. Djwa in '"A New Soil and a Sharp Sun"' links the beginnings of imagism to the northern landscape, but without any reference to Aboriginal culture (p. 7).

113 Castro, *Interpreting the Indian*, 31–2. He cites George W. Cronyn, 'Indian Melodists and Mr. Untermeyer,' *Dial* (23 August 1919), 162–3, 31.

114 Kenny, *On Second Thought*, 21–2.

115 N. Hamilton, 'Pauline Johnson Honored but Not for Her Poetry,' *VS* (10 March 1961), 1; Davies, 'Writer's Diary,' *VP* (8 April 1961), 19; Richler, 'Headdresses Jingled but Highbrows Stayed Away,' *VS* (10 May 1961), 5; Pacey, *Creative Writing in Canada*, 68; NAC, Pacey Papers, MG 30 D339, vol. 2, Pacey to Mrs Olive Dickason, 6 March 1961. See also Rashley's *Poetry in Canada*, which barely acknowledges Johnson because she doesn't suit his organizational scheme, and Bissell's *Great Canadian Writing*, which omits Johnson from his selection of seventy-five men and only nine women.

116 H. Lutz, 'Canadian Native Literature and the Sixties: A Historical and Bibliographical Survey,' 167–92.

117 C. Lillard, 'A Choice of Lens,' 155.

118 L. Monkman, *A Native Heritage*; Goldie, *Fear and Temptation*.

119 M. Harry, 'Literature in English by Native Canadians,' 146–53; G.W. Lyon, 'Pauline Johnson: A Reconsideration,' 136–59; N. Shrive, 'What Happened to Pauline?' 25–38.

120 See Leighton, '"Performing" Pauline Johnson: Representations of "the Indian Poetess" in the Periodical Press, 1892–95,' and Rose, 'Pauline Johnson: New World Poet.'

121 Acoose, *Neither Indian Princesses nor Easy Squaws*, 65–6, 106–7.

122 For example, see Monique Mojica's brilliant play, *Princess Pocahontas and the Blue Spots* (1991).

123 Both poems were selected by Grant for *Our Bit of Truth* and for Moses and Goldie's *Anthology of Canadian Native Literature in English*. Grant also includes the story 'Catharine of the "Crow's Nest."' Moses and Goldie add the canoeing poems 'Shadow River' and 'The Song My Paddle Sings,' as well as the story 'We-hro's Sacrifice.'

124 Atwood, 'A Double-Bladed Knife: Subversive Laughter in Two Stories by Tom King,' 243. Atwood's lectures were published as *Strange Things* (1995).

See Petrone, *Native Literature* and Petrone, ed., *First People, First Voices*; Grant, *Our Bit of Truth*; and the first edition of Moses and Goldie, *An Anthology of Canadian Native Literature in English*. Francis's *The Imaginary Indian* keeps Johnson more consistently in sight – due, perhaps, to his Vancouver perspective.

125 Johnson is the subject of several recent dissertations at American universities. A. LaVonne Brown Ruoff, at the University of Illinois (Chicago), has been the most dedicated Johnson scholar. Entries on Johnson or selections from her work appear in many recent American publications, including *Oxford Companion to Women Writers of the United States* (1995), *Dictionary of Literary Biography* no. 175, *Native American Writers of the United States* (1997), Bernd C. Peyer, ed., *The Singing Spirit: Early Short Stories by North American Indians* (1989), Paula Gunn Allen, ed., *Voice of the Turtle: American Indian Literature 1900–70* (1994), A. LaVonne Brown Ruoff's bibliography of 'American Indian Literature' in A.L.B. Ruoff and Jerry Ward, eds., *Redefining American Literary History* (1990), and Ruoff's 'Early Native American Women Authors: Jane Johnston Schoolcraft, Sarah Winnemucca, S. Alice Callahan, E. Pauline Johnson, and Zitkala-Sa' in K. Killcup ed., *Nineteenth-Century American Women Writers* (1988).

126 R. Stacy's 'Afterword' to *Iroquois Fires* emphasizes Winslow's oratorical ability, finding her less conventional and less sentimental (p. 144) than Johnson. Like Winslow, Loretta Jobin cites Johnson as an inspiration (see Perrault and Vance, eds., *Writing the Circle*, 122), as does Kenny (*On Second Thought*, 21–2). Thomas King's presentation of Johnson in *Green Grass, Running Water* is a little enigmatic, as is Chief Lindsay Marshall's poem, 'My Paddle Does Not Sing' (*Clay Pots and Bones* [1997], 82).

127 Interview with Lee Maracle (27 October 1990) in Lutz, *Contemporary Challenges*, 171; Brant, *Writing as Witness*, 6–8.

128 Crate, *Pale as Real Ladies*, 7–8, 27, 33, 56–8.

129 Brant, *Writing as Witness*, 5.

4: 'The most interesting English poetess now living'

The quotation in the chapter title comes from an article by T. Watts-Dunton in the *Atheneum* (28 September 1889), 412.

1 The first edition of 1912 contained twenty late poems; four more were added in 1916, and one more in 1917.

2 See Mrs W.G. Foster, *The Mohawk Princess* (1931), 193–96. A partial list of published poems compiled by McRaye is at Queen's (coll. 2001b; box 39; file 3). As well, there are many unreliable references to periodicals where

she is reported to have published, and there remains the possibility of
anonymous publication.

3 AO, E. Johnson, 'Chiefswood,' ts, p. 106.
4 AO, Johnson Papers, Johnson to O'Brien, 6 October 1903.
5 Keller, *Pauline*, 195.
6 University of Guelph, L.M. Montgomery Papers, Price Record Book. See
   Gerson, 'The Business of a Woman's Life: Money and Motive in the Careers
   of Early Canadian Women Writers' in Potvin and Williamson, eds., *Women's
   Writing and the Literary Institution/L'écriture au féminin et l'institution littéraire*,
   77–94.
7 Keller, *Pauline*, 85–6, speculates that *The White Wampum* was published on
   commission, with the author paying the costs, but according to experts on
   the Bodley Head, by the time Johnson's book appeared, John Lane normally
   offered 'straight royalties on copies sold.' Stetz and Lasner, *England in the
   1890s*, 3.
8 UTFRBR, J.E. Wetherell Papers, Johnson to Wetherell, 28 April 1893.
9 Adams, *Sir Charles God Damn*, 64.
10 See 'Rondeau' ('Some bittersweet ...') (1889), 'At Husking Time' (1891),
   'Rondeau: The Skater' (1892), 'Rondeau: Crow's Nest Pass' (1894).
11 Logan and French, in *Highways of Canadian Literature*, described her as a
   balladist (p. 126). The first known musical setting of one of her poems is
   'Life,' with music by Arthur E. Fisher; see *Musical Journal* (15 July 1887),
   108–9; the most recent is the 1994 recording of 'The Song My Paddle Sings'
   by the group Tamarack on the Grand. Foster, in *The Mohawk Princess*,
   describes others (p. 111).
12 Keller, *Pauline*, 152–60.
13 McRaye, *Pauline Johnson and Her Friends*, 55.
14 Keller, *Pauline*, 267–8. She speculates that the subject of the photo is Charles
   Wuerz.
15 McRaye, *Pauline Johnson and Her Friends*, 37. This poem, 'Ex Voto,' does
   not appear in *Poems* (1904) published by Tucker's friends after his death.
   The frontispiece photograph clearly disqualifies him as the handsome blond
   canoeist.
16 Keller, *Pauline*, 53. Mrs W. Garland Foster in *The Mohawk Princess* notes, in a
   rather protective manner, 'Some curiosity has been indulged in regarding
   Pauline Johnson's love affairs. That she had them, should go without saying,
   in the case of one who radiated energy and vitality as she did. Fascinating in
   person, charming in conversation, with a tempting trick of repartee it could
   not have been otherwise. There were several engagements, but something
   always intervened ...' (105).

17 VCA 554-B-4, Canadian Women's Press Club Papers, Memorial Scrapbook, 1910–1930.

18 'Day Dawn.'

19 The editing of the poem, from the first to the final version, emphasizes the concluding sense of loss. The sexual downfall of the apparently liberated New Woman is a common subject of the fiction of the 1890s. See Ardis, *New Woman, New Novels*, Grant Allen, *The Woman Who Did* (1895), and Olive Schreiner, *The Story of an African Farm* (1883).

20 Stetz, 'Sex, Lies, and Printed Cloth: Bookselling at the Bodley Head in the Eighteen-Nineties,' 71–86. Stetz elsewhere describes Lane as attracting 'not the elite, but the would-be elite: writers and illustrators mainly from the lower-middle or solidly middle classes, who were themselves rebels, climbers, and poseurs, eager to establish themselves as a cultural vanguard to be reckoned with. Many of these were, moveover, artists with varying political agendas and interests in social reform. Some were working purely for change in aesthetic standards, some for the equality of women, some for the levelling of the class system, and some for the forging of cultural ties between England and the rest of Europe.' Stetz and Lasner, *England in the 1890s*, viii.

21 R. Miles, 'George Egerton, Bitextuality and Cultural (Re)Production in the 1890s,' *Women's Writing* 3, no. 3 (1996), 246.

22 Showalter, ed., Introduction to *Daughters of Decadence*, xi.

23 No other accounts or records corroborate the story of the intervention of Clement Scott that appears in Thompson's 1904 *McMaster University Monthly* article which contains significant errors about other details of Johnson's life. Note that in Hector Charlesworth's version (*Candid Chronicles*), John Davidson is the major intervenor, while McRaye also mentions Richard Le Gallienne (*Pauline Johnson and Her Friends*, 51). An 1897 interview with the *Chicago Tribune* cites Andrew Lang and Sir Frederick Leighton as Johnson's advisers, MUL, Johnson Papers, clipping, 'Poetess of the Iroquois' (28 January 1897).

24 Sandra M. Gilbert and Susan Gubar, eds., *The Norton Anthology of Literature by Women*, 2nd ed. (1996), 1011. *The Norton Anthology* represents this period with very few women poets. There are no articles on poetry in the special issue of *Women's Writing* devoted to the New Woman.

25 Logan and French, *Highways of Canadian Literature*, 196.

26 Hale, 'The White Wampum,' *The Critic* (New York) (4 June 1895), 4.

27 MUL, Johnson Papers, review of *The White Wampum, Manchester Guardian* (16 July 1895), clipping. See also *Times Literary Supplement* (4 December 1913), 590: 'Love ... makes her momentarily perfect as a poetess.'

28 Charlesworth, 'The Indian Poetess: A Study,' *Lake Magazine* 1 (September 1892), 81–7.

29 See, for example, Lionel Makovski's editorial in the *VP*, describing her as 'absolutely natural and simple in her love of happiness,' as well as willing to sacrifice herself for her friends (8 March 1913), 6.
30 Lyon, 'Pauline Johnson: A Reconsideration,' 141.
31 Logan and French, *Highways of Canadian Literature*, 196.
32 'A Mohawk Princess,' *Times Literary Supplement* (4 December 1913), 590. Mrs Siddons, with whom Johnson was compared with some frequency, was the leading Shakespearean tragic actress of her time, especially known for her performance of Lady Macbeth.
33 MUL, Johnson Papers, 'Johnson-Smily Entertainment,' n.p., undated.
34 'The Indian Poetess: A Study'; Miss Pauline Johnson's Poems,' *CM* 5 (September 1895), 479.
35 'A Poet of the Prairie. Miss E. Pauline Johnson: "Tekahionwake,"' *Black and White* 28 (December 1895), 839.
36 Review of *The White Wampum* in *The Academy* (17 August 1895).
37 *TW* (25 June 1885), 474; Wetherald, 'Conquering Heroes,' ibid. (23 July 1885).
38 The Cypress Hills was the site of a massacre of thirty-six Assiniboine by American wolf hunters and provided one justification for John A. Macdonald's creation of the North-West Mounted Police. The Sioux or the Dakota were allied to the British during the War of 1812, only to be betrayed by the Treaty of Ghent two years later. After the Battle of the Little Big Horn in 1876, the Americans drove some Sioux, including Sitting Bull, into Canada. Note that *Flint and Feather* introduces the erroneous spelling 'Cyprus.'
39 Frye, 'Preface to an Uncollected Anthology,' *The Bush Garden*, 171–2.
40 Anderson, in *When Passion Reigned: Sex and the Victorians*, notes that romance on the river was a common motif in Victorian popular culture (although not as common as courting at the piano). While Benidickson (*Idleness, Water and a Canoe*, 12–16) questions the logistics of the canoe as a trysting-place, one of our students has testified that anything is possible in a canoe.
41 Lyon, 'Pauline Johnson: A Reconsideration,' 148.
42 In her later series, 'With Barry in the Bow' (1896–7), the female narrator is in the stern because she has far greater experience than her younger cousin Barry. Note how Michael Ondaatje uses the image of the single woman in her canoe in *The English Patient* (1992; reprint Vintage 1996), 292, 296, to represent Clara as a figure of maternal safety and mobility.
43 For further discussion of a Canadian woman author's presentation of erotic landscape, see Irene Gammel, '"My Secret Garden": Dis/Pleasure in L.M.

Montgomery and F.P. Grove,' *English Studies in Canada* 25 (March 1999): 36–65.

44 Logan and French, *Highways of Canadian Literature*, 203; A. Buckley, 'The Spectator,' *Daily News-Advertiser* (Vancouver) (16 March 1913).

45 N. Hamilton, 'Pauline Johnson Honored But Not for Her Poetry,' *VS* (10 March 1961), 1; R. Davies, 'Writer's Diary,' *VP* (8 April 1961), 19.

46 Logan and French, *Highways of Canadian Literature*, 196.

47 See, for example, her letter to Henry O'Brien of 4 February 1894, deploring her failure to act 'the true poet,' and regretfully justifying her need to 'play to the public' and engage in 'literary pot boiling.' As we lack details of the occasion which generated this response, we cannot place her reply in context, nor identify the extent to which her defensive language mirrors his accusations. We can, however, suggest that this letter represents another instance of playing to an audience. Here, her attempt to dispell 'the ever recurring haunting memory of your silent disapproval' reflects the larger cultural issue of the elevation of 'real poetry' over the audience's laughter at 'some of my brainless lines and business.' AO, Johnson Papers.

48 Charlesworth, 'The Indian Poetess: A Study,' 82.

49 Thanks to Wendy Smith, student in English 804, Simon Fraser University, 1996, for this insight.

50 'Reckless Young Canada,' (1892).

51 'With Paddle and Peterboro' (1890); 'Charming Word Pictures' (1890); 'With Canvas Overhead' (1890); 'Striking Camp' (1891).

52 'Outdoor Pastimes for Women' (December 1892).

53 Benidickson, *Idleness, Water, and a Canoe*, 157.

54 'A Pictorial Poem and a Picture,' *Canadian Club*, 12 Dec. 1912, in Toronto Public Library, Canadian Literature Scrapbook, p. 75.

55 'Canoeing' (1891). A similar passing reference to her Native background appears in 'With Barry in the Bow. Act III' (1897).

56 'The Game of Lacrosse,' *Detroit Free Press* (1892).

57 'A Brother Chief' (1892). Her reference to her mother's 'clear blue English eyes' looking at '"our" chief' enhances the ambiguity of her self-representation, allowing her to appear Caucasian to the general American public (who did not like Indians), while at the same time being truthful to those who knew her.

58 'Canoe and Canvas III. The Leap of the Sainte Marie' (1895).

59 'With Barry in the Bow. Act V' (1897), p. 271; 'With Barry in the Bow. Act III' (1897), p. 32; 'With Barry in the Bow. Act II. Scene: The Great Northland' (1897).

60 'The Battleford Trail,' written 1902 and apparently unpublished, ms. Vancouver Public Library; 'The Cariboo Trail' (1906); 'The Traffic of the Trail' (1906); 'The Southward Trail' (1908); 'The Chinook Wind' (1909); 'Coaching on the Cariboo Trail' (1914).

61 *Pauline*, 130–1. In addition to Keller's sources, *The Cleveland World* reported that she was 'engaged upon her first lengthy prose story,' a serial entitled 'Direlict' [*sic*] (9 January 1896); the Grand Rapids *Democrat* reported that 'Her writings are now accepted by the Harper Brothers' (18 November 1896). In January of 1898, according to a Winnipeg reporter, she was on her way to New York 'where she intends to interview Harper's with the idea of publishing a book of poems,' clipping unidentified Winnipeg newspaper (17 January 1898). In 1899 H.G. Paine of Harper's expressed interest in her proposed book of short stories and asked to see the manuscript, H.G. Paine to E. Pauline Johnson, 14 June 1899; all MUL, Johnson Papers.

62 Interestingly, Johnson's argument was already anticipated by *Grip*, which in 1890 published 'Mabel, The Dog-Catcher's Daughter,' an anonymous parody of conventional fiction, which concludes, 'The Algonquin maiden was exposed as a fraud by Miss Pauline Johnson ....' (18 June 1890). Thanks to Klay Dyer for this reference.

63 Pratt, *Imperial Eyes*, 6–7.

64 Parker, *The Translation of a Savage*, 119, 187.

65 MUL, Johnson Papers, Account statements from *Daily Express*. A fifth story, 'Witchcraft and the Winner,' was refused and remained unpublished.

66 L. Makovski, 'Former *Province* Editor Recalls Acquaintances,' *VP* (10 March 1961), 119.

67 We would like to thank Ruth Derksen, a student in English 804 at Simon Fraser University, for pointing out the poetic qualities of Johnson's prose in this piece.

68 MUL, Johnson Papers, financial statements from David Cook, 1907.

69 Ibid., Elizabeth Ansley to Johnson, 8 November 1905.

70 'The Broken Barrels,' chapter one (1909).

71 'Maurice of His Majesty's Mails' (1906), 'Little Wolf-Willow' (1907), 'The Wolf-Brothers' (1910), and 'The Little Red Messenger' (1913).

72 'A Night with "North Eagle"' (1908), 'The Scarlet Eye' (1908), and 'The Shadow Trail' (1907).

73 'Our Iroquois Compatriots' (1891); 'A Glimpse at the Grand River Indians' (1892), 7; 'A Pagan in St. Paul's Cathedral' (1906); 'The Great New Year White Dog: Sacrifice of the Onandagas' (1911). Perhaps due to later sensitivities, the white dog feast becomes transmuted to the feast of the white doe. See Winslow, *Iroquois Fires*, 79.

74 Acadia University Archives, J.D. Logan Papers, Johnson to Musson Book Company, 26 January 1910. The Johnson papers at McMaster contain an undated list of twenty-five stories, in Johnson's handwriting, which includes six early *Boys' World* stories (1907–8), three early pieces from the *Mother's Magazine* (1907), her four pieces from the London *Express* (1906), and an assortment of other titles, some of which seem never to have been published (e.g., 'The Tossing of a Rose,' 'Witchcraft and the Winner') while several others have either not survived, or were retitled for publication.

75 Keller ascribes the production of both *The Shagganappi* and *The Moccasin Maker* to 'the ladies of the Press Club,' *Pauline*, 260. Evelyn Johnson says that Pauline intended to leave her the copyright of *The Moccasin Maker*, but she never received anything from Johnson's last books. See AO, Evelyn Johnson, 'Chiefswood,' ms, p. 112.

76 In 1911 or 1912, four members of the Vancouver branch of the Canadian Women's Press Club, 'Isabel Ecclestone MacKay, Mrs. W. J. Holt Murison, Miss Laverock, and Miss MacLean, were appointed as a committee to co-operate with the Women's Canadian Club in collecting and preparing her unpublished manuscripts for publication.' CWPC Memorial Scrapbook, VCA, 554-B-4, p. 5. This group is generally identified as instrumental in the publication of *Legends of Vancouver* and *Flint and Feather*, but their connection with *The Shagganappi* and *The Moccasin Maker* remains unknown.

77 MUL, Johnson Papers, Elizabeth Ansley to Johnson, 26 March and 13 August 1907.

78 'Current News of Interest to Mothers,' *MM* (December 1906), 51.

79 MUL, Johnson Papers, verso of Elizabeth Ansley to Johnson, 26 March 1907.

80 See 'Mothers of a Great Red Race' (1908).

81 'The Prayers of the Pagan' (1907).

82 'Mothers of a Great Red Race' (1908).

83 'Outdoor Occupations' (1908) (note the echo of the title of one of C.G.D. Roberts's best-known books of animal stories, *The Kindred of the Wild* of 1902); 'Heroic Indian Mothers' (1908).

84 S.K. Harris, 'Evaluating Women's Fiction' in Warren, ed., *The (Other) American Tradition*, 273; Dobson, 'The American Renaissance Re-envisioned,' idid., 170, 171.

85 'The Great Deep Water: A Legend of "The Flood"' (1912).

86 Sioui, *For an Amerindian Autohistory*, trans. S. Fischman (1992), 15 and passim; Sioui, 'Why Canada Should Look for, Find, Recognize and Embrace Its True, Aboriginal Roots,' 45–54. See also Acoose, *Neither Indian Princesses nor Easy Squaws*, 53–4.

87 For example, the narrative style of Tom King's novel, *Green Grass, Running Water* (1993), reflects the narratives of story-teller Harry Robinson, as recorded by W. Wickwire in *Write It on Your Heart* (1989).

88 Fee, 'Writing Orality: Interpreting Literature in English by Aboriginal Writers in North America, Australia, and New Zealand,' 24, 34; Arnold Krupat, 'Introduction,' *New Voices in Native American Literary Criticism*, xix. See also his *Ethnocriticism: Ethnography, History, Literature*.

89 At the conference on 'Perspectives on Native American Oral Literature,' held at the University of British Columbia, 5–8 March 1998, participants constantly called attention to the peculiarity of the term.

90 Questionable is the assertion that 'My mother-tongue is the Mohawk' in B.J. Thompson's 'Pauline Johnson: Tekahionwake,' *McMaster University Monthly* (December 1904), and also Johnson's claim to be translating A'bram's story from 'the quaint and beautiful Mohawk.' Given the amount of press coverage Johnson received, mention of her fluency in Mohawk would likely have recurred frequently if it had been the case. On the importance of language to the Mohawk, see Valentine, 'Performing Native Identities,' *Papers of the Twenty-Fifth Algonquian Conference*.

91 'My Mother' (1909).

92 One includes Mohawk words for father, master, lord, moon, and star ('Ojistoh'); another, on the back of a letter fragment dated 1896, cites Mohawk words for star, wolf, the flyer, flower, deer, pilgrim, running, beaver, otter, and road; see MUL, Johnson Papers. In contrast, the parents of Bernice Loft Winslow ('Dawendine,' b. 1902) insisted that their children attain basic fluency in the five languages still in use on the Six Nations Reserve; see *Iroquois Fires*, 19.

93 'Indian Medicine Men and their Magic' (1892).

94 'Canadian Fiction,' *TG* (13 June 1903), 13.

95 See Ong, *Orality and Literacy*, 125–6.

96 Mackay, 'Pauline Johnson: A Reminiscence,' *CM* 41 (July 1913), 273–4.

97 Brown, '"Legends of Vancouver,"' *VP* (18 June 1929).

98 Alfred Buckley, 'The Spectator,' *Vancouver News-Advertiser* (23 March 1913), 23.

99 Marshall, 'The Re-Presented Indian: Pauline Johnson's "Strong Race Opinion,"' 119.

100 Our thanks to Sarah Parry for her work on the *Vancouver Province* while a student in English 809, Simon Fraser University, 1998.

101 McEvoy, 'Introduction' to *Legends of Vancouver* (1911), v.

5: 'Canadian Born'

1 Chucky Beaver, 'Proud Indian' quoted in Neuenfeldt, 'First Nations and Métis Songs as Identity Narratives,' 212.
2 Johnson, 'My Mother' (1909).
3 Quoted in E.T. Seton, 'Tekahionwake,' *The Shagganappi*, 5–6.
4 McRaye, *Pauline Johnson and Her Friends*, xii.
5 B. Godard, 'The Politics of Representation. Some Native Canadian Women Writers' in New, ed., *Native Writers and Canadian Writing*, 197.
6 Evans, *Frontier Theatre*, 184. See Twain, 'The Noble Red Man.'
7 Charles Mair, 'Pauline Johnson: An Appreciation,' *CM* (July 1913), 281.
8 Leacock as quoted in Monkman, *A Native Heritage*, 7.
9 See, for example, C. Morgan, 'Wampum and Waffle-Irons: Gender and National Identities in the Writing of Canadian Popular History, 1880s-1930s,' paper presented to the meetings of the Canadian Historical Association in 1996; Dianne M. Hallman, 'Cultivating a Love of Canada through History: Agnes Maule Machar, 1837–1927'; Beverly Boutilier, 'Women's Rights and Duties: Sarah Anne Curzon and the Politics of Canadian History'; and Jean Barman, '"I walk my own track in life & no mere male can bump me off it": Constance Lindsay Skinner and the Work of History'; all in Boutilier and Prentice, eds., *Creating Historical Memory.*
10 T. Nicks, 'Dr Oronhyatekha's History Lessons: Reading Museum Collections as Texts' in Brown and Vibert, eds., *Reading beyond Words*, 483.
11 As quoted in L.P. Valentine, 'Performing Native Identities,' *Papers of the Twenty-Fifth Algonquian Conference*, ed. W. Cowan, 482.
12 Sheridan, *Along the Faultlines*, 121–2.
13 J. Sharpe, 'Figures of Colonial Resistance' in Ashcroft et al., eds., *The Post-colonial Studies Reader*, 99.
14 J.E. Logan, 'National Literature' (21 August 1884), quoted in Monkman, *A Native Heritage*, 108.
15 Hale, ed., *The Iroquois Book of Rites*, iii–iv.
16 For the invocation of the Native, see Nelles, *The Art of Nation-Building: Pageantry and Spectacle at Quebec's Tercentenary.*
17 'Forty-Five Miles on the Grand' (1892).
18 'The Tribe of Tom Longboat' (1908).
19 'With Barry in the Bow.' Act III (1897).
20 'Fate of the Red Man,' *Ottawa Daily Free Press* (21 June 1894). 3.
21 Introduction to 'The Lady of the Lake,' *The Complete Poetical Works of Scott* (Boston: Houghton Miffin, 1900), 153.

22 'Tekahionwake,' *The Sketch* (London) (13 June 1894).

23 See Francis, *The Imaginary Indian*, 122.

24 Garth Grafton [S.J Duncan],' Saunterings,' *TG* (21 October 1886).

25 See C.G.D. Roberts, 'An Ode for the Canadian Confederacy' (1886), 'Canada' (1886), in D. Pacey and G. Adams, eds., *Collected Poems of Sir Charles G.D. Roberts*.

26 'The Iroquois of the Grand River' (1894). For a reminder of recurring military interests, see 'Warriors of the Iroquois (of the Silver Covenant Chain)' in Winslow, *Iroquois Fires*.

27 'Trails of the Old Tillicums' (1910).

28 NAC, Wilfrid Laurier Papers, E. Pauline Johnson to Wilfrid Laurier, 7 July 1910.

29 'The Old Lady of the Siwashes,' *VW* (5 March 1910). Líxwelut is called Agnes May in this article, suggesting again how little settler society knew its Aboriginal neighbours.

30 'With Barry in the Bow. Act III (1897).

31 'The Six Nations' (1895). Compare this with the portrait of the Iroquois as 'a ravening pack' in 'At the Long Sault: May, 1660,' edited by Duncan Campbell Scott from notes by Archibald Lampman.

32 'A Glimpse of the Grand River Indians' (1892).

33 'The Six Nations' (1895).

34 For an impassioned presentation of Native ways as a corrective to European thought and practice, whose lack of reference to Johnson signals her general invisibility among many late-twentieth century First Nations advocates, see Sioui, *For an Amerindian Autohistory*.

35 'The Iroquois of the Grand River' (1894).

36 'We-hro's Sacrifice' (1907).

37 'E. Pauline Johnson,' *Onward* 19 (April 1913), 122.

38 MUL, Walter McRaye Papers, Johnson, 'Witchcraft and the Winner,' unpub. ms.

39 'The Game of Lacrosse' (1892).

40 See, for example, 'The Potlatch' (1910). Generosity has been regularly counted a strength by Native advocates. See, for example, Deloria, *Speaking of Indians* and George Copway, *Life, Letters and Speeches*, ed. A.L.B. Ruoff and D. Smith.

41 VCA, Johnson Papers, Johnson, 'The Stings of Civilization' unpublished ms. Similar themes recur in the work of current First Nations authors, such as Lee Maracle's 1993 novel *Ravensong*.

42 'The Sea-Serpent' (1910).

43 'Heroic Indian Mothers' (1908); MUL, McRaye Papers, Johnson, 'Witchcraft and the Winner,' unpublished ms.

44 'A Brother Chief' (1892).

45 'A Glimpse of the Grand River Indians' (1892).

46 NAC, Wilfrid Laurier Papers, Johnson to Wilfrid Laurier, 18 January 1909; J.T. Gilkison (compiler), *Narrative Visit of the Governor-General and the Countess of Dufferin to the Six Nations Indians August 25, 1874* (1875), 11.

47 Quoted in Seton, 'Tekahionwake,' 5–6.

48 AO, E. Pauline Johnson Papers, Johnson to Henry O'Brien, 23 August, c. 1894. For similar discomfort with her own Mixed-race origins, see the Black feminist activist Ida B. Wells (1862–1931), in Ware, *Beyond the Pale*, 203.

49 'A Brother Chief' (1892); Brant, *Writing as Witness*, 21.

50 Monture-Angus, *Thunder in My Soul*, 47; Damm, 'Says Who: Colonialism, Identity and Defining Indigenous Literature' in Armstrong, ed., *Looking at the Words of Our People*, 19; Seesequasis, 'The Republic of Tricksterism,' in Moses and Goldie, eds., *An Anthology of Canadian Native Literature in English*, 411–16.

51 G. Viswananthan, 'The Beginnings of English Literary Study in British India' in Ashcroft et al., eds., *The Post-colonial Studies Reader*, 437.

52 'A Poet of the Prairie. Miss E. Pauline Johnson: "Tekahionwake,"' *Black and White* (28 December 1895).

53 Quoted in Ware, *Beyond the Pale*, 177. See also the similar response of the earlier Ojibwa traveller, George Copway, *Running Sketches of Men and Places ... in England, France, Gemany, Belgium, and Scotland* (1851).

54 *Set in Authority* (1906, reprinted 1996), 225.

55 AO, Johnson Papers, Johnson to O'Brien, 29 June 1894. See also her professed intimidation by her English publisher, in Keller, *Pauline*, 82–3.

56 T. Watts-Dunton, 'Introduction,' *Flint and Feather*. See his original review in *Athenaeum* (28 September 1889), 411–13.

57 'Some People I Have Met' (1899), 1. Aberdeen is not explicitly identified but the reference is clear.

58 D. Cannadine, 'The Context, Performance and Meaning of Ritual: The British Monarchy and the "Invention of Tradition," *c.* 1820–1977,' in Hobsbawm and Ranger, eds., *The Invention of Tradition*, 121.

59 'For Queen and Country, May 24th' (1890). See also Sui Sin Far's ironical observation that the fact of a Chinese empress did not seem to have made much of an impact on Europeans. Annette White-Parks, *Sui Sin Far/Edith Maude Eaton: A Literary Biography*, 111.

60 'A Pagan in St. Paul's' (1906).

61 F.G. Scott, 'Wahonomin. Indian Hymn to the Queen' in Lighthall, ed., *Songs of the Great Dominion*, 58.

62 MUL, Johnson Papers, Box 4, file 5, clipping, *Dundee Evening Telegraph* (4 July 1906).

63 On the meaning of the Mountie myth, see Walden, *Visions of Order* and, more recently, M. Dawson, '"That Nice Red Coat Goes to My Head Like Champagne": Gender, Anti-modernism and the Mountie Image, 1880–1960,' 119–39. While Dawson pays important attention to issues of masculinity, he overlooks Johnson's portrait of the Mounties. At least in her short story Mother o' the Men, women are significant actors, not merely props for the presentation of an idealized masculinity.

64 See McClung, *In Times Like These* (1915) and *The Next of Kin* (1917).

65 'Calgary of the Plains.' On the general preoccupation with the shortcomings of the city, see Rutherford, ed., *Saving the Canadian City*; on tory imperialists as reformers, see Berger, *The Sense of Power*, chapter 7.

66 J. Stevinson, 'Friends Pay Tribute to Indian Poetess on Anniversary of Death,' *Calgary Herald* (5 March 1932).

67 'With Barry in the Bow ... Interlude between Acts II and III' (1896). Johnson echoes the earlier observation of Susanna Moodie, who is so appalled at the behaviour of Irish steerage passengers upon her ship's arrival at Grosse Isle that she declares the Europeans to be 'wild savages,' in contrast to the Indians who are 'nature's gentlemen.' *Roughing It in the Bush*, 29–31.

68 AO, Johnson Papers, Johnson to O'Brien, 6 October 1903.

69 'Canada' (1908).

70 VCA, Johnson Collection, Johnson, 'The Battleford Trail,' incomplete and undated but c. 1902.

71 The anecdote, with its emphasis, occurs in the note to the poem.

72 Berger, *The Sense of Power*, 128.

73 'Deadman's Island' (1910); 'Autumn's Orchestra' (1908).

74 AO, Johnson Papers, Johnson to O'Brien, 23 August [1894].

75 MUL, Johnson Papers, box 4, file 5, newspaper clipping, undated and unplaced.

76 'The Brotherhood' (1910).

77 MUL, Johnson Papers, box 4, file 5, clipping titled 'Music and Drama,' identified Winnipeg and dated 17 January 1898.

78 McRaye, *Town Hall Tonight* (1929), 32.

79 'Brandon' (1912); 'The Traffic of the Trail' (1906).

80 'A Toast' (1903).

81 C. Batke, '"Overcoming All Obstacles": The Assimilation Debate in Native

American Women's Journalism of the Dawes Era' in H. Jaskoski, ed., *Early Native American Writing*, 192.
82 J.E. Chute, 'A Unifying Vision: Shingwaukonse's Plan for the Future of the Great Lakes Ojibwa,' 79. See also her *The Legacy of Shingwaukonse*. Brant-Sero, 'Views of a Mohawk Indian (From Toronto *Evening Telegram*, 18 January 1901),' 161.
83 For a powerful reminder of Indian diversity, see D.A. Mihesuah, 'Commonality of Difference: American Indian Women and History,' 92.
84 Culleton, *In Search of April Raintree*, 116.

Appendix

1 For example, it has not been possible to verify claims that Johnson published frequently in the *Boston Evening Transcript* and the *Pall Mall Gazette*. It is possible that some of this work may have been anonymous.
2 Cited by Reville, *History of the County of Brant*, 632. Reville, who later married Jean Morton, the addressee of the poem, claims this poem appeared in *Gems of Poetry* in 1883, and was Johnson's first published work. A 'Partial List of Published Poems' (typescipt in McRaye Papers, Queen's University) cites *Gems of Poetry*, 1884. Waldie ('The Iroquois Poetess') reports seeing a clipping, with notes and corrections in Johnson's hand, in the Brant Historical Society Museum. *Gems of Poetry* has been searched unsuccessfully.
3 Published under this title in Marcus Van Steen, *Pauline Johnson, Her Life and Work* (Toronto: Musson, 1965), 130.
4 In the Chiefswood scrapbook (see note 24 below), Johnson changed the title to 'The Lumberman's Christmas,' under which name it appeared on her programs from 1892.
5 A different version, an undated typescript titled 'Misguided,' survives in the Brant County Museum; see Waldie, 'The Iroquois Poetess' 69.
6 An undated typescript version, titled 'If I Could Only Know,' survives in the Frank Yeigh Papers, NAC.
7 Three verses of this poem, without title, appeared in the *OAC Review* 18, no. 7 (April 1906), 308.
8 The 'Monthly Record' was paginated independently from the regular issues of *Outing*, and often omitted from the bound volumes (including those microfilmed by UMI). Johnson's column appeared in February, March, April, May, June, July, August, October, and December. A portion of the first column was reprinted in an unidentified Toronto newspaper; clipping, 'The Snowshoe Girl,' Johnson collection, McMaster University.

9 Several verses appeared under the title 'Outlook,' *OAC Review* 24, no. 10 (July 1912), 544.

10 This column appeared in February, March, May, and July.

11 An undated fair copy is in the Chiefswood scrapbook.

12 An undated fair copy of the calendar version is in the Chiefswood scrapbook, slightly different from the later version in *Canadian Born*.

13 An undated fair copy, slightly different, is in the Chiefswood scrapbook.

14 Undated clipping, Chiefswood scrapbook. According to Johnson, the poem was written in June 1895; see AO, Johnson to O'Brien, 9 June 1895.

15 During Johnson's tour of the Maritime provinces, the poem appeared on the same date in other Halifax newspapers, less lavishly illustated than in the *Herald*. The Johnson papers at Trent include a broadside of 'Canadian Born' dated 1900; she first recited it in 1897.

16 Unidentified clipping, McMaster University, Pauline Johnson Collection. Internal evidence points to 1901: the poem celebrates the ascension of 'the King of England,' the 'son of a woman dear, and dead,' whose Empire extends to 'the South, in its silken harness,' the latter referring to the recent victory of Britain in South Africa.

17 Johnson claimed that 'half the poems it contains were accepted by *Harper's* and brought some excellent notice,' AO, Johnson to Harry O'Brien, 9 October 1903. However, a thorough search of *Harper's Weekly* confirms only two poems, both published in 1896: 'The Corn Husker' and 'Lullaby of the Iroquois.'

18 The first part was reprinted under the title 'C.P.R. Westbound,' *OAC Review* 17, no. 8 (May 1905), 460

19 This anonymous article preceeds her identified piece,'The Traffic of the Trail.' Copies of both are in the Johnson collection, MUL.

20 The context is an article covering the visit of Prince Fushimi to Calgary.

21 A 'Partial List of Published Poems,' (typescript in McRaye Papers, Queen's University Archives), erroneously identifies the source of a clipping in the Johnson papers at McMaster University as *Smart Set*, 1912.

22 There are two versions of this poem. Under the title 'In Heidelberg,' the *Canadian Magazine* reproduces the text of the manuscript titled 'To. C.H.W.,' McMaster University, Walter McRaye Collection, Box 1, folder 14. Foster (p. 104) and Keller (p. 158) cite a different version, under the title 'Heidelburgh.'

23 The content of this poem suggests that it dates from the Russo-Japanese conflict of 1905. On a manuscript copy at McMaster University appear the crossed-out words: 'For Competition in "Topical" verse.' The first stanza,

untitled, appeared in 1907 in a Calgary newspaper article on the visit of Prince Fushimi.

24 This scrapbook is currently in the Chiefswood Collection at the Woodland Cultural Centre Museum. It seems to have been compiled by Johnson, then blue-pencilled by Hector Charlesworth, with an aim to selecting and editing her early periodical poems for book publication. A pair of epigraphs, Johnson's answered by Charlesworth's, appear on the first page.

25 An undated clipping is also in the Johnson Papers at Trent University; Johnston cites 1890.

26 'Both Sides' and 'Disillusioned' are anonymous. They may have been pasted into Johnson's scrapbook not because she wrote them, but because they refer to a relationship between a young man and a woman five years his senior, much like Johnson's relationship with Hector Charlesworth, who clearly had a hand in compiling the scrapbook and editing the poems.

27 Johnston cites 1889, perhaps inferred from the dates of other items on the same page.

28 In a scrapbook in the McRaye Collection.

29 A search of the microfilmed *Boston Evening Transcript* for the likely years (1890–1) proved fruitless. The source of the clipping in the Johnson papers at McMaster University seems to be the *Brantford Courier*, citing the *Transcript*.

30 Written in an album for Jean Morton; cited by Reville, *The History of the County of Brant*, 631.

31 In the St Mary's Museum, St Mary's, Ontario; first cited by Sheila Johnston, *Buckskin and Broadcloth*, 57.

32 Written in Jean Morton's autograph album; cited by Waldie, 'The Iroquois Poetess,' 68.

33 Poem to Peggy Webling written on birchbark, cited by Keller, *Pauline*, 211.

34 MUL, Walter J. McRaye Collection, Box 1, folder 14; addressee identified as Charles Wuerz by Keller, *Pauline*, 158.

35 Walter J. McRaye Collection, Box 1 folder 14; rejected by London *Daily Express*, MUL, Johnson Collection, *Daily Express* to Johnson, August 1906; on list of titles, *c.* 1908.

36 MUL, Johnson Collection, Box 6, blue scrapbook.

37 Johnson's epigraph to the Chiefswood scrapbook, *c.* 1893–4?

38 Vancouver Public Library, NW 921, J66b.

39 NAC, Frank Yeigh Papers, MG 30 D 58, typescript.

40 Written c. 1895 to Gerald Wilkes, young son of Johnson's canoeing friend, Florence Wilkes; manuscript owned by John Wilkes; copy at Chiefswood Museum.

41 Manuscript at MUL, Johnson Collection, Box 1, folder 10; on list of stories, c. 1908.

42 VCA, Add Mss 336, vol. 24, f. 206.

43 MUL, Pauline Johnson Collection.

44 MUL, Walter J. McRaye Collection, Box 1, folder 14; published after Johnson's death as 'In Heidelberg,' *CM*, Nov. 1913, 53.

45 NAC, Pauline Johnson Collection, MG 30 D 93.

46 MUL, Pauline Johnson Collection, Box 1, folder 8.

47 Titles noted down by reporters are often impressionistic rather than exact; as many of the clipped reviews and programs in the Johnson Papers at McMaster and Trent Universities remain undated, the cited dates should be viewed as approximate.

48 AO, cited in letter, Johnson to O'Brien, 4 Februrary 1894.

49 Written for the Summerland Development Corporation according to Keller, *Pauline*, 196. The phrase 'Canada for the Canadians' occurs several times in the 1903 poem 'Made in Canada.'

Bibliography

Major Archival Collections

Acadia University Archives:
J.D. Logan Papers

Brant County Museum and Archives (Brant Historical Society):
Johnson Family Collection

Brantford Public Library:
Clipping Files

Metro Toronto Library:
Canadian Literature Scrapbooks

McGill University Library, Rare Books and Special Collections:
W.D. Lighthall Papers

McMaster University Library, William Ready Division of Archives and Research
Collections:
Pauline Johnson Collection
Walter McRaye Collection

National Archives of Canada:
Department of Indian Affairs: RG 10
Emily Pauline Johnson Papers: MG 30 D93
Sir Wilfrid Laurier Papers: MG 26 G
Gertrude O'Hara Papers: MG 22 A 14

Duncan Camphell Scott Papers: MG 30 D 100
Clifford Sifton Papers: MG 27 II D 15
Ernest Thompson Seton Papers: MG 29 D 108
Sir William Van Horne Papers: MG 29 A 60
John Willison Papers: MG 30 D 29
Frank Yeigh Papers: MG 30 D 58

Public Archives of British Columbia:
Add Mss 2753 (Makovski)

Public Archives of New Brunswick:
Wood Family Papers: MC218, MS 16

Public Archives of Ontario:
Emily Pauline Johnson Papers, Accession 16603; MU4553 (letters to Arthur Henry O'Brien)
'Chiefswood' by Evelyn Johnson, typescript, Accession 13601; MU4642

Royal Ontario Museum:
The Chiefswood Collection

Queen's University Archives:
Lorne Pierce Papers
Walter McRaye Papers
W.W. Campbell Papers
John Garvin Papers

Saskatchewan Archives Board:
Kate Simpson-Hayes Papers

Southwest Museum Library and Museum:
Pauline Johnson letters

Trent University Archives:
Pauline Johnson Collection acc 89-013

University of New Brunswick, Harriet Irving Library:
Annie Harvey (Ross) Foster Hanley fonds, MG L 7

University of Toronto, Thomas Fisher Rare Books Room:
J.E. Wetherell Papers

Vancouver City Archives:
Canadian Women's Press Club (Vancouver Branch)
Pacific Press Clipping File
Pauline Johnson Collection, Add MSS 678

Vancouver Public Library:
Johnson-Higginbotham correspondence, NW 921 J664

Woodland Cultural Centre Museum:
Chiefswood Collection

Selected Books, Theses, and Articles

Acoose, Janice/Misko-Kisikawihkwe (Red Sky Woman). *Iskwewak – Kah' Ki Yaw Ni Wahkomakanak: Neither Indian Princesses nor Easy Squaws*. Toronto: Women's Press, 1995
Adams, John Coldwell. *Sir Charles God Damn: The Life of Sir Charles G.D. Roberts*. Toronto: University of Toronto Press, 1986
Albers, Patricia C. 'From Illusion to Illumination: Anthropological Studies of American Indian Women.' In *Gender and Anthropology: Critical Reviews for Research and Teaching*. Ed. Sandra Morgan. Washington: American Anthropological Association, 1989
Albers, Patricia C., and William R. James. 'Illusion and Illumination: Visual Images of American Indian Women in the West.' In *The Women's West*. Ed. Susan Armitage and Elizabeth Jameson. Norman: University of Oklahoma Press, 1987: 35–50
Allen, Paula Gunn, ed. *Voice of the Turtle: American Indian Literature 1900–70*. New York: Ballentine, 1994
Anderson, Benedict. *Imagined Communities: Reflections on the Origin and Spread of Nationalism*. London: New Left Books, 1983
Anderson, Kay J. *Vancouver's Chinatown: Racial Discourse in Canada, 1875–1980*. Montreal: McGill-Queen's University Press, 1991
Anderson, Patricia. *When Passion Reigned: Sex and the Victorians*. New York: Basic Books, 1995
Anon. 'Azakia. A Canadian Story.' *Nova Scotia Magazine* 4, no. 6 (June 1791): 353–7
Ardis, Ann L. *New Women, New Novels: Feminism and Early Modernism*. New Brunswick, NJ: Rutgers University Press, 1990
– '"Shakespeare" and Mrs Grundy: Redefining Literary Value in the 1890s.' In *Transforming Genres: New Approaches to British Fiction of the 1890s*. Ed. Nikki Lee Manos and Meri-Jane Rochelson. New York: St Martin's Press, 1994: 1–20

Armstrong, Jeannette. 'Writing from a Native Woman's Perspective.' In *In the Feminine*. Ed. Ann Dybikowski et al. Edmonton: Longspoon, 1985: 55–7

Ashcroft, Bill, Gareth Griffiths, and Helen Tiffin, eds. *The Post-Colonial Studies Reader*. London: Routledge, 1995

– *The Empire Writes Back: Theory and Practice in Post-Colonial Literatures*. London: Routledge, 1993

Atwood, Margaret. 'A Double-Bladed Knife: Subversive Laughter in Two Stories by Tom King.' *Canadian Literature* 124–5 (1990): 243–50

– *Strange Things: The Malevolent North in Canadian Literature*. Toronto: Oxford University Press, 1995

– ed. *New Oxford Book of Canadian Verse*. Toronto: Oxford University Press, 1982

Ayre, John. 'Canadian Writers of the Past. IX. Pauline Johnson.' *Canadian Forum* 14 (October 1933): 17

Bacchi, Carol Lee. *Liberation Deferred? The Ideas of the English-Canadian Suffragists, 1877–1918*. Toronto: University of Toronto Press, 1983

Backhouse, Constance. *Petticoats and Prejudice: Women and Law in Nineteenth-Century Canada*. Toronto: Women's Press for The Osgoode Society, 1991

Ball, Christine. 'Female Sexual Ideologies in Mid- to Late-Nineteenth-Century Canada.' *Canada Journal of Women and the Law* 1, no. 2 (1986): 324–38

Ballstadt, Carl, ed. *The Search for English-Canadian Literature*. Toronto: University of Toronto Press, 1975

Ballstadt, Carl, Elizabeth Hopkins, and Michael A. Peterman, eds. *I Bless You in My Heart: Selected Correspondence of Catharine Parr Traill*. Toronto: University of Toronto Press, 1996

Barman, Jean. 'Invisible Women: Aboriginal Mothers and Mixed-Race Daughters in Rural Pioneer British Columbia.' In *Beyond the City Limits: Essays from British Columbia*. Ed. R.W. Sandwell. Vancouver, UBC Press, 1998.

– '"I walk my own track in life and no mere male can bump me off it": Constance Lindsay Skinner and the Work of History.' In *Creating Historical Memory: English-Canadian Women and the Work of History*. Ed. Beverly Boutilier and Alison Prentice. Vancouver: UBC Press, 1997: 129–63

– 'Lost Okanagan: In Search of the First Settler Families.' *Okanagan History* 60 (1996): 8–20

– 'Taming Aboriginal Sexuality: Gender, Power, and Race in British Columbia, 1850–1900.' *BC Studies* 115–16 (Fall–Winter 1997–8): 237–66

– *The West beyond the West: A History of British Columbia*. Toronto: University of Toronto Press, 1991

Barnett, Louise K. *The Ignoble Savage: American Literary Racism, 1790–1890*. Westport, CT: Greenwood Press, 1975

Bataille, Gretchen M., and Kathleen Mullen Sands. *American Indian Women: Telling Their Lives.* Lincoln: University of Nebraska Press, 1984

Batker, Carol. '"Overcoming All Obstacles": The Assimilation Debate in Native American Women's Journalism of the Dawes Era.' In *Early Native American Writing: New Critical Essays.* Ed. Helen Jaskoski. Cambridge: Cambridge University Press, 1996: 190–203

Beauchamp, W.M. 'Iroquois Women.' 1900. Reprinted in *Iroquois Women: An Anthology.* Ed. William Guy Spittal. Ohsweken, ON: Iroqrafts, 1990

Beaver, George. 'Early Iroquoian History in Ontario.' *Ontario History* 85, no. 3 (September 1993): 223–9

Belier, Patricia. 'Passing Through ... From Town Hall to Opera House.' *Officers' Quarterly* 11, no. 3 (Summer 1995): 10–12

– 'Passing Through: Pictures from the Life of Mrs W. Garland Foster (née Annie H. Ross).' *Officers' Quarterly* 12, no. 2 (Spring 1996): 7–9

Belsey, Catherine. *Critical Practice.* London: Methuen, 1980

Benidickson, Jamie. *Idleness, Water, and a Canoe: Reflections on Paddling for Pleasure.* Toronto: University of Toronto Press, 1997

Berger, Carl. *The Sense of Power: Studies in the Ideas of Canadian Imperialism 1867–1914.* Toronto: University of Toronto Press, 1970

Berger, Carl, and Ramsay Cook, eds. *The West and the Nation: Essays in Honour of W.L. Morton.* Toronto: McClelland and Stewart, 1976

Berkhofer, Robert F. *The White Man's Indian: Images of the American Indian from Columbus to the Present.* New York: Knopf, 1978

Bieder, Robert E. 'The Representations of Indian Bodies in Nineteenth-Century American Anthropology.' *American Indian Quarterly* 20, no. 2 (Spring 1996): 165–79

– *Science Encounters the Indian, 1820–1880: The Early Years of American Ethnology.* Norman: University of Oklahoma Press, 1986

Billington, Ray A. *Land of Savagery, Land of Promise.* New York: Norton, 1981

Billson, Janet Mancini. 'Keepers of the Culture: Attitudes towards Women's Liberation and the Women's Movement in Canada.' *Women & Politics* 14, no. 1 (1994): 1–34

Bissell, Claude, ed. *Great Canadian Writing: A Century of Imagination.* Toronto: Canadian Centennial Publishing Company, 1966

Blackstone, Sarah J. *Buckskins, Bullets, and Business: A History of Buffalo Bill's Wild West.* New York: Greenwood, 1986

Boone, Laurel, ed. *Collected Letters of Charles G.D. Roberts.* Fredericton: Goose Lane Editions, 1989

Bordo, Jonathon. 'Jack Pine: Wilderness Sublime or the Erasure of the

Aboriginal Presence for the Landscape.' *Journal of Canadian Studies* 27, no. 4 (Winter 1992–3): 98–128

Bourinot, Arthur S. *The Letters of Edward William Thomson to Archibald Lampman (1891–1897)*. Ottawa: A.S. Bourinot, 1957

Boutilier, Beverly, and Alison Prentice, eds. *Creating Historical Memory: English-Canadian Women and the Work of History*. Vancouver: UBC Press, 1997

Bowerbank, Sylvia, and Dolores Nawagesic Wawia. 'Literature and Criticism by Native and Métis Women of Canada.' *Feminist Studies* 20, no. 3 (Fall 1994): 565–81

Boyle, David. 'On the Paganism of the Civilised Iroquois of Ontario.' *Journal of the Anthropological Institute of Great Britain and Ireland*. 30, no. 3 (1900): 263–73

Brant, Beth. *Writing as Witness: Essay and Talk*. Toronto: Women's Press, 1994

Brant-Sero, John Ojijatekha. 'The Six-Nations Indians in the Province of Ontario, Canada.' *Journals and Transactions of the Wentworth Historical Society* 2 (1899): 62–73

– 'Some Descendants of Joseph Brant.' *Papers and Records of the Ontario Historical Society* 1 (1899): 113–17

– 'Views of a Mohawk Indian (from Toronto *Evening Telegram*, 18 January 1901).' *Journal of American Folklore* 18 (January–March 1905): 160–2

Bremer, Richard G. *Indian Agent and Wilderness Scholar: The Life of Henry Rowe Schoolcraft*. Mount Pleasant: Clark Historical Library, Central Michigan University, 1987

Brinton, D.G. 'Horatio Hale.' *The American Anthropologist* 10 (January 1897): 25–7

Brown, Alanna K. 'Mourning Dove's The House of Little Men.' *Canadian Literature* 144 (Spring 1995): 49–60

– 'Mourning Dove's Canadian Recovery Years, 1917–1919.' In *Native Writers and Canadian Writing*. Ed. W.H. New. Vancouver: UBC Press, 1990. Special issue of *Canadian Literature* 124–5: 113–32

Brown, Jennifer. *Strangers in Blood: Fur Trade Company Families in Indian Country*. Vancouver: University of British Columbia Press, 1980

Brown, Jennifer S.H., and Elizabeth Vibert. *Reading beyond Words: Contexts for Native History*. Peterborough, ON: Broadview, 1996

Brown, Mary M. 'Entertainers of the Road.' In *Early Stages: Theatre in Ontario, 1800–1914*. Ed. Ann Saddlemyer. Toronto: University of Toronto Press, 1990: 123–65

Buerger, Geoffrey E. 'Eleazer Williams: Elitism and Multiple Identity on Two Frontiers.' In *Being and Becoming Indian: Biographical Studies of North American Frontiers*. Ed. James A. Clifton. Chicago: Dorsey, 1989: 112–36

Burgess, Marilyon, and Gail Guthrie Valaskakis. *Indian Princesses and Cowgirls: Stereotypes from the Frontier.* Montreal: Oboro, 1995

Burley, David G. *A Particular Condition in Life: Self-Employment and Social Mobility in Mid-Victorian Brantford, Ontario.* Toronto: University of Toronto Press, 1993

Burton, Antoinette. *Burdens of History: British Feminists, Indian Women, and Imperial Culture, 1865–1915.* Chapel Hill: University of North Carolina Press, 1994

Butler, Judith. 'Performative Acts and Gender Constitution: An Essay in Phenomenology and Feminist Theory.' In *Performing Feminisms: Feminist Critical Theory and Theatre.* Ed. Sue-Ellen Case. Baltimore: Johns Hopkins University Press, 1990: 270–82

Callahan, S. Alice. *Wynema: A Child of the Forest.* Ed. A. LaVonne Brown Ruoff. Lincoln: University of Nebraska Press, 1997

Cameron, Agnes Deans. *The New North: An Account of a Woman's 1908 Journey through Canada to the Arctic.* Rev. ed. Ed. David R. Richeson. Saskatoon: Western Producer Prairie Books, 1986

Campbell, Maria. *Halfbreed.* Halifax: Formac, 1983

Campbell, Marjorie Freeman. 'The Lyric Voice of Canada's Indians.' *Globe Magazine,* 25 February 1961: 11, 20–1

Campbell, Sandra, and Lorraine McMullen, eds. *New Women: Short Stories by Canadian Women, 1900–1920.* Ottawa: Carleton University Press, 1991

Camper, Carol, ed. *Miscegenation Blues: Voices of Mixed Race Women.* Toronto: Sister Vision Press, 1994

Canfield, Gae Whitney. *Sarah Winnemucca of the Northern Paiutes.* Norman: University of Oklahoma Press, 1983

Cannadine, David. 'The Context, Performance and Meaning of Ritual: The British Monarchy and the "Invention of Tradition," c. 1820–1977.' In *The Invention of Tradition.* Ed. Eric Hobsbawm and Terence Ranger. Cambridge: Cambridge University Press, 1983: 101–64

Carr, Helen. *Inventing the American Primitive.* Cork: Cork University Press, 1996

Carter, Sarah. *Capturing Women: The Manipulation of Cultural Imagery in Canada's Prairie West.* Montreal: McGill-Queen's University Press, 1997

– 'Categories and Terrains of Exclusion: Constructing the "Indian Woman" in the Early Settlement Era of Western Canada.' *Great Plains Quarterly* 13 (1993): 147–61

– *Lost Harvests: Prairie Indian Reserve Farmers and Government Policy.* Montreal: McGill-Queen's University Press, 1990

Castro, Michael. *Interpreting the Indian: Twentieth-Century Poets and the Native American.* Albuquerque: University of New Mexico Press, 1983

Chalmers, John W. 'Tekahionwake.' *Alberta Historical Review* 22 (Summer 1974): 24–5

Champagne, Duane. 'American Indian Studies Is for Everyone.' *American Indian Quarterly* 20, no. 1 (Spring 1996): 77–82

Chaput, Donald. 'Charlotte de Rocheblave: Métisse Teacher of the Teachers.' *The Beaver* (Autumn 1977): 55–8

– 'The "Misses Nolin" of Red River.' *The Beaver* (Winter 1975): 14–17

Charlesworth, Hector. 'The Canadian Girl: An Appreciative Medley.' *Canadian Magazine* 1 (1893): 186–93

– *Candid Chronicles.* Toronto: Macmillan, 1925

– 'The Indian Poetess: A Study.' *Lake Magazine* (Sept. 1892): 81–7

– 'Miss Pauline Johnson's Poems.' *Canadian Magazine* 5 (1895): 478–80.

– [pseud. Touchstone]. 'Baton and Buskin,' *Vancouver Province*, 6 October 1894

Chatterjee, Partha. *Nationalist Thought and the Colonial World: A Derivative Discourse?* London: Zed, 1986

Chute, Janet E. *The Legacy of Shingwaukonse: A Century of Native Leadership.* Toronto: University of Toronto Press, 1998

– 'A Unifying Vision: Shingwaukonse's Plan for the Future of the Great Lakes Ojibwa.' *Journal of the CHA* New Series, 7 (1996): 55–80

Clark, Jerry E., and Martha Ellen Webb. 'Susette and Susan La Flesche: Reformer and Missionary.' In *Being and Becoming Indian: Biographical Studies of North American Frontiers.* Ed. James A. Clifton. Chicago: Dorsey, 1989: 137–59

Clifton, James A. 'Alternate Identities and Cultural Frontiers.' In *Being and Becoming Indian: Biographical Studies of North American Frontiers.* Ed. James A. Clifton. Chicago: Dorsey, 1989: 1–37

– ed. *Being and Becoming Indian: Biographical Sketches of North American Indians.* Chicago: Dorsey, 1989

– ed. *The Invented Indian: Cultural Fictions and Government Policies.* New Brunswick, NJ: Transaction Publishers, 1994

Cole, Douglas. *Captured Heritage: The Scramble for Northwest Coast Artifacts.* Vancouver: UBC Press, 1995

– 'The Origins of Canadian Anthropology.' *Journal of Canadian Studies* 8, no. 1 (February 1973): 33–54

Cole, Douglas, and Ira Chaikin. *An Iron Hand upon the People: The Law against the Potlatch on the Northwest Coast.* Vancouver: Douglas & McIntyre, 1990

Collett, Anne. 'Pauline Tekahionwake Johnson: Her Choice of Form.' *Kunapipi* 19, no. 1 (1997): 59–66

Collins, Patricia Hill. 'Toward a New Vision: Race, Class and Gender as Categories of Analysis and Connection.' *Race, Sex & Class* 1, no. 1 (Fall 1993): 23–45

Colombo, John Robert. *Songs of the Indians* I. Ottawa: Oberon, 1983

Comeau-Vasilopoulos, Gayle. 'Oronhyatekha (meaning "burning cloud," baptized Peter Martin).' *Dictionary of Canadian Biography* 13: 791–5

Conrad, Margaret. 'Recording Angels: The Private Chronicles of Women from the Maritimes Provinces of Canada, 1750–1950.' In *The Neglected Majority: Essays in Canadian Women's History*. Ed. Alison Prentice and Susan Mann Trofimenkoff. Vol. 2. Toronto: McClelland and Stewart, 1985: 41–60

– '"Sundays Always Make Me Think of Home": Time and Place in Canadian Women's History.' In *Rethinking Canada: The Promise of Women's History*. Ed. Veronica Strong-Boag and Anita Clair Fellman. 2nd ed. Toronto: Copp Clark Pitman, 1991: 97–112

Converse, Harriet. 'Myths and Legends of the New York State Iroquois.' *New York State Museum Bulletin*. Ed. A.C. Parker. 125: 5–195

Cook-Lynn, Elizabeth. 'American Indian Intellectualism and the New Indian Story.' *American Indian Quarterly* 20, no. 1 (Winter 1996): 57–76

Cooper, Carol. 'Native Women of the Northern Pacific Coast: An Historical Perspective, 1830–1900.' *Journal of Canadian Studies* 27, no. 4 (Winter 1992/3): 44–75

Copway, George. *Running Sketches of Men and Places in England, France, Germany, Belgium, and Scotland*. New York: J.C. Rilker, 1851

Crate, Joan. *Pale as Real Ladies: Poems for Pauline Johnson*. Iderton, ON: Brick Books, 1989

Creese, Gillian, and Daiva Stasiulus. 'Intersections of Gender, Race, Class and Sexuality.' *Studies in Political Economy: A Socialist Review* 51 (Fall 1996): 5–14

Cunningham, Gail. *The New Woman and the Victorian Novel*. London: Macmillan, 1978

Damm, Kateri. 'Says Who: Colonialism, Identity and Defining Indigenous Literature.' In *Looking at the Words of Our People: First Nations Analysis of Literature*. Ed. J. Armstrong. Penticton, BC: Theytus, 1993

Daniells, Roy. 'Minor Poets 1880–1920.' In *Literary History of Canada*. Gen. ed. Carl F. Klink. Toronto: University of Toronto Press, 1966: 422–30

Dault, Gary Michael. 'On Side with the Good Mind.' *Globe and Mail*, 10 May 1997: C9

Davies, Barrie. '"We Hold a Vaster Empire Than Has Been": Canadian Literature and the Canadian Empire.' *Studies in Canadian Literature* 14, no. 1 (1989): 18–29

Davis, Marilyn I., ed. *Stories Subversive: Through the Field with the Gloves Off. Short Fiction by Nellie L. McClung*. Ottawa: Carleton University Press, 1996

Davis, Tracy C. *Actresses as Working Women: Their Social Identity in Victorian Culture*. New York: Routledge, 1991

Dawson, Michael. '"That Nice Red Coat Goes to My Head Like Champagne": Gender, Anti-Modernism and the Mountie Image, 1880–1960.' *Journal of Canadian Studies*, 32, no. 3 (1997): 119–39

Deacon, W.A. *Poteen: A Pot-Pourri of Canadian Essays.* Ottawa: Graphic, 1920

Dean, Misao. *A Different Point of View: Sara Jeannette Duncan.* Montreal: McGill-Queen's University Press, 1991

Deloria, Ella Cara. *Speaking of Indians.* Vermillion: Dakota, 1979

Devens, Carol. *Countering Colonization: Native American Women and the Great Lakes Missions, 1630–1900.* Berkeley: University of California Press, 1992

Dewart, Edwart Hartley. *Selections from Canadian Poets.* Montreal: Lovell, 1864

Dickason, Olive. *Canada's First Nations: A History of Founding Peoples.* Toronto: McClelland and Stewart, 1992

Dippie, Brian W. *The Vanishing American: White Attitudes and U.S. Indian Policy.* Middletown: Wesleyan University Press, 1982

Djwa, Sandra. '"A New Soil and a Sharp Sun": The Landscape of a Modern Canadian Poetry.' *Modernist Studies* 2, no. 2 (1977): 3–17

– '"Who Is This Man Smith": Second and Third Thoughts on Canadian Modernism.' In *Inside the Poem: Essays and Poems in Honour of Donald Stephens.* Ed. W.H. New. Toronto: Oxford University Press, 1992: 205–15

Donaldson, Laura E. *Decolonizing Feminisms: Race, Gender, and Empire-building.* Chapel Hill: University of North Carolina Press, 1992

Donovan, Kathleen. *Feminist Readings of Native American Literature: Coming to Voice.* Tucson: University of Arizona Press, 1998

Downie, Jill. *Passionate Pen: The Life and Times of Faith Fenton.* Toronto: HarperCollins, 1996

Doyle, James. *Annie Howells and Achille Fréchette.* Toronto: University of Toronto Press, 1979

– 'Sui Sin Far and Onoto Watanna: Two Early Chinese-Canadian Authors.' *Canadian Literature* 140 (Spring 1994): 50–8

Drees, Laurie Meijer. 'Introduction to Documents One through Five: Nationalism, the League of Nations and the Six Nations of Grand River.' *Native Studies Review* 10, no. 1 (1995): 75–88

Dudek, Louis, and Michael Gnarowski, eds. *The Making of Modern Poetry in Canada.* Toronto: Ryerson, 1970

Duncan, Sara Jeannette. *Set in Authority.* 1906. Reprint, Peterborough: Broadview, 1996

– *A Social Departure: How Orthodocia and I Went around the World by Ourselves.* London: Chatto & Windus, 1890

– 'Woman's World,' *Globe,* 14 Oct 1886

Dunham, Mabel. *Grand River.* Toronto: McClelland and Stewart, 1945

Ebersole, Gary L. *Captured by Texts: Puritan to Postmodern Images of Indian Captivity.* Charlottesville: University Press of Virginia, 1995

Emberley, Julia V. 'Aboriginal Women's Writing and the Cultural Politics of Representation.' In *Women of the First Nations: Power, Wisdom, and Strength.* Ed. Christine Miller et al. Winnipeg: University of Manitoba Press, 1996

– *Thresholds of Difference: Feminist Critique, Native Women's Writings, Postcolonial Theory.* Toronto: University of Toronto Press, 1993

Evans, Chad. *Frontier Theatre: A History of Nineteenth-Century Theatrical Entertainment in the Canadian Far West and Alaska.* Victoria: Sono Nis, 1983

Feldman, Egal. *The Dreyfus Affair and the American Conscience 1895–1906.* Detroit: Wayne State University Press, 1981

Felski, Rita. *The Gender of Modernity.* Cambridge: Harvard University Press, 1995

Fenton, William N. 'Horatio Hale.' In *The Iroquois Book of Rites.* Ed. Horatio Hale. Toronto: University of Toronto Press, 1963

– ed. *Parker on the Iroquois.* Syracuse, NY: Syracuse University Press, 1958

– ed. *Symposium on Local Diversity in Iroquois Culture.* Smithsonian Institution. Washington, Bureau of American Ethnology. Bulletin 149, 1951

Files, Angela E.M. 'The Loyalist Lineage of Native Poetess Pauline Johnson.' In *Loyalist Families of the Grand River Branch, United Empire Loyalists' Association of Canada.* Toronto: Pro Familia Publishing, 1991: 307–19

Finkel, Alvin, et al. *History of the Canadian Peoples.* Vol. 2. *1867 to the Present.* Toronto: Copp Clark Pitman, 1993

Fisher, Robin. 'Su-á-pu-luck (Joseph Capilano).' *Dictionary of Canadian Biography* 13: 998–9

Fiske, Jo-Anne. 'Aboriginal Women and the Discourses of Nationhood.' *Studies in Political Economy: A Socialist Review* 51 (Fall 1996): 65–95

– 'Pocahontas's Granddaughters: Spiritual Transition and Tradition of Carrier Women of British Columbia.' *Ethnohistory* 43, no. 4 (Fall 1996): 663–81

– 'The Womb Is to the Nation as the Heart Is to the Body: Ethnopolitical Discourses of the Canadian Indigenous Women's Movement.' *Studies in Political Economy* 51 (Fall 1996): 65–92

Fixico, Donald L. 'Ethics and Responsibilities in Writing American Indian History.' *American Indian Quarterly* 20, no. 1 (Winter 1996): 29–39

Forster, J.W.L. *Under the Studio Light.* Toronto: Macmillan, 1928

Foster, Martha Harroun. 'Lost Women of the Matriarchy: Iroquois Women in the Historical Literature.' *American Indian Culture and Research Journal* 19, no. 3 (1995): 121–40

Foster, Michael K., Jack Campisi, and Marianne Mithun, eds. *Extending the Rafters: Interdisciplinary Approaches to Iroquoian Studies.* Albany: State University of New York Press, 1984

Foster, Mrs W. Garland. *The Mohawk Princess: Being Some Account of the Life of Teka-hionwake (E. Pauline Johnson)*. Vancouver: Lions' Gate Publishing, 1931
– 'Pauline Johnson's Gift to Vancouver.' *The Canadian Bookman* (June 1936): 6–7
Francis, Daniel. *The Imaginary Indian: The Image of the Indian in Canadian Culture.* Vancouver: Arsenal Pulp Press, 1993
Freeman, Barbara M. *Kit's Kingdom: The Journalism of Kathleen Blake Coeman.* Ottawa: Carleton University Press, 1989
Friesen, Gerald. 'John Norquay.' *Dictionary of Canadian Biography* 11: 642–7
Frye, Northrop. 'Preface to an Uncollected Anthology.' *The Bush Garden: Essays on the Canadian Imagination.* Toronto: Anansi, 1971: 163–80
Furnier, Suzanne, and Ernie Crey. *Stolen from Our Embrace: The Abduction of First Nations Children and the Restoration of Aboriginal Communities.* Vancouver: Douglas & McIntyre, 1997
Gagan, Rosemary R. *A Sensitive Independence: Canadian Methodist Women Missionaries in Canada and the Orient, 1881–1925.* Montreal: McGill-Queen's University Press, 1992
Geller, Peter. '"Hudson's Bay Company Indians": Images of Native People and the Red River Pageant.' In *Dressing in Feathers: The Construction of the Indian in American Popular Culture.* Ed. Elizabeth Bird. Boulder, CO: Westview, 1996: 65–77
Georgi-Findlay, Brigitte. 'The Frontiers of Native American Women's Writing: Sarah Winnemucca's *Life among the Piutes*.' In *New Voices in Native American Literary Criticism.* Ed. Arnold Krupat. Washington: Smithsonian Institution Press, 1993: 222–52
Gerson, Carole. 'Anthologies and the Canon of Early Canadian Women Writers.' In *Re(Dis)covering Our Foremothers: Nineteenth-Century Canadian Women Writers.* Ed. Lorraine McMullen. Ottawa: University of Ottawa Press, 1989: 55–76
– 'The Business of a Woman's Life: Money and Motive in the Careers of Early Canadian Women Writers.' In *Women's Writing and the Literary Institution.* Ed. C. Potvin and J. Williamson. Edmonton: Research Institute for Comparative Literature, University of Alberta, 1992: 77–94
– 'Canadian Women Writers and American Markets.' In *Context North America.* Ed. Camille R. LaBossière. Ottawa: University of Ottawa Press, 1994: 107–18
– 'Nobler Savages: Representations of Native Women in the Writings of Susanna Moodie and Catharine Parr Trail.' *Journal of Canadian Studies* 32, no. 2 (Summer 1997): 5–21
– 'Sarah Binks and Edna Jaques: Gender, Parody, and the Construction of Literary Value.' *Canadian Literature* 134 (1992): 62–73

- 'Some Notes Concerning Pauline Johnson.' *Canadian Notes and Queries* 34 (Autumn 1985): 16–19
- 'Wild Colonial Girls: New Women of the Empire, 1883–1901.' *Journal of Commonwealth and Postcolonial Studies* 3, no. 1 (Fall 1995): 61–71
Gerson, Carole, and Gwendolyn Davies, eds. *Canadian Poetry: From the Beginnings through the First World War.* Toronto: McClelland and Stewart, 1994.
Gibson, Arrell Morgan. *The American Indian: Prehistory to the Present.* Lexington, MA.: D.C. Heath, 1980
Gilbert, Sandra M., and Susan Gubar, eds. *The Norton Anthology of Literature by Women.* New York: Norton, 1985, 1996
Gilkison, J.T., comp. *Narrative Visit of the Governor-General and the Countess of Dufferin to the Six Nations, August 25, 1874.* n.p., 1875
Godard, Barbara. 'The Politics of Representation: Some Native Canadian Women Writers.' In *Native Writers and Canadian Writing.* Ed. W.H. New. Vancouver: UBC Press, 1990. Special issue of *Canadian Literature,* 124–5: 183–225
- *Talking about Themselves: The Literary Productions of the Native Women of Canada.* CRIAW Papers, No. 11. Ottawa, July 1985
Goldenweiser, A.A. 'Functions of Women in Iroquois Society.' (1914) In *Iroquois Women: An Anthology.* Ed. William Guy Spittal. Ohsweken, ON: Iroqrafts, 1990
Goldie, Terry. *Fear and Temptation: The Image of the Indigene in Canadian, Australian, and New Zealand Literatures.* Montreal: McGill-Queen's University Press, 1989
Gould, Janice. 'The Problem of Being "Indian": One Mixed-Blood's Dilemma.' In *De/Colonizing the Subject: The Politics of Gender in Women's Autobiography.* Ed. Sidonie Smith and Julia Watson. Minneapolis: University of Minnesota Press, 1992: 81–7
Grant, Agnes. 'Contemporary Native Women's Voices in Literature.' In *Native Writers and Canadian Writing.* Ed. W.H. New. Vancouver: UBC Press, 1990. Special issue of *Canadian Literature,* 124–5: 124–32
- *Native Literature in the Curriculum.* Winnipeg: University of Manitoba Press, 1986.
- 'Reclaiming the Lineage House: Canadian Native Women Writers.' *SAIL* 6, no. 1 (Spring 1994): 43–62
- ed. *Our Bit of Truth: An Anthology of Canadian Native Literature.* Winnipeg: Pemmican, 1990
Grant, John W. *Moon of Wintertime: Missionaries and the Indians of Canada in Encounter since 1534.* Toronto: University of Toronto Press, 1984
Graymont, Barbara, ed. *Fighting Tuscarora: The Autobiography of Chief Clinton Rickard.* Syracuse: Syracuse University Press, 1973

Green, Gretchen. 'Gender and the Longhouse: Iroquois Women in a Changing Culture.' In *Women and Freedom in Early America*. Ed. Larry D. Eldridge. New York: New York University Press, 1997: 7–25
– 'Molly Brant, Catharine Brant, and Their Daughters: A Study in Colonial Acculturation.' *Ontario History* 81, no. 3 (September 1989): 235–50
Green, Rayna. 'The Pocahontas Perplex: The Image of Indian Women in American Culture.' *Massachusetts Review* 16, no. 4 (1975): 698–714
– *That's What She Said: Contemporary Poetry and Fiction by Native American Women*. Bloomington: Indiana University Press, 1984
– 'The Tribe Called Wannabee: Playing Indian in America and Europe.' *Folklore* 995 (1988): 30–55
Greenhill, Pauline, and Diane Tye, eds. *Undisciplined Women: Tradition and Culture in Canada*. Montreal: McGill-Queen's University Press, 1997
Griffin, Gabrielle, ed. *Difference in View: Women and Modernism*. London: Taylor and Francis, 1994
Gundy, H. Pearson. 'Molly Brant – Loyalist.' *Ontario History* 45, no. 3 (1953): 97–108
Haig-Brown, Celia. 'Border Work.' In *Native Writers and Canadian Writing*. Ed. W.H. New. Vancouver: UBC Press, 1990. Special edition of *Canadian Literature*, 124–5: 229–41
– 'Choosing Border Work.' *Canadian Journal of Native Education* 19, no. 1 (1992): 96–116
Hale, Horatio. 'Chief George H.M. Johnson – Onwanonsyshon: His Life and Work among the Six Nations.' *Magazine of American History* February 1885: 131–42
– 'An Iroquois Condoling Council: A Study of Aboriginal American Society and Government.' *Transactions of the Royal Society of Canada*, 2nd Series (1895–96), Vol. 1, Section 2: 45–65
– 'Miss E. Pauline Johnson.' *The Critic* (New York), 4 January 1896: 7–8
– 'The White Wampum.' *The Critic* (New York), 4 June 1896: 4–5
– ed. *The Iroquois Book of Rites*. 1883. New York: AMS Press, 1969
Hale, Katherine [Amelia Garvin]. *Canadian Cities of Romance*. Toronto: McClelland and Stewart, 1922
Hall, Tony. 'The Politics of Monarchy.'' *Canadian Forum* (April 1998): 6–8
Hallman, Dianne M. 'Cultivating a Love of Canada through History: Agnes Maule Machar, 1837–1927.' In *Creating Historical Memory: English-Canadian Women and the Work of History*. Ed. Beverly Boutilier and Alison Prentice. Vancouver: UBC Press, 1996: 25–50
Hamilton, A.C. 'Northrop Frye as a Canadian Critic.' In *Canadian Literature: Introductory and Critical Essays*. Ed. Sang Ran Lee, Kwangsook Chung, and

Myungsoon Shin. Seoul: Center for Canadian Studies, Institute of East and West Studies, 1990: 1–20

Hanley, Ann [Mrs W. Garland Foster]. 'Pauline.' *Canadian Author & Bookman* 42, no. 18 (Spring 1968): 18

Harper, Frances E.W. *Complete Poems of Frances E.W. Harper.* Ed. Maryemma Graham. New York: Oxford University Press, 1988

Harris, Cole. *The Resettlement of British Columbia: Essays on Colonialism and Geographical Change.* Vancouver: UBC Press, 1997

Harris, Susan K. '"But is it any *good?*" Evaluating Nineteenth-Century American Women's Fiction.' In *The (Other) American Tradition.* Ed. Joyce Warren. New Brunswick, NJ: Rutgers University Press, 1993: 263–79

Harry, M. 'Literature in English by Native Canadians.' *Studies in Canadian Literature* 10, no. 1–2 (1985): 146–53

Harsh, Constance D. *Subversive Heroines: Feminist Resolutions of Soical Crisis in the Condition-of-England Novel.* Ann Arbor: University of Michigan Press, 1994

Hauptman, Laurence M. 'Designing Woman: Minnie Kellogg, Iroquois Leader.' In *Indian Lives: Essays on Nineteenth- and Twentieth-Century Native American Leaders.* Ed. L.G. Moses and Raymond Wilson. Albuquerque: University of New Mexico Press, 1985: 159–88

– *The Iroquois Struggle for Survival: World War II to Red Power.* Syracuse: Syracuse University Press, 1986

Hawkes, Arthur. *The Birthright: A Search for the Canadian Canadian and the Larger Loyalty.* Toronto: J.M. Dent & Sons, 1919

Hayball, Gwen. 'Agnes Deans Cameron 1863–1912.' *BC Historical News* 7, no. 2 (February 1974): 18–25

Hewitt, J.N.B. 'Status of Woman in Iroquois Polity before 1784.' 1933. Reprinted in *Iroquois Women: An Anthology.* Ed. William Guy Spittal. Ohsweken, ON: Iroqrafts, 1990

Hill, Asa R. 'The Historical Position of the Six Nations.' *Papers and Records of the Ontario Historical Society* 19 (1922): 103–9

Hill, B.E. 'The Grand River Navigation Company and the Six Nations Indians.' *Ontario History* 63, no. 1 (1971): 31–40

Hinsley, Curtis. 'Digging for Identity: Reflections on the Cultural Background of Collecting.' *American Indian Quarterly* 20, no. 2 (Spring 1996): 180–95

Hobsbawm, Eric. 'Identity Politics and the Left.' *New Left Review* 217 (May/June 1996): 38–47

Hobsbawm, Eric, and Terence Ranger, eds. *The Invention of Tradition.* Cambridge: Cambridge University Press, 1983

Hochbruck, Wolfgang. 'Cultural Authenticity and the Construction of Pan-Indian Metanarrrative.' In *Cultural Difference and the Literary Text: Pluralism and the Limits of Authenticity in North American Literatures.* Ed. Winfried Siemerling and Katrin Schwenk. Iowa City: University of Iowa Press, 1996: 18–28

Hutcheon, Linda. 'Frye Recoded: Postmodernity and the Conclusions.' In *The Legacy of Northrop Frye.* Ed. Alvin A. Lee and Robert D. Denham. Toronto: University of Toronto Press, 1994: 110–21

Ignace, Ron, George Speck, and Renée Taylor. 'Some Native Perspectives on Anthropology and Public Policy.' In *Anthropology, Public Policy and Native Peoples in Canada.* Ed. Noel Dyck and James B. Waldram. Montreal: McGill-Queen's University Press, 1993: 166–91

Jannetta, Amando E. 'Métis Autobiography: The Emergence of a Genre amid Alienation, Resistance and Healing in the Context of Maria Campbell's *Halfbreed* (1973).' *International Journal of Canadian Studies* 12 (Fall 1995): 169–81

Jasen, Patricia. *Wild Things: Nature, Culture, and Tourism in Ontario, 1790–1914.* Toronto: University of Toronto Press, 1995

Jenness, Diamond. *The Indians of Canada.* 1932. 7th edition. Toronto: University of Toronto Press, 1980

Jhappan, Radha. 'Race and Gender Essentialism.' *Studies in Political Economy: A Socialist Review* 51 (Fall 1996): 15–63

Johnson, E. Pauline. Works currently in print. For all other publications, see pp. 219–36.

– *Flint and Feather.* 1912. Reprint, Toronto: Guardian Printing for Chiefswood National Historic Site, 1997

– *Legends of Vancouver.* 1911. Reprint, Vancouver: Douglas and MacIntyre, 1997

– *The Moccasin Maker.* 1913. Reprint, with Introduction, Annotation, and Bibliography by A. LaVonne Brown Ruoff. Norman: University of Oklahoma Press, 1998

Johnson, Evelyn H.C. 'Chief John Smoke Johnson: Sakayengwaraton – "Disappearing of the Indian Summer Mist."' *Papers and Records of the Ontario Historical Society* 12 (1914): 102–13

– 'Grandfather and Father of E. Pauline Johnson.' *Archaelogical Report of the Ontario Department of Education* 36 (1928): 44–7

– 'The Martin Settlement.' *Papers and Records of the Brant Historical Society* 2 (1908–11): 55–64

Johnston, C.M. *Brant Country: A History 1784–1945.* Toronto: Oxford University Press, 1967

Johnston, Dorothy E. 'Evelyn Johnson Remembers Her Sister.' *Early Canadian Life,* April 1980, B6.

Johnston, Jean. 'Molly Brant: Mohawk Matron.' *Ontario History* 61, no. 2 (1964): 105–23

Johnston, Sheila M.F. *Buckskin and Broadcloth: A Celebration of E. Pauline Johnson – Tekahionwake 1861–1913*. Toronto: Natural Heritage Books, 1997

Jones, Robin. 'Johnson, E. Pauline (1861–1913).' In *Oxford Companion to Women's Writing in the US*. Ed. Cathy N. Davidson and Linda Wagner-Martin. New York: Oxford University Press, 1995: 446–7

Kanitkar, Helen. '"Real True Boys": Moulding the Cadets of Imperialism.' In *Dislocating Masculinity: Comparative Ethnographies*. Ed. Andrea Cornwall and Nancy Lindisfarne. London: Routledge, 1994: 184–96

Keen, Dorothy, and Martha McKeon as told to Mollie Gillen. 'The Story of Pauline Johnson, Canada's Passionate Poet.' *Chatelaine*, Part 1, Feb. 1966: 39–42, 44, 49; Part. 2, March 1966: 95–8, 100

Keller, Betty C. *Black Wolf: The Life of Ernest Thomson Seton*. Vancouver: Douglas & McIntyre, 1984

– *Pauline: A Biography of Pauline Johnson*. Vancouver: Douglas & McIntyre, 1981

– 'On Stage Now! The Chastely Voluptuous Weblings.' *The Beaver* 66, no. 2 (April–May 1986): 13–18

– 'On Tour with Pauline Johnson.' *The Beaver* 66, no. 6 (Dec. 1986–January 1987): 19–25

Kempster, Janet, and Gary Muir. *Brantford: Grand River Crossing*. Burlington: Windor Publications, 1986

Kenny, Maurice. *On Second Thought: A Compilation*. Norman: University of Oklahoma Press, 1995

Kidwell, Clara Sue. 'Indian Women as Cultural Mediators.' *Ethnohistory* 39, no. 2 (Spring 1992): 97–107

Killan, Gerald. *David Boyle: From Artisan to Archaeologist*. Toronto: University of Toronto Press, 1983

– *Preserving Ontario's Heritage: A History of the Ontario Historical Society*. Ottawa: Love Printing, 1976

King, Cecil. 'J.-B. Assiginack: Arbiter of Two Worlds.' *Ontario History* 86, no. 1 (March 1994): 33–51

King, Thomas, Cheryl Calver, and Helen Hoy. *The Native in Literature*. Oakville, ON: ECW, 1987

Klein, Laura F., and Lillian A. Ackerman, eds. *Women and Power in Native North America*. Norman: University of Oklahoma Press, 1995

Klinck, Carl F., gen. ed. *Literary History of Canada*. Toronto: University of Toronto Press, 1967

Knowles, Norman. *Inventing the Loyalists: The Ontario Loyalist Tradition and the Creation of Usable Pasts*. Toronto: University of Toronto Press, 1997

Koss, Stephen. *The Pro-Boers: The Anatomy of an Anti-War Movement*. Chicago: University of Chicago Press, 1973

Krupat, Arnold. *Ethnocriticism: Ethnography, History, Literature.* Berkeley: University of California Press, 1992
– Introduction. *New Voices in Native American Literary Criticism.* Washington: Smithsonian Institution Press, 1993
– *The Turn to the Native: Studies in Criticism and Culture.* Lincoln: University of Nebraska Press, 1996
Kulchyski, Peter. 'Some Questions and Issues about the New Nationalism.' *Journal of Canadian Studies* 31, no. 3 (Fall 1996): 189–96
Lampman, Archibald. *At the Long Sault and Other New Poems.* Foreword by Duncan Campbell Scott. Toronto: Ryerson Press, 1943
Landsman, Gail H. 'The "Other" as Political Symbol: Images of Indians in the Woman Suffrage Movement.' *Ethnohistory* 39, no. 3 (Summer 1992): 247–84
Lang, Marjory. 'Separate Entrances: The First Generation of Canadian Women Journalists.' In *Re(Dis)covering Our Foremothers: Nineteenth-Century Canadian Women Writers.* Ed. Lorraine McMullen. Ottawa: University of Ottawa Press, 1989: 77–90
– *Women Who Made the News: Female Journalists in Canada, 1880–1945.* Montreal: McGill-Queen's University Press, 1999
Lang, Marjory, and Linda Hale. 'Women of *The World* and Other Dailies: The Lives and Times of Vancouver Newspaperwomen in the First Quarter of the Twentieth Century.' *BC Studies* 85 (May 1990): 3–23
LaRocque, Emma. 'The Colonization of a Native Woman Scholar.' In *Women of the First Nations: Power, Wisdom, and Strength.* Ed. Christine Miller et al. Winnipeg: University of Manitoba Press, 1996: 11–18
Lawrence, Elizabeth Atwood. *Rodeo: An Anthropologist Looks at the Wild and the Tame.* Knoxville: University of Tennessee Press, 1982
Le Vay, John. *Margaret Anglin: A Stage Life.* Toronto: Simon & Pierre, 1989
Leacock, Stephen. 'Greater Canada: An Appeal.' In *The Social Criticism of Stephen Leacock.* Ed. A. Bowker. Toronto: University of Toronto Press, 1973: 3–11
Ledger, Sally. *The New Woman: Fiction and Feminism at the fin de siècle.* Manchester: Manchester University Press, 1997
Lee, Betty. *Love and Whiskey: The Story of the Dominion Drama Festival and the Early Years of Theatre in Canada 1606–1972.* Toronto: Simon & Pierre, 1982
Leighton, Douglas. 'George Henry Martin Johnson. (Onwanonsyshon).' *Dictionary of Canadian Biography* XI: 451–3
– 'Abram (Abraham) Nelles.' *Dictionary of Canadian Biography* XI: 639–40
– 'John Johnson (Sakayengwaraton, Shakoyen'kwarahton, usually known as Smoke Johnson).' *Dictionary of Canadian Biography* XI: 453–4
Leighton, Mary Elizabeth. '"Performing" Pauline Johnson: Representations

of "the Indian Poetess" in the Periodical Press, 1892–95.' *Essays on Canadian Writing* 65 (Fall 1998): 141–64

Lenskyj, Helen. 'Femininity First: Sport and Physical Education for Ontario Girls, 1890–1930.' *Canadian Journal of History of Sport* 13, no. 2 (December 1982): 4–17

– 'Moral Physiology in Physical Education and Sport for Girls in Ontario, 1890–1930.' *Proceedings. 5th Canadian Symposium on the History of Sport and Physical Education.* Toronto: University of Toronto Press, 1982: 139–50

– 'Training for "True Womanhood": Physical Education for Girls in Ontario Schools, 1890–1920.' *Historical Studies in Education* 2, no. 2 (Fall 1990): 205–23

Lenton-Young, Gerald. 'Variety Theatre.' In *Early Stages: Theatre in Ontario 1800–1914.* Ed. Ann Saddlemyer. Toronto: University of Toronto Press, 1990: 166–213

Leprohon, Rosanna. *The Poetical Works of Mrs. Leprohon.* Montreal: Lovell, 1881

Li, Victor. 'Selling Modernism: Resisting Commodification, Commodifying Resistance.' *English Studies in Canada* 19, no. 1 (1993): 35–44

Lighthall, William Douw, ed. *Songs of the Great Dominion.* London: Walter Scott, 1889

Lillard, Charles. 'Choice of Lens.' *Canadian Literature* 118 (Autumn 1988): 154–5

Ling, Amy, and Annette White-Parks, eds. *Mrs. Spring Fragrance and Other Writings.* Urbana: University of Illinois Press, 1995

Litt, Paul. 'The Cultivation of Progress: Sara Jeannette Duncan's Social Thought.' *Ontario History* 80, no. 2 (June 1988): 97–119

Livingston, Lili Cockerille. *American Indian Ballerinas.* Norman: University of Oklahoma Press, 1997

Logan, J.D., and D.G. French. *Highways of Canadian Literature.* Toronto: McClelland and Stewart, 1929

Loosley, Elizabeth. 'Pauline Johnson 1861–1913.' In *The Clear Spirit: Twenty Canadian Women and Their Times.* Ed. Mary Quayle Innis. Toronto: University of Toronto Press, 1966: 74–90

Luke, Carmen. 'White Women in Interracial Families: Reflections on Hybridization, Feminine Identities, and Racialized Othering.' *Feminist Issues* 14, no. 2 (Fall 1994): 49–72

Lundgren, Jodi. '"Being a Half-breed": Discourses of Race and Cultural Syncreticity in the Works of Three Metis Women Writers.' *Canadian Literature* 144 (Spring 1995): 61–79

Lutz, Harmut. 'Canadian Native Literature and the Sixties: A Historical and Bibliographical Survey.' *Canadian Literature* 152–3 (Spring/Summer 1997): 167–92

– *Contemporary Challenges: Conversations with Canadian Native Authors.* Saskatoon: Fifth House, 1991

Lyon, George W. 'Pauline Johnson: A Reconsideration.' *Studies in Canadian Literature* 15, no. 2 (1990): 136–59

MacDonald, Mary Lu. 'Red and White; Black, White and Grey Hats.' In *Native Writers and Canadian Writing.* Ed. W.H. New. Vancouver: UBC Press, 1990. Special issue of *Canadian Literature,* 124–5: 92–111

MacDonald, Robert H. *Sons of the Empire: The Frontier and the Boy Scout Movement, 1890–1918.* Toronto: University of Toronto Press, 1993

Mackay, Isabel Ecclestone. 'Pauline Johnson: A Reminiscence.' *Canadian Magazine* 41 (1913): 273–8

– 'A Romance of Yesterday.' *Globe* (Toronto), 30 November 1912

Mackenzie, J.B. *The Six Nations Indians in Canada.* Toronto: Hunter Rose, 1896

– *Thanendanega: An Historico-military Drama.* Toronto: William Briggs, 1898

– *A Treatise on the Six-Nations Indians.* Toronto: Guardian Printing Office, 1882

Maclean, John. *Canadian Savage Folk: The Native Tribes of Canada.* Toronto: William Briggs, 1896

MacMechan, Archibald. *Headwaters of Canadian Literature.* Toronto: McClelland, 1924

MacMillan, Carrie, Lorraine McMullen, and Elizabeth Waterston. *Silenced Sextet: Six Nineteenth-Century Canadian Women Novelists.* Montreal: McGill-Queen's University Press, 1992

MacMullen, John. *The History of Canada from Its Discovery to the Present Time.* Brockville, ON: McMullen and Co., 1868

Mair, Charles. 'An Appreciation.' *The Moccasin Maker.* E. Pauline Johnson. Toronto: Briggs, 1913: 9–19

Mandel, Eli, and David Taras, eds. *A Passion for Identity: An Introduction to Canadian Studies.* Toronto: Methuen, 1987

Mangum, Teresa. 'Style Wars of the 1890s: The New Woman and the Decadent.' In *Transforming Genres: New Approaches to British Fiction of the 1890s.* Ed. Nikki Lee Manos and Meri-Jane Rochelson. New York: St Martin's Press, 1994: 47–66

Manos, Nikki Lee, and Meri-Jane Rochelson, eds. *Transforming Genres: New Approaches to British Fiction of the 1890s.* New York: St Martin's Press, 1994

Maracle, Brian. *Back on the Rez: Finding the Way Home.* Toronto: Viking, 1996

Mark, Joan. *A Stranger in Her Native Land: Alice Fletcher and the American Indians.* Lincoln: University of Nebraska Press, 1988

Marsh, Edith L. 'The County History as a Factor in Social Progress.' *Papers and Records of the Ontario Historical Society* 12 (1915): 53–7

Marshall, Christine Lowella. 'The Re-Presented Indian: Pauline Johnson's

"Srong Race Opinion" and Other Forgotten Discourses.' unpublished diss.,
University of Arizona, 1997
Martin, Calvin. *The American Indian and the Problem of History*. New York: Oxford
University Press, 1987
– 'The Metaphysics of Writing Indian-White History.' In *The American Indian
and the Problem of History*. Ed. Martin Calvin. New York: Oxford University
Press, 1987: 27–34
Mathur, Mary E. Fleming. 'The Iroquois in Ethnography.' *The Indian Historian* 2,
no. 3 (Fall 1969): 12–18
McBride, Bunny. *Molly Spotted Elk: A Penobscot in Paris*. Norman: University of
Oklahoma Press, 1995
McClintock, Anne. *Imperial Leather: Race, Gender and Sexuality in the Colonial
Conquest*. London: Routledge, 1995
McClung, Nellie L. *The Stream Runs Fast*. Toronto: Thomas Allen, 1945
– *In Times Like These*. 1915. Reprint, Toronto: University of Toronto Press, 1971
McCrone, Kathleen. *Sport and the Physical Emancipation of English Women, 1870–
1914*. London: Routledge, 1988
McDonald, Robert A.J. *Making Vancouver: Class, Status, and Social Boundaries,
1863–1913*. Vancouver: UBC Press, 1996
McGrath, Ann, and Winona Stevenson. 'Gender, Race, and Policy: Aboriginal
Women and the State in Canada and Australia.' *Labour* 38 (Fall 1996): 37–53
McKay, Ian. *The Quest of the Folk: Antimodernism and Cultural Selection in Twentieth-
Century Nova Scotia*. Montreal: McGill-Queen's University Press, 1994
McLaren, Angus. *The Trials of Masculinity: Policing Sexual Boundaries, 1870–1930*.
Chicago: University of Chicago Press, 1997
McMullen, Lorraine., ed. *Re(Dis)covering Our Foremothers: Nineteenth-Century Cana-
dian Women Writers*. Ottawa: University of Ottawa Press, 1989
McMullin, Stanley E. 'Grey Owl (Archibald Stansfeld Belaney).' *Dictionary of Lit-
erary Biography* 92. Detroit: Gale, 1990: 137–42
McNab, David. 'George Martin (known in Mohawk as "Shononhsé:se").' *Dictio-
nary of Canadian Biography* VIII: 619–21
McRaye, Walter. *Pauline Johnson and Her Friends*. Toronto: Ryerson, 1947
– *Town Hall Tonight*. Toronto: Ryerson, 1929
Meyer, Bruce. 'Frank Prewett.' *Profiles in Canadian Literature* 7 (1991): 57
Mihesuah, Devon A. 'Commonality of Difference: American Indian Women and
History.' *American Indian Quarterly* 20, no. 1 (Winter 1996): 15–27
– *Cultivating the Rosebuds: The Education of Women at the Cherokee Female Seminary,
1851–1909*. Urbana: University of Illinois Press, 1993
– 'Voice, Interpretations, and the "New Indian History."' *American Indian Quar-
terly* 20, no. 1 (Winter 1996): 91–108

Miller, Christine, et al., eds. *Women of the First Nations: Power, Wisdom, and Strength.*
Winnipeg: University of Manitoba Press, 1996

Miller, J.R. *Canada and the Aboriginal Peoples 1867–1927.* Booklet No. 57. Ottawa:
Canadian Historical Association, 1997

– 'Reading Photographs, Reading Voices: Documenting the History of Native
Residential Schools.' In *Reading beyond Words: Contexts for Native History.* Ed.
Jennifer S.H. Brown and Elizabeth Vibert. Peterborough, ON: Broadview,
1996: 460–81

– *Shingwauk's Vision: A History of Native Residential Schools.* Toronto: University of
Toronto Press, 1996

– *Skyscrapers Hide the Heavens: A History of Indian-White Relations in Canada.*
Toronto: University of Toronto Press, 1989

Miller, Jay. 'Mourning Dove: The Author as Cultural Mediator.' In *Being and
Becoming Indian: Biographical Studies of North American Frontiers.* Ed. James A.
Clifton. Chicago: Dorsey, 1989: 160–82

Millman, T.R. 'Frederick Augustus O'Meara.' *Dictionary of Canadian Biography*
XI: 653–5

– 'Adam Elliot (Elliot).' *Dictionary of Canadian Biography* X: 269–70

Mills, Sara. *Discourses of Difference: An Analysis of Women's Travel Writing and Colonialism.* London: Routledge, 1993

Mitchinson, Wendy. *The Nature of Their Bodies: Women and Their Doctors in Victorian
Canada.* Toronto: University of Toronto Press, 1991

Mohica, Monique. *Princess Pocahontas and the Blue Spots.* Toronto: Women's Press,
1991

Monkman, Leslie, and Douglas Daymond, eds. *Towards a Canadian Literature:
Essays, Editorials and Manifestos.* Ottawa: Tecumseh, 1984

Monkman, Leslie. *A Native Heritage: Images of the Indian in English-Canadian
Literature.* Toronto: University of Toronto Press, 1981

Montgomery, Malcolm. 'The Legal Status of the Six Nations Indians in Canada.'
Ontario History 55, no. 2 (1963): 92–105

– 'Historiography of the Iroquois Indians 1925–1963.' *Ontario History* 55, no. 4
(1963): 247–57

Montour, Enos T. *The Feathered U.E.L.'s.* Toronto: United Church of Canada, 1973

Monture, Ethel Brant. *Canadian Portraits: Brant, Crowfoot, Oronyatekha: Famous
Indians.* Toronto: Clarke, Irwin, 1960

Monture-Angus, Patricia. *Thunder in My Soul.* Halifax: Fernwood, 1995

Moodie, Susanna. *Life in the Clearings versus the Bush.* 1852. Reprint, Toronto:
McClelland and Stewart, 1989

Moray, Gerta. 'Wilderness, Modernity and Aboriginality in the Paintings of
Emily Carr.' *Journal of Canadian Studies* 33, no. 2 (1998): 43–65

Morgan, Cecilia. 'Aboriginal Travellers and Colonial Subjects? Pauline Johnson

and John Brant-Sero in Imperial London, 1890s–1900s.' Unpublished paper presented at Canadian Historical Association meetings, 1999
– 'Wampum and Waffle-Irons: Gender and National Identities in the Writing of Canadian Popular History, 1880s–1930s.' Unpublished paper presented at Canadian Historical Association meetings, 1996
Moses, Daniel David, and Terry Goldie, eds. *An Anthology of Canadian Native Literature in English.* 2nd ed. Toronto: Oxford University Press, 1998
Moses, L.C. *Wild West Shows and the Images of American Indians 1883–1933.* Albuquerque: University of New Mexico Press, 1996
Moylan, Michele. 'Materiality as Performance: The Forming of Helen Hunt Jackson's *Ramona.*' In *Reading Books: Essays on the Material Text and Literature in America.* Ed. Michelè Moylan and Lane Stiles. Amherst: University of Massachusetts Press, 1996: 223–47
Mulvihill, James. 'The "Canadian Bookman" and Literary Nationalism.' *Canadian Literature* 107 (Winter 1985): 48–59
Murphy, Emily. *Janey Canuck in the West.* 1910. Reprint, Toronto: McClelland and Stewart, 1975
Muszynski, A. *Cheap Wage Labour: Race and Gender in the Fisheries of British Columbia.* Montreal: McGill-Queen's University Press, 1996
Namias, June. *White Captives: Gender and Ethnicity on the American Frontier.* Chapel Hill: University of North Carolina Press, 1993
Nash, Roderick, ed. *The Call of the Wild (1900–1916).* New York: George Braziller, 1970
– *Wilderness and the American Mind.* New Haven: Yale University Press, 1973
Nettels, Elsa. *Language, Race, and Social Class in Howells's America.* Lexington: University Press of Kentucky, 1988
Nelles, H.V. *The Art of Nation-Building: Pageantry and Spectacle at Quebec's Tercentenary.* Toronto: University of Toronto Press, 1999
Neuenfeldt, Karl. 'First Nations and Métis Songs as Identity Narratives.' *International Journal of Canadian Studies* 12 (Fall 1995): 201–20
New, W.H., ed. *Native Writers and Canadian Writing.* Vancouver: UBC Press, 1990. Special issue of *Canadian Literature,* No. 124–5 (Spring-Summer 1990)
Newell, Diane. *The Tangled Webs of History: Indians and the Law in Canada's Pacific Coast Fisheries.* Toronto: University of Toronto Press, 1993
Nicks, Trudy. 'Dr Oronhyatekha's History Lessons: Reading Museum Collections as Texts.' In *Reading beyond Words: Contexts for Native History.* Ed. Jennifer S.H. Brown and Elizabeth Vibert. Peterborough: Broadview, 1996: 482–508
Noon, John A. *Law and Government of the Grand River Iroquois.* New York: Viking Fund Publications in Anthropology 12, 1949
O'Brien, Susie. '"Please Eunice, Don't Be Ignorant": The White Reader as Trickster in Lee Maracle's Fiction.' *Canadian Literature* 144 (Spring 1995): 82–96

Ong, Walter. *Orality and Literacy.* London: Methuen, 1982

Owram, Douglas. *Promise of Eden.* Toronto: University of Toronto Press, 1980

Pacey, Desmond. *Creative Writing in Canada.* Toronto: Ryerson, 1961

Page, Robert. *The Boer War and Canadian Imperialism.* Ottawa: Canadian Historical Association, 1987

Paget, Amelia M. *The People of the Plains.* Toronto: Ryerson, 1909

Pannekoek, Frits. 'The Anglican Church and the Disintegration of Red River Society, 1818–1870.' In *The West and the Nation: Essays in Honour of W.L. Morton.* Ed. Carl Berger and Ramsay Cook. Toronto: McClelland and Stewart, 1976: 72–90

Parker, Andrew, et al., eds. Introduction. *Nationalities and Sexualities.* New York: Routledge, 1992

Parker, Gilbert. Introduction. *The Moccasin Maker,* by E. Pauline Johnson. Toronto: Briggs, 1913: 5–8.

– *The Translation of a Savage.* New York: Appleton, 1893; Reprint, New York: Appleton, 1898.

Parr, Joy. *Labouring Children: British Immigrant Apprentices to Canada, 1869–1924.* Toronto: University of Toronto Press, 1994

Payment, Diane. '"La vie en rose"? Métis Women at Batoche, 1870–1920.' In *Women of the First Nations: Power, Wisdom, and Strength.* Ed. Christine Miller et al. Winnipeg: University of Manitoba Press, 1996

Perkins, David. *Is Literary History Possible?* Baltimore: Johns Hopkins University Press, 1992

Perrault, Jeanne, and Sylvia Vance, eds. *Writing the Circle: Native Women of Western Canada.* Edmonton: NeWest, 1990

Perry, Adele. '"Oh I'm Just Sick of the Faces of Men": Gender Imbalance, Race, Sexuality, and Sociability in Nineteenth-Century British Columbia.' *BC Studies* 105–6 (Spring/Summer 1995): 27–43

Peterson, Jacqueline, and Jennifer S. Brown, eds. *The New Peoples: Being and Becoming Métis in North America.* Winnipeg: University of Manitoba Press, 1985

Petrone, Penny. 'Brant-Sero, John Ojijatekha.' *Dictionary of Canadian Biography* XIV: 137–9

– *Native Literature in Canada: From the Oral Tradition to the Present.* Toronto: Oxford University Press, 1990

– ed. *First People, First Voices.* Toronto: University of Toronto Press, 1991

Peyer, Bernd C., ed. *The Singing Spirit: Early Short Stories by North American Indians.* Tucson: University of Arizona Press, 1989

Pierce, Lorne. *An Outline of Canadian Literature.* Toronto: Ryerson, 1927

Plant, Richard. 'Chronology: Theatre in Ontario to 1914.' In *Early Stages: Theatre in Ontario 1800–1914.* Ed. Ann Saddlemyer. Toronto: University of Toronto Press, 1990: 289–346

Potter-Mackinnon, Janice. *While the Women Only Wept: Loyalist Refugee Women in Eastern Ontario*. Montreal: McGill-Queen's University Press, 1993

Pratt, Mary Louise. *Imperial Eyes: Travel Writing and Transculturation*. London: Routledge, 1992

Prentice, Alison, et al. *Canadian Women: A History*. 2nd ed. Toronto: Harcourt Brace, 1996

Prewett, Frank. *Collected Poems of Frank Prewett*. London: Cassell, 1964

Raffan, James. *Bark, Skin and Cedar: Exploring the Canoe in Canadian Experience*. Toronto: HarperCollins, 1999

Ramusack, Barbara, and Antoinette Burton. 'Feminism, Imperialism and Race: A Dialogue Between India and Britain.' *Women's History Review* 3, no. 4 (1994): 469–81

Randle, Martha Champion. 'Iroquois Women, Then and Now' (1951). In *Symposium on Local Diversity in Iroquois Culture*. Ed. William N. Fenton. Smithsonian Institution. Washington: Bureau of American Ethnology, Bulletin 149, 1951: 167–80

Rashley, R.E. *Poetry in Canada: The First Three Steps*. Toronto: Ryerson Press, 1958

Rasporich, Beverly. 'Native Women Writing: Tracing the Patterns.' *Canadian Ethnic Studies* 28, no. 1 (1996): 37–50

Ray, Arthur J. *I Have Lived Here since the World Began: An Illustrated History of Canada's Native People*. Toronto: Key Porter, 1997

Reade, John. I. 'The Half Breed.' *Transactions of the Royal Society of Canada*. Section 2 (1885): 1–21

– 'The Literary Faculty of the Native Races of America.' *Transactions of the Royal Society of Canada*. Section 2 (1884): 17–30

Reid, Jennifer. *Myth, Symbol, and the Colonial Encounter: British and Mi'kmaq in Acadia, 1700–1867*. Ottawa: University of Ottawa Press, 1995

Reville, F. Douglas. *History of the County of Brant*. Brantford: Hurley Printing Co., 1920

Riley, Glenda. *Women and Indians on the Frontier 1825–1915*. Albuquerque: University of New Mexico Press, 1984

Roberts, Barbara. 'Women against War, 1914–1918: Francis Beynon and Laura Hughes.' In *Up and Doing: Canadian Women and Peace*. Ed. Janice Williamson and Deborah Gorham. Toronto: Women's Press, 1989: 48–65

Roberts, Charles G.D. *Collected Poems of Sir Charles G.D. Roberts*. Ed. Desmond Pacey and Graeme Adams. Wolfville, NS: Wombat Press, 1985.

Roemer, Kenneth. Introduction. *Native American Writers of the United States (Dictionary of Literary Biography*, vol. 175). Detroit: Gale Reserve, 1997

Rogers, Edward S., and Donald B. Smith, eds. *Aboriginal Ontario: Historical Perspectives on the First Nations*. Toronto: Dundurn Press, 1994

Rose, Alex, ed. *Nisga'a: People of the Nass River.* Vancouver: Douglas & McIntyre, 1993

Rose, Marilyn. 'Emily Pauline Johnson.' *Dictionary of Canadian Biography* XIV: 536–8

– 'Pauline Johnson: New World Poet.' *British Journal of Canadian Studies* 12, no. 2 (1997): 298–307

Rose, Sonya O. *Limited Livelihoods: Gender and Class in Nineteenth-Century England.* Berkeley: University of California Press, 1992

Rubin, Don, ed. *Canadian Theatre History: Selected Readings.* Toronto: Copp Clark Pitman, 1996

Ruoff, A. Lavonne Brown. *American Indian Literatures: An Introduction, Bibliographic Review, and Selected Bibliography.* New York: Modern Language Association of America, 1990

– 'Early Native American Women Authors: Jane Johnston Schoolcraft, Sarah Winnemucca, S. Alice Callahan, E. Pauline Johnson, and Zitkala-Sa.' In *Nineteenth-Century American Women Writers.* Ed. Karen Killcup. Cambridge, MA: Blackwells, 1988: 81–111

– 'E. Pauline Johnson (Tekahionwake) (10 March 1861–7 March 1913).' In *Native American Writers of the United States (Dictionary of Literary Biography,* vol. 175). Ed. Kenneth M. Roemer. Detroit: Gale Reserve, 1997: 131–6

– 'Justice for Indians and Women: The Protest Fiction of Alice Callahan and Pauline Johnson.' *World Literature Today* 66, no. 2 (1992): 249–55

– ed. *The Moccasin Maker,* by E. Pauline Johnson. 1913. Reprint, Norman: University of Oklahoma Press, 1998

Ruoff, A. LaVonne Brown, and Donald Smith, eds. *Life, Letters and Speeches of George Copway.* Lincoln: University of Nebraska Press, 1977

Ruoff, A. LaVonne Brown, and Jerry Ward, eds. *Redefining American Literary History.* New York: Modern Language Association of America, 1990

Rutherford, Paul, ed. *Saving the Canadian City: The First Phase, 1880–1920.* Toronto: University of Toronto Press, 1976

Ryan, Allan J. *The Trickster Shift: Humour and Irony in Contemporary Native Art.* Vancouver: UBC Press, 1999

Saddlemyer, Ann. *Early Stages: Theatre in Ontario 1800–1914.* Toronto: University of Toronto Press, 1990

Said, Edward. *Culture and Imperialism.* New York: Vintage Books, 1994

– *Orientalism: Western Representations of the Orient.* London: Routledge & Kegan Paul, 1978

Salem, Lisa. '"Her Blood Is Mingled with Her Ancient Foes": The Concepts of Blood, Race, and "Miscegenation" in the Poetry and Short Fiction of Duncan Campbell Scott.' *Studies in Canadian Literature* 18, no. 1 (1993): 99–111

Salem-Wiseman, Lisa. '"Verily the White Man's Ways Were the Best": Duncan Campbell Scott, Native Culture and Assimilation.' *Studies in Canadian Literature* 21, no. 1 (1996): 120–42

Saywell, John T., ed. *The Canadian Journal of Lady Aberdeen, 1893–98.* Toronto: Champlain Society, 1960

Schneider R., and G. Gottfriedson. *In Honour of Our Grandmothers.* Penticton: Theytus, 1994

Schoeman, Karel. *Only an Anguish to Live Here: Olive Schreiner and the Anglo Boer War, 1899–1902.* Cape Town: Human and Rousseau, 1992

Scott, Duncan Campbell. 'The Aboriginal Races,' *Annals of the American Academy of Political and Social Science* 107 (May 1923): 63–6

– 'Indian Affairs, 1763–1841.' In *Canada and Its Provinces.* Ed. Adam Shortt and Arthur Doughty. Vol. 4. Toronto: Brook & Co, 1914: 695–725

Scott, Frank, et al. *New Provinces.* 1936. Toronto: University of Toronto Press, 1976

Scott, Jack. 'The Passionate Princess.' *Maclean's Magazine,* 1 April 1952: 12–13, 54–5, 57

Seesequasis, Paul. 'The Republic of Tricksterism.' In *An Anthropology of Canadian Native Literature in English.* Ed. Daniel Moses and Terry Goldie. 2nd ed. Toronto: Oxford University Press, 1998: 411–16

Seton, Ernest Thompson, 'Tekahionwake (Pauline Johnson).' *The Shagganappi,* by E. Pauline Johnson. Toronto: Briggs, 1913: 5–7

Sharpe, Jenny. 'Figures of Colonial Resistance.' In *The Post-colonial Studies Reader.* Ed. B. Ashcroft, G. Griffiths, and H. Tiffin. London: Routledge, 1995: 99–103

Sheridan, Susan. *Along the Faultlines: Sex, Race and Nation in Australian Women's Writing 1880s–1930s.* St Leonards, Australia: Allen & Unwin, 1995

Sherzer, Joel, and Anthony C. Woodbury, eds. *Native American Discourse: Poetics and Rhetoric.* Cambridge: Cambridge University Press, 1987

Shields, David S. *Oracles of Empire: Poetry, Politics, and Commerce in British America, 1690–1750.* Chicago: University of Chicago Press, 1990

Shimony, Annemarie Anrod. *Conservatism among the Iroquois at the Six Nations Reserve.* Syracuse, NY: Syracuse University Press, 1994

Shoemaker, Nancy. 'The Rise or Fall of Iroquois Women.' *Journal of Women's History* 2, no. 3 (Winter 1991): 39–57

– ed. *Negotiators of Change: Historical Perspectives on Native American Women.* New York: Routledge, 1995

Showalter, Elaine, ed. *Daughters of Decadence: Women Writers at the Fin-de-Siècle.* New Brunswick, NJ: Rutgers University Press, 1993

Shrive, Norman. *Charles Mair: Literary Nationalist.* Toronto: University of Toronto Press, 1965

– 'What Happened to Pauline?' *Canadian Literature* 13 (1962): 25–38

Sioui, George E. *For An Amerindian Autohistory: An Essay on the Foundations of a Social Ethic.* Montreal: McGill-Queen's University Press, 1992
– 'Why Canada Should Look for, Find, Recognize and Embrace Its True, Aboriginal Roots,' *Canadian Issues/Thèmes Canadiens* 20 (1998): 45–54
Skinner, James M. 'The Silent Enemy: A Forgotten Chapter in the Screen History of the Canadian Indian.' *Ontario History* 71, no. 3 (September 1979): 159–67
Smith, Donald B. 'Elizabeth Field (Eliza) (Jones; Carey).' *Dictionary of Canadian Biography* XI: 316–17
– *From the Land of Shadows: The Making of Grey Owl.* Saskatoon: Prairie Producer Books, 1990
– 'From Sylvester Long to Chief Long Lance.' In *Being and Becoming Indian.* Ed. James A. Clifton. Chicago: Dorsey, 1989: 183–203
– 'Fred Loft.' In *The Encyclopedia of North American Indians.* Ed. Frederick E. Hoxie. Boston: Houghton Mifflin, 1996: 344–5
– *Long Lance: The True Story of an Imposter.* Toronto: Macmillan, 1982
– 'Nahnebahucquay (... known as Catherine Sutton ...).' *Dictionary of Canadian Biography* IX: 590–1
– 'Peter Edmund Jones (Kahkewaquonaby).' *Dictionary of Canadian Biography* XIII: 530–1
– *Sacred Feathers: The Reverend Peter Jones (Kahkewaquonaby) and the Mississauga Indians.* Toronto: University of Toronto Press, 1987
Smith, Erica. '"Gentlemen, This Is No Ordinary Trial": Sexual Narratives in the Trial of the Reverend Corbett, Red River, 1863.' In *Reading beyond Words: Contexts for Native History.* Ed. Jennifer S.H. Brown and Elizabeth Vibert. Peterborough: Broadview, 1996: 364–80
Smith, Gordon J. 'Captain Joseph Brant's Status as a Chief, and Some of His Descendants.' *Papers and Records of the Ontario Historical Society* 12 (1914): 89–101
– 'Land Tenure in Brant County (March 14, 1910).' *Papers and Records of the Brant Historical Society* 2 (1908–11): 31–43
Smith, Michael J. 'Graceful Athleticism or Robust Womanhood: The Sporting Culture of Women in Victorian Nova Scotia, 1870–1914.' *Journal of Canadian Studies* 23, no. 1–2 (Spring/Summer 1988): 120–37
Smith, Susan L. 'Whitewashing Womanhood: The Politics of Race in Writing Women's History.' *Canadian Review of Comparative Literature* (March 1995): 93–103
Smith-Rosenberg, Carroll. 'Captured Subjects/Savage Others: Violently Engendering the New American.' *Gender and History* 5, no. 2 (Summer 1993): 177–95

Smits, David D. 'The "Squaw Drudge": A Prime Index of Savagism.' *Ethnohistory* 29, no. 4 (1982): 281–306

Snell, James G. '"The White Life for Two": The Defense of Marriage and Sexual Morality in Canada, 1890–1914.' *Social History* 16, no. 31 (May 1983): 111–28

Snow, Dean. *The Iroquois.* Oxford: Blackwell, 1994

Spittal, William Guy, ed. *Iroquois Women: An Anthology.* Ohsweken, ON: Iroqrafts, 1990

Sprague, D.N. *Canada and the Métis, 1869–1885.* Waterloo, ON: Wilfrid Laurier University Press, 1988

St Peter, Christine. 'Feminist Afterwords: Revisiting Copper Woman.' In *Undisciplined Women: Tradition and Culture in Canada.* Ed. Pauline Greenhill and Diane Tye. Montreal: McGill-Queen's University Press, 1997: 65–72

Staats, Sheila. 'The Six Nations Council House: Historic Building at Ohsweken.' *Ontario History* 85, no. 3 (Sept. 1993): 213–22

Stedman, Raymond William. *Shadows of the Indian: Stereotypes in American Culture.* Norman: University of Oklahoma Press, 1982

Stetz, Margaret Diane. 'New Grub Street and the Woman Writer of the 1890s.' In *Transforming Genres: New Approaches to British Fiction of the 1890s.* Ed. Nikki Lee Manos and Meri-Jane Rochelson. New York: St Martin's Press, 1994: 21–46

– 'Sex, Lies, and Printed Cloth: Bookselling at the Bodley Head in the Eighteen-Nineties.' *Victorian Studies* 35 (Autumn 1991): 71–86

Stetz, Margaret Diane, and Mark Samuels Lasner. *England in the 1890s.* Washington, DC: Georgetown University Press, 1990

Stevenson, Lionel. *Appraisals of Canadian Literature.* Toronto: Macmillan, 1926

Stevenson, O.J. *A People's Best.* Toronto: Musson, 1927

Stevenson, Winona. 'The Journals and Voices of a Church of England Native Catechist: Askenootow (Charles Pratt), 1851–1884.' In *Reading beyond Words: Contexts for Native History.* Ed. Jennifer S.H. Brown and Elizabeth Vibert. Peterborough, ON: Broadview, 1996: 304–29

Stevinson, Jean. 'Canada's Famous Indian Poetess.' *Lethbridge Herald*, 21 March 1931: 3–4

– 'Friends Pay Tribute to Indian Poetess on Anniversary of Death,' *Calgary Herald*, 5 March 1932.

Stocking, Jr, George W. *Victorian Anthropology.* New York: Free Press, 1987

Stoler, Ann Laura. *Race and the Education of Desire.* Durham: Duke University Press, 1995

Stonechild, Blair, and Bill Waiser. *Loyal till Death: Indians and the North-West Rebellion.* Calgary: Fifth House, 1997

Stringer, Arthur. 'Wild Poets I've Known.' *Saturday Night*, 11 October 1941: 29

Strong-Boag, Veronica. 'Claiming a Place in the Nation: Citizenship Education and the Challenge of Feminists, Natives, and Workers in Post-Confederation Canada.' *Canadian and International Education* 25, no. 2 (1997): 128–45
– 'Contested Space: The Politics of Canadian Memory.' *Journal of the Canadian Historical Association* New Series 5 (1994): 3–17
– '"Every a Crusader": Nellie McClung, First-Wave Feminist.' In *Rethinking Canada: The Promise of Women's History.* Ed. V. Strong-Boag, and A.C. Fellman. Toronto: Oxford University Press, 1997: 271–84
– '"Home Dreams": Women and the Suburban Experiment in Canada, 1945–60.' *Canadian Historical Review* 72, no. 4 (Dec 1991): 471–504
– 'Independent Women and Problematic Men: First and Second Wave Anti-Feminism in Canada from Goldwin Smith to Betty Steele.' *Histoire sociale/ Social History* 29, no. 57 (May 1996): 1–22
– 'Pulling in Double Harness or Hauling a Double Load: Women, Work and Feminism on the Canadian Prairie.' *Journal of Canadian Studies* 21, no. 3 (1986): 32–52
Strong-Boag, Veronica, and Anita Clair Fellman, eds. *Rethinking Canada: The Promise of Women's History.* 3rd ed. Toronto: Oxford University Press, 1997
Stuart, E. Ross. *The History of Prairie Theatre: The Development of Theatre in Alberta, Manitoba, and Saskatchewan, 1833–1982.* Toronto: Simon & Pierre, 1984
Tausky, Thomas E. 'In Search of a Canadian Liberal: The Case of Sara Jeannette Duncan.' *Ontario History* 83, no. 2 (June 1991): 85–107
– *Sara Jeannette Duncan: Novelist of Empire.* Port Credit, ON: P.D. Meany Publishers, 1980
Taylor, Drew Hayden. *Funny, You Don't Look Like One: Observations from a Blue-eyed Ojibway.* Penticton, BC: Theytus, 1996
Tennant, Paul. *Aboriginal Peoples and Politics: The Indian Land Question in British Columbia, 1849–1989.* Vancouver: UBC Press, 1990
Thompson, Bertha Jean (later Stevinson). 'Pauline Johnson: Tekahionwake.' *McMaster University Monthly* (Dec. 1904): 104–7
Thurston, John. *The Work of Words: The Writing of Susanna Strickland Moodie.* Montreal: McGill-Queen's University Press, 1996
Tilton, Robert. *Pocahontas: The Evolution of an American Narrative.* Cambridge: Cambridge University Press, 1994
Tippett, Maria. *Making Culture: English-Canadian Institutions and the Arts before the Massey Commission.* Toronto: University of Toronto Press, 1990
Titley, E. Brian. *A Narrow Vision: Duncan Campbell Scott and the Administration of Indian Affairs in Canada.* Vancouver: UBC Press, 1986
Tooker, Elisabeth. 'Women in Iroquois Society.' In *Extending the Rafters: Inter-disciplinary Approaches to Iroquoian Studies.* Ed. Michael K. Foster, Jack Campisi,

and Marianne Mithun. Albany: State University of New York Press, 1984: 109–23

Trigger, Bruce G. 'The Historians' Indian: Native Americans in Canadian Historical Writing from Charlevoix to the Present.' *Canadian Historical Review* 68, no. 3 (1986): 315–42

Trimble, W.C. *Illustrated Historical Atlas of Brant County, Ontario.* 1875. Reprint, Belleville, ON: Mika, 1972

Trinh T. Minh-ha. *Framer Framed.* New York: Routledge, 1992

Turnbull, Elsie G. 'Recollections of Marie Houghton Brent.' *British Columbia Historical News* 18, no. 2 (1984): 21–2

Twain, Mark, 'The Noble Red Man.' 1870. Reprinted in S.F. Tropp, *Shaping Tradition: Art and Diversity in the Essay.* Fort Worth: Harcourt Brace Jovanovich, 1992, 251–4

Unrau, William E. *Mixed Bloods and Tribal Dissolution: Charles Curtis and the Quest for Indian Identity.* Laurence: University of Kansas Press, 1989

Valaskasis, Gail Guthrie. 'Sacajawea and Her Sisters: Images and Indians.' In *Indian Princesses and Cowboys: Stereotypes from the Frontier.* Montreal: Oboro, 1995: 11–40

Valentine, Lisa Philips. 'Performing Native Identities.' *Papers of the Twenty-Fifth Algonquian Conference.* Ed. W. Cowan. Ottawa: Carleton University Press, 1994: 482–92

Valverde, Marianna. *The Age of Light, Soap, and Water: Moral Reform in English Canada, 1885–1925.* Toronto: McClelland and Stewart, 1991

Van Kirk, Sylvia. *'Many Tender Ties': Women in Fur-Trade Society, 1670–1870.* Winnipeg: Watson & Dwyer, 1980

– '"The Reputation of a Lady": Sarah Ballenden and the Foss-Pelly Scandal.' *Manitoba History* 11 (Spring 1986): 4–11

– 'Toward a Feminist Perspective in Native History.' In *Papers of the Eighteenth Algonquian Conference.* Ed. William Cowan. Ottawa: Carleton University Press, 1987: 377–89

– 'Tracing the Fortunes of Five Founding Families of Victoria.' *BC Studies* (Fall-Winter 1997–8): 148–79

– '"What if Mama is an Indian?": The Cultural Ambivalence of the Alexander Ross Family.' In *The Developing West: Essays on Canadian History in Honor of Lewis H. Thomas.* Ed. J.E. Foster. Edmonton: University of Alberta Press, 1983: 123–36

Van Steen, Marcus. *Pauline Johnson: Her Life and Work.* Toronto: Musson, 1965

Vautier, Marie. 'Comparative Postcolonialism and the Amerindian in English-speaking Canada and Quebec.' *Canadian Ethnic Studies* 28, no. 3 (1996): 4–15

Viswanathan, Gauri. 'The Beginning of English Literary Study in British India.'

In *The Post-colonial Studies Reader*, Ed. B. Ashcroft, G. Griffiths, and H. Tiffin. London: Routledge, 1995: 431–7

Wadland, John. *Ernest Thompson Seton: Man in Nature and the Progressive Era, 1880–1915*. New York: Arno, 1978

Wagner, Sally Roesch. 'The Root of Oppression is the Loss of Memory: The Iroquois and the Early Feminist Vision.' In *Iroquois Women: An Anthology*. Ed. William Guy Spittal. Ohsweken, ON: Iroqrafts, 1990

Walden, Keith. *Visions of Order.* Toronto: Butterworth, 1982

Waldie, Jean H. *Brant County: The Story of Its People*. Vol. 1. Paris, ON: Brant Historical Society, 1984

– 'The Iroquois Poetess, Pauline Johnson.' *Ontario History* 40 (1948): 65–75

Ware, Vron. *Beyond the Pale: White Women, Racism and History.* London: Verso, 1992

Warne, Randi R. *Literature as Pulpit: The Christian Social Activism of Nellie L. McClung.* Waterloo: Wilfrid Laurier University Press, 1993

Warren, Joyce, W., ed. *The (Other) American Traditions: Nineteenth-Century Women Writers.* New Brunswick, NJ: Rutgers University Press, 1993

Watson, Scott. 'Race, Wilderness, Territory and the Origins of Canadian Landscape Painting.' *Semiotext(e)* 6, no. 2 (1994): 93–104

Watt, William (compiler). *The City of Brantford, Canada: The Telephone City of the West.* Brantford, 1886

Watts-Dunton, Theodore. 'Introduction. In Memorium: Pauline Johnson.' *Flint and Feather,* by E. Pauline Johnson. Toronto: Musson, 1917: 1–10.

Weaver, Sally M. 'The Iroquois: The Consolidation of the Grand River Reserve in the Mid-Nineteenth Century, 1847–1875.' In *Aboriginal Ontario: Historical Perspectives on the First Nations*. Eds. Edward S. Rogers and Donald B. Smith. Toronto: Dundurn Press, 1994: 182–212

– 'The Iroquois: The Grand River Reserve in the Late Nineteenth and Early Twentieth Centuries, 1875–1945.' In *Aboriginal Ontario: Historical Perspectives on the First Nations*. Eds. Edward S. Rogers and Donald B. Smith. Toronto: Dundurn Press, 1994: 213–57

– *Medicine and Politics among the Grand River Iroquois: A Study of the Non-Conservatives*. Ottawa: National Museums of Canada, Publications in Ethnology, No. 4, 1972

– 'Seth Newhouse and the Grand River Confederacy at Mid-Nineteenth Century.' In *Extending the Rafters: Interdisciplinary Approaches to Iroquoian Studies*. Ed. Michael K. Foster, Jack Campisi, and Marianne Mithun. Albany: State University of New York Press, 1984: 165–82

Weir, F.G. 'Great Indian Characters.' *Onward*, 19 April 1930: 15–16

Welsh, Christine. 'Voices of the Grandmothers: Reclaiming a Métis Heritage.' *Canadian Literature* 131 (Winter 1991): 15–24

Wescott (Athabascan/Yup'ik), Brian. 'Indian Princesses on Parade.' *The Runner* 1, no. 3 (Summer 1994): 4–8, 10–11, 54–5

Wexler, J.P. *Who Paid for Modernism: Art, Money and the Fiction of Conrad, Joyce, and Lawrence.* Fayetteville: University of Arkansas Press, 1997

Whale, R.R. 'A Short Sketch of Chief G.H.M. Johnson of the Six Nations Indians.' *Archaelogical Report of the Ontario Department of Education* 36 (1928): 40–7

White-Parks, Annette. *Sui Sin Far/Edith Maude Eaton: A Literary Biogaphy.* Urbana: University of Chicago Press, 1995

Wickwire, Wendy. Introduction to *Write It on Your Heart: The Epic World of an Okanagan Storyteller*, by Harry Robinson. Vancouver: Talonbooks/Theytus, 1989: 9–28

Wilson, Angela Cavender. 'American Indian History or Non-Indian Perceptions of American Indian History?' *American Indian Quarterly* 20, no. 1 (Winter 1996): 3–4

Wilson, Daniel. *Prehistoric Man: Researches into the Origin of Civilisation in the Old and the New World.* London: Macmillan, 1876

Wilson, Ethel. 'The Princess.' *Canadian Literature* 12 (Summer 1961): 60–1

Wilson, Stephen. *Ideology and Experience: Anti-Semitism in France at the Time of the Dreyfus Affair.* London: Associated University Presses, 1982

Winslow, Bernice Loft. *Iroquois Fires: The Six Nations Lyrics and Lore of Dawendine (Bernice Loft Winslow).* Ottawa: Penumbra, 1995

Wright, Donald. A. 'W.D. Lighthall and David Ross McCord: Antimodernism and English-Canadian Imperialism, 1880s–1918.' *Journal of Canadian Studies* 32, no. 2 (Summer 1997): 134–53

Young, Robert J.C. *Colonial Desire: Hybridity in Theory, Culture and Race.* London: Routledge, 1995

Young-Ing, Gregory. 'I Am Mixed Blood.' In *Seventh Generation: Contemporary Native Writing.* Ed. and compiled by Heather Hodgson. Penticton, BC: Theytus, 1989: 48–9

Illustration Credits

Index

Bhabha, Homi, 36
bicycles, and the New Woman, 153
Big Bear, 149, 216
Billson, Janet Mancini, 90
Birney, Earle, 12, 130
Black Woman's era of writing, in the
   United States, 78
Blacks in Canada, 42, 184; in John-
   son's writing, 208, 213
Boadicea, 116, 191
Boas, Franz, 176
Bodley Head (publisher), 144,
   266n. 7
bohemianism, 75; in Johnson's writ-
   ing, 76, 140, 153, 157
Borden, Prime Minister Robert, 55–6
Boyle, David (anthropologist), 40, 41
Boys' World, 78, 87–9, 92, 135, 164,
   166–71
Brant, Beth, 12, 134
Brant, Catharine, 44
Brant, Joseph: depictions of, in early
   Canadian writing, 21, 183; Johnson
   on, 41, 57, 147–8, 191–2; statue and
   commemoration of, 32, 35; and the
   United Empire Loyalists, 34
Brant, Molly, 44
Brant Amateurs, 104
Brant County Museum, 169
Brant Historical Society, 41, 54
Brantford, 34–5, 191
Brantford Canoe Club, 80, 159
Brantford Collegiate, 51, 63
Brantford Expositor, 136
Brantford Local Council of Women,
   64
Brantford Young Ladies College,
   38
Brant-Sero, John (Ojijatekha), 35–6,
   43, 111, 216, 257n. 43

British Empire: Canadian loyalty to,
   212; and Iroquois as allies, 192;
   Johnson's support for, 200
Brooke, Frances, 44
Brown, J.N.J., 176
Buffalo Bill Cody, Wild West Show,
   35, 111
Buffalo Child Long Lance (Sylvester
   Long), 45, 125
Burns, Robert, 149, 190
Butler, Judith, 112

Callaghan, S. Alice, 60, 94, 129
Cameron, Agnes Deans, 80
Campbell, William Wilfred, 101, 103,
   118–19, 123, 153
Canada First, 23
Canadian Authors' Association, 123
Canadian Bookman, 125
Canadian Expeditionary Force, 67
Canadian Forum, 125, 127
Canadian Indian Research and Aid
   Society (CIRAS), 28
Canadian Magazine, 29, 60, 103, 136,
   166,
Canadian Manufacturer's Associa-
   tion, 69; Johnson's performance at,
   210
Canadian Women's Press Club, 65,
   69, 140–1
canoeing, 80, 103, 140, 159, 160; as
   Canadian icon, 153; and eroticism,
   142; in Johnson's work, 101, 115,
   140, 141; and nature, 153; and
   women, 81, 153, 157, 159; and
   women's sexuality, 154
Capilano, Joe. *See* Su-á-pu-luck
Capilano, Mary Agnes. *See* Líxwelut
Capilano, Mathias, 30, 64, 193, 215
Carey, Pauline: *Pauline Johnson*, 131

Leprohon, Rosanna Mullins, 44, 94,
101
Lighthall, W.D., 117–19; *The Master of
Life*, 21; *Songs of the Great Dominion*,
21, 101, 110, 202
Lillard, Charles, 131
Livesay, Dorothy, 126
Líxwelut (Mary Agnes Capilano), 29,
64, 173; as 'the Grand Old Woman'
of British Columbia, 193
Loft, Chief Frederick Ogilvie, 38–9,
56
Loft family, of Six Nations, 111
Loft Winslow, Bernice (Dawendine),
12
Logan, J.D., 98, 145, 185; and French,
and the 'School of Canadian
Poetry,' 124, 145
London Express, 137
Long, Sylvester. *See* Buffalo Child
Long Lance
Longfellow. *See Hiawatha*
Loyalist centennials, 183
Lutz, Hartmut, 130
Lyon, George W., 131, 146

Macdonald, John A., 210
MacLean, Isabel, 60
MacLean, John (Canadian ethnolo-
gist), on Joseph Brant, 34
Maclean's, list of the 100 most impor-
tant Canadians, 6
MacMechan, Archibald: *Headwaters of
Canadian Literature*, 262n. 92
MacMurchy, Dr Helen, 54
Macphail, Andrew, 61
Machar, Agnes Maule, 60, 94, 101,
118, 183
Mackay, Isabel Ecclestone, 105, 121,
136

Maguire, Eileen, 65
Mair, Charles, 23, 67, 182, 188;
'Tecumseh,' 194. *See also* Tecumseh
Makovski, Lionel, 66, 117, 177
Maracle, Floretta, 38
Maracle, Lee, 4, 134
marriage, interracial: in Johnson's
writing, 21, 24–5, 28, 85–6, 93, 164
Marshall, Christine, 176
Martin, Catherine Rollston (Wan-o-
wen-re-teh), 46
Martin, Helen, 46, 47
Martin, Jacob, 48
Martin, Dr Peter. *See* Oronhyatekha
Martin, Sophie, 45
masculinity, 89, 276n. 63 *See also* men
matriarchy, 33–4, 60
McBride, Premier Richard, 79
McClung, Nellie, 70, 94, 121, 123,
126, 172, 183, 207; friendship with
Johnson, 64, 66; *In Times Like These*,
103
McEvoy, Bernard, 177, 186
McGill University, 38, 125
McIlwraith, Jean, 94
McLachlan, Alexander: 'The Anglo-
Saxon,' 179
McLean Paget, Amelia: *The People of
the Plains*, 30–1
McRaye, Walter, 24, 64, 67, 97, 140,
180, 209, 213–15; *Pauline Johnson
and Her Friends*, 140, 262n. 92; performance of William Henry Drummond's French Canada poems,
120, 181
men, European: and interracial
unions, 25; in Johnson's writing,
85–6, 88–9, 93; and sports, in
Johnson's writing, 82–3. *See also*
masculinity

STUDIES IN GENDER AND HISTORY

General editors: Franca Iacovetta and Karen Dubinsky